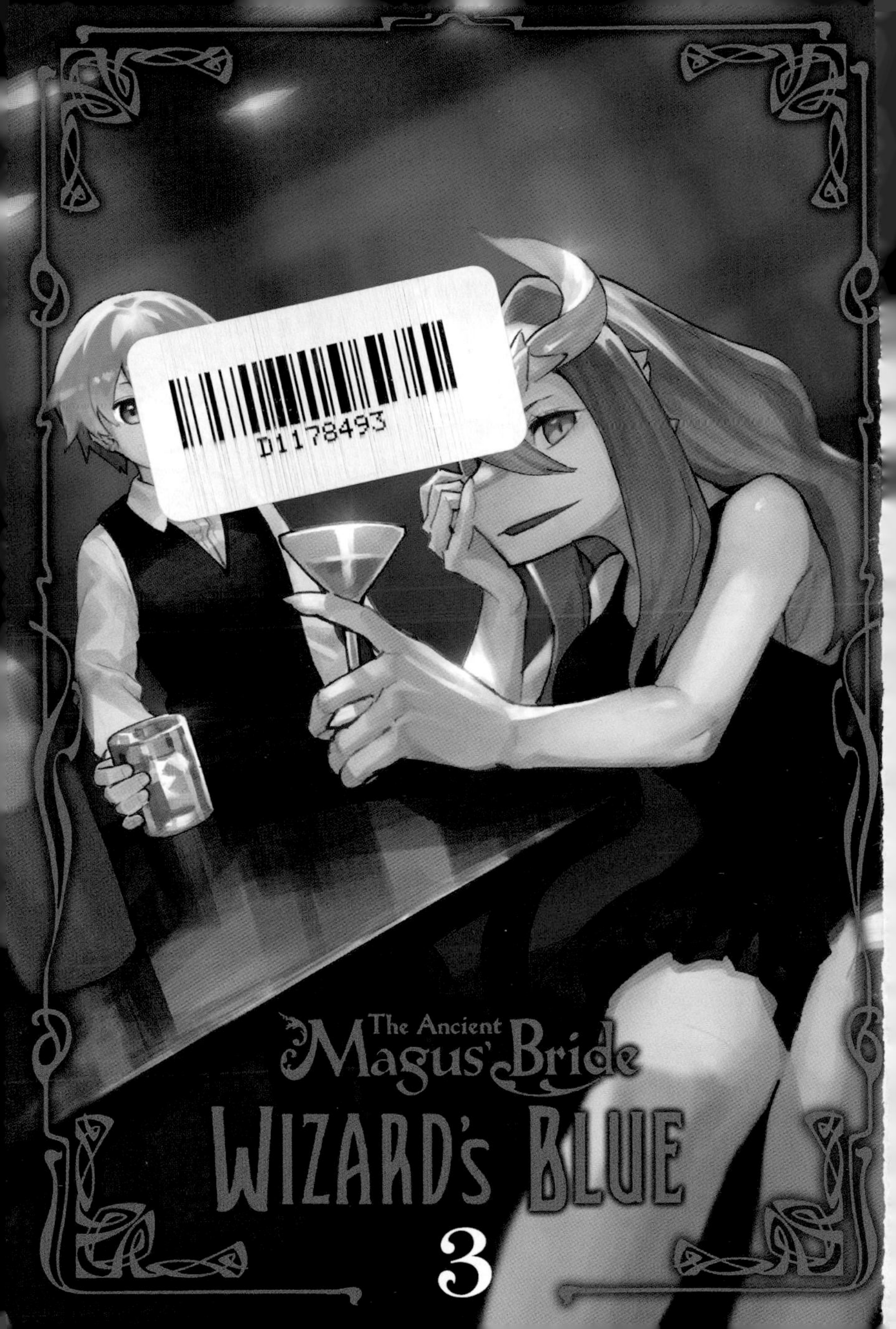
The Ancient Magus' Bride
WIZARD's BLUE
3

The Ancient Magus' Bride
WIZARD's BLUE
3

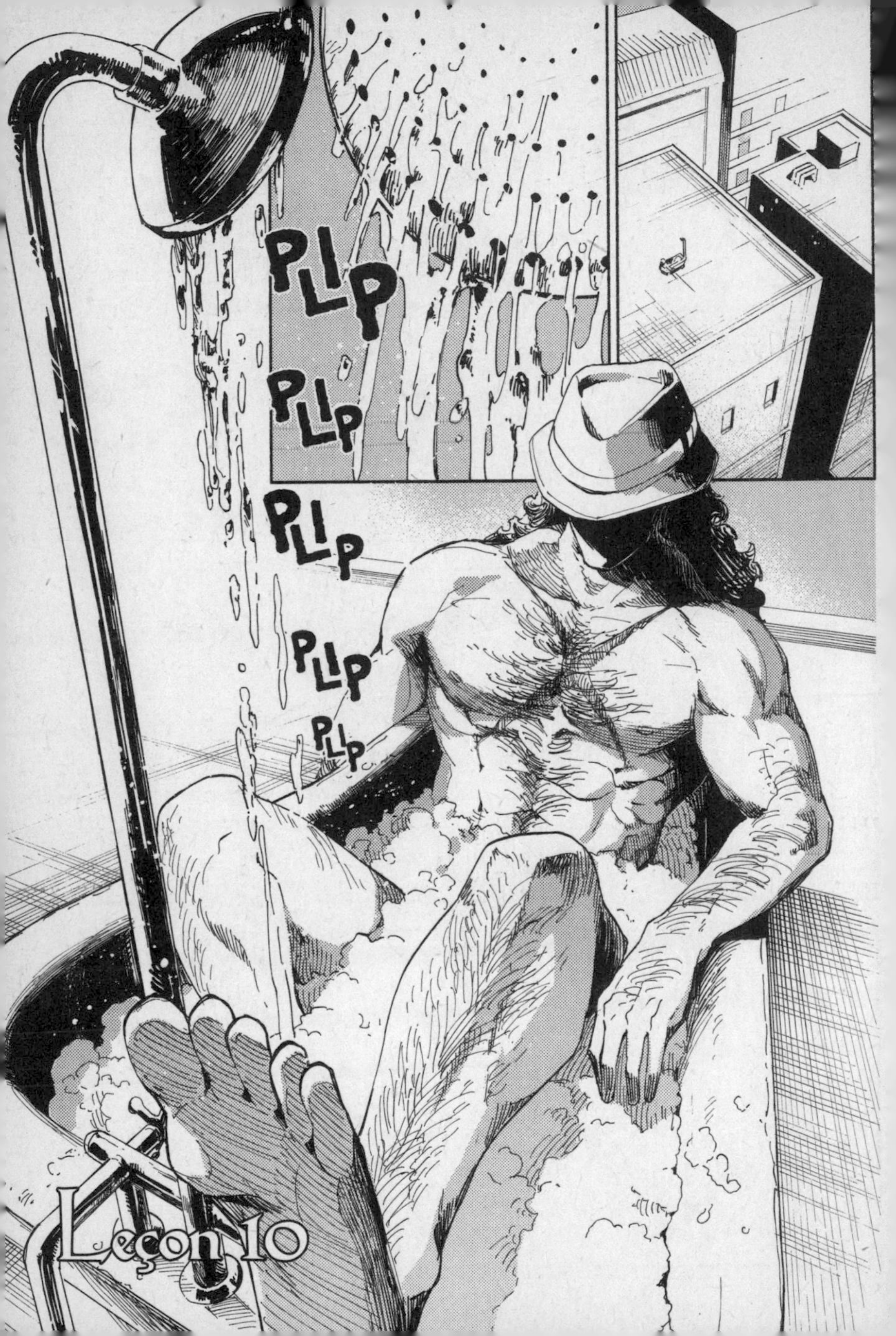
PLIP
PLIP
PLIP
PLIP
PLIP
Leçon 10

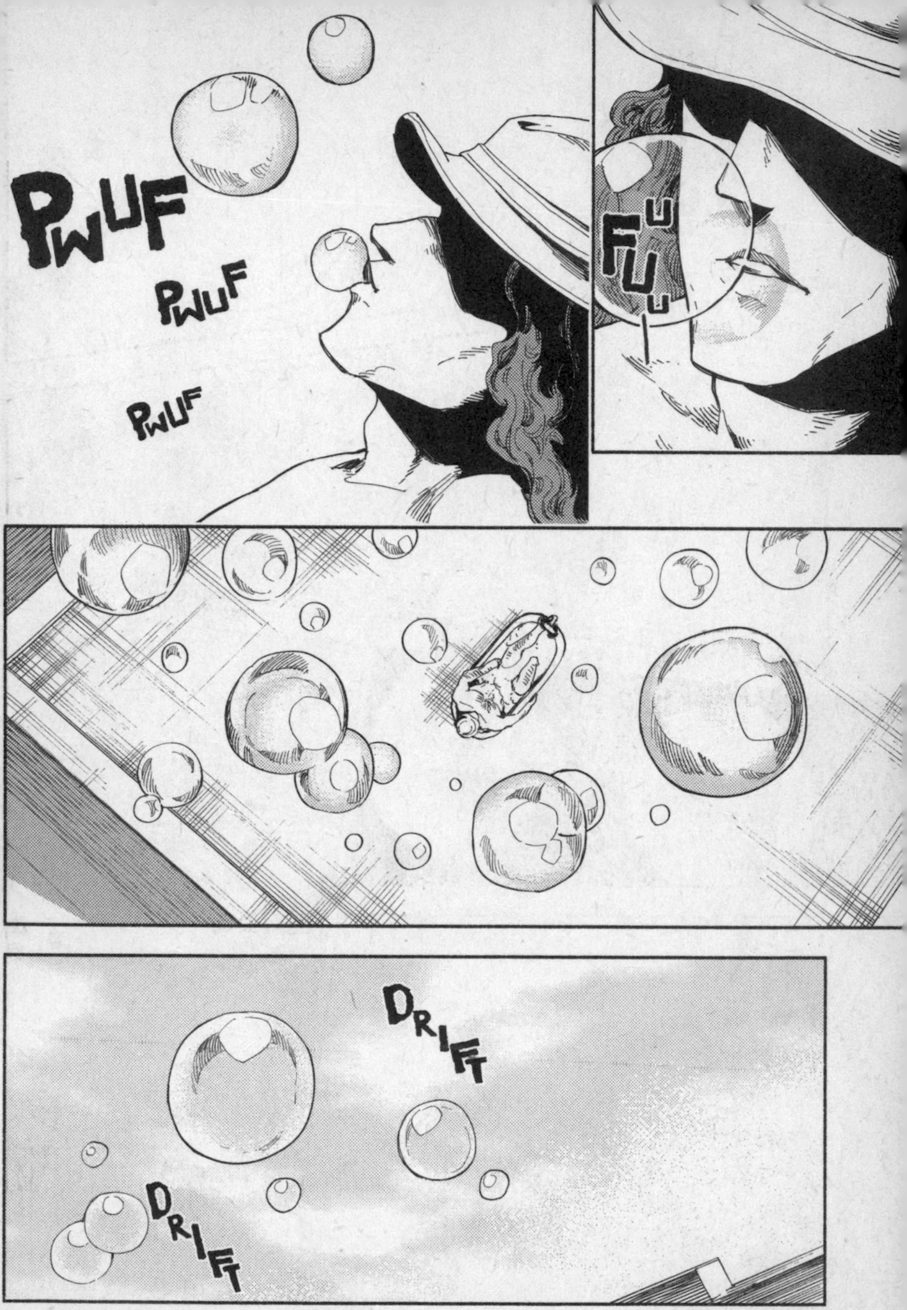
FUUUU
PWUF
PWUF
PWUF
DRIFT
DRIFT

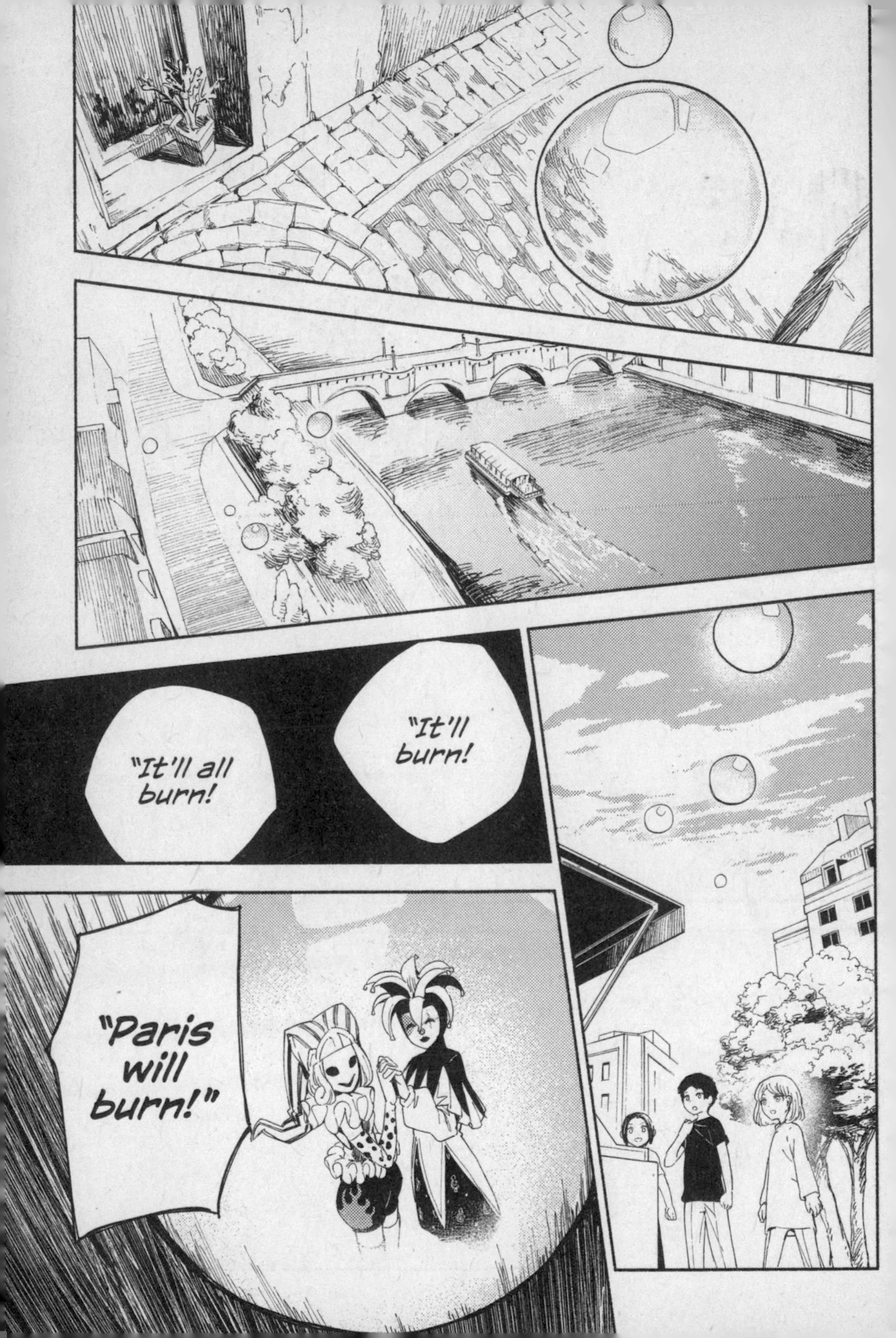
"It'll
burn!
"It'll all
burn!
"Paris
will
burn!"

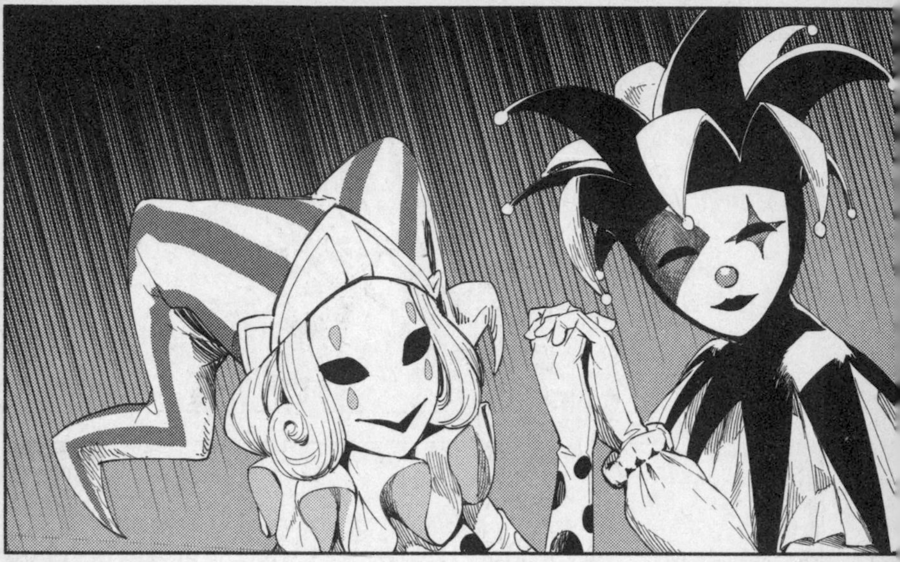

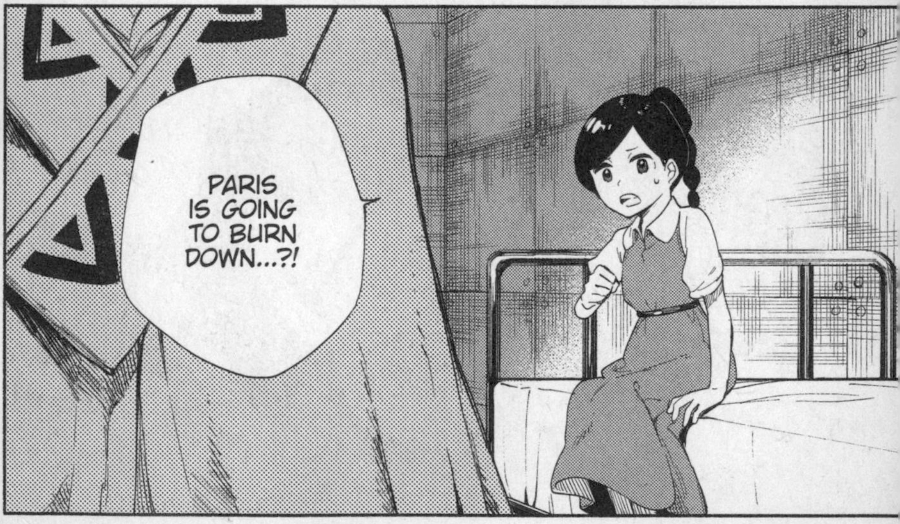
PARIS IS GOING TO BURN DOWN...?!

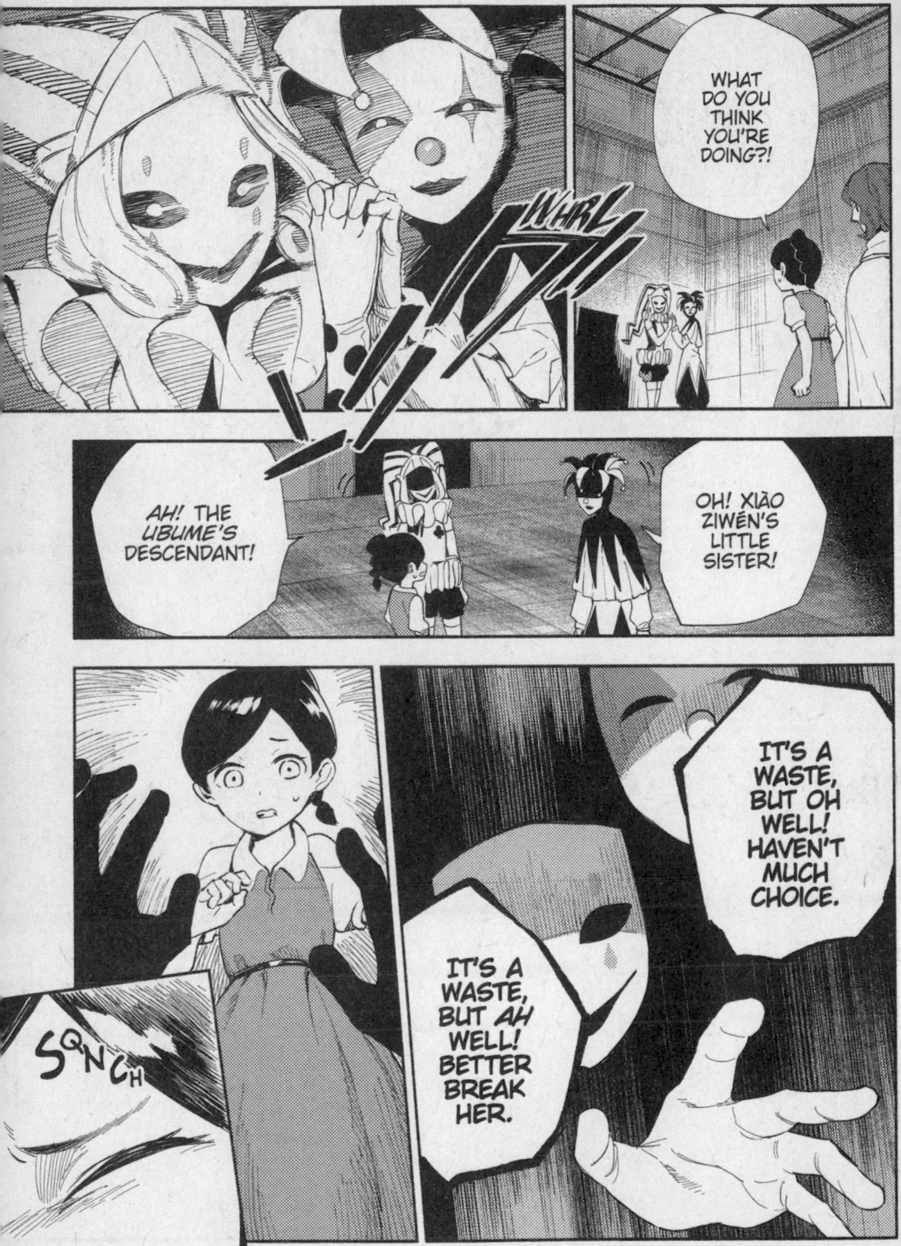
WHAT DO YOU THINK YOU'RE DOING?!
WHIRL
OH! XIÀO ZIWÉN'S LITTLE SISTER!
AH! THE UBUME'S DESCENDANT!
IT'S A WASTE, BUT OH WELL! HAVEN'T MUCH CHOICE.
IT'S A WASTE, BUT AH WELL! BETTER BREAK HER.
SQNCH

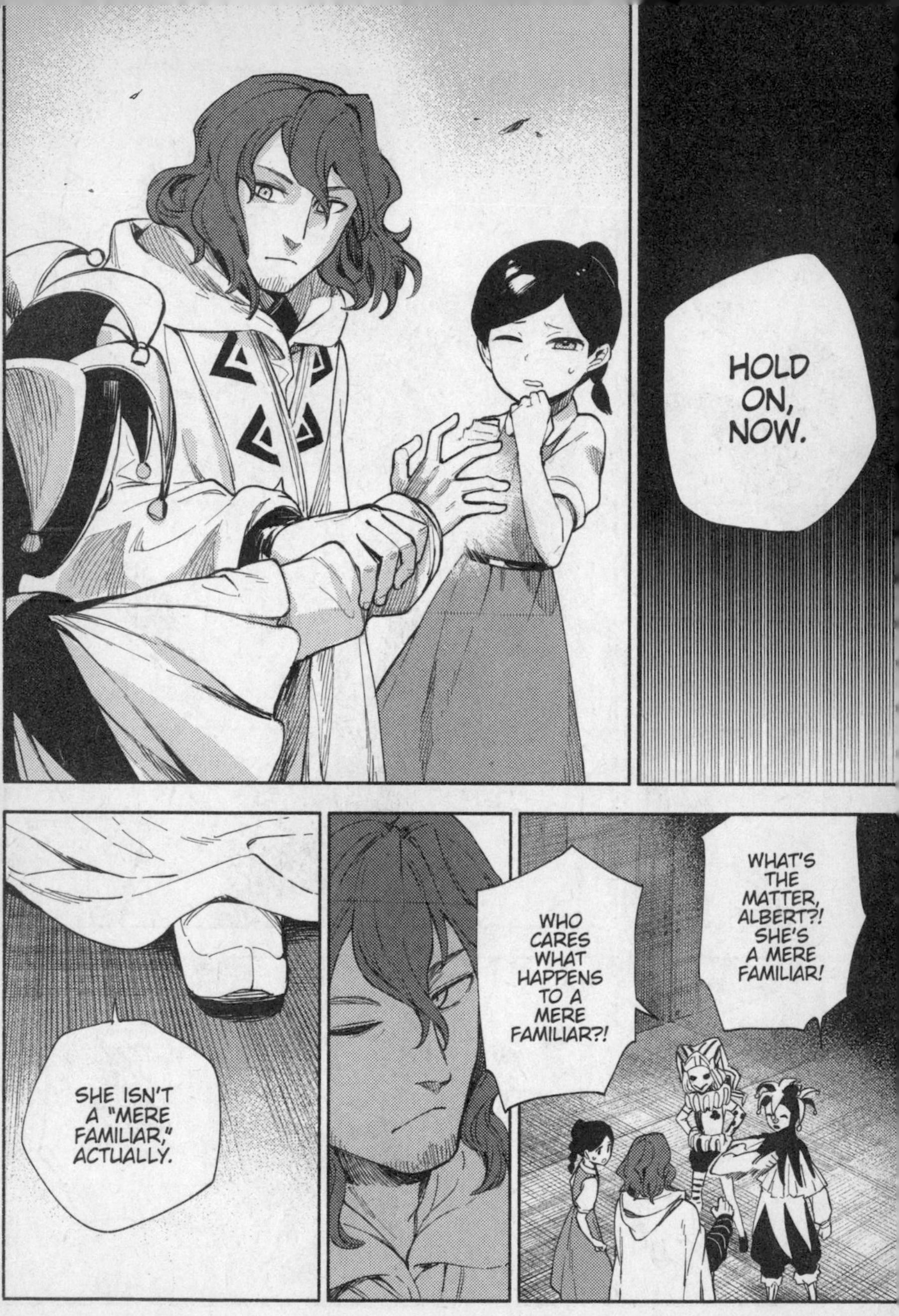
HOLD ON, NOW.
WHAT'S THE MATTER, ALBERT?! SHE'S A MERE FAMILIAR!
WHO CARES WHAT HAPPENS TO A MERE FAMILIAR?!
SHE ISN'T A "MERE FAMILIAR," ACTUALLY.

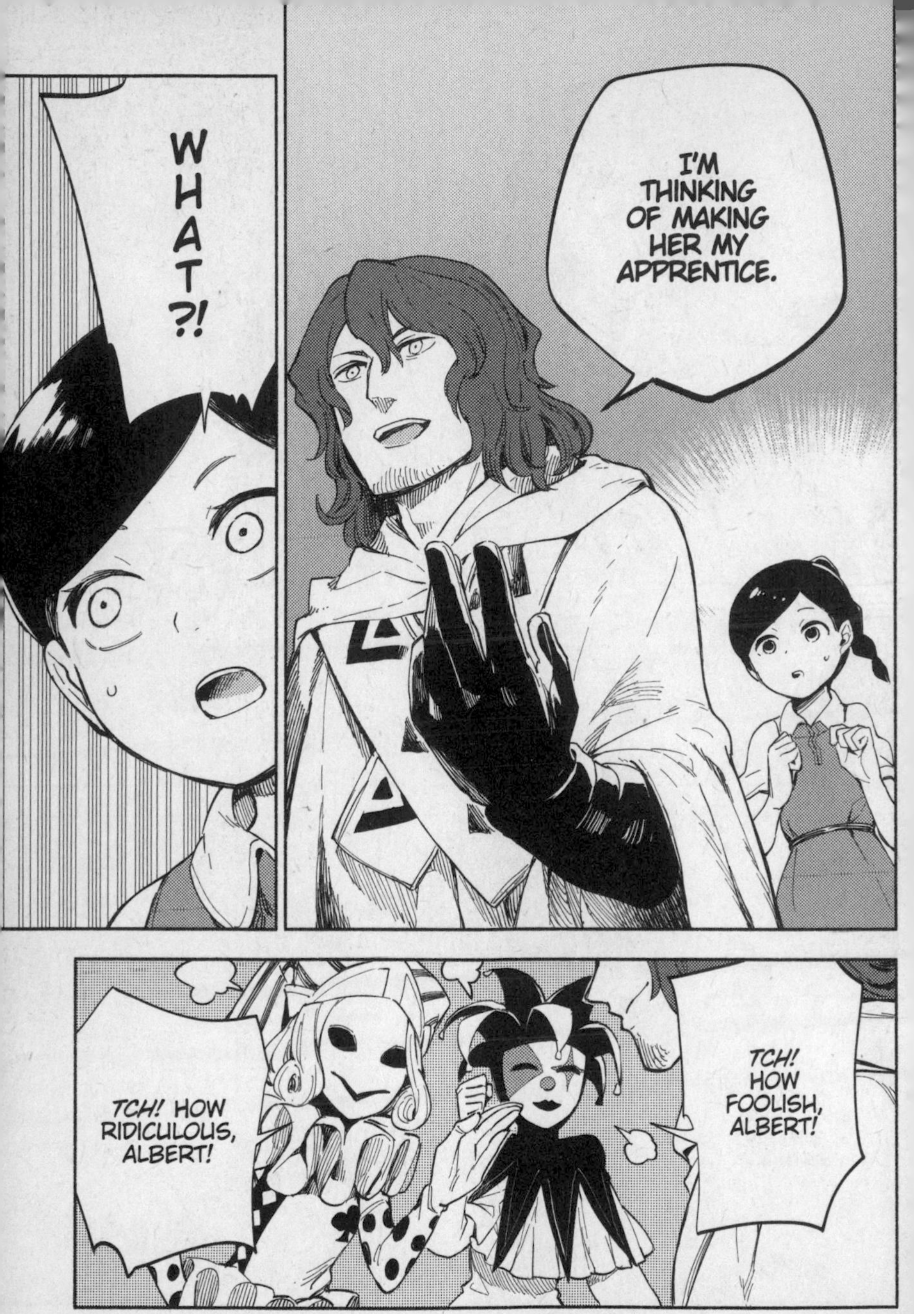
I'M THINKING OF MAKING HER MY APPRENTICE.
WHAT?!
TCH! HOW FOOLISH, ALBERT!
TCH! HOW RIDICULOUS, ALBERT!

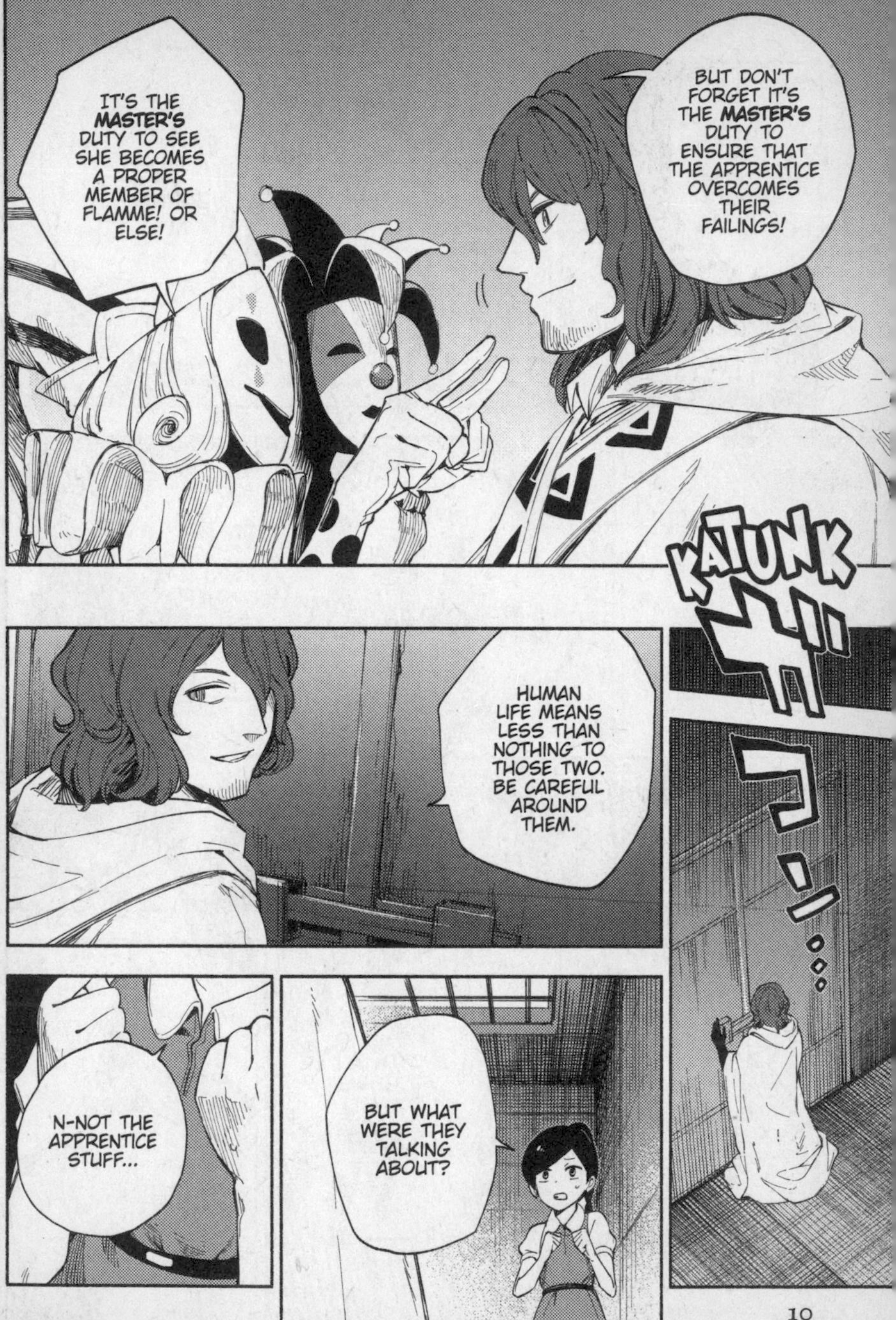
BUT DON'T FORGET IT'S THE **MASTER'S** DUTY TO ENSURE THAT THE APPRENTICE OVERCOMES THEIR FAILINGS!
IT'S THE **MASTER'S** DUTY TO SEE SHE BECOMES A PROPER MEMBER OF FLAMME! OR ELSE!
KATUNK
HUMAN LIFE MEANS LESS THAN NOTHING TO THOSE TWO. BE CAREFUL AROUND THEM.
BUT WHAT WERE THEY TALKING ABOUT?
N-NOT THE APPRENTICE STUFF...

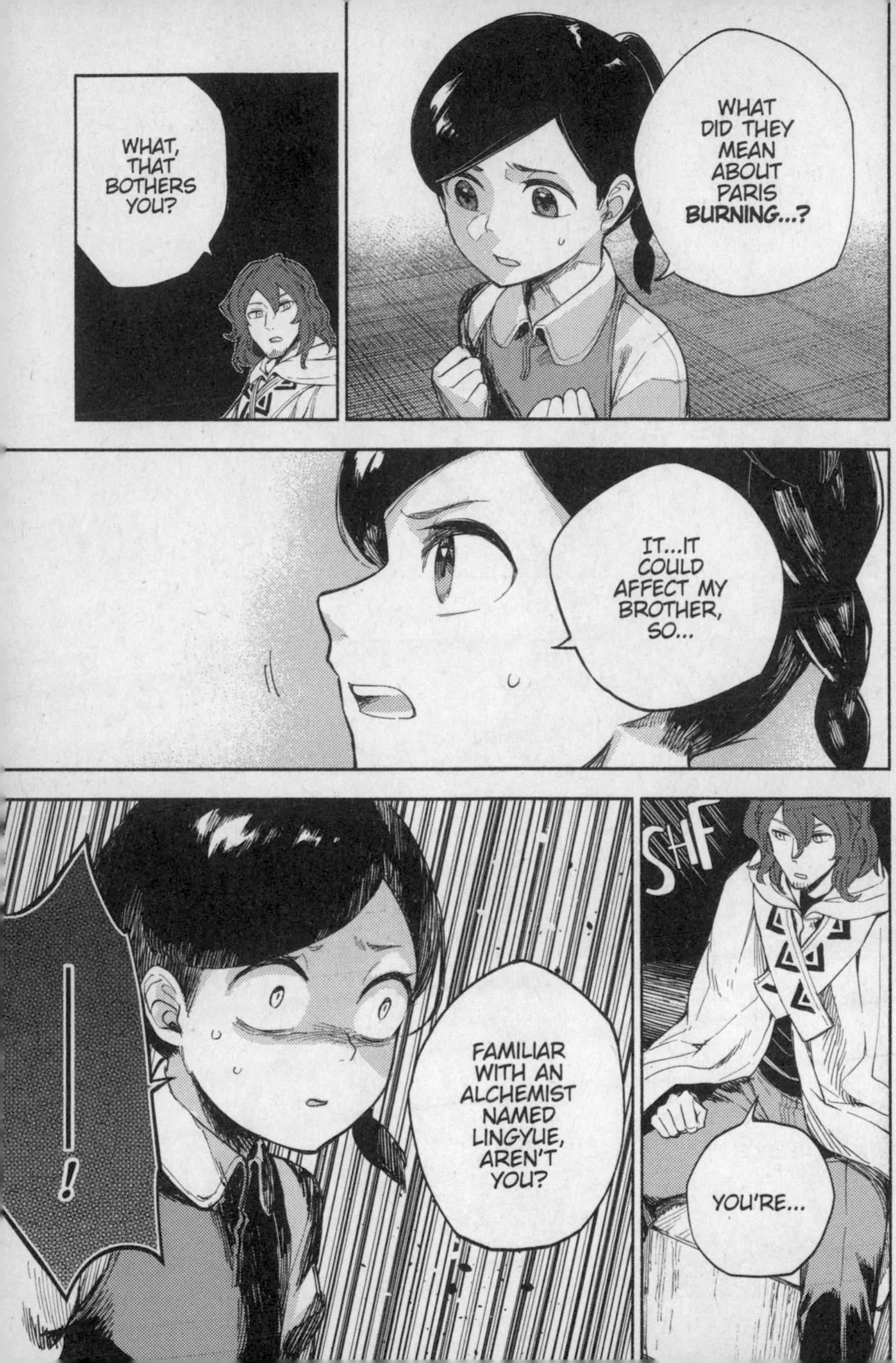
WHAT DID THEY MEAN ABOUT PARIS BURNING...?
WHAT, THAT BOTHERS YOU?
IT...IT COULD AFFECT MY BROTHER, SO...
SHF
YOU'RE...
FAMILIAR WITH AN ALCHEMIST NAMED LINGYUE, AREN'T YOU?
—!

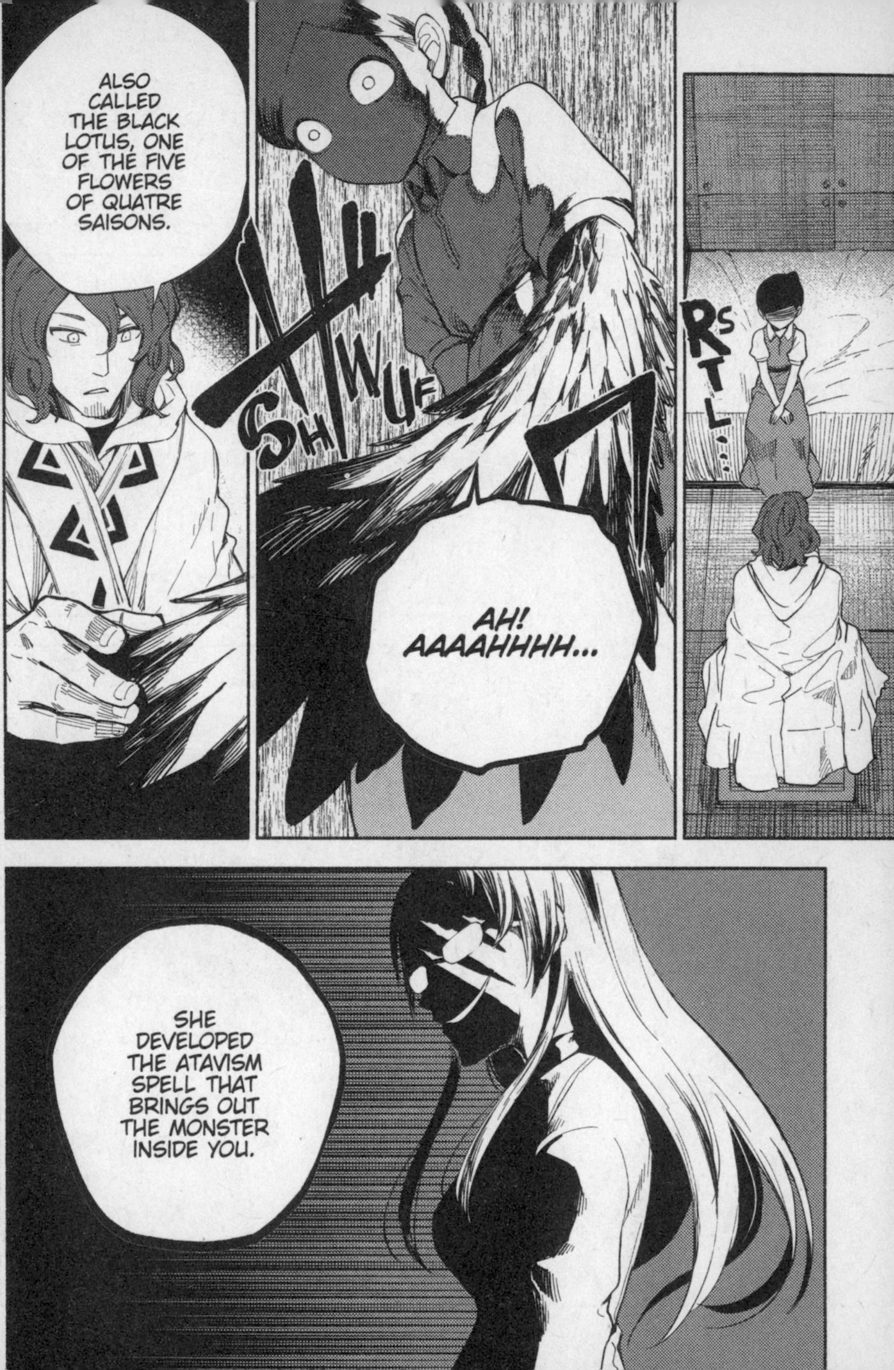
RSTL...
SHWUF
AH! AAAAHHHH...
ALSO CALLED THE BLACK LOTUS, ONE OF THE FIVE FLOWERS OF QUATRE SAISONS.
SHE DEVELOPED THE ATAVISM SPELL THAT BRINGS OUT THE MONSTER INSIDE YOU.

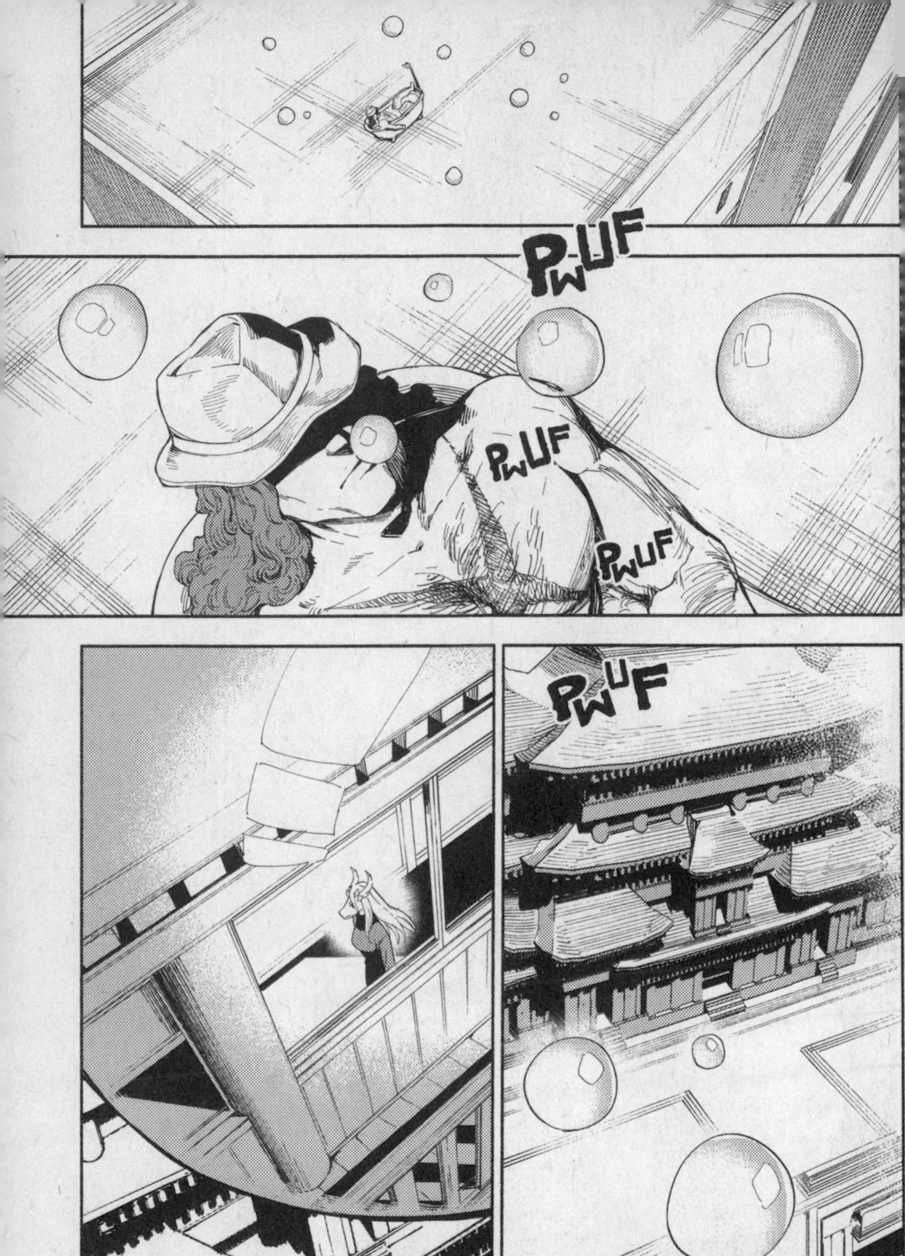
PWUF
PWUF
PWUF
PWUF

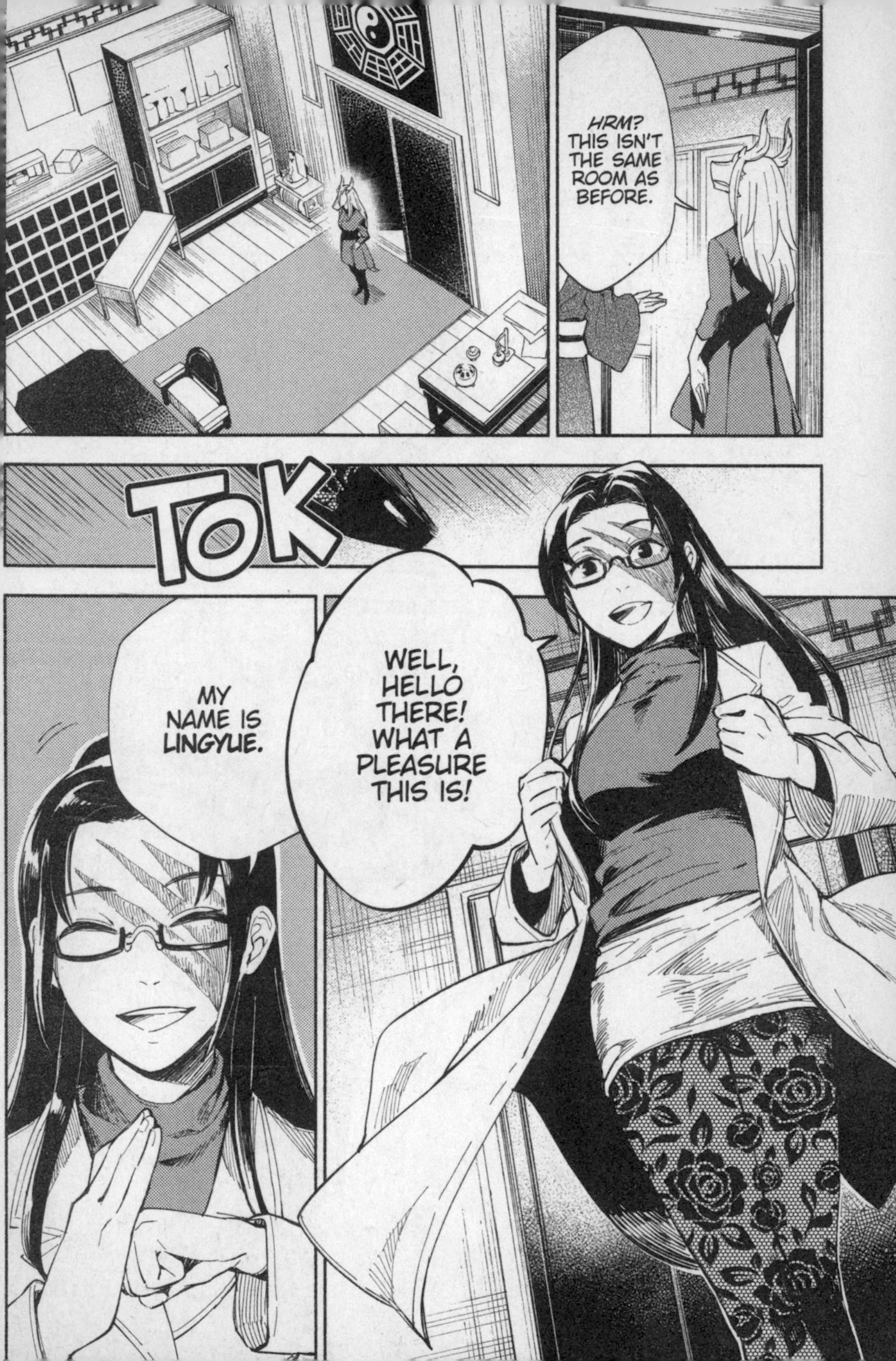
HRM? THIS ISN'T THE SAME ROOM AS BEFORE.
TOK
WELL, HELLO THERE! WHAT A PLEASURE THIS IS!
MY NAME IS LINGYUE.

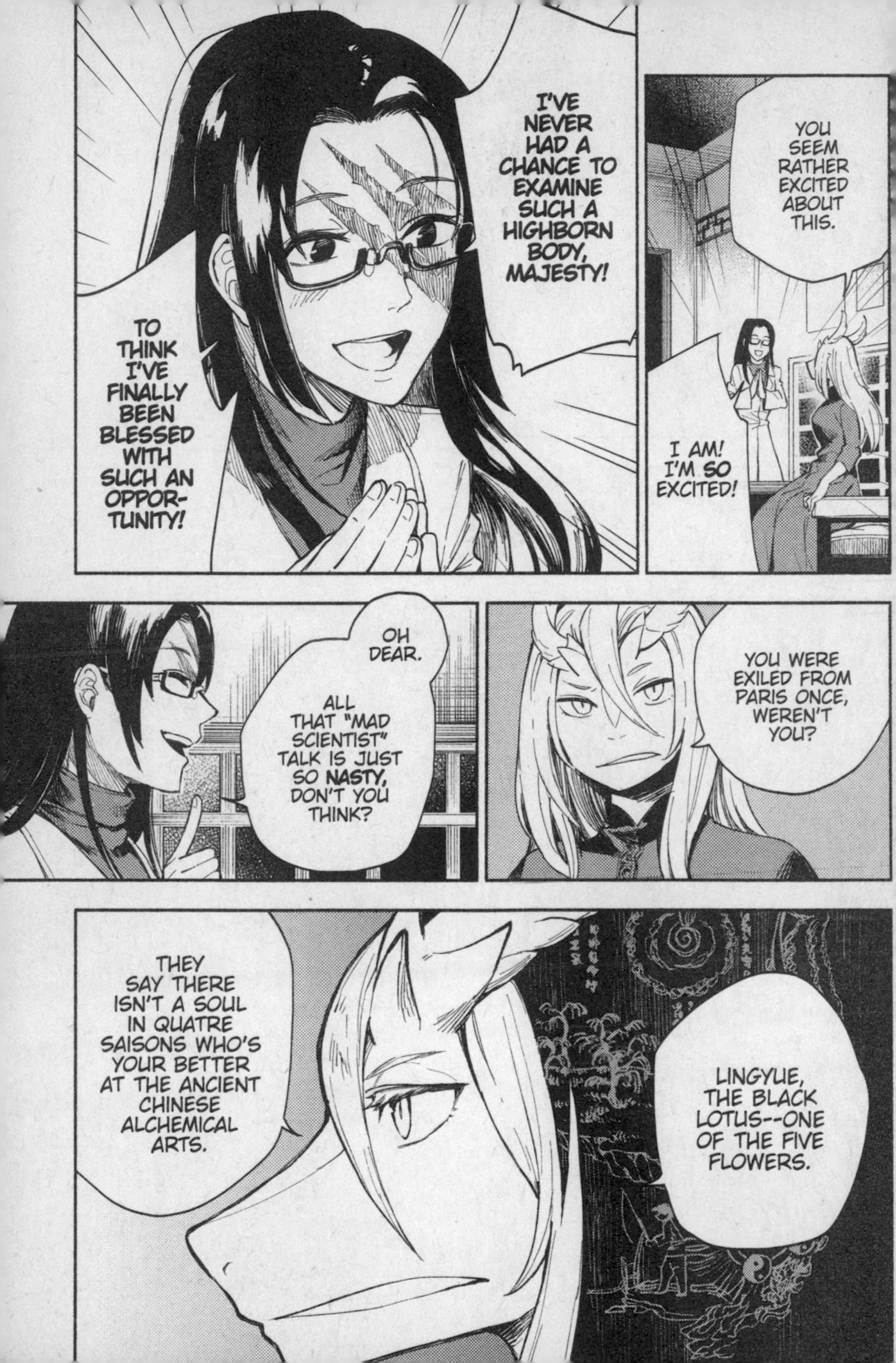
YOU SEEM RATHER EXCITED ABOUT THIS.
I AM! I'M SO EXCITED!
I'VE NEVER HAD A CHANCE TO EXAMINE SUCH A HIGHBORN BODY, MAJESTY!
TO THINK I'VE FINALLY BEEN BLESSED WITH SUCH AN OPPOR-TUNITY!
YOU WERE EXILED FROM PARIS ONCE, WEREN'T YOU?
OH DEAR.
ALL THAT "MAD SCIENTIST" TALK IS JUST SO NASTY, DON'T YOU THINK?
LINGYUE, THE BLACK LOTUS--ONE OF THE FIVE FLOWERS.
THEY SAY THERE ISN'T A SOUL IN QUATRE SAISONS WHO'S YOUR BETTER AT THE ANCIENT CHINESE ALCHEMICAL ARTS.

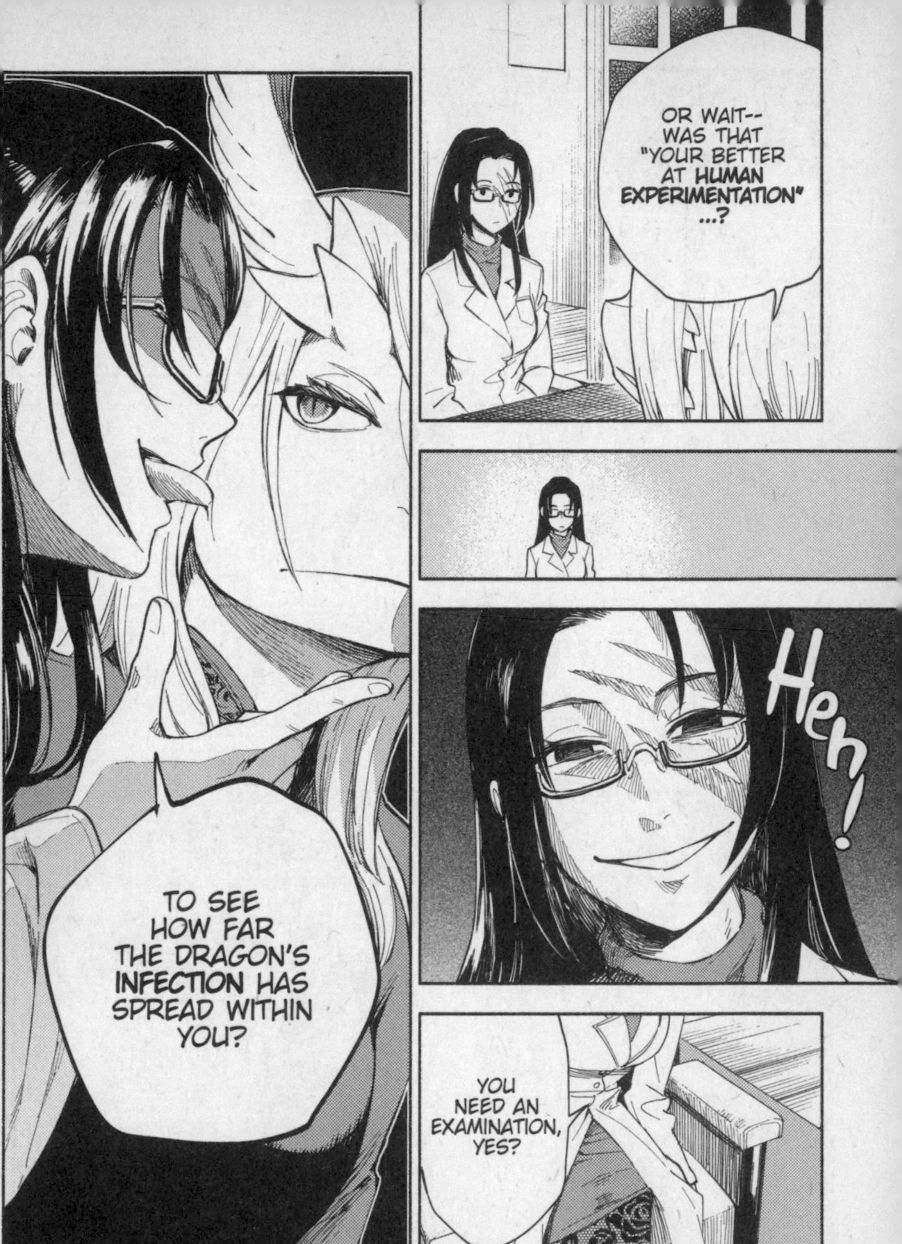

OR WAIT-- WAS THAT "YOUR BETTER AT HUMAN EXPERIMENTATION" ...?
Hen!
YOU NEED AN EXAMINATION, YES?
TO SEE HOW FAR THE DRAGON'S INFECTION HAS SPREAD WITHIN YOU?

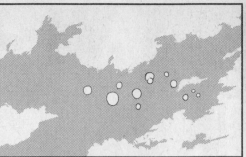

LINGYUE, THE BLACK LOTUS?!

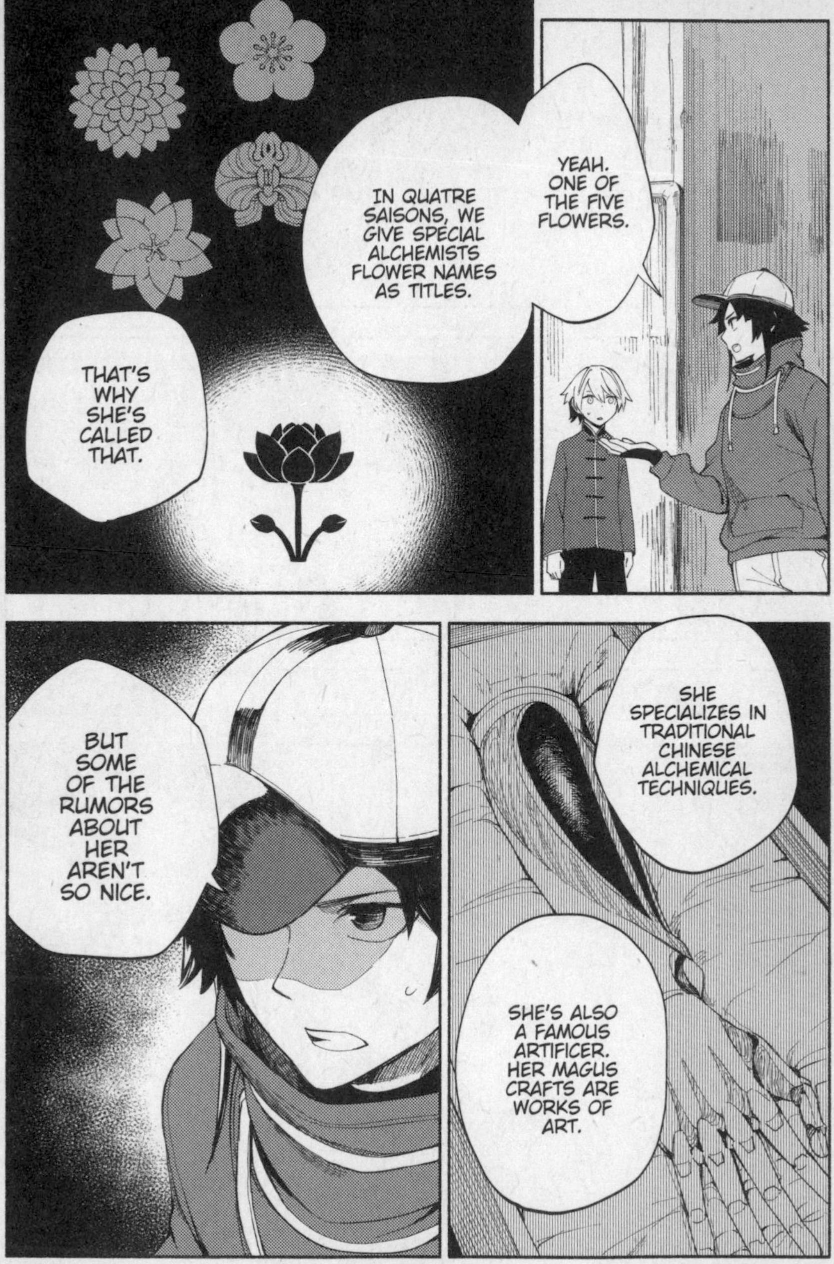
YEAH. ONE OF THE FIVE FLOWERS.
IN QUATRE SAISONS, WE GIVE SPECIAL ALCHEMISTS FLOWER NAMES AS TITLES.
THAT'S WHY SHE'S CALLED THAT.
SHE SPECIALIZES IN TRADITIONAL CHINESE ALCHEMICAL TECHNIQUES.
SHE'S ALSO A FAMOUS ARTIFICER. HER MAGUS CRAFTS ARE WORKS OF ART.
BUT SOME OF THE RUMORS ABOUT HER AREN'T SO NICE.

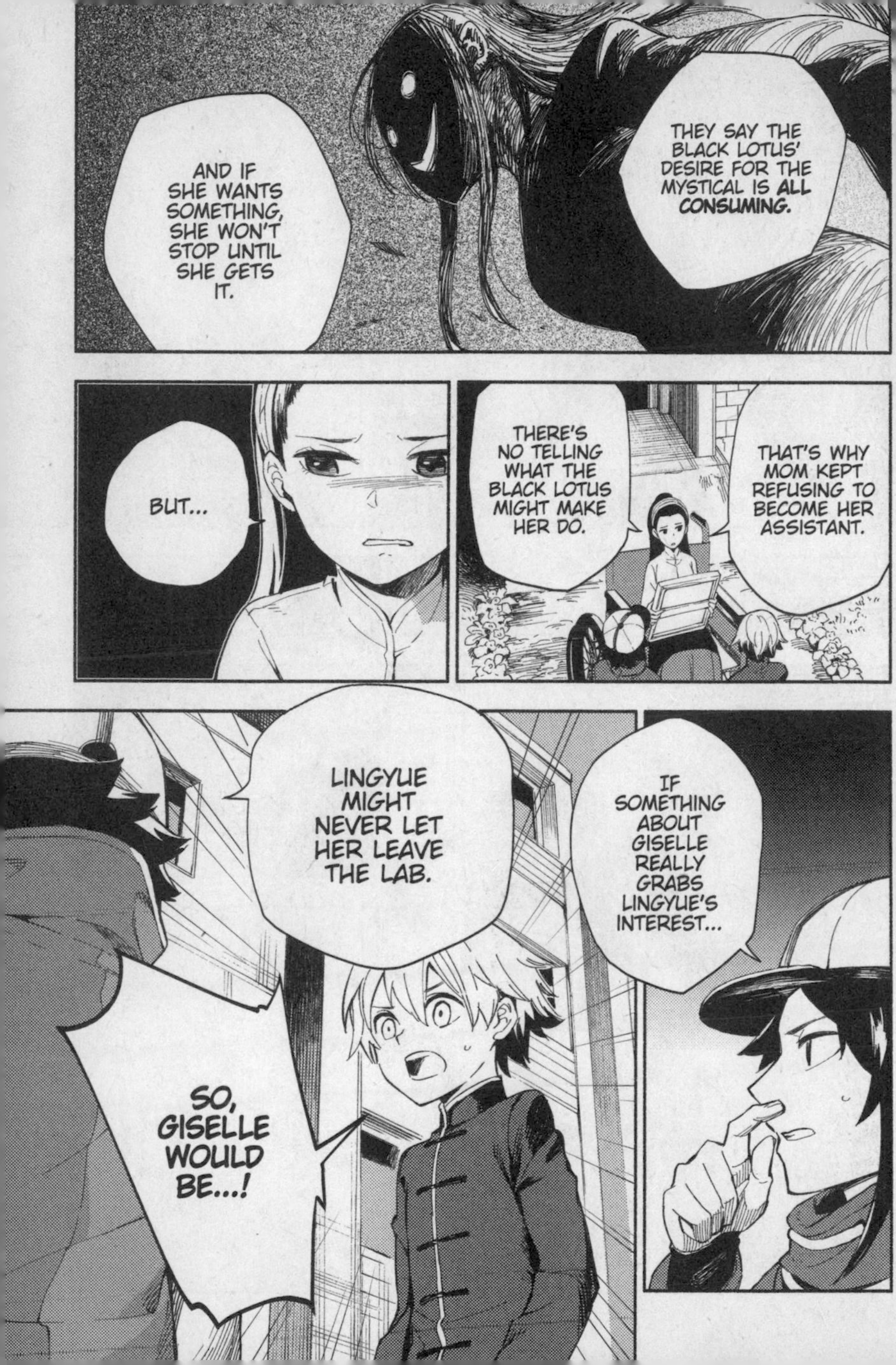
THEY SAY THE BLACK LOTUS' DESIRE FOR THE MYSTICAL IS ALL CONSUMING.
AND IF SHE WANTS SOMETHING, SHE WON'T STOP UNTIL SHE GETS IT.
THAT'S WHY MOM KEPT REFUSING TO BECOME HER ASSISTANT.
THERE'S NO TELLING WHAT THE BLACK LOTUS MIGHT MAKE HER DO.
BUT...
IF SOMETHING ABOUT GISELLE REALLY GRABS LINGYUE'S INTEREST...
LINGYUE MIGHT NEVER LET HER LEAVE THE LAB.
SO, GISELLE WOULD BE...!

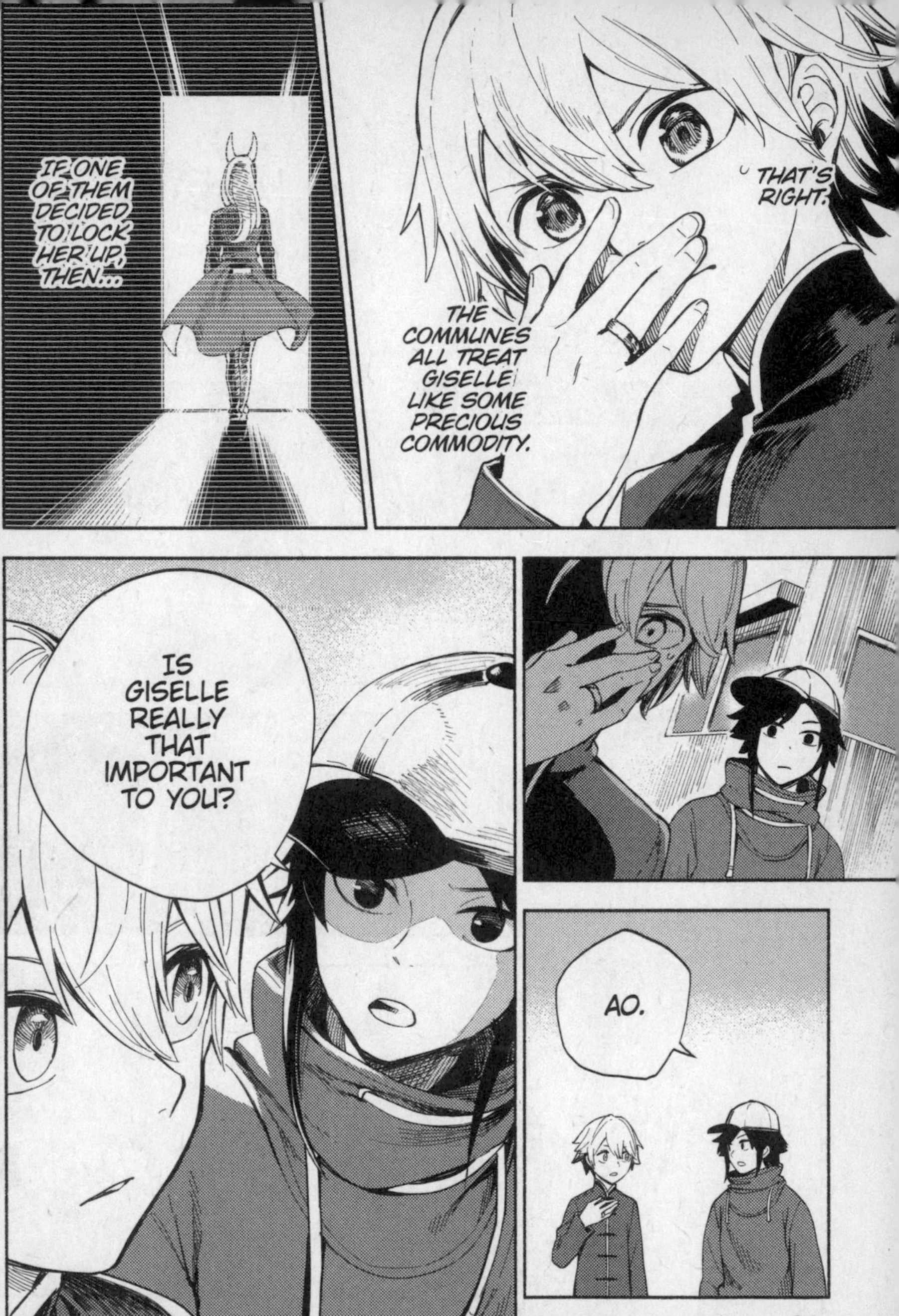
THAT'S RIGHT.
THE COMMUNES ALL TREAT GISELLE LIKE SOME PRECIOUS COMMODITY.
IF ONE OF THEM DECIDED TO LOCK HER UP, THEN...
AO.
IS GISELLE REALLY THAT IMPORTANT TO YOU?

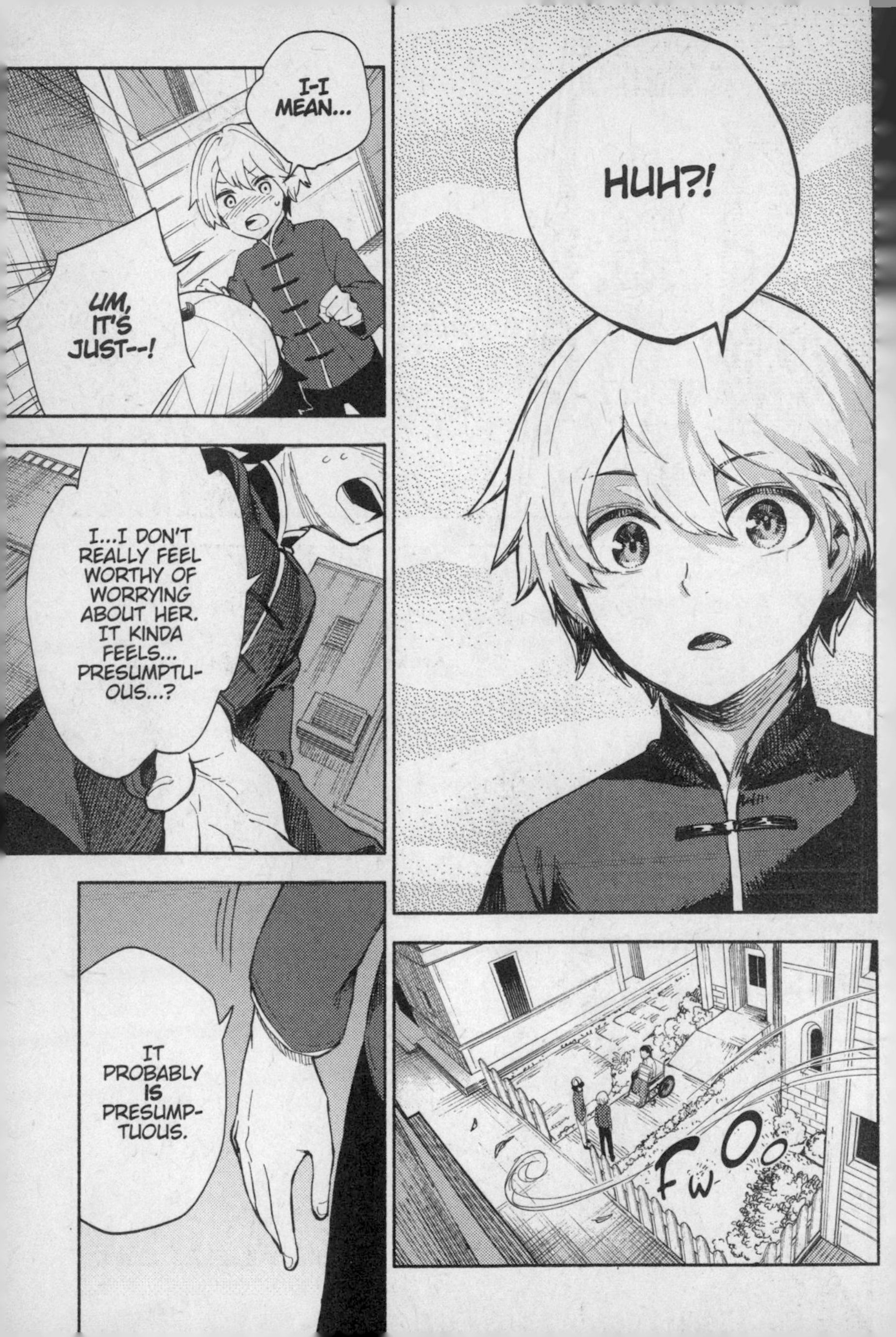
HUH?!
I-I MEAN...
UM, IT'S JUST--!
I...I DON'T REALLY FEEL WORTHY OF WORRYING ABOUT HER. IT KINDA FEELS... PRESUMPTUOUS...?
FWOO
IT PROBABLY IS PRESUMPTUOUS.

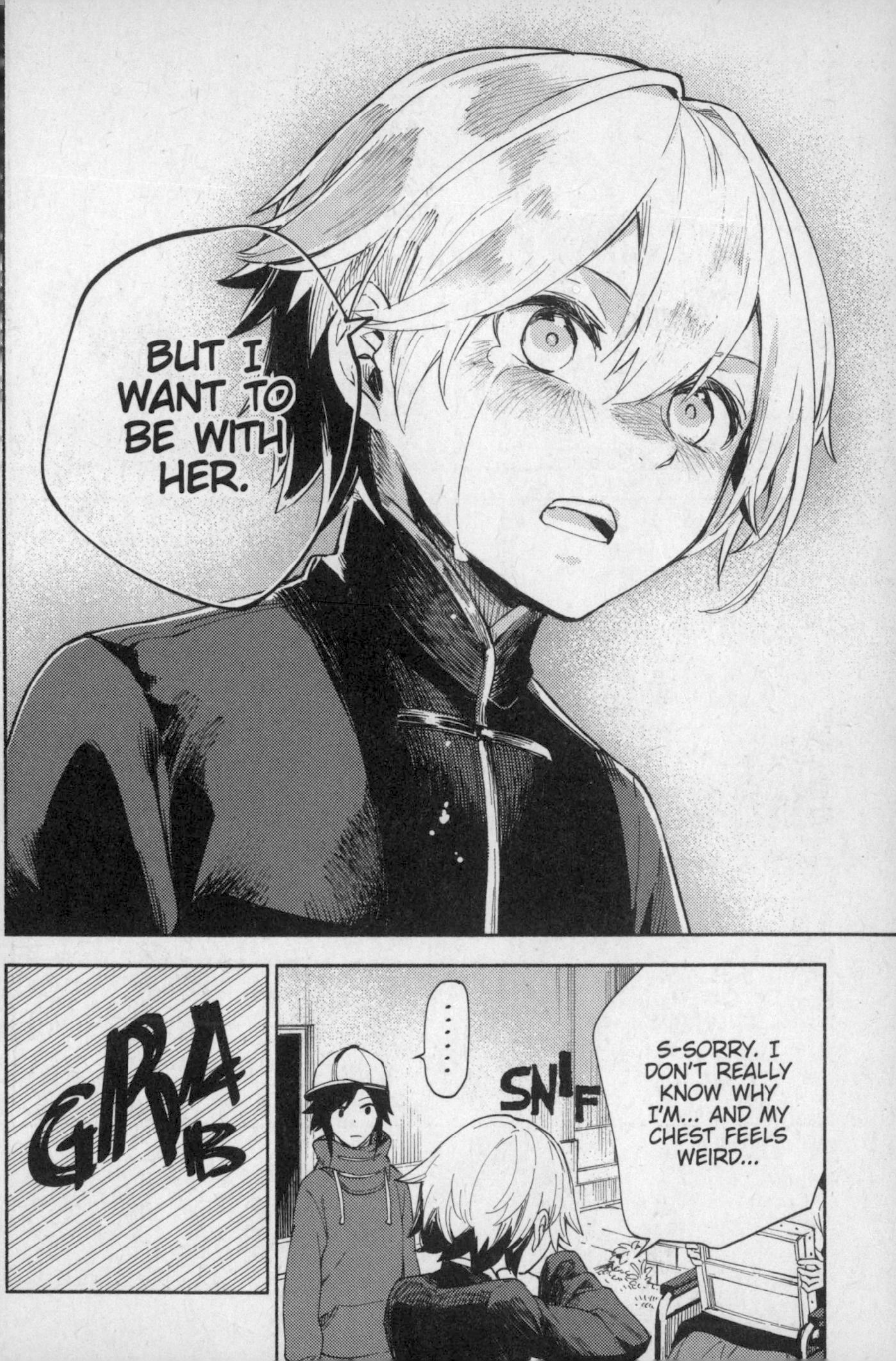
BUT I WANT TO BE WITH HER.
S-SORRY. I DON'T REALLY KNOW WHY I'M... AND MY CHEST FEELS WEIRD...
......
SNIF
GRAB

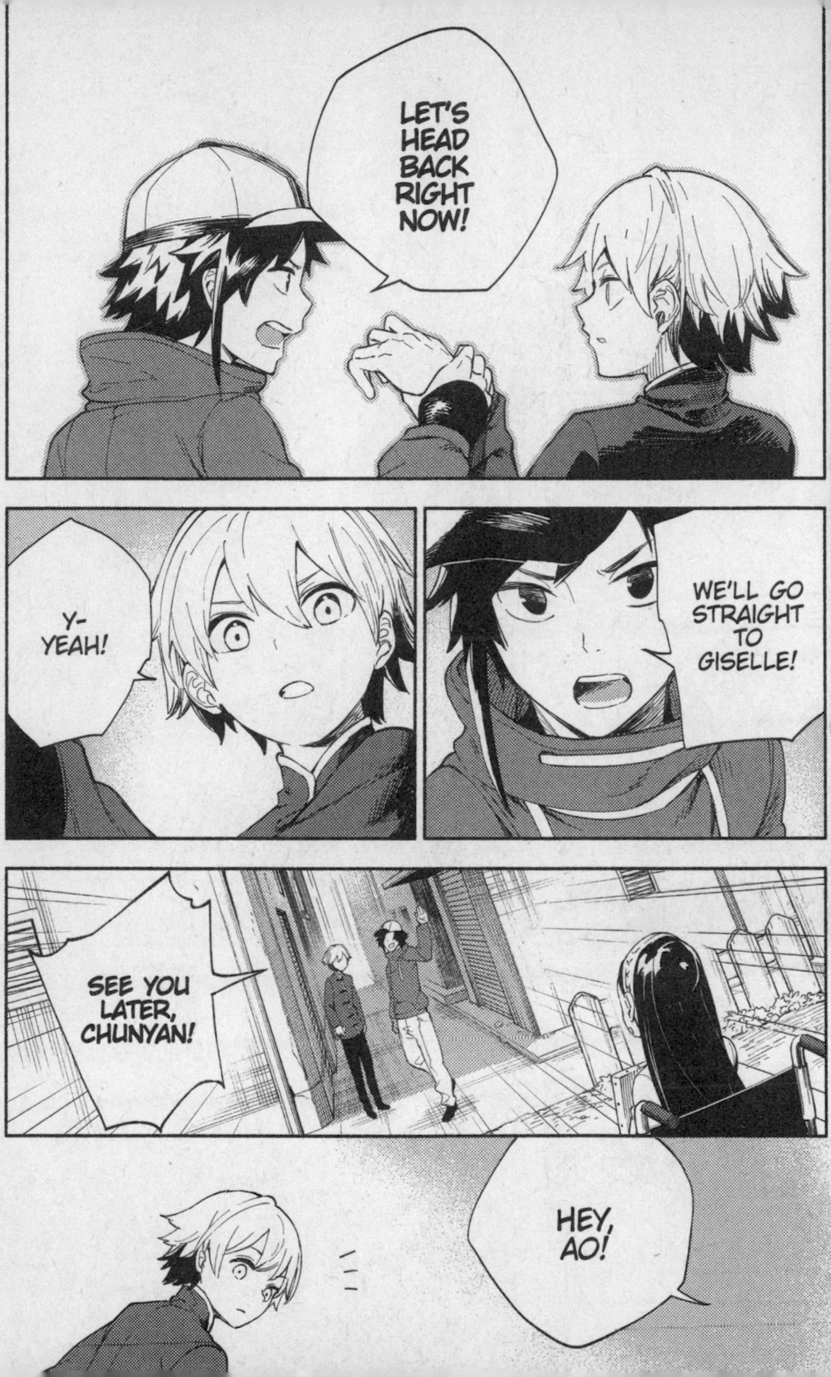
LET'S HEAD BACK RIGHT NOW!
WE'LL GO STRAIGHT TO GISELLE!
Y-YEAH!
SEE YOU LATER, CHUNYAN!
HEY, AO!

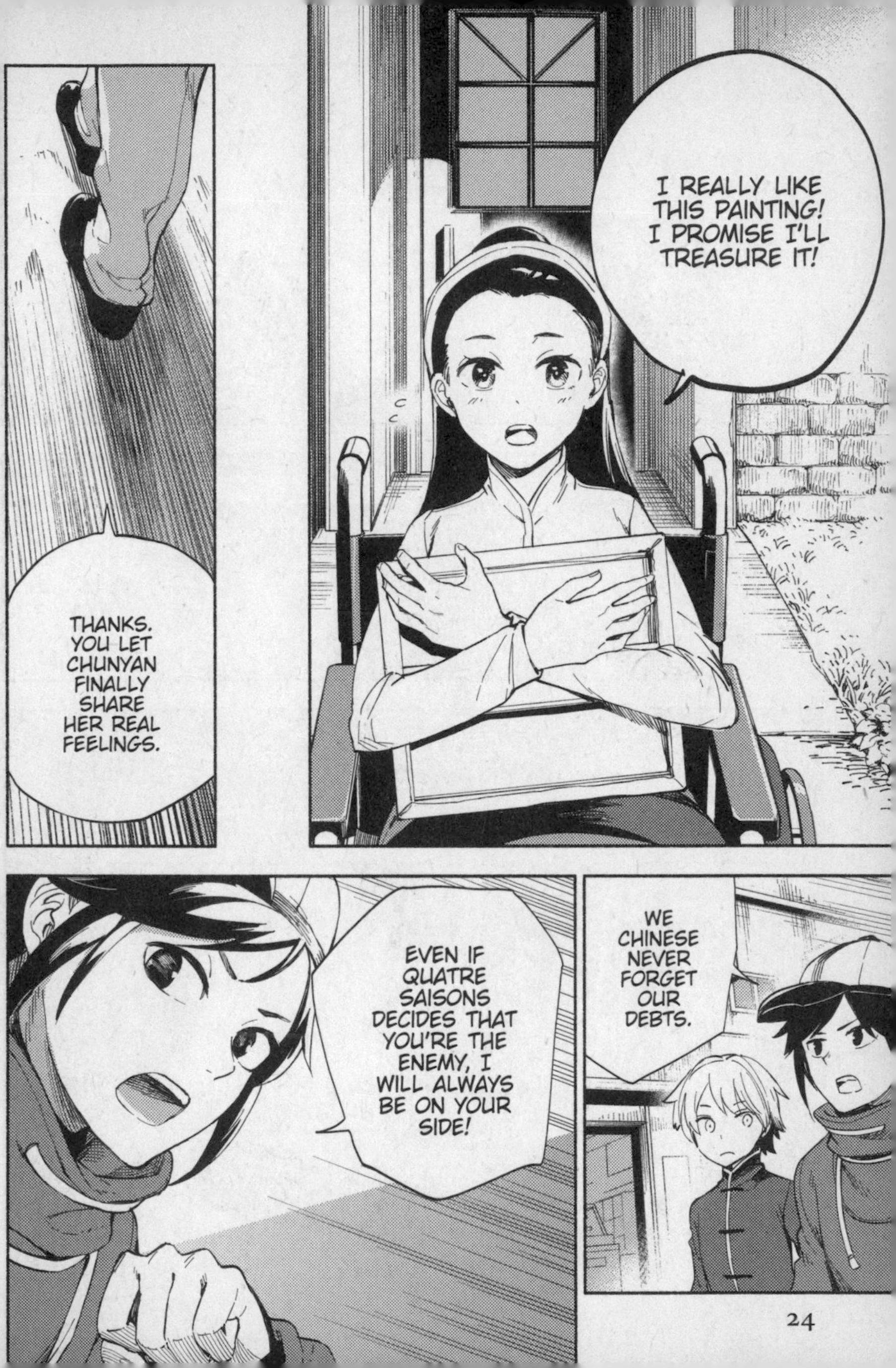
I REALLY LIKE THIS PAINTING! I PROMISE I'LL TREASURE IT!
THANKS. YOU LET CHUNYAN FINALLY SHARE HER REAL FEELINGS.
WE CHINESE NEVER FORGET OUR DEBTS.
EVEN IF QUATRE SAISONS DECIDES THAT YOU'RE THE ENEMY, I WILL ALWAYS BE ON YOUR SIDE!

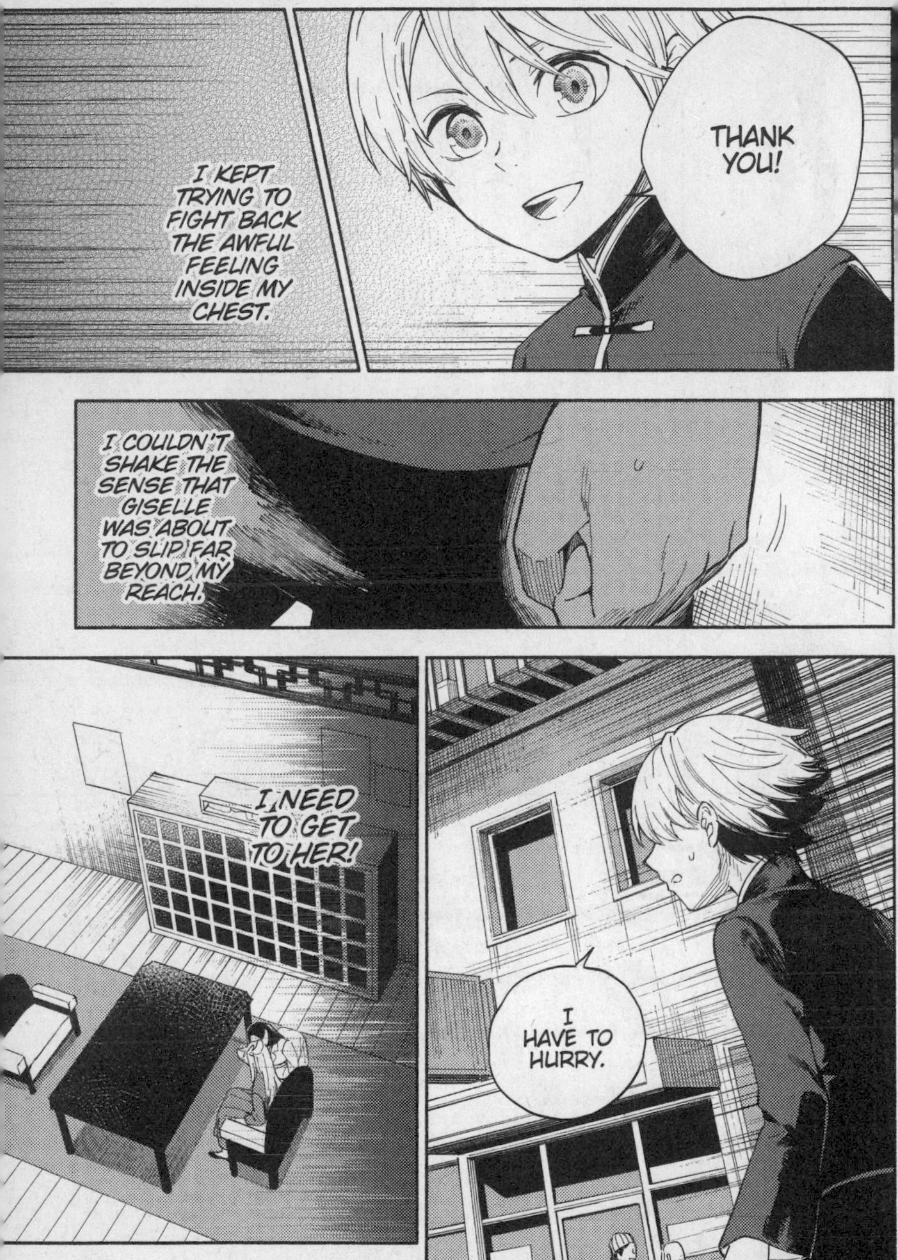
THANK YOU!
I KEPT TRYING TO FIGHT BACK THE AWFUL FEELING INSIDE MY CHEST.
I COULDN'T SHAKE THE SENSE THAT GISELLE WAS ABOUT TO SLIP FAR BEYOND MY REACH.
I HAVE TO HURRY.
I NEED TO GET TO HER!

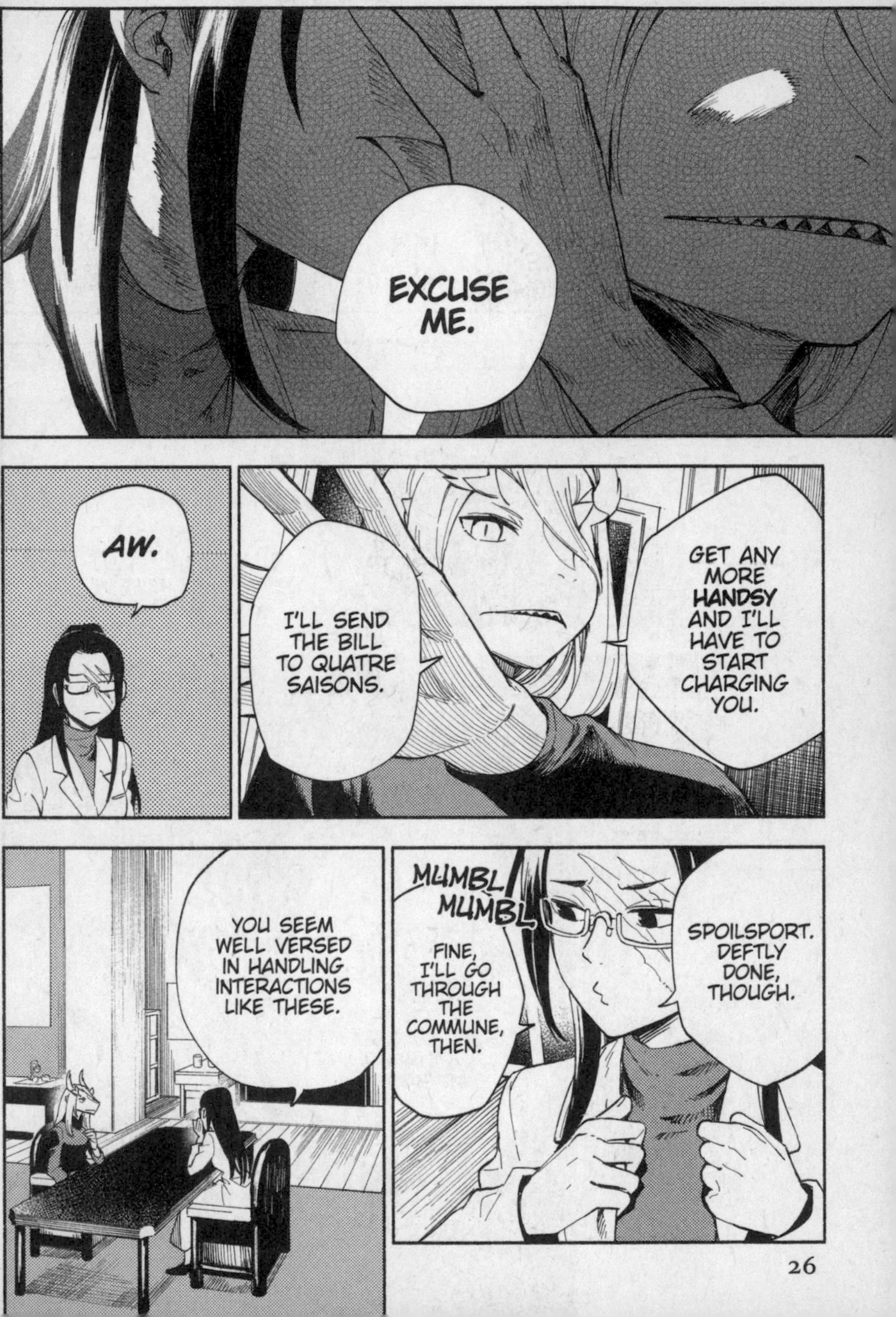
EXCUSE ME.
GET ANY MORE HANDSY AND I'LL HAVE TO START CHARGING YOU.
I'LL SEND THE BILL TO QUATRE SAISONS.
AW.
SPOILSPORT. DEFTLY DONE, THOUGH.
MUMBL MUMBL
FINE, I'LL GO THROUGH THE COMMUNE, THEN.
YOU SEEM WELL VERSED IN HANDLING INTERACTIONS LIKE THESE.

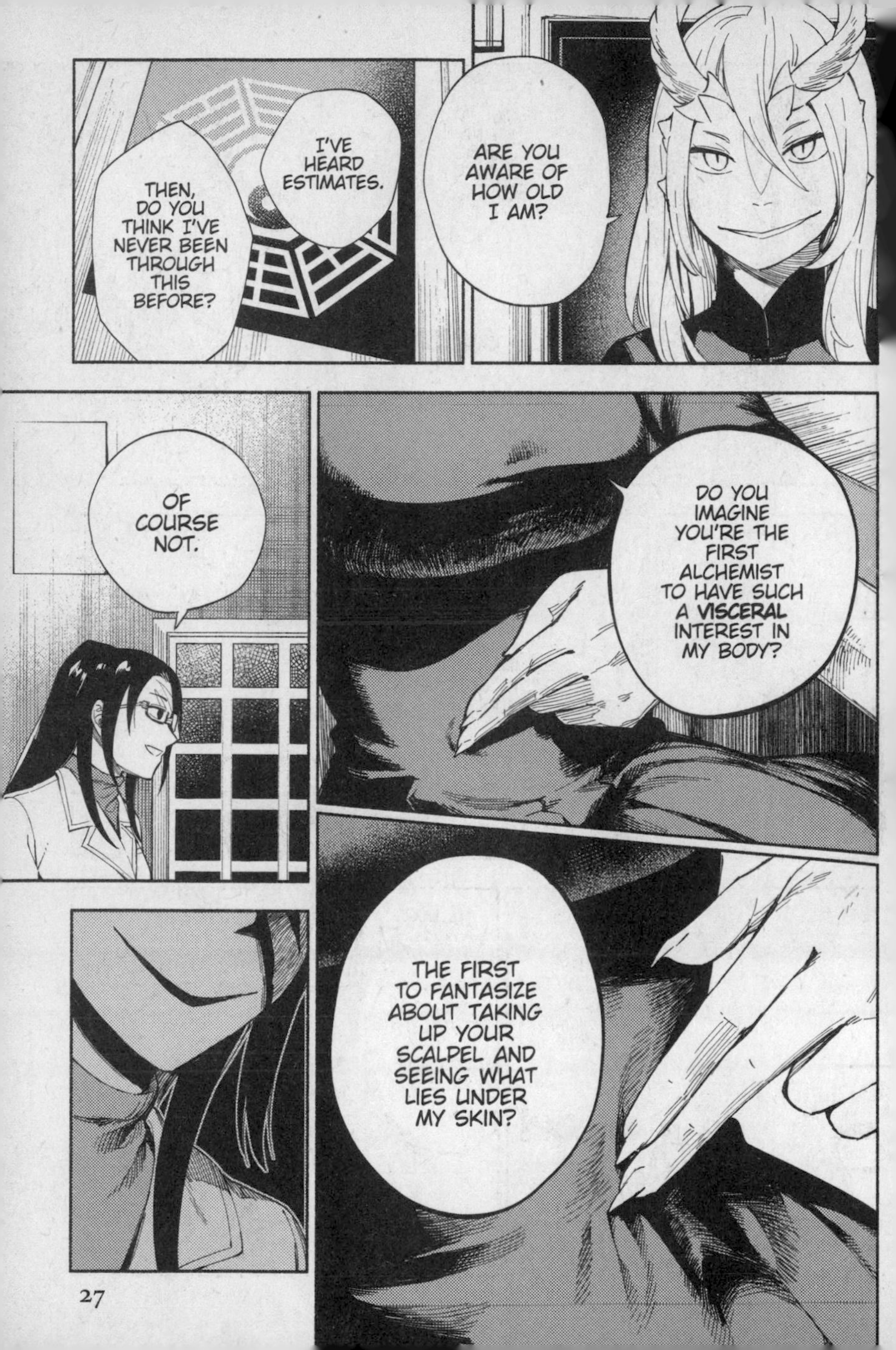
ARE YOU AWARE OF HOW OLD I AM?
I'VE HEARD ESTIMATES.
THEN, DO YOU THINK I'VE NEVER BEEN THROUGH THIS BEFORE?
DO YOU IMAGINE YOU'RE THE FIRST ALCHEMIST TO HAVE SUCH A **VISCERAL** INTEREST IN MY BODY?
OF COURSE NOT.
THE FIRST TO FANTASIZE ABOUT TAKING UP YOUR SCALPEL AND SEEING WHAT LIES UNDER MY SKIN?

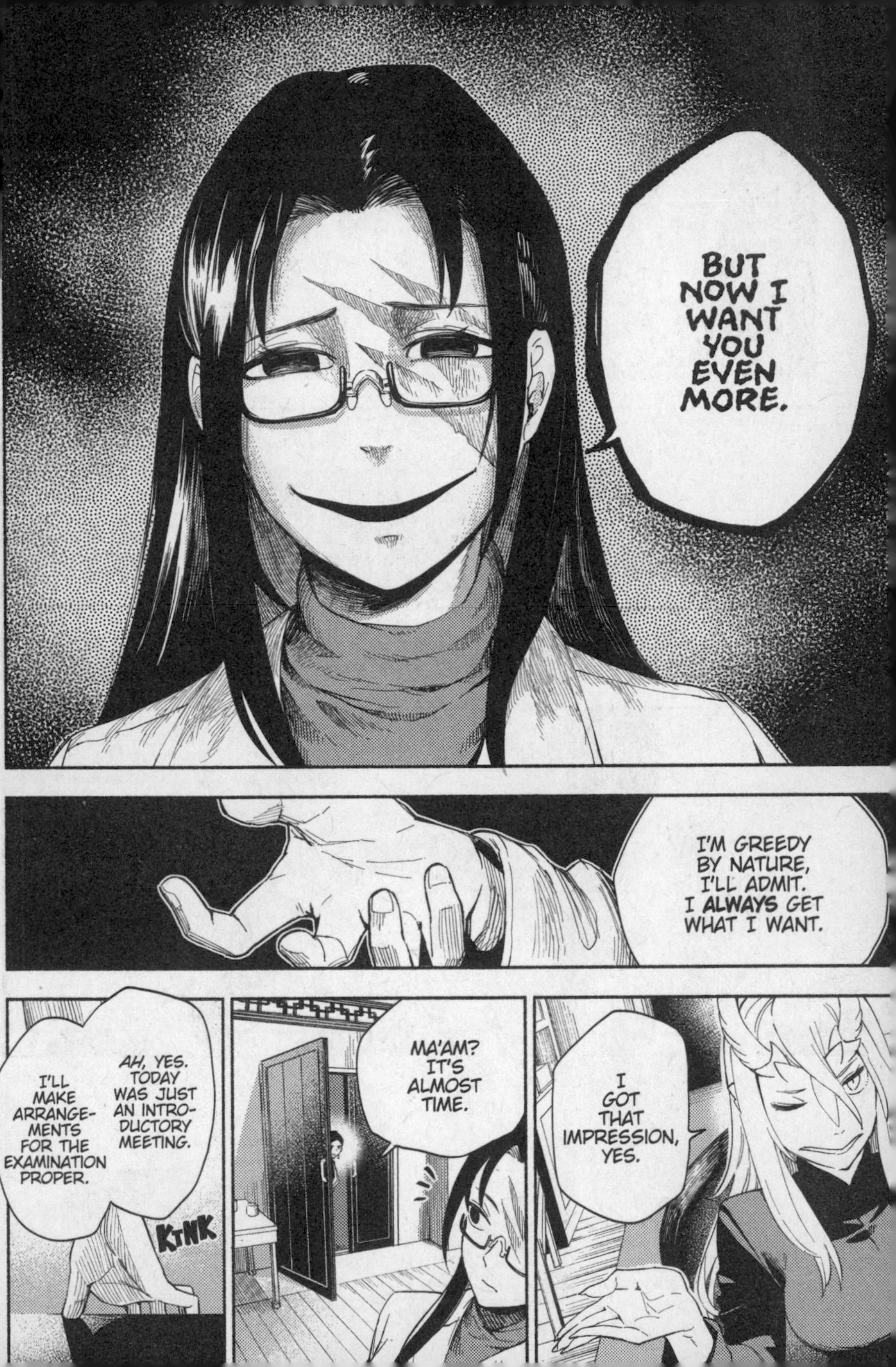
BUT NOW I WANT YOU EVEN MORE.
I'M GREEDY BY NATURE, I'LL ADMIT. I ALWAYS GET WHAT I WANT.
I GOT THAT IMPRESSION, YES.
MA'AM? IT'S ALMOST TIME.
AH, YES. TODAY WAS JUST AN INTRODUCTORY MEETING.
I'LL MAKE ARRANGEMENTS FOR THE EXAMINATION PROPER.
KTNK

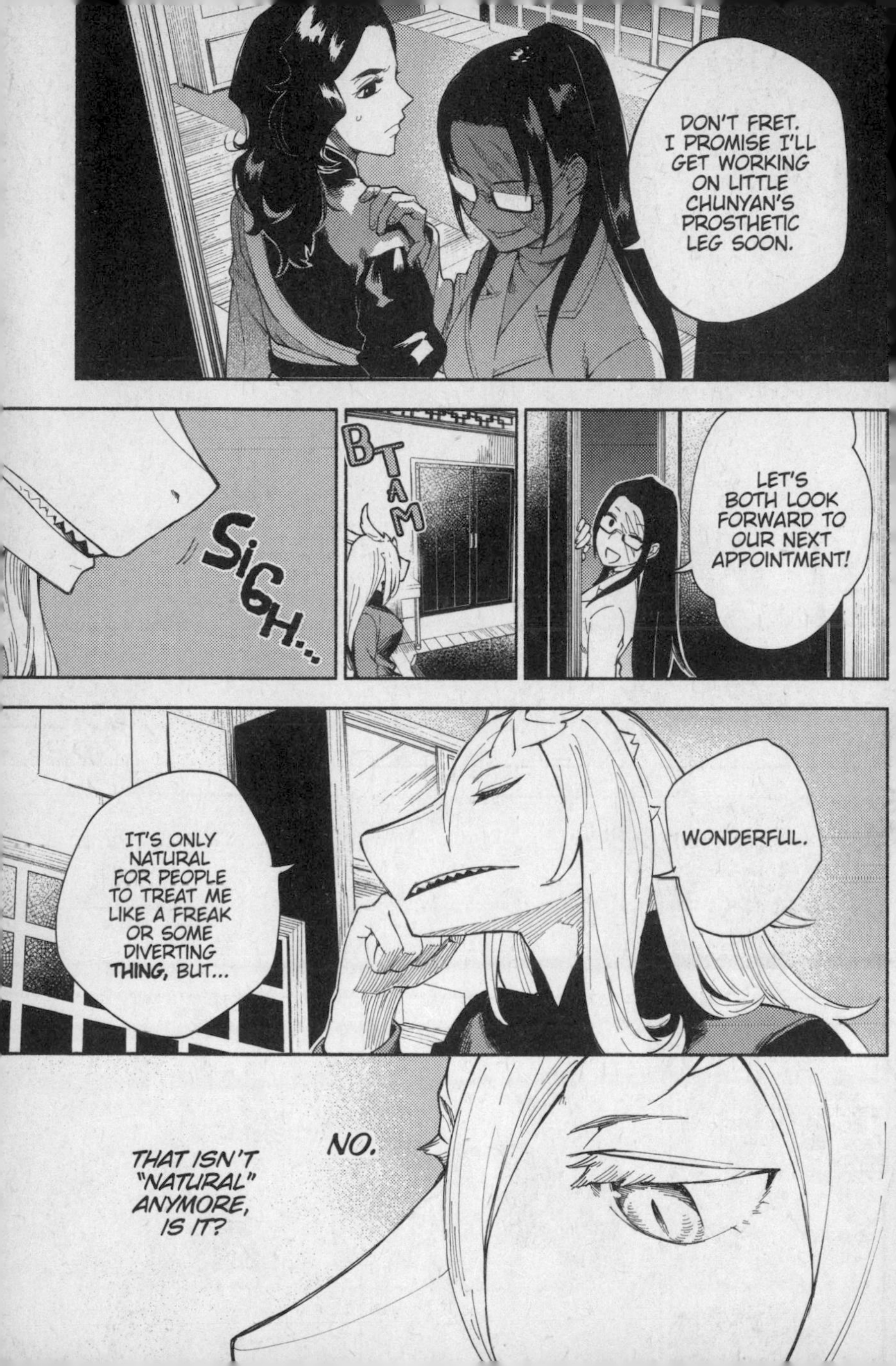
DON'T FRET. I PROMISE I'LL GET WORKING ON LITTLE CHUNYAN'S PROSTHETIC LEG SOON.
LET'S BOTH LOOK FORWARD TO OUR NEXT APPOINTMENT!
BTAM
SIGH...
WONDERFUL.
IT'S ONLY NATURAL FOR PEOPLE TO TREAT ME LIKE A FREAK OR SOME DIVERTING THING, BUT...
NO.
THAT ISN'T "NATURAL" ANYMORE, IS IT?

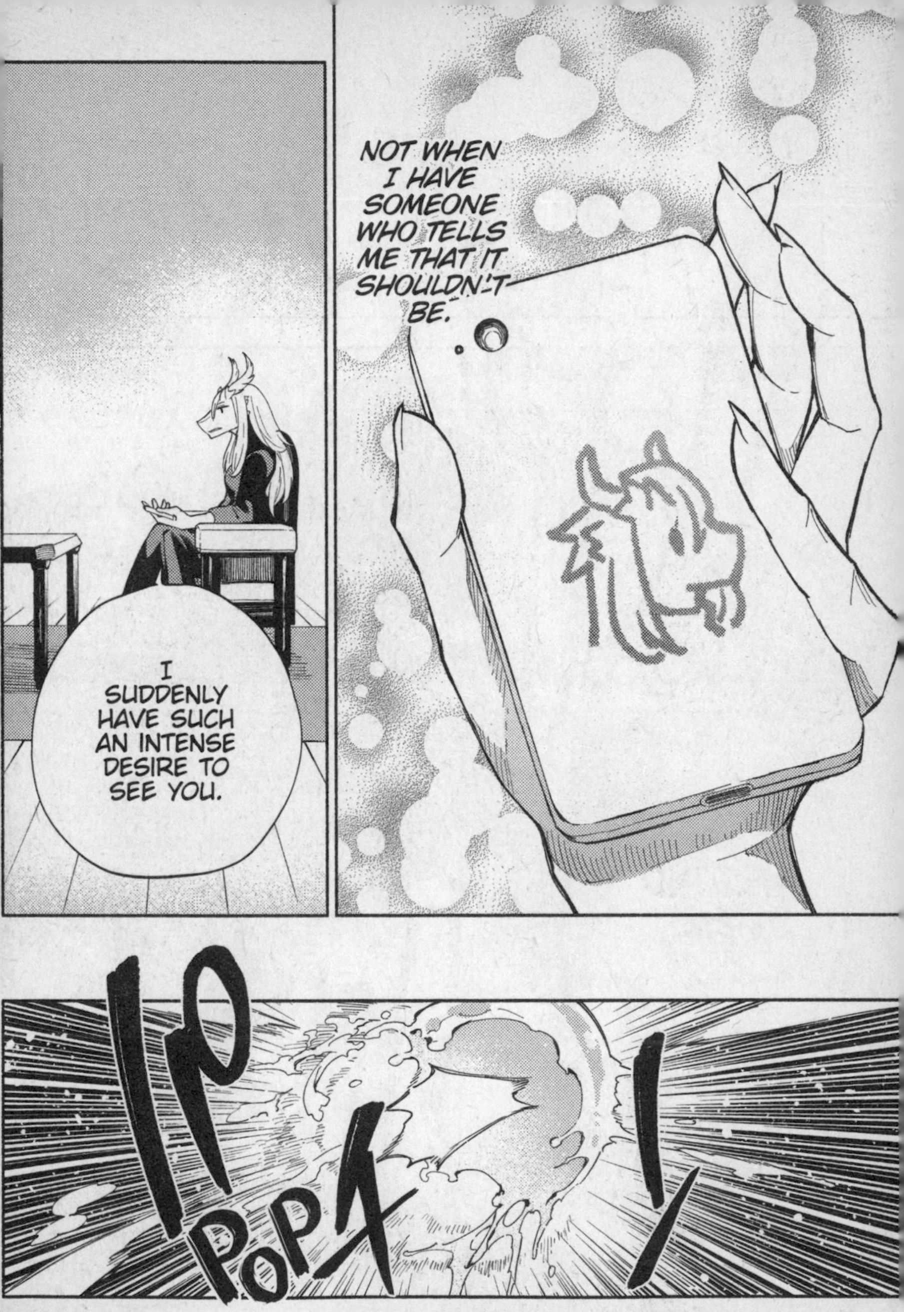
NOT WHEN I HAVE SOMEONE WHO TELLS ME THAT IT SHOULDN'T BE.
I SUDDENLY HAVE SUCH AN INTENSE DESIRE TO SEE YOU.
POP!

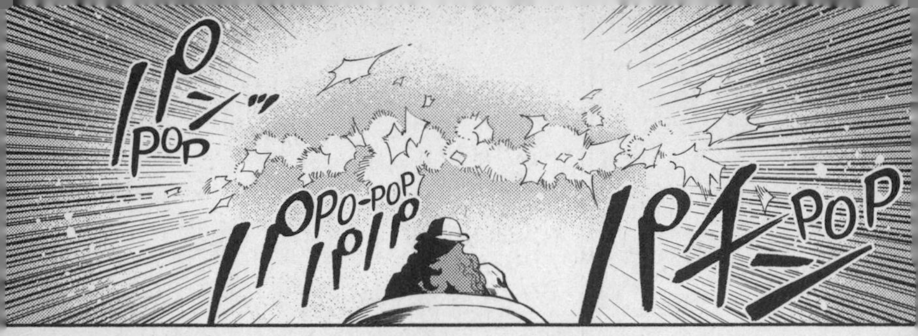
POP
PO-POP
POP

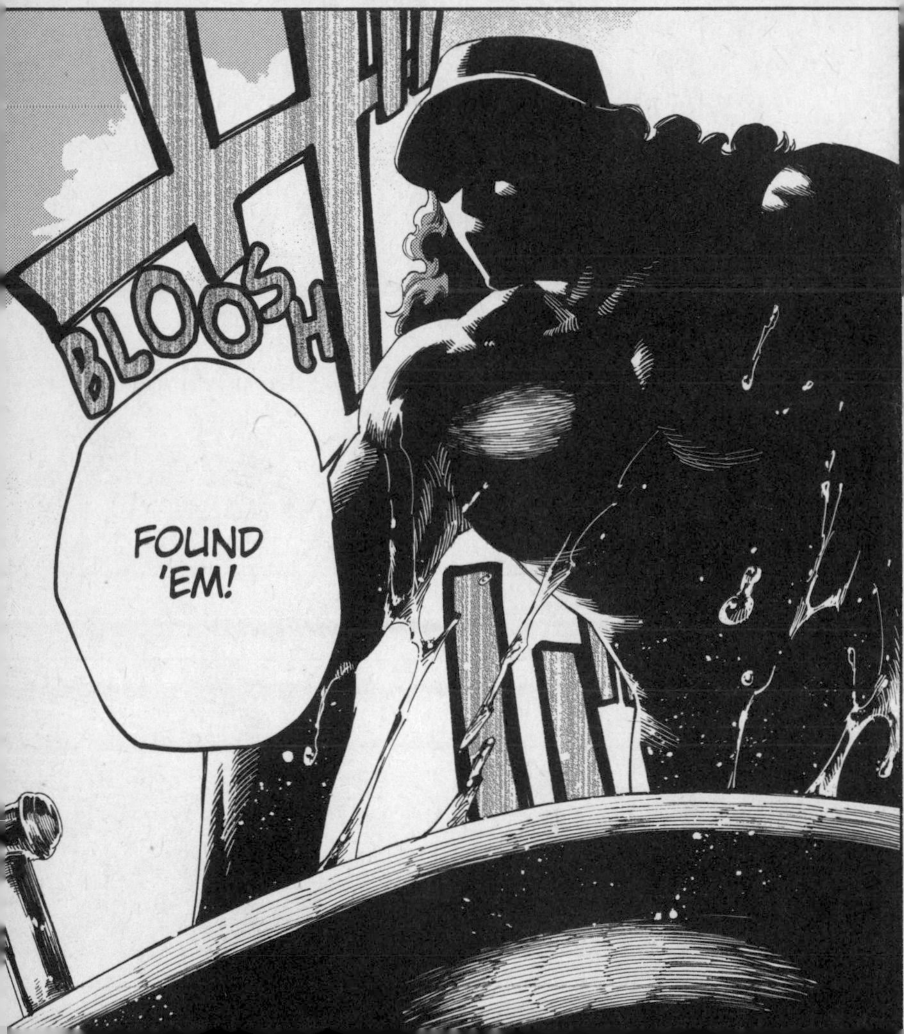
BLOOSH
FOUND 'EM!

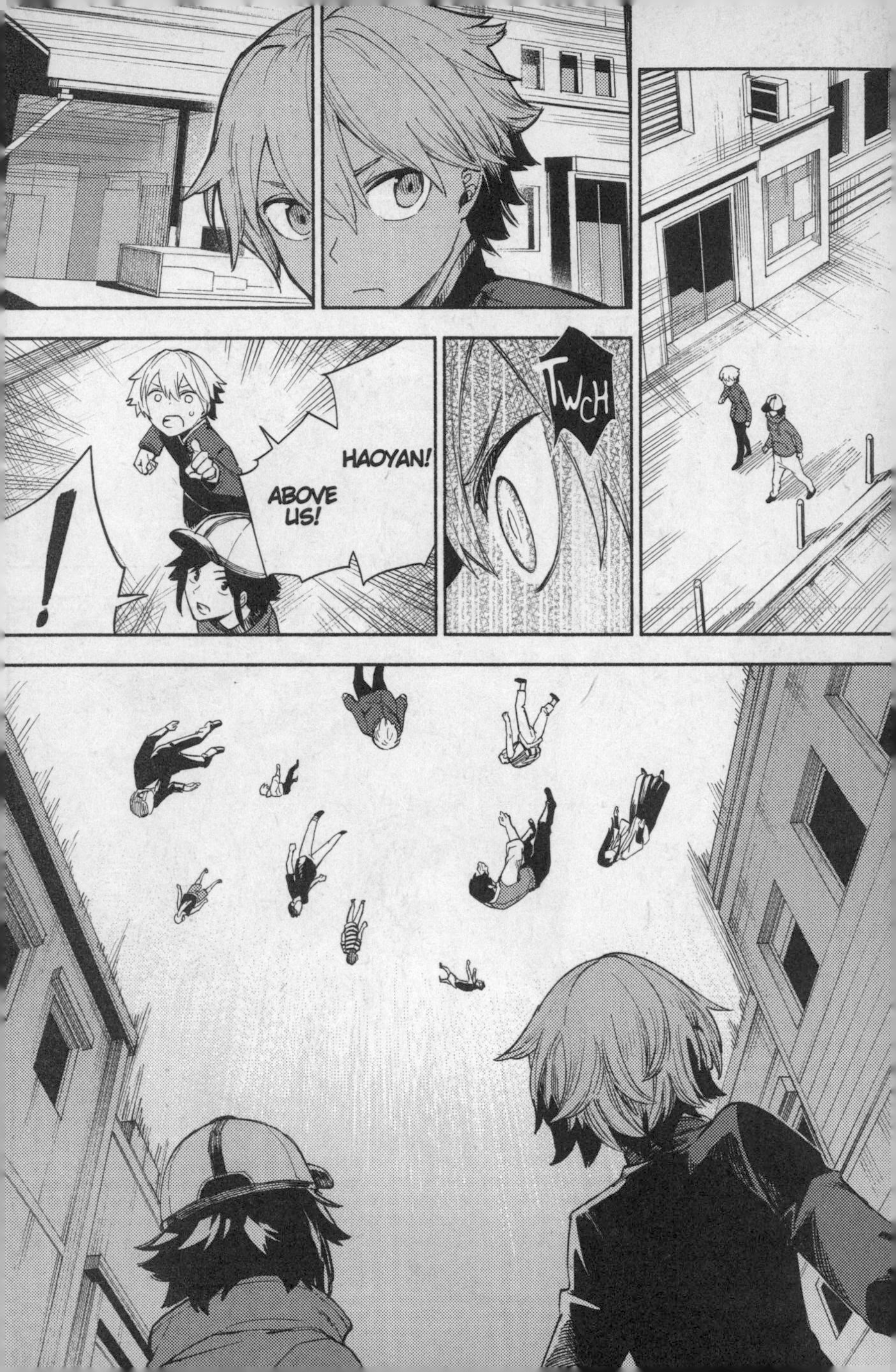
TWCH
HAOYAN!
ABOVE US!
!

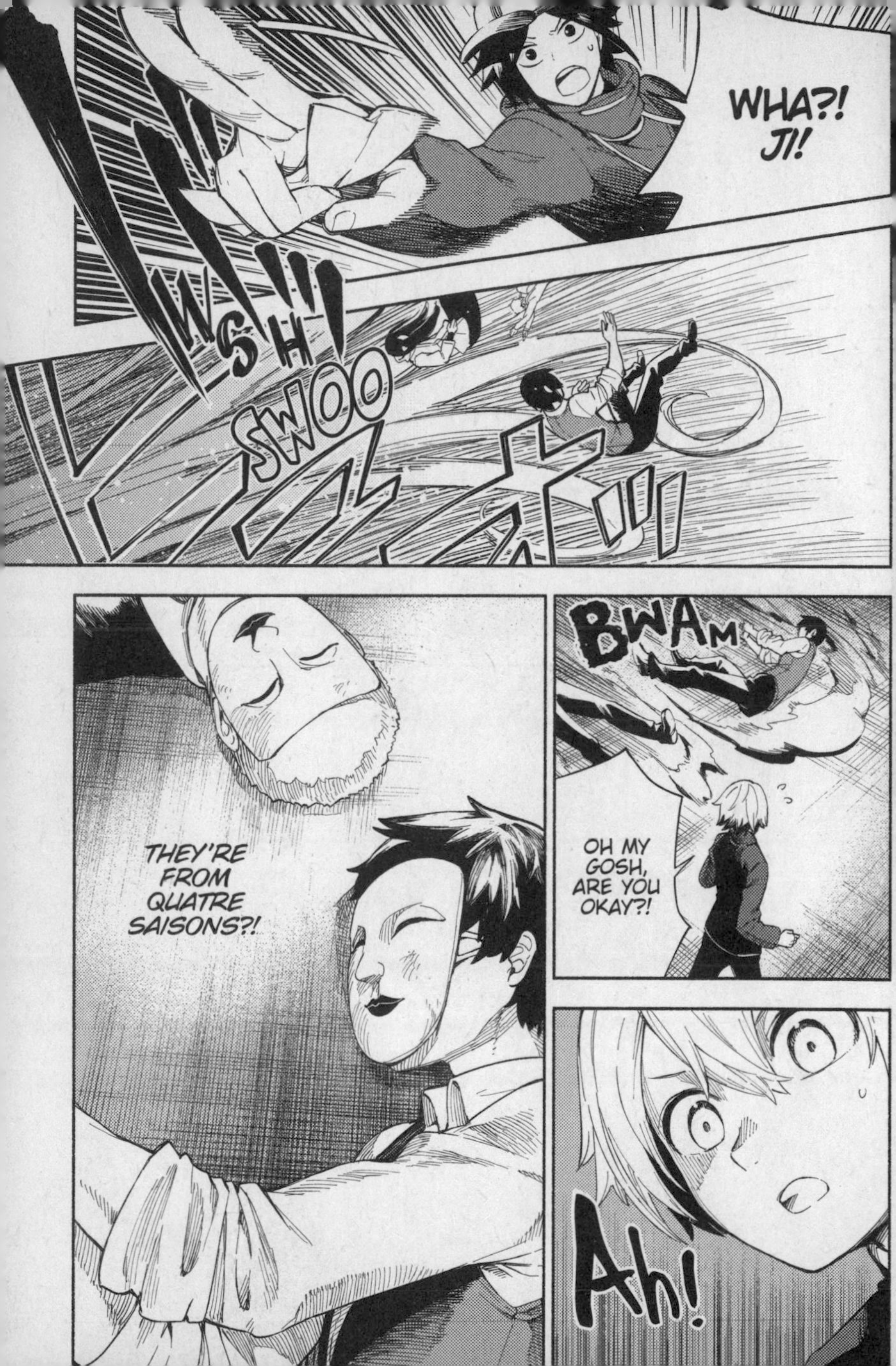
WHA?! JI!
WSH!!
SWOO
BWAM
OH MY GOSH, ARE YOU OKAY?!
Ah!
THEY'RE FROM QUATRE SAISONS?!

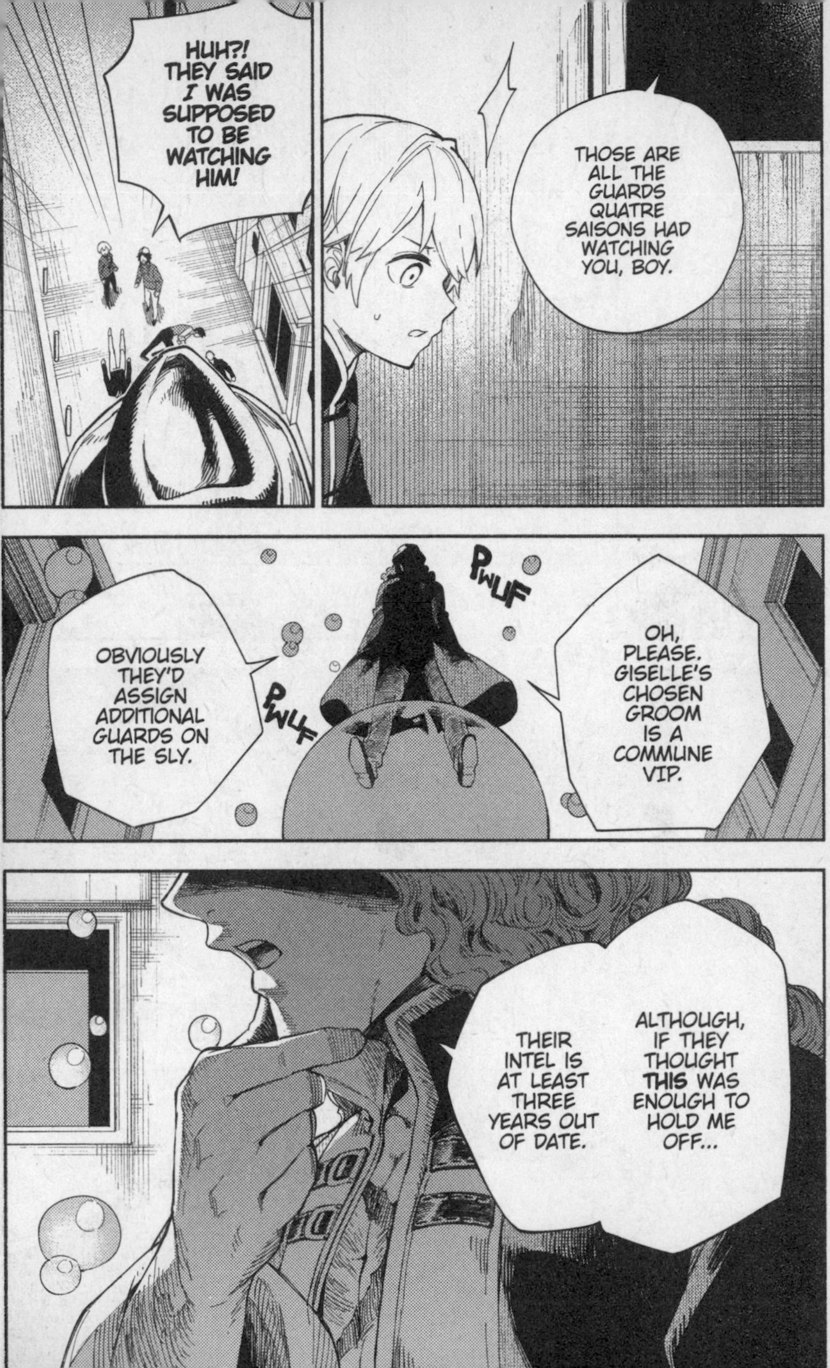
THOSE ARE ALL THE GUARDS QUATRE SAISONS HAD WATCHING YOU, BOY.
HUH?! THEY SAID I WAS SUPPOSED TO BE WATCHING HIM!
PWUF
OH, PLEASE. GISELLE'S CHOSEN GROOM IS A COMMUNE VIP.
OBVIOUSLY THEY'D ASSIGN ADDITIONAL GUARDS ON THE SLY.
PWUF
ALTHOUGH, IF THEY THOUGHT **THIS** WAS ENOUGH TO HOLD ME OFF...
THEIR INTEL IS AT LEAST THREE YEARS OUT OF DATE.

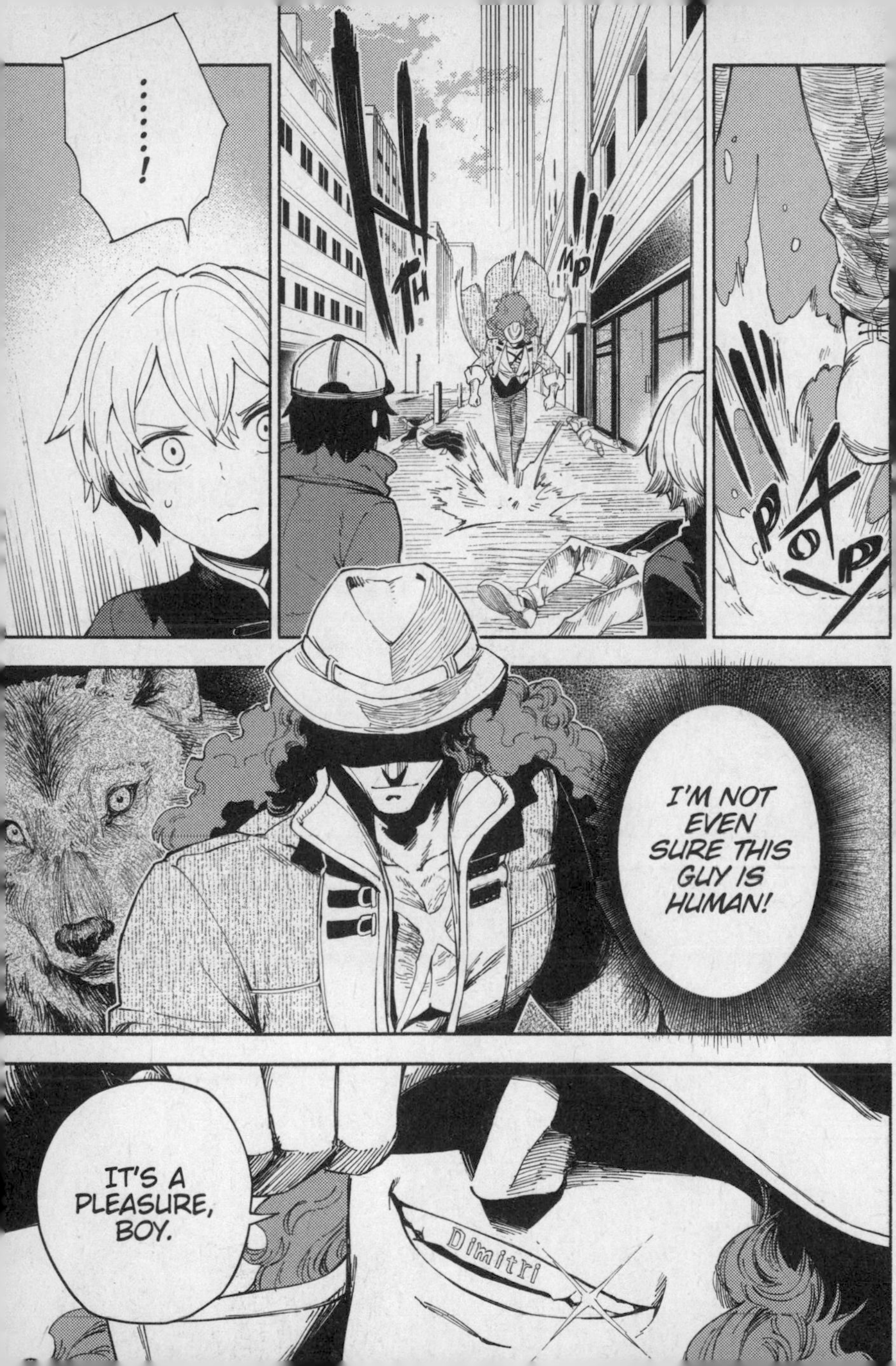
POP
......!
I'M NOT EVEN SURE THIS GUY IS HUMAN!
IT'S A PLEASURE, BOY.
Dimitri

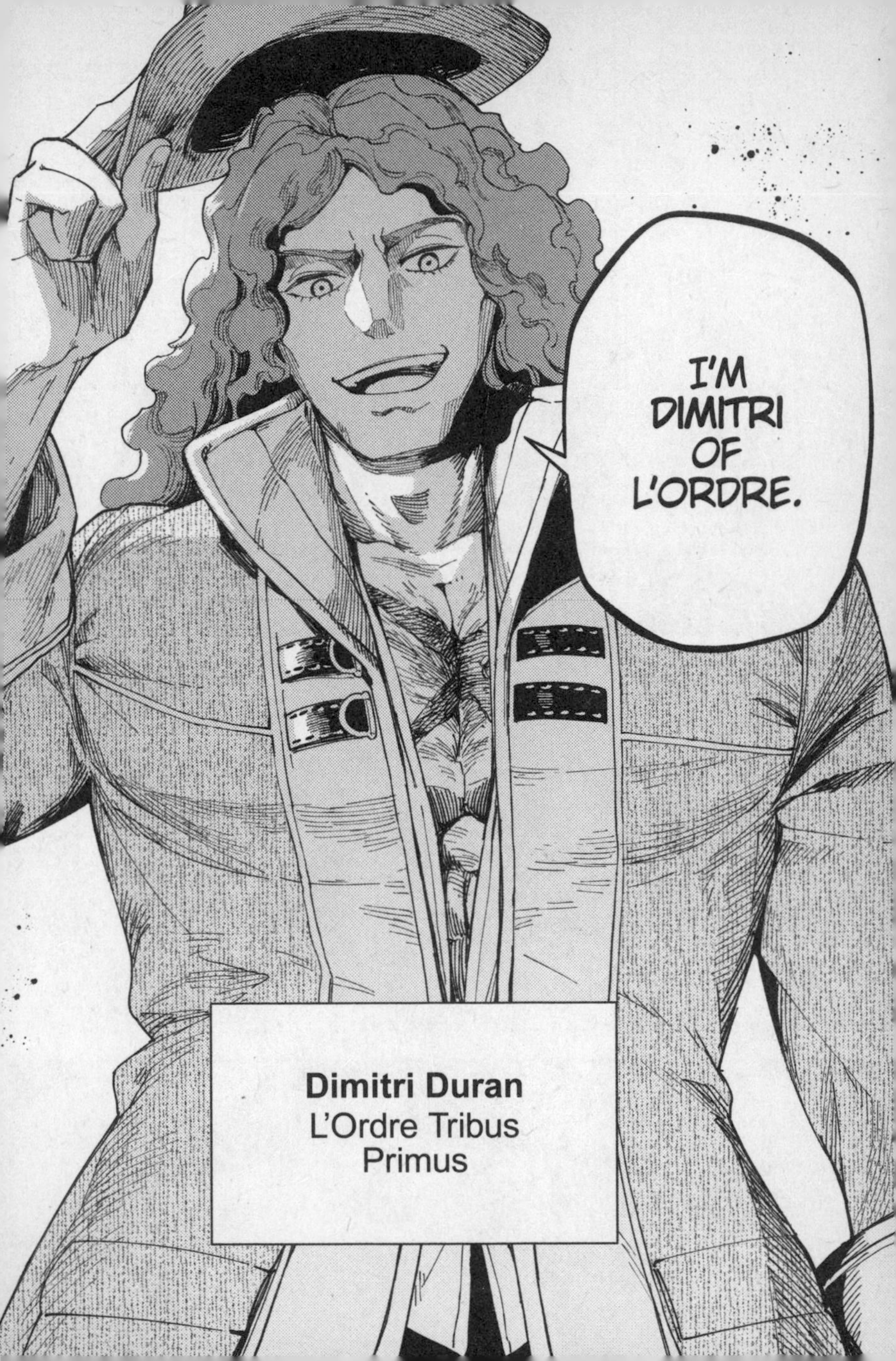
I'M DIMITRI OF L'ORDRE.
Dimitri Duran
L'Ordre Tribus Primus

The Ancient Magus' Bride

WIZARD's BLUE

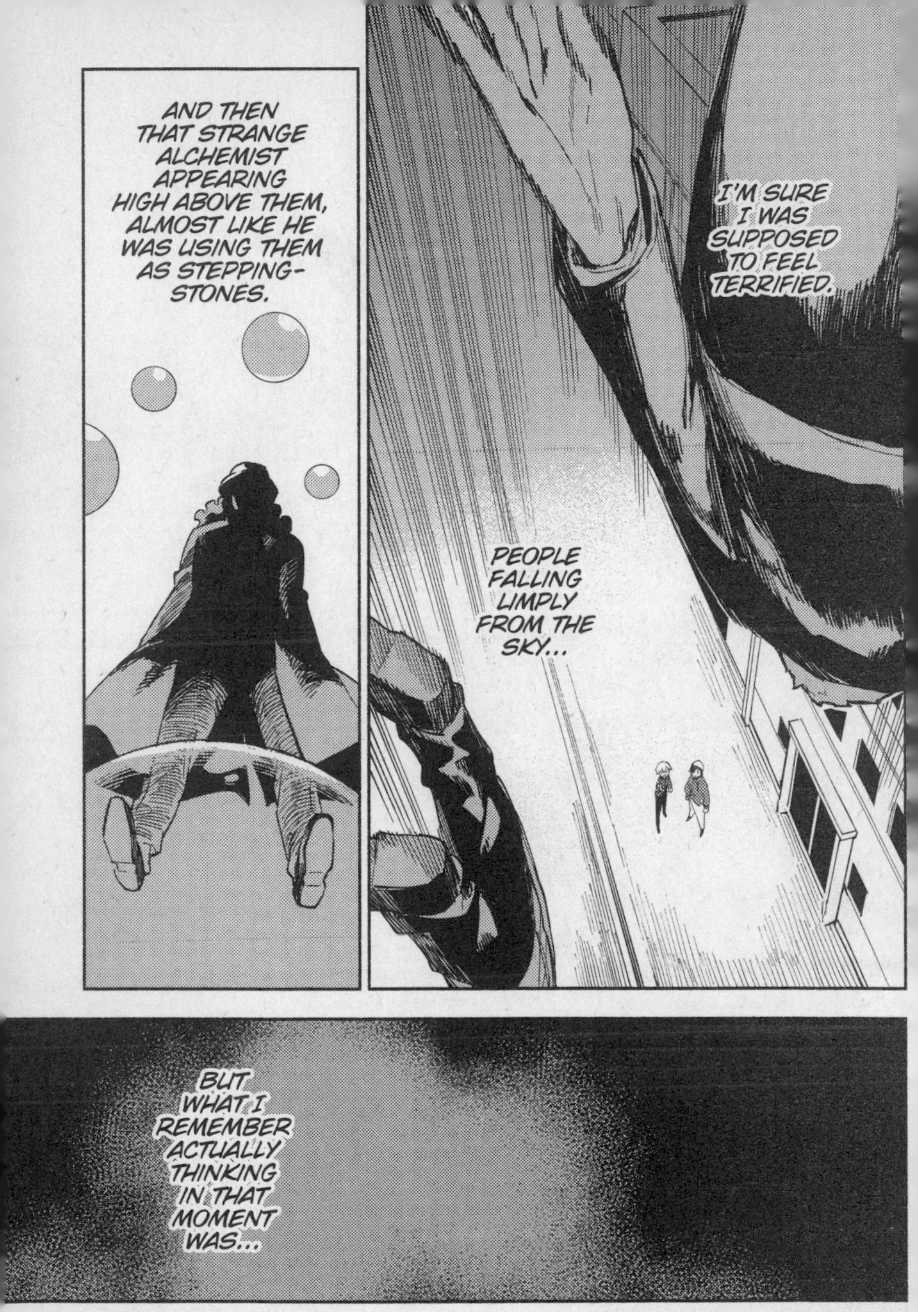
I'M SURE I WAS SUPPOSED TO FEEL TERRIFIED.
PEOPLE FALLING LIMPLY FROM THE SKY...
AND THEN THAT STRANGE ALCHEMIST APPEARING HIGH ABOVE THEM, ALMOST LIKE HE WAS USING THEM AS STEPPING-STONES.
BUT WHAT I REMEMBER ACTUALLY THINKING IN THAT MOMENT WAS...

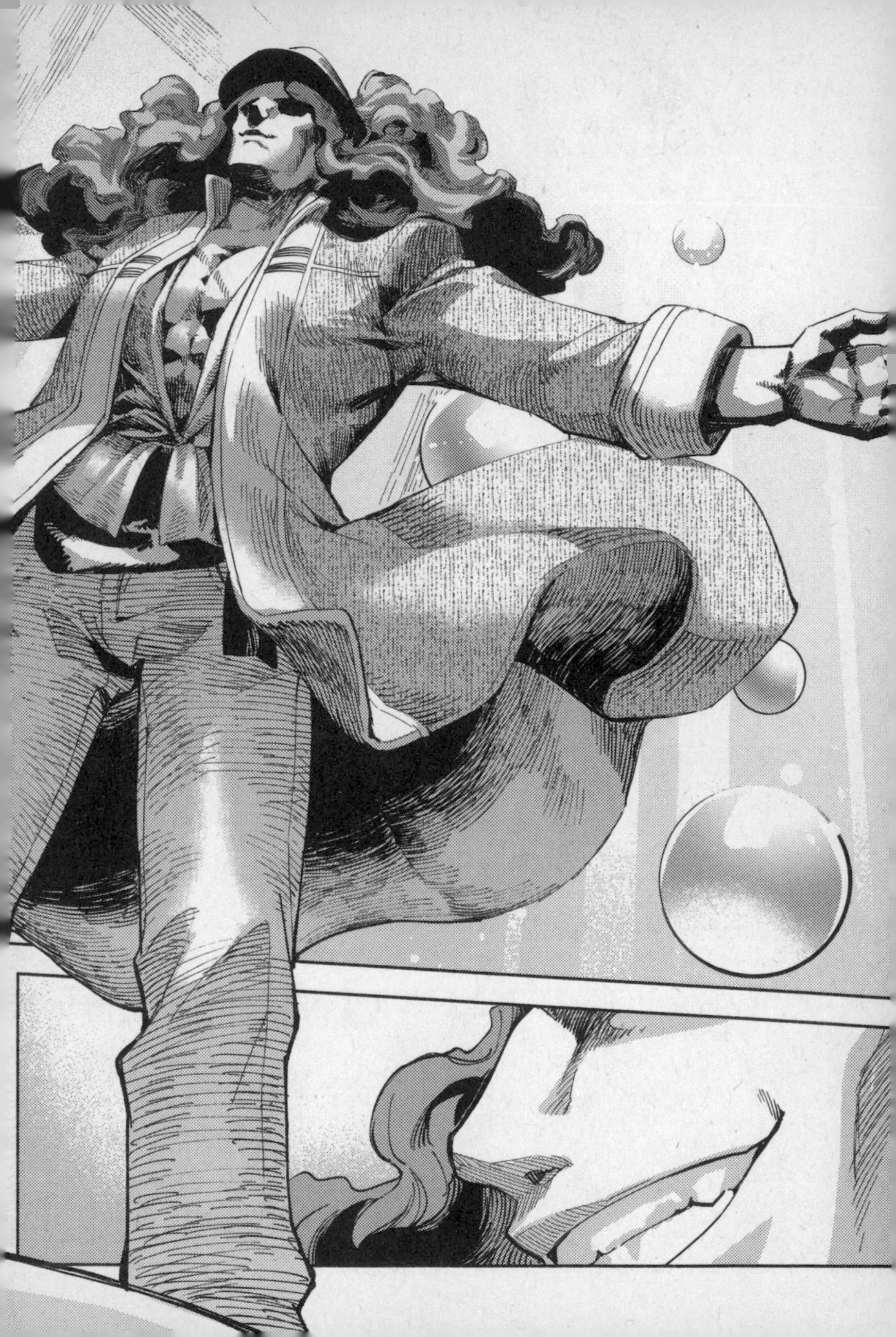

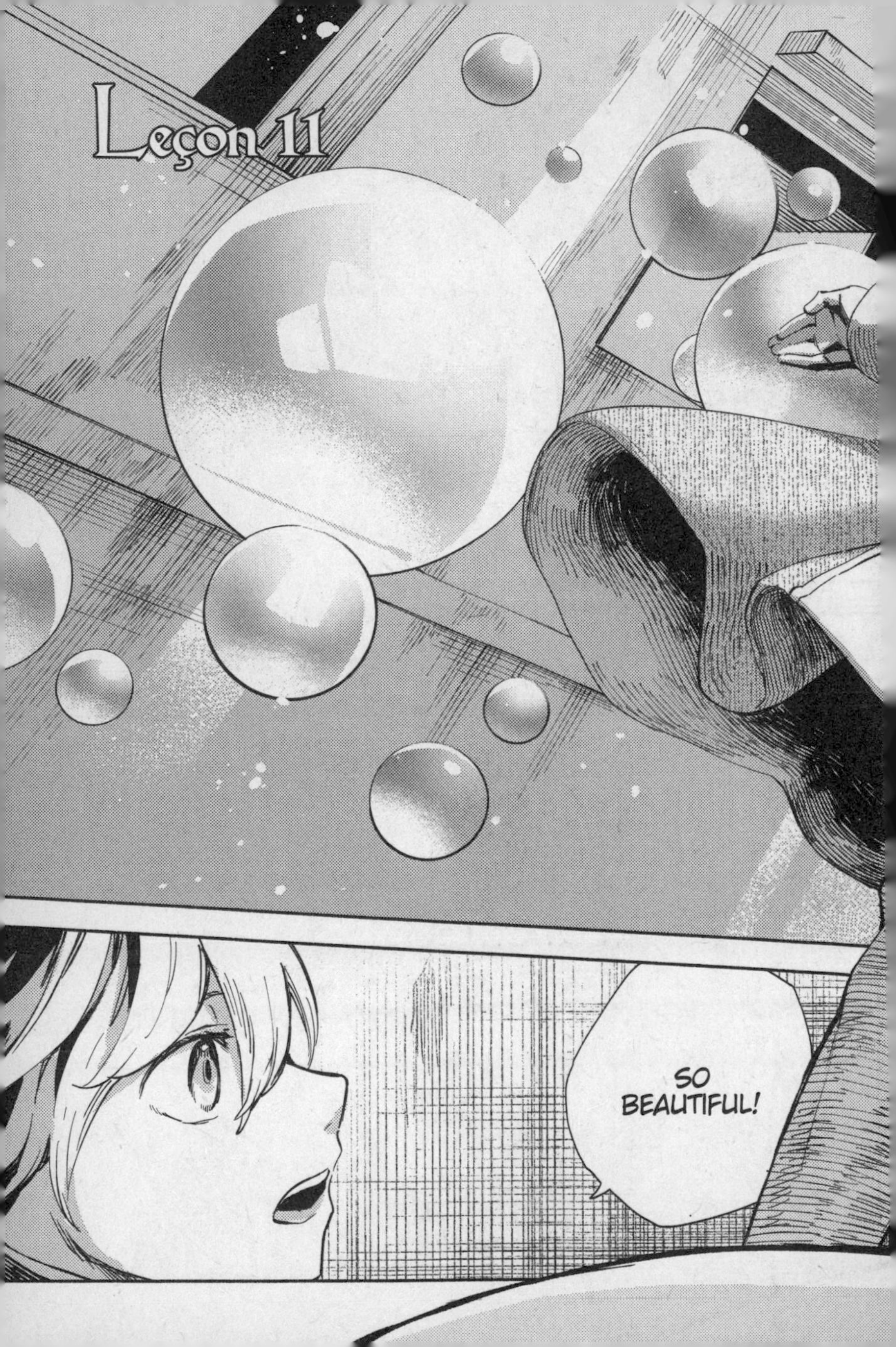
Leçon 11
SO BEAUTIFUL!

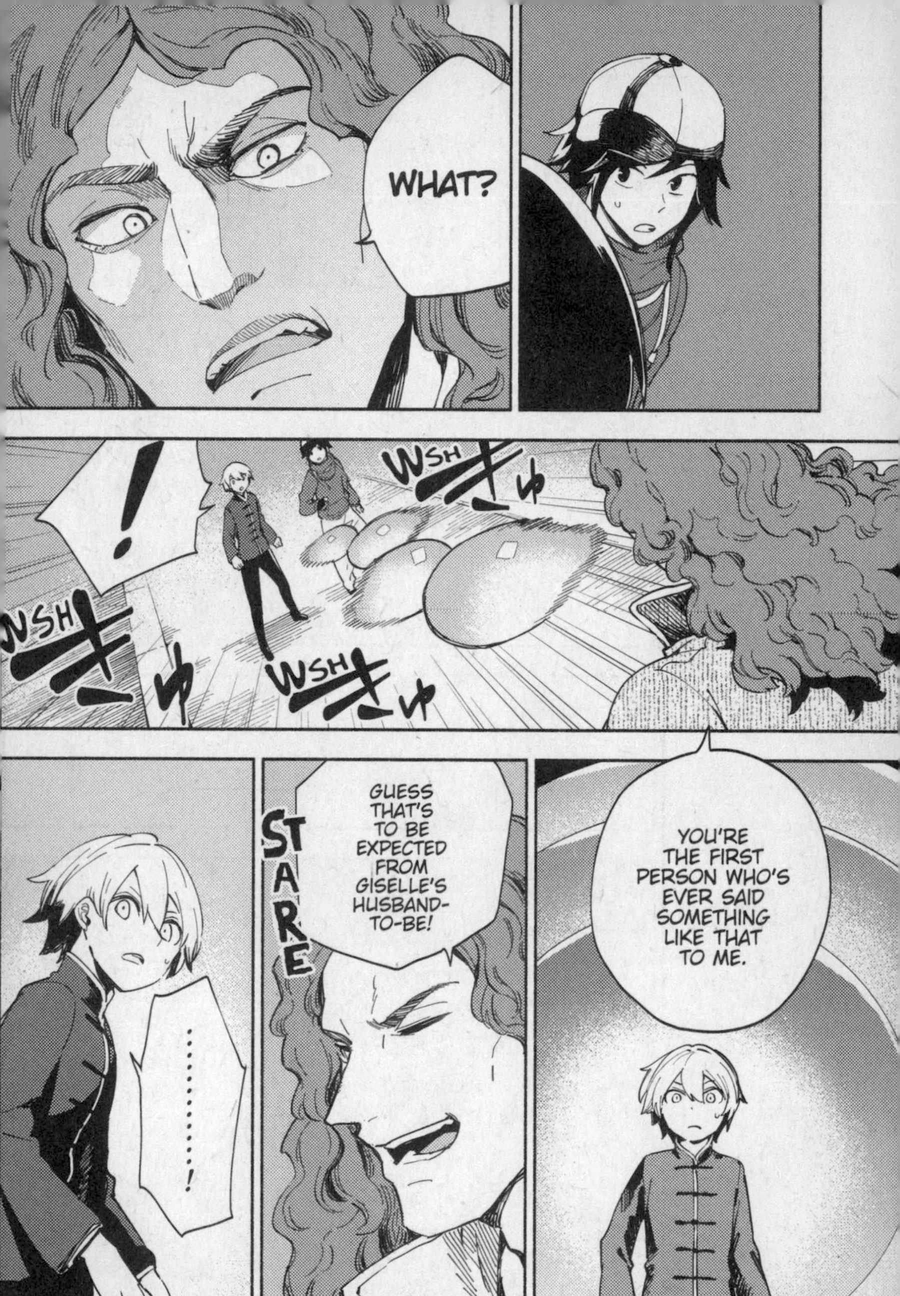
WHAT?
WSH
!
WSH
WSH
YOU'RE THE FIRST PERSON WHO'S EVER SAID SOMETHING LIKE THAT TO ME.
STARE
GUESS THAT'S TO BE EXPECTED FROM GISELLE'S HUSBAND-TO-BE!
......!

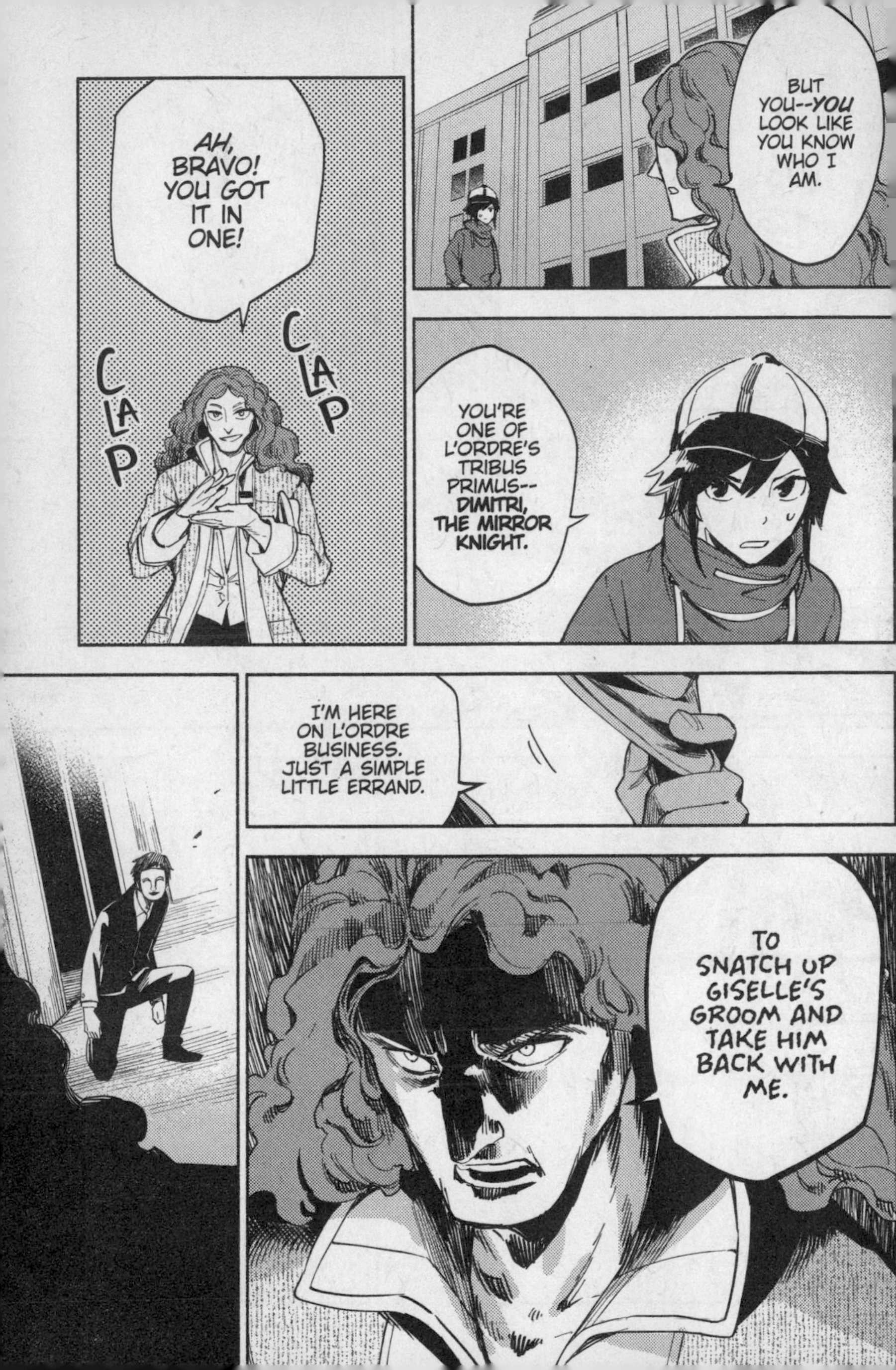
BUT YOU--YOU LOOK LIKE YOU KNOW WHO I AM.
YOU'RE ONE OF L'ORDRE'S TRIBUS PRIMUS-- DIMITRI, THE MIRROR KNIGHT.
AH, BRAVO! YOU GOT IT IN ONE!
CLAP
CLAP
I'M HERE ON L'ORDRE BUSINESS. JUST A SIMPLE LITTLE ERRAND.
TO SNATCH UP GISELLE'S GROOM AND TAKE HIM BACK WITH ME.

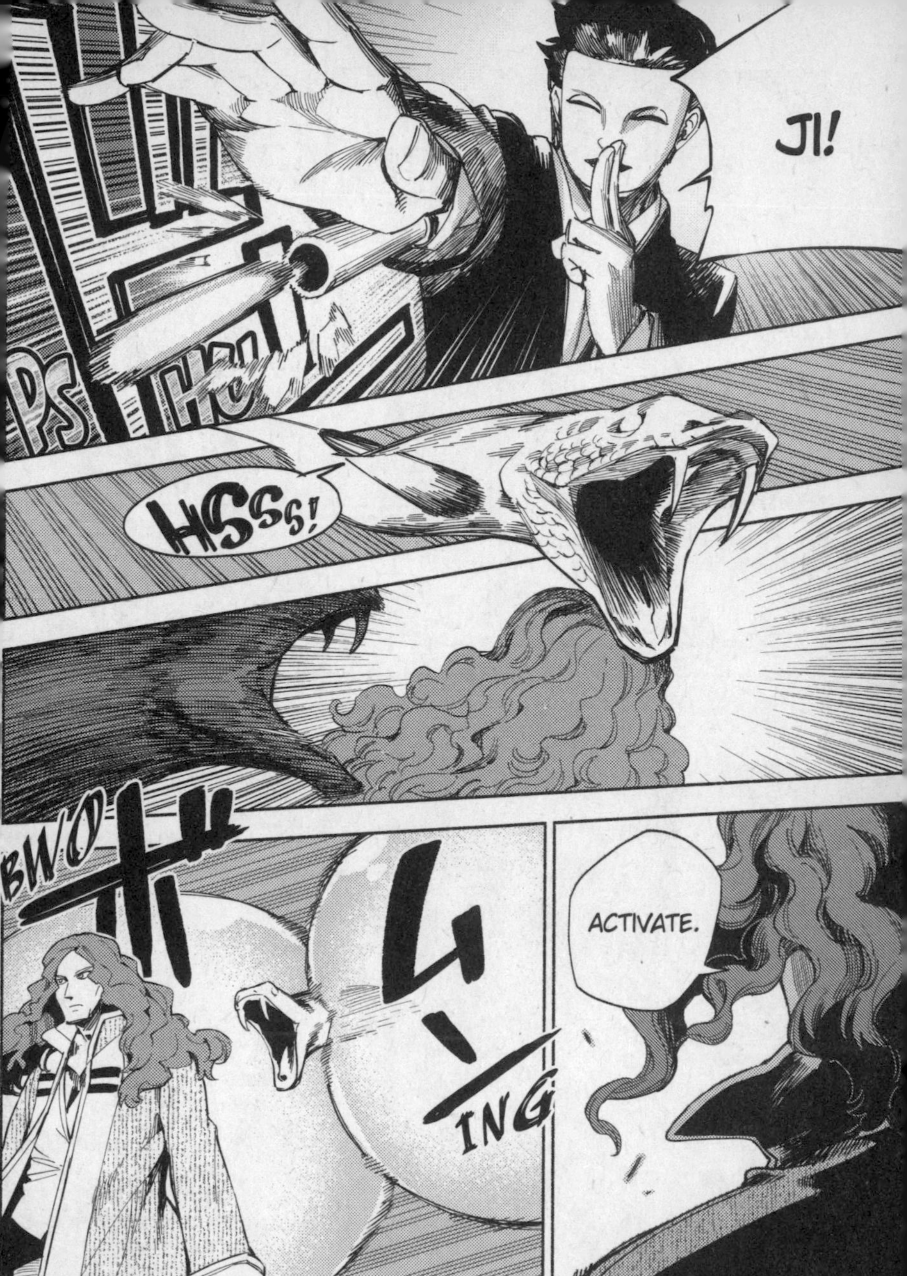
JI!
HSSS!
ACTIVATE.
BWO
ING

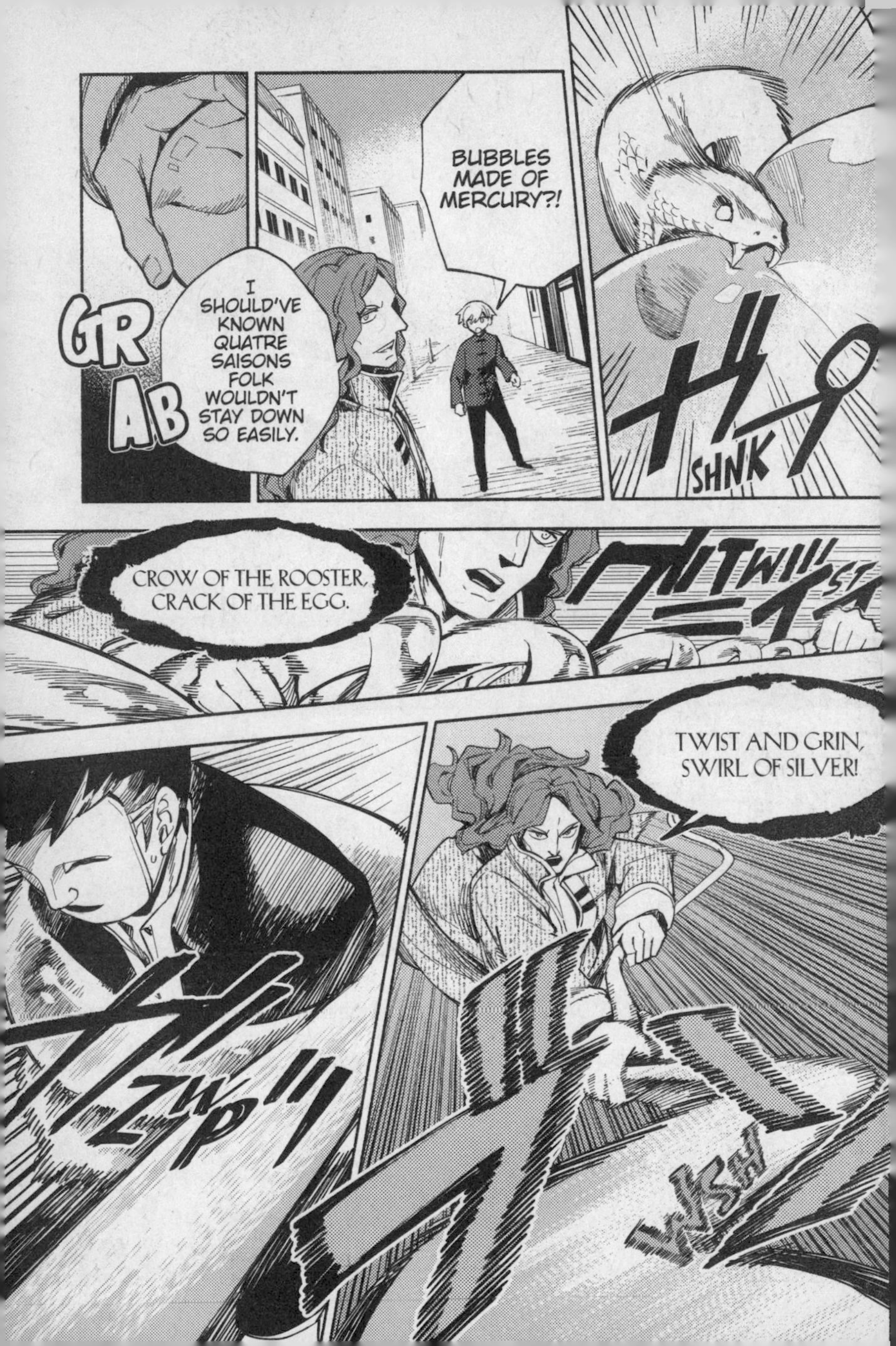
SHNK
BUBBLES MADE OF MERCURY?!
I SHOULD'VE KNOWN QUATRE SAISONS FOLK WOULDN'T STAY DOWN SO EASILY.
GRAB
CROW OF THE ROOSTER, CRACK OF THE EGG.
TWIST AND GRIN, SWIRL OF SILVER!

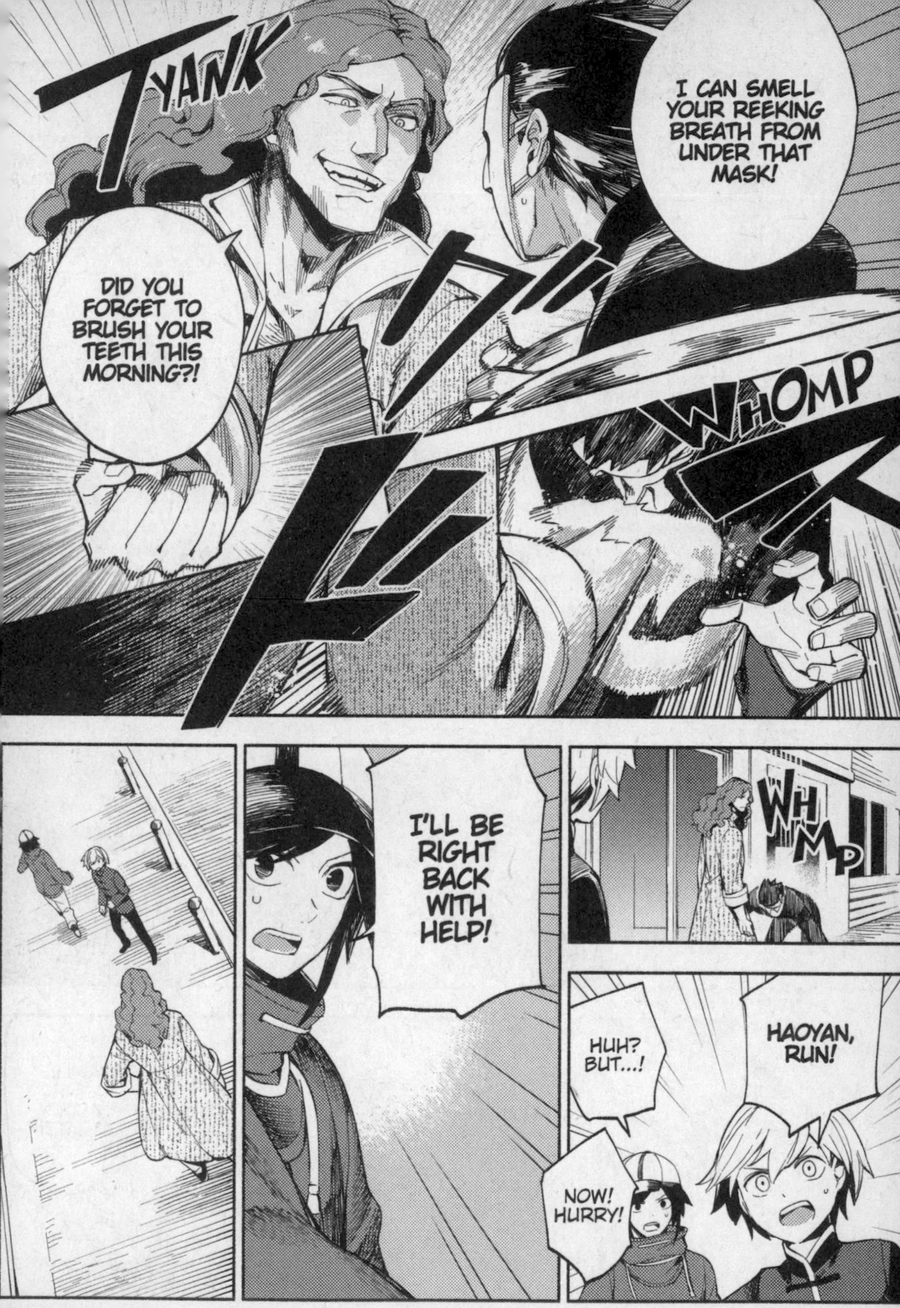
I CAN SMELL YOUR REEKING BREATH FROM UNDER THAT MASK!
YANK
DID YOU FORGET TO BRUSH YOUR TEETH THIS MORNING?!
WHOMP
WHMP
HAOYAN, RUN!
HUH? BUT...!
NOW! HURRY!
I'LL BE RIGHT BACK WITH HELP!

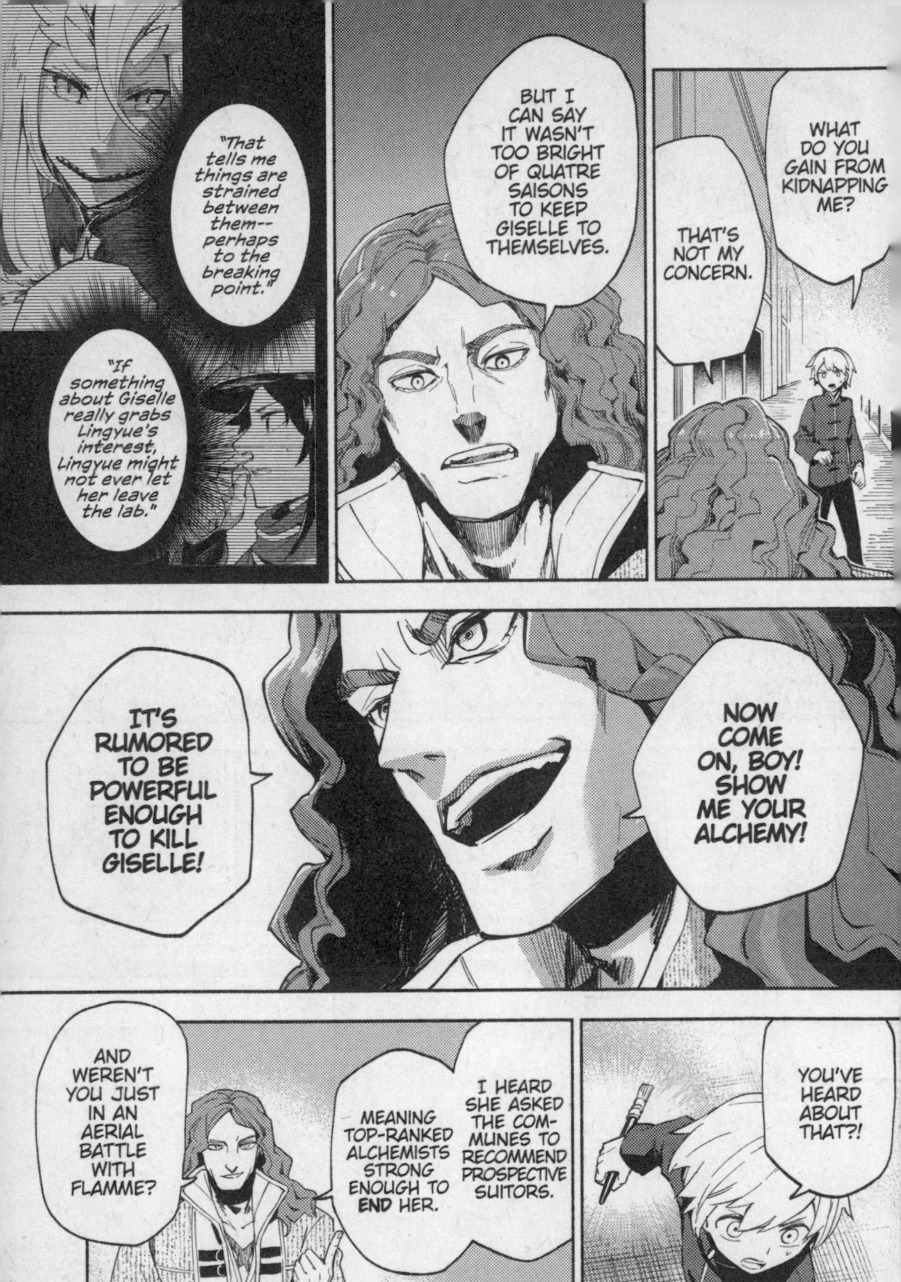
WHAT DO YOU GAIN FROM KIDNAPPING ME?
THAT'S NOT MY CONCERN.
BUT I CAN SAY IT WASN'T TOO BRIGHT OF QUATRE SAISONS TO KEEP GISELLE TO THEMSELVES.
"That tells me things are strained between them--perhaps to the breaking point."
"If something about Giselle really grabs Lingyue's interest, Lingyue might not ever let her leave the lab."
NOW COME ON, BOY! SHOW ME YOUR ALCHEMY!
IT'S RUMORED TO BE POWERFUL ENOUGH TO KILL GISELLE!
YOU'VE HEARD ABOUT THAT?!
I HEARD SHE ASKED THE COM-MUNES TO RECOMMEND PROSPECTIVE SUITORS.
MEANING TOP-RANKED ALCHEMISTS STRONG ENOUGH TO END HER.
AND WEREN'T YOU JUST IN AN AERIAL BATTLE WITH FLAMME?

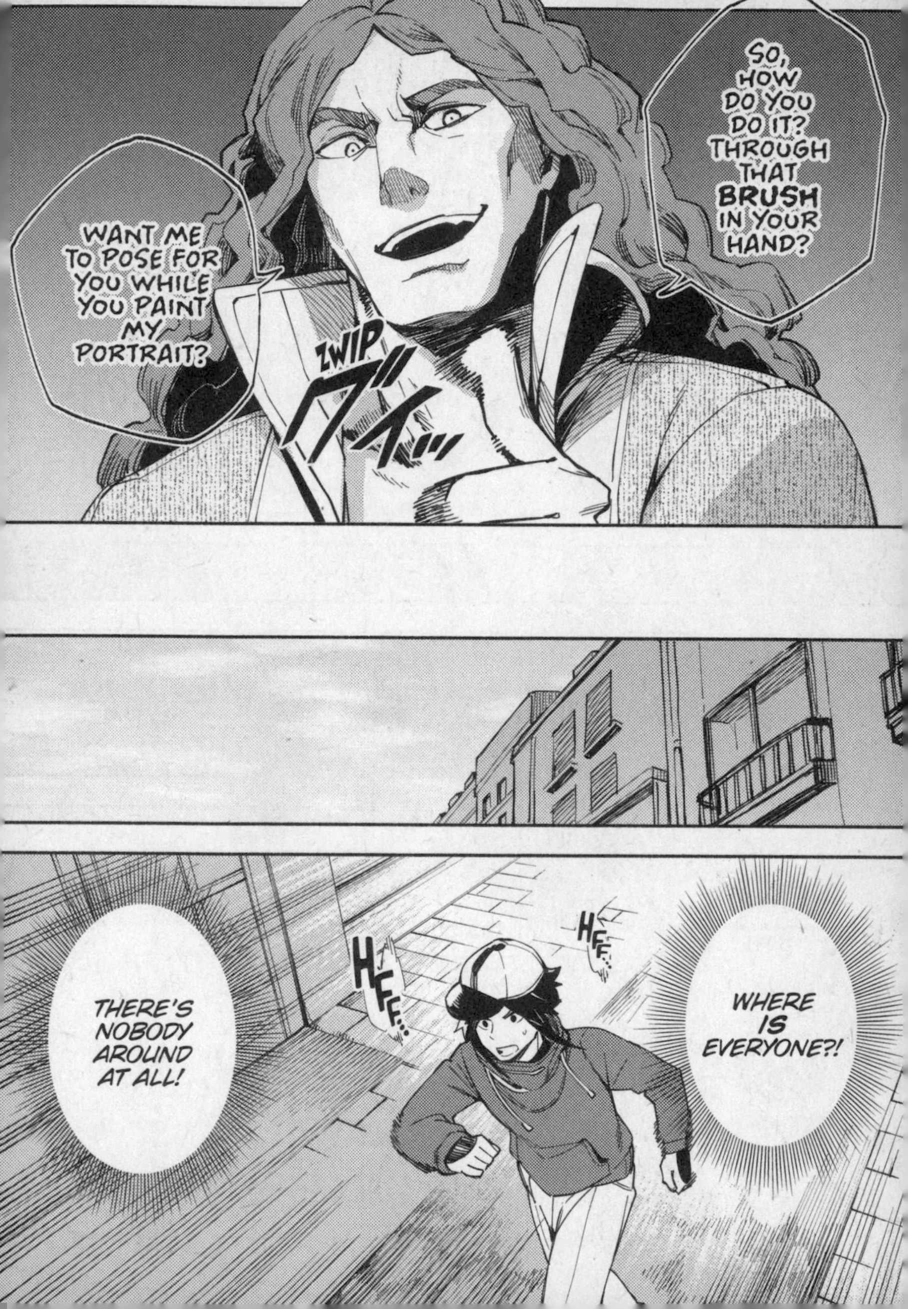
SO, HOW DO YOU DO IT? THROUGH THAT BRUSH IN YOUR HAND?
WANT ME TO POSE FOR YOU WHILE YOU PAINT MY PORTRAIT?
ZWIP
WHERE IS EVERYONE?!
HFF...
HFF...
THERE'S NOBODY AROUND AT ALL!

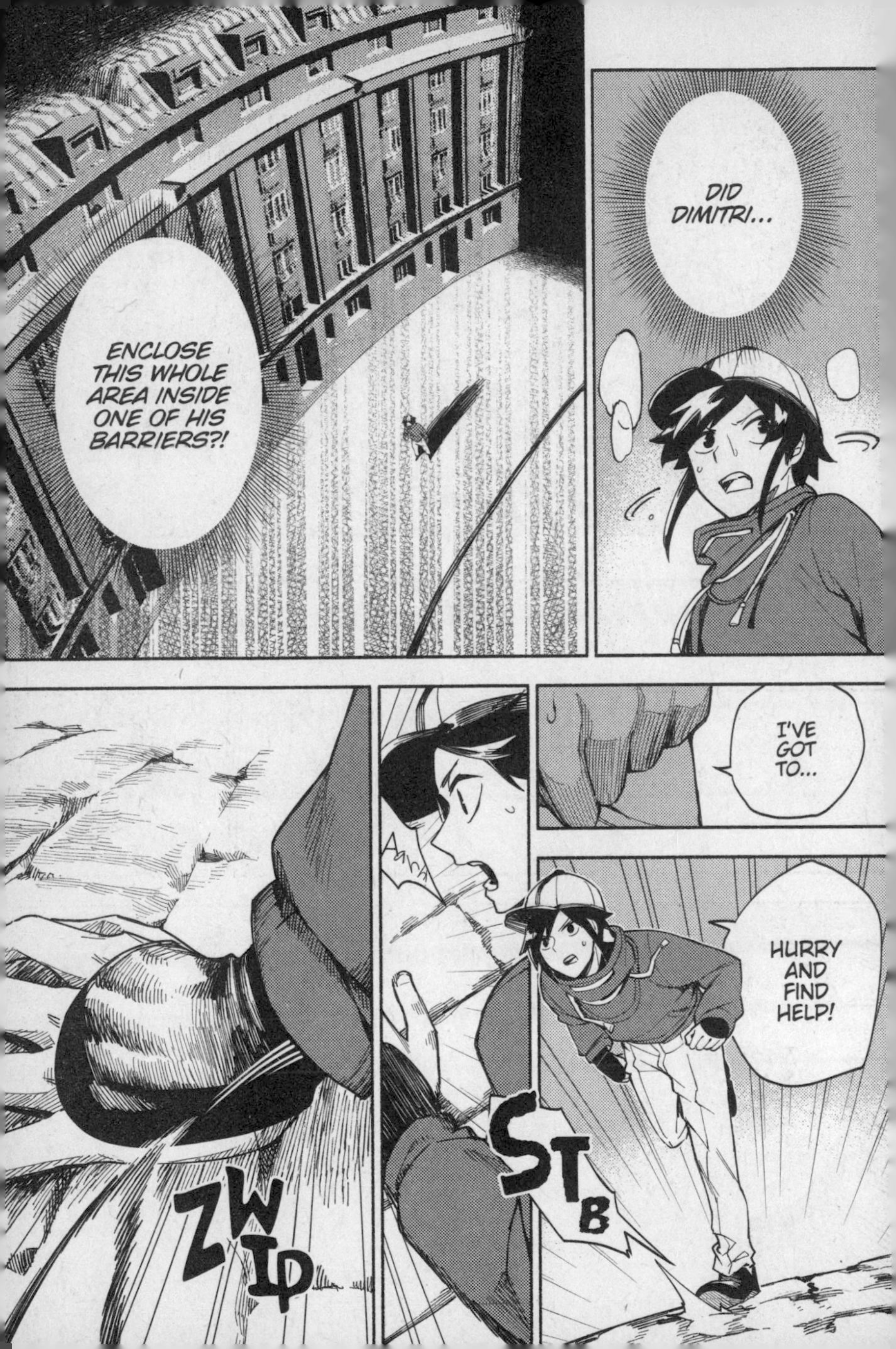
DID DIMITRI...
ENCLOSE THIS WHOLE AREA INSIDE ONE OF HIS BARRIERS?!
I'VE GOT TO...
HURRY AND FIND HELP!
STB
ZWIP

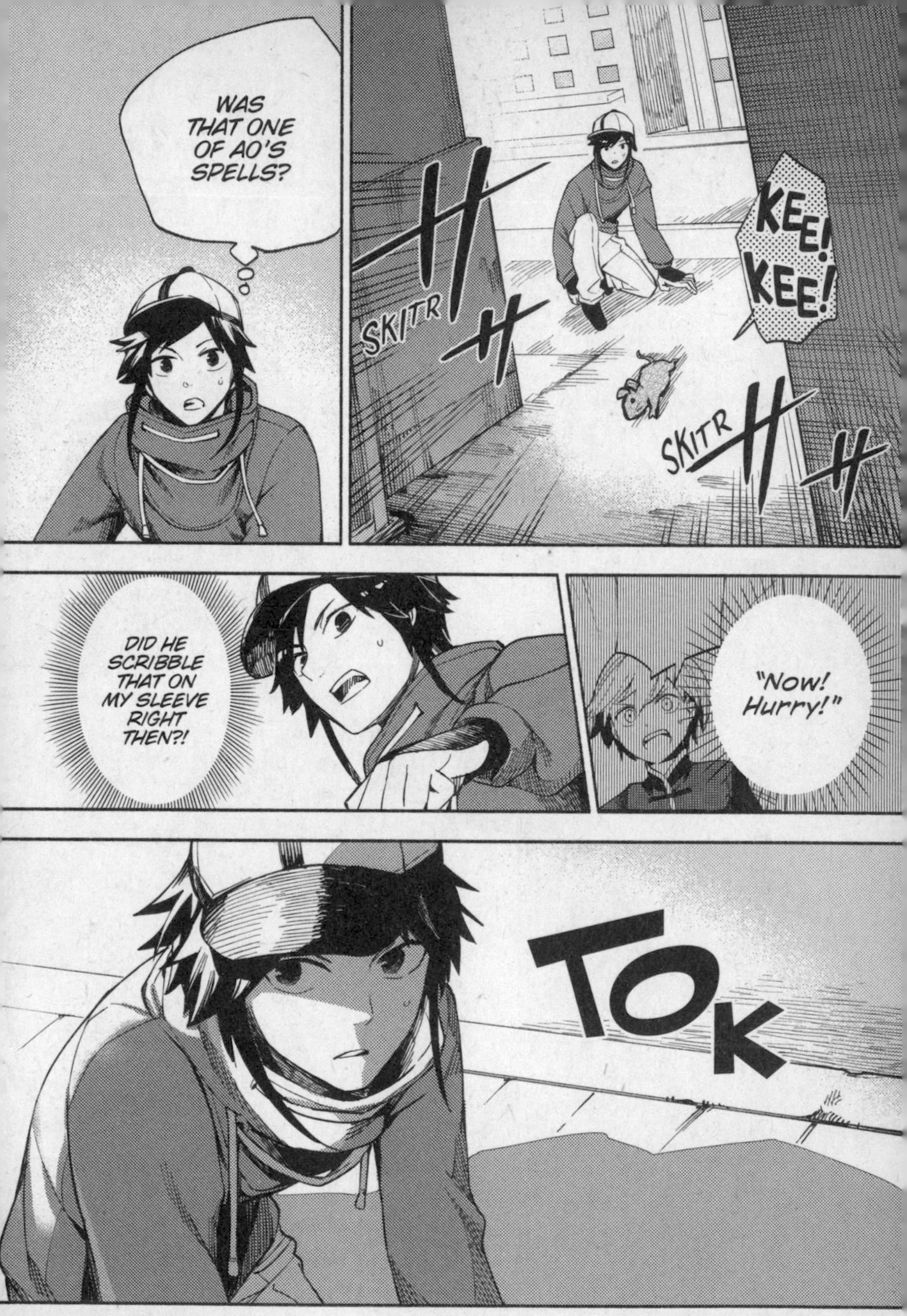
KEE! KEE!
SKITR
SKITR
WAS THAT ONE OF AO'S SPELLS?
"Now! Hurry!"
DID HE SCRIBBLE THAT ON MY SLEEVE RIGHT THEN?!
TOK

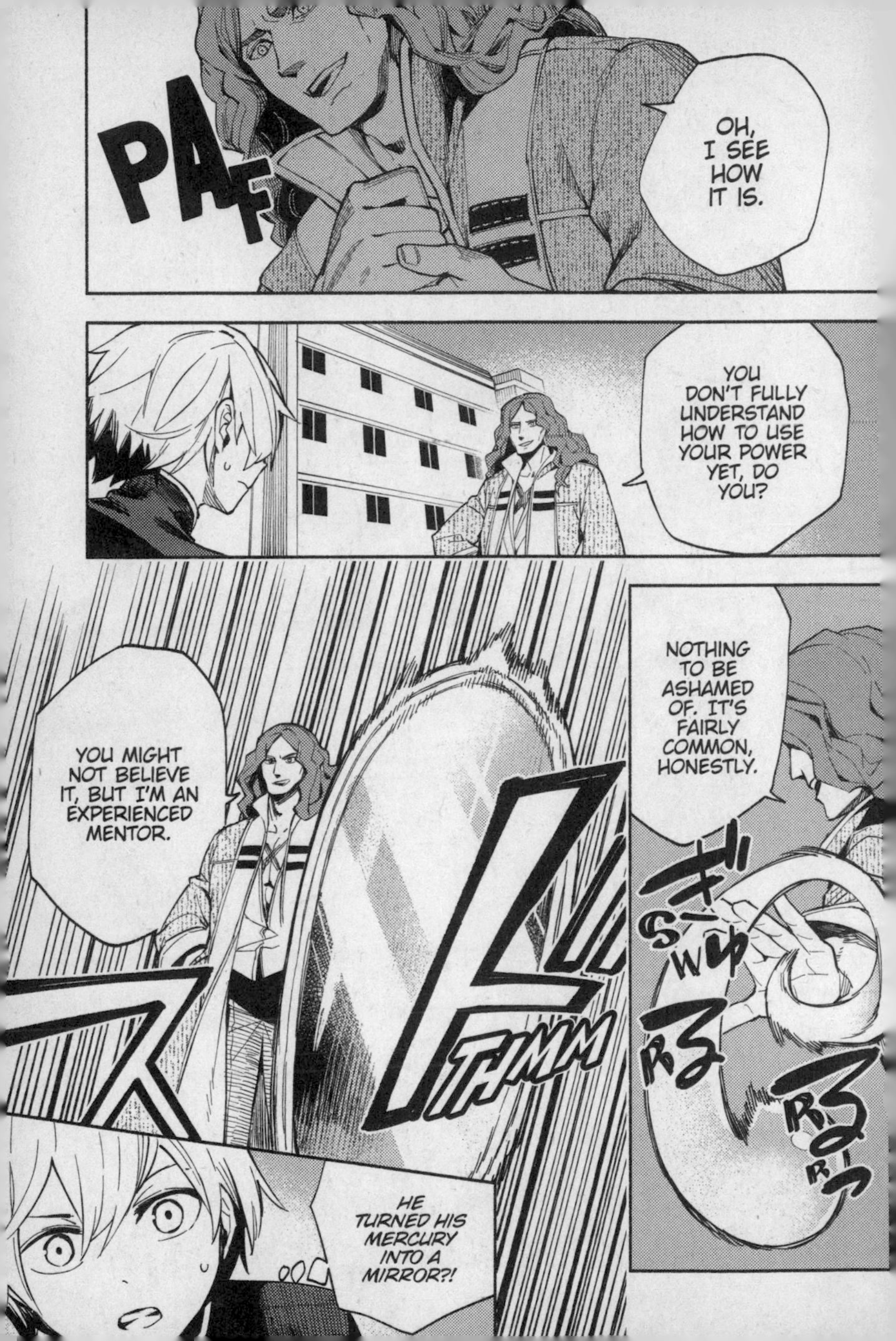
PAF
OH, I SEE HOW IT IS.
YOU DON'T FULLY UNDERSTAND HOW TO USE YOUR POWER YET, DO YOU?
NOTHING TO BE ASHAMED OF. IT'S FAIRLY COMMON, HONESTLY.
YOU MIGHT NOT BELIEVE IT, BUT I'M AN EXPERIENCED MENTOR.
THMM
HE TURNED HIS MERCURY INTO A MIRROR?!

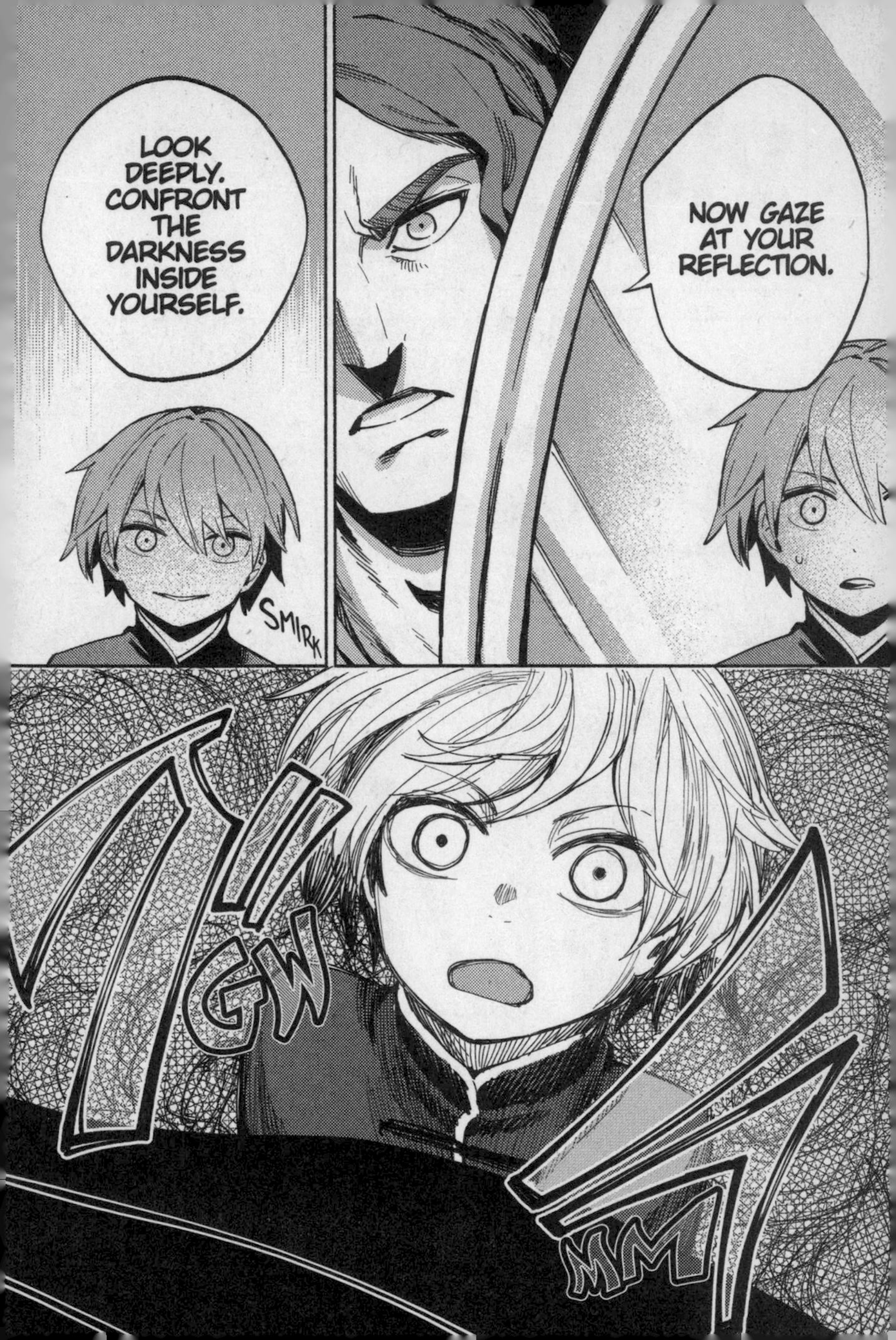
NOW GAZE AT YOUR REFLECTION.
LOOK DEEPLY. CONFRONT THE DARKNESS INSIDE YOURSELF.
SMIRK
GW
MM

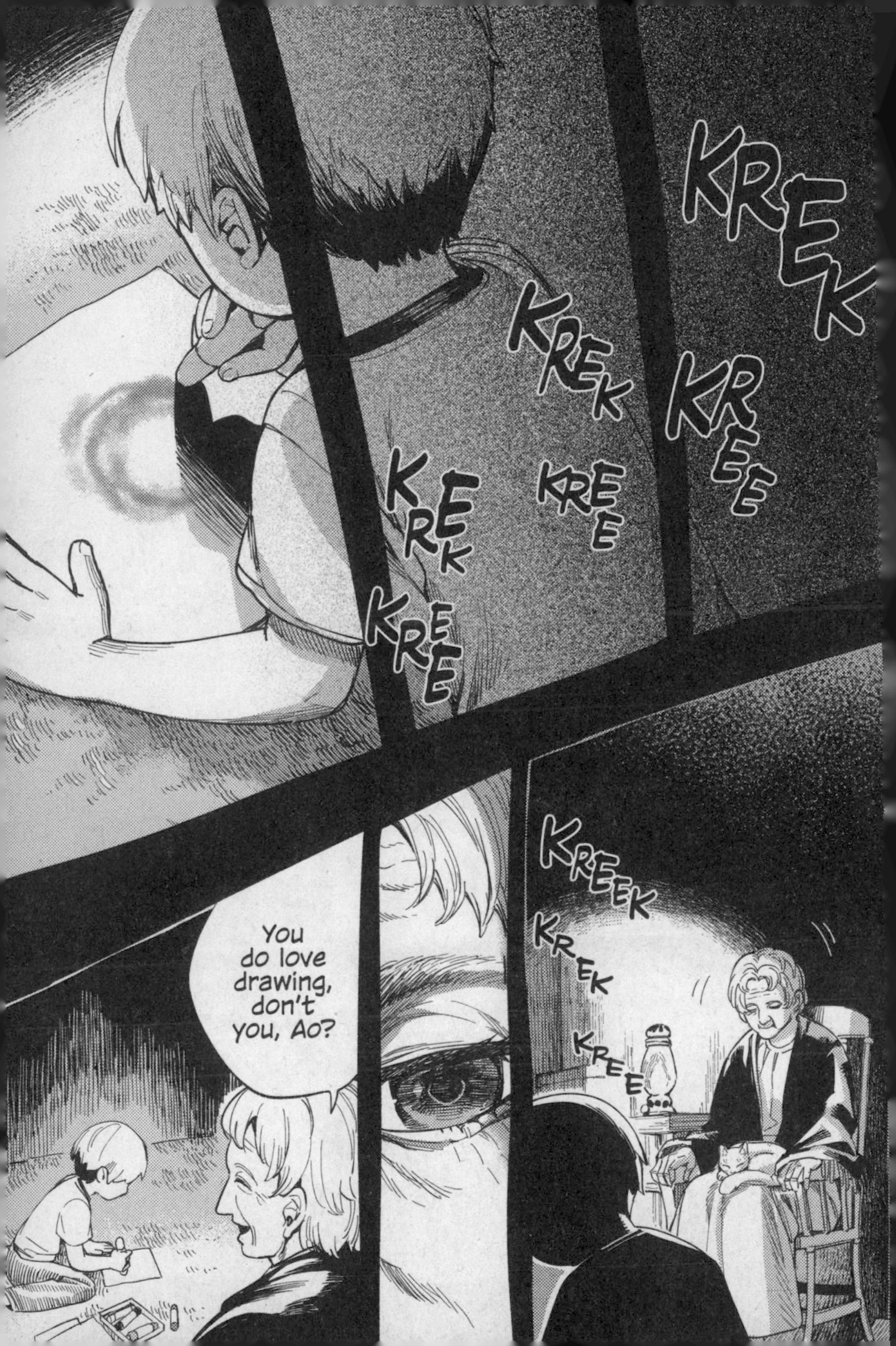

KREK
KREEE
KREK
KREE
KREK
KREE
KREEK
KREK
KREE
You do love drawing, don't you, Ao?

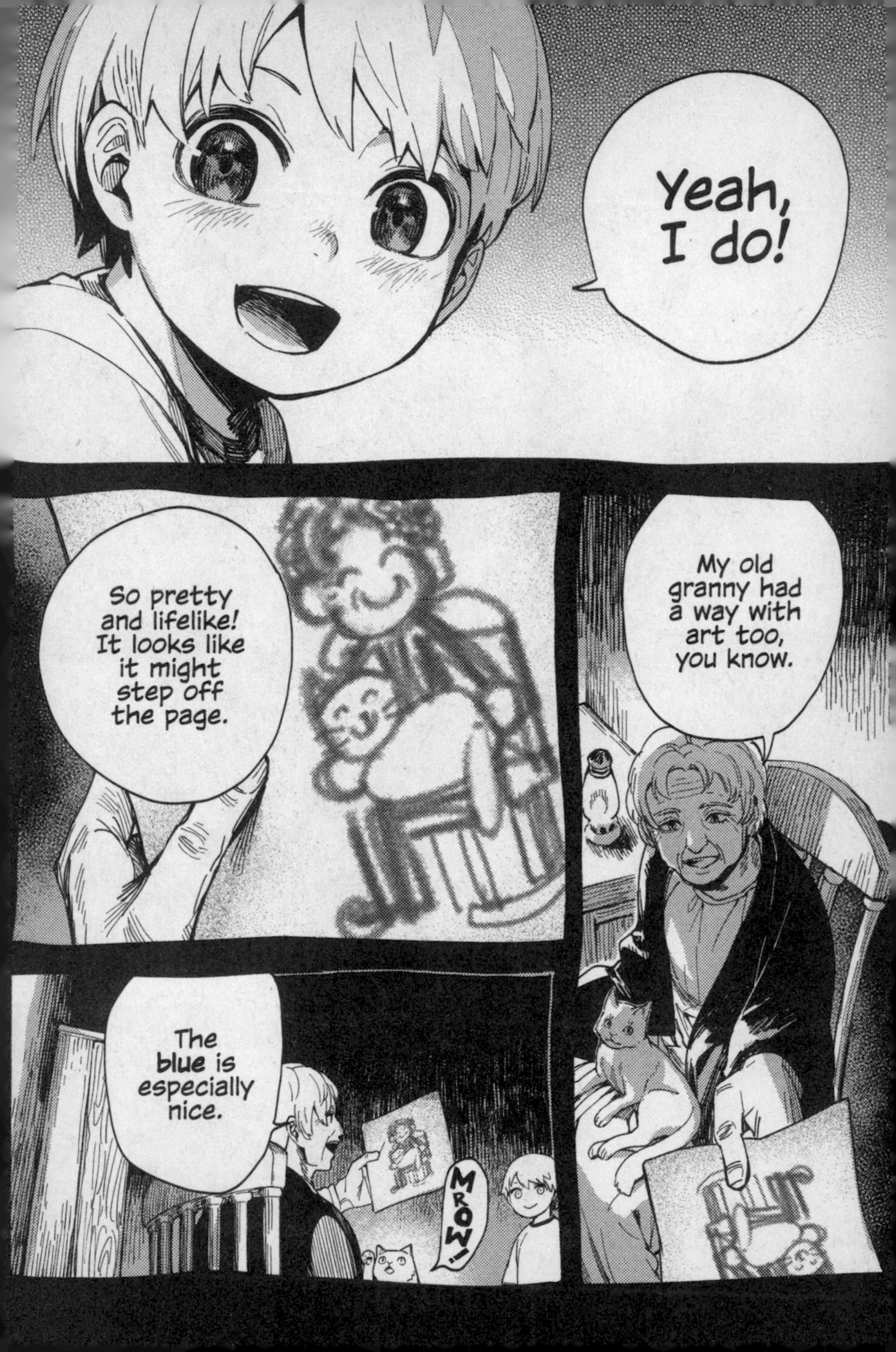
Yeah, I do!
My old granny had a way with art too, you know.
So pretty and lifelike! It looks like it might step off the page.
The blue is especially nice.
MROW!

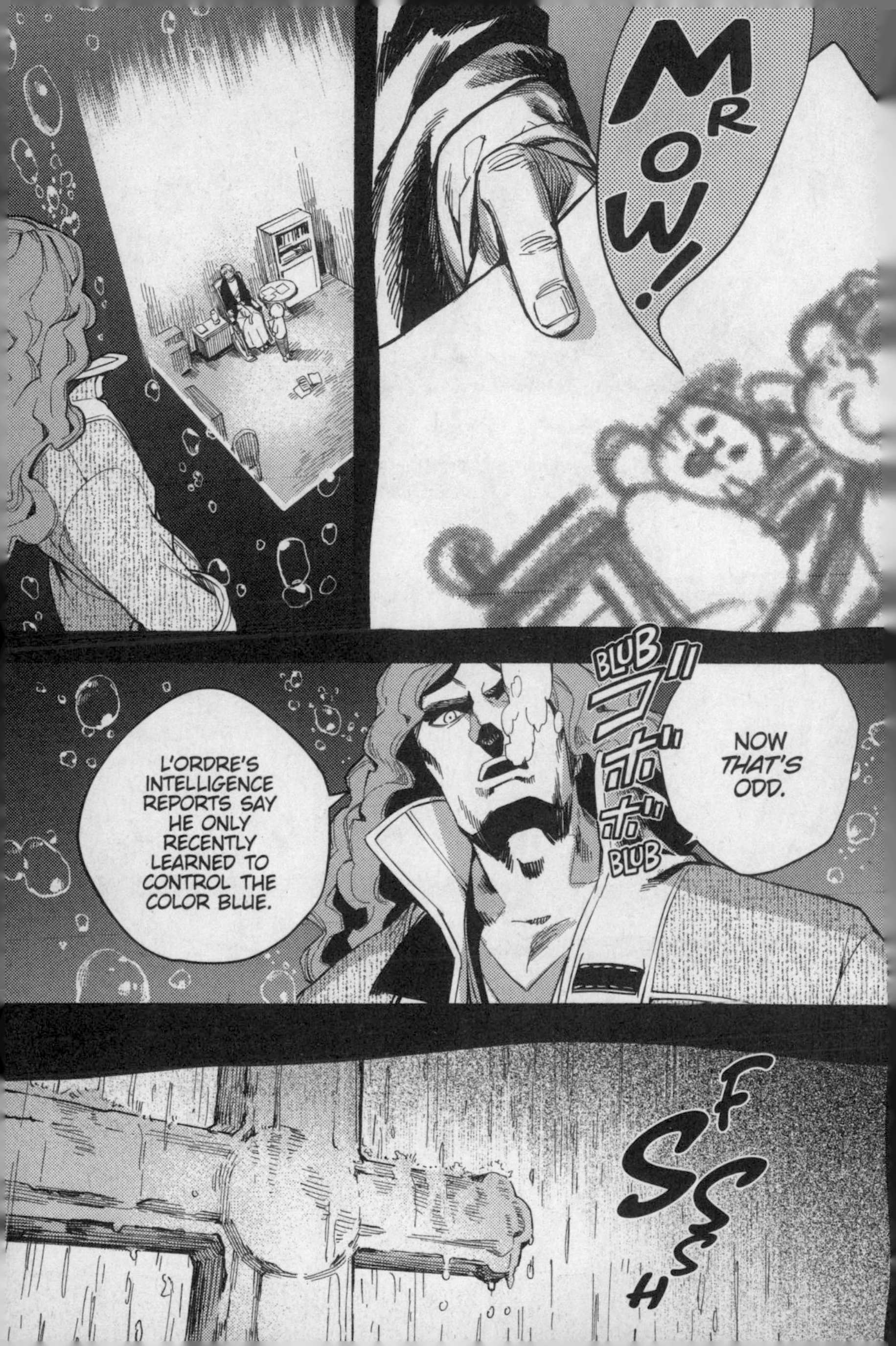
MROW!
BLUB
BLUB
NOW THAT'S ODD.
L'ORDRE'S INTELLIGENCE REPORTS SAY HE ONLY RECENTLY LEARNED TO CONTROL THE COLOR BLUE.
FSSSH

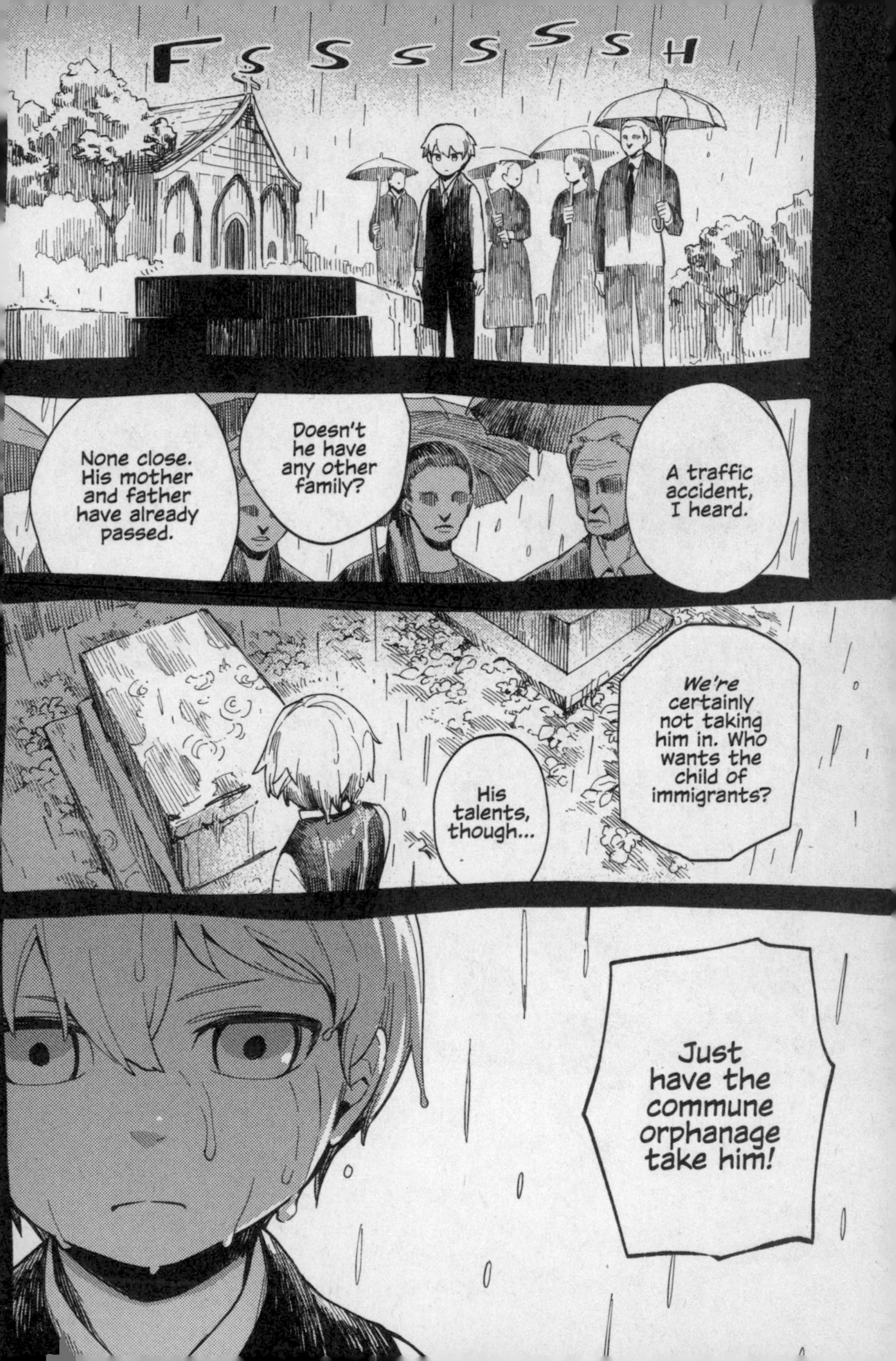
FSSSSSSH
A traffic accident, I heard.
Doesn't he have any other family?
None close. His mother and father have already passed.
We're certainly not taking him in. Who wants the child of immigrants?
His talents, though...
Just have the commune orphanage take him!

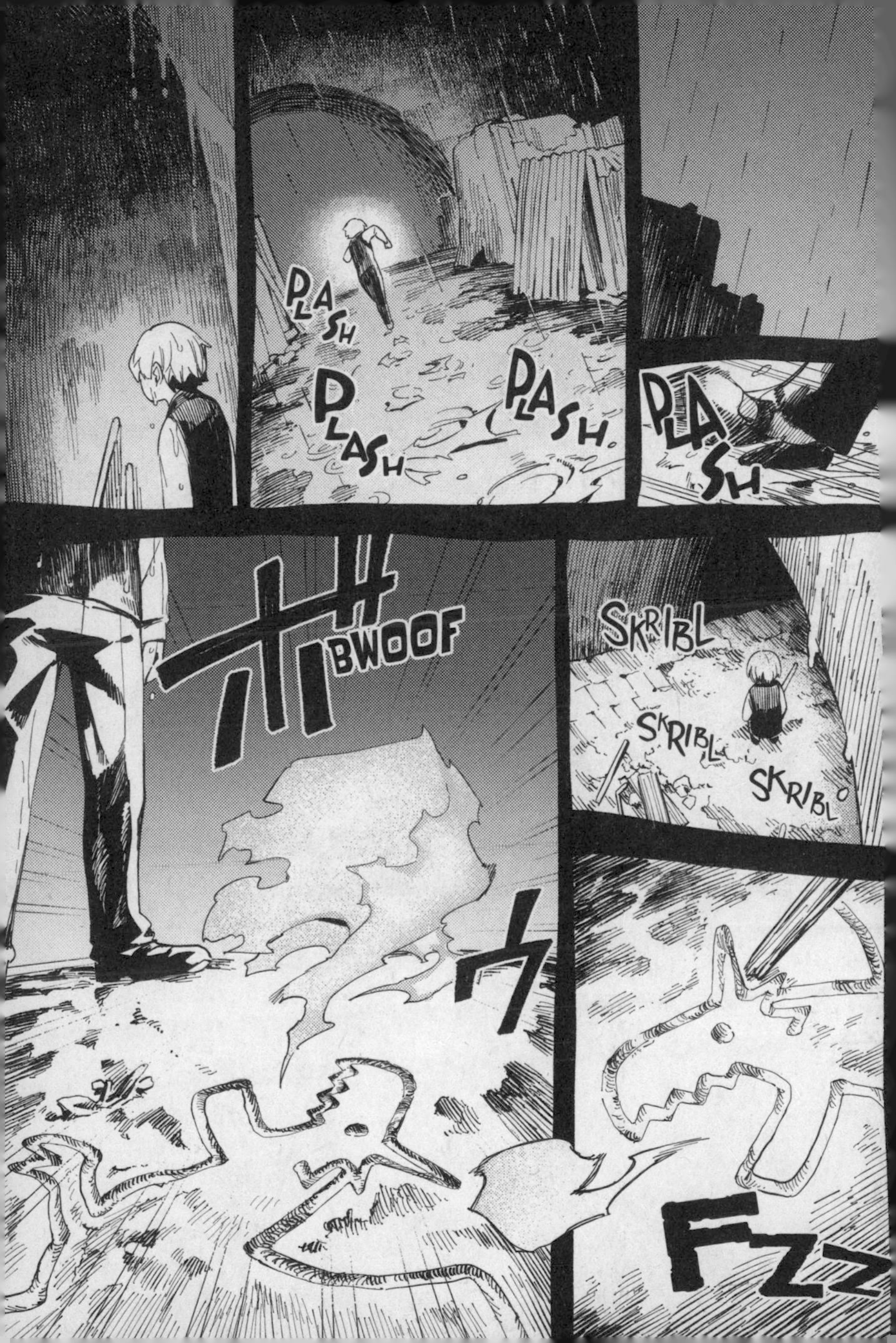
PLASH
PLASH
PLASH
PLASH
SKRIBL
SKRIBL
SKRIBL
FZZ
BWOOF

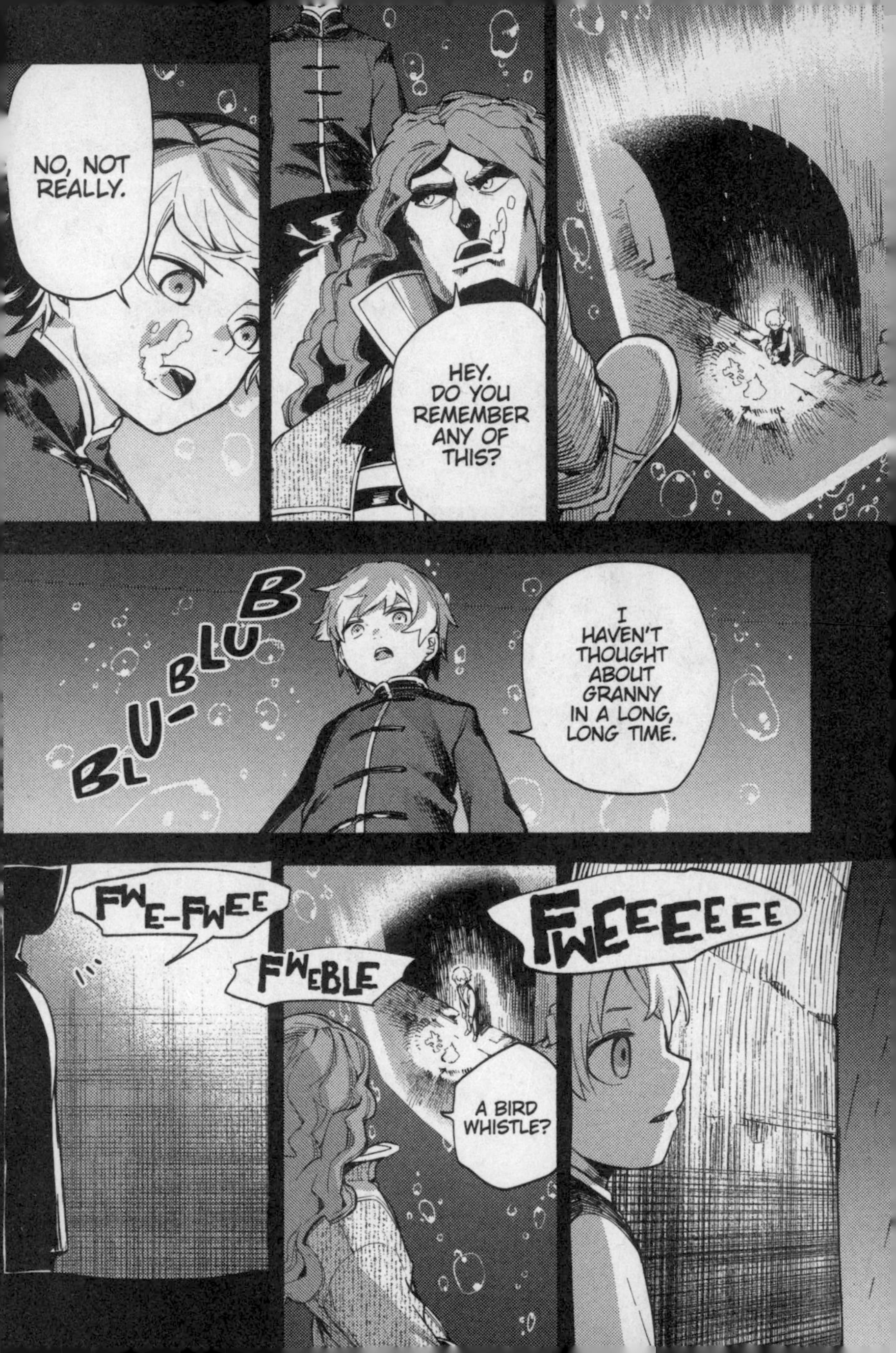
HEY. DO YOU REMEMBER ANY OF THIS?
NO, NOT REALLY.
I HAVEN'T THOUGHT ABOUT GRANNY IN A LONG, LONG TIME.
BLU-BLUB
FWEEEEEEE
FWEBLE
A BIRD WHISTLE?
FWE-FWEE

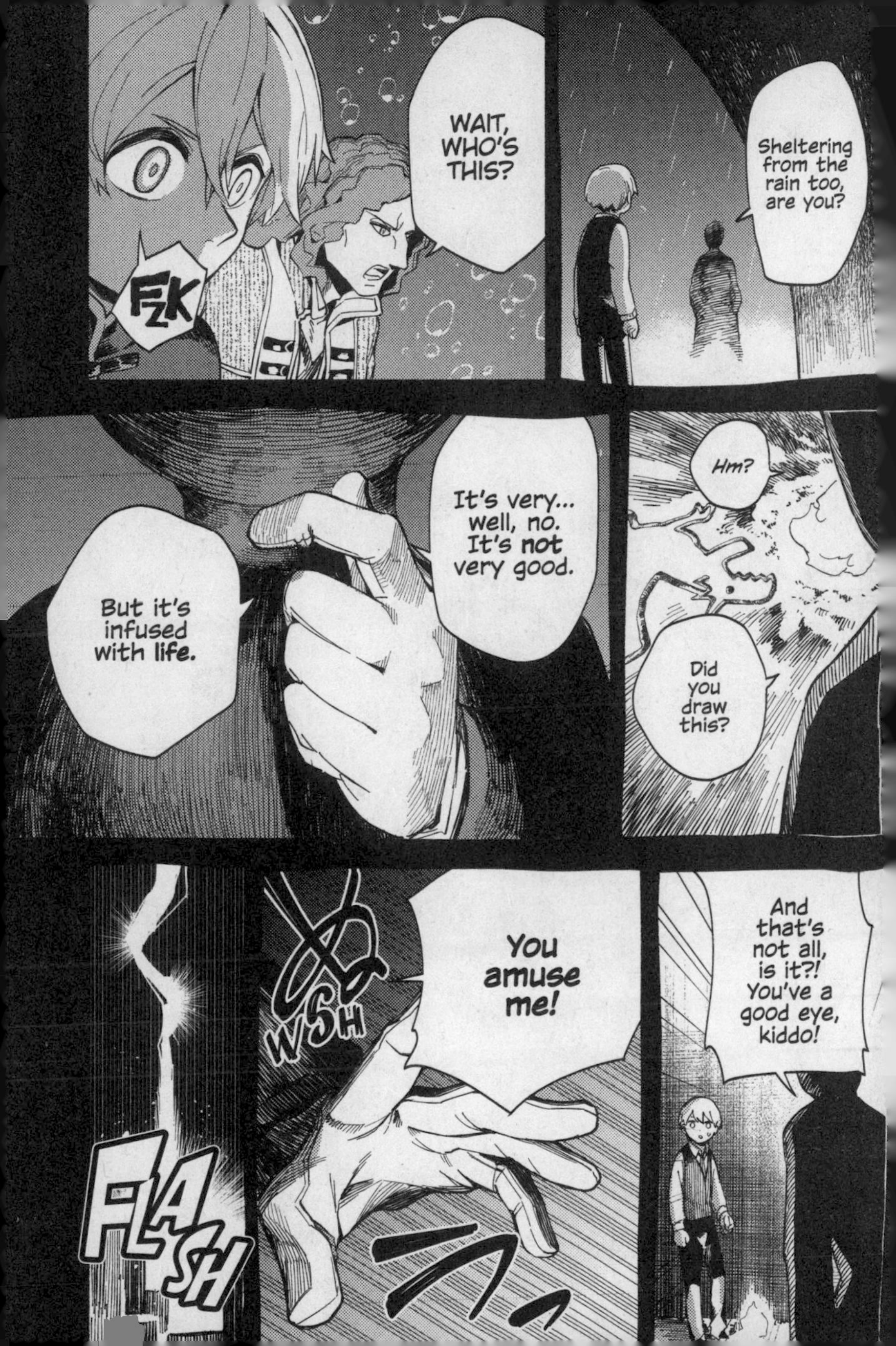
Sheltering from the rain too, are you?
WAIT, WHO'S THIS?
FZK
Hm?
Did you draw this?
It's very... well, no. It's not very good.
But it's infused with life.
And that's not all, is it?! You've a good eye, kiddo!
You amuse me!
WSH
FLASH

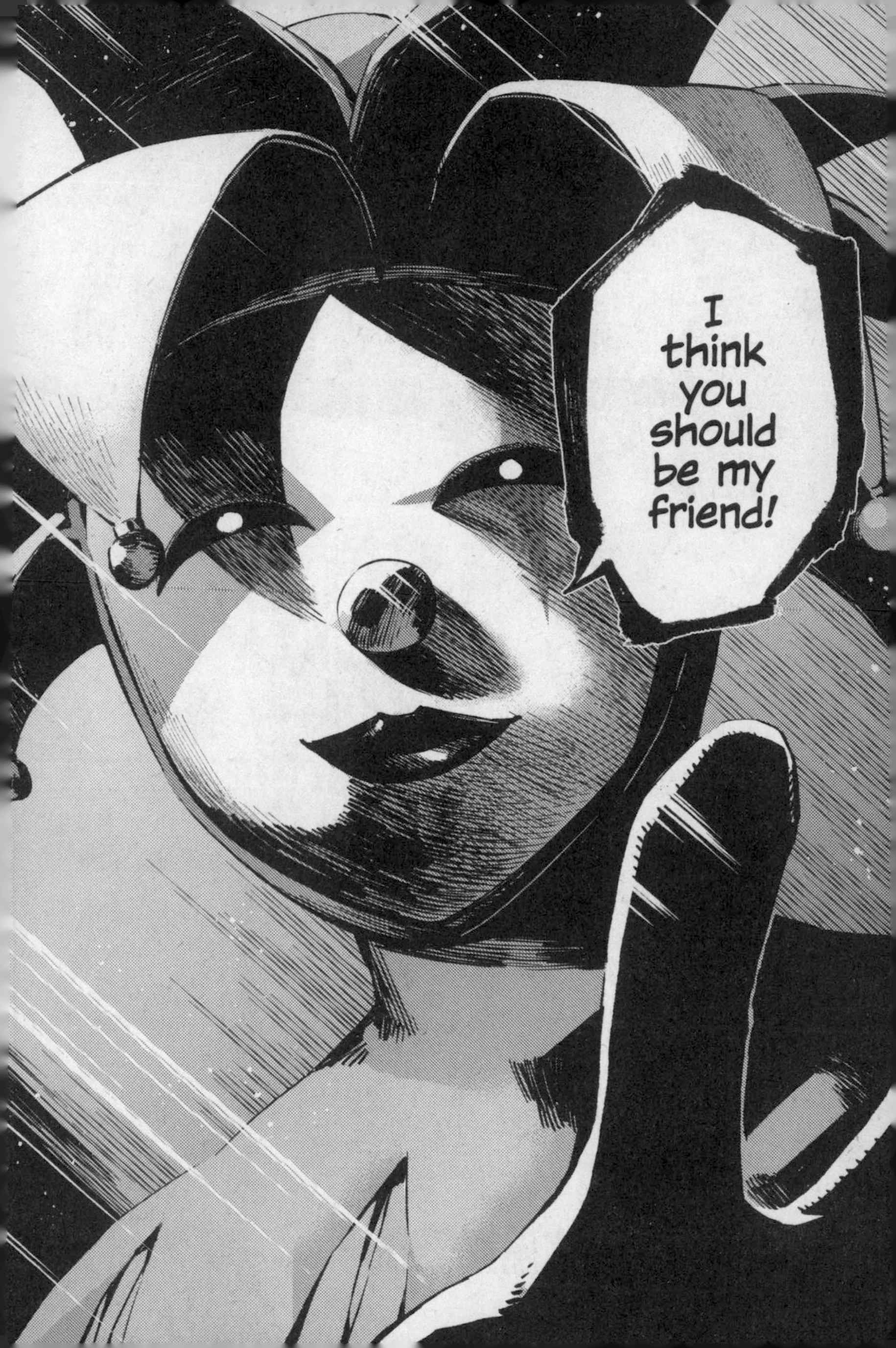
I think you should be my friend!

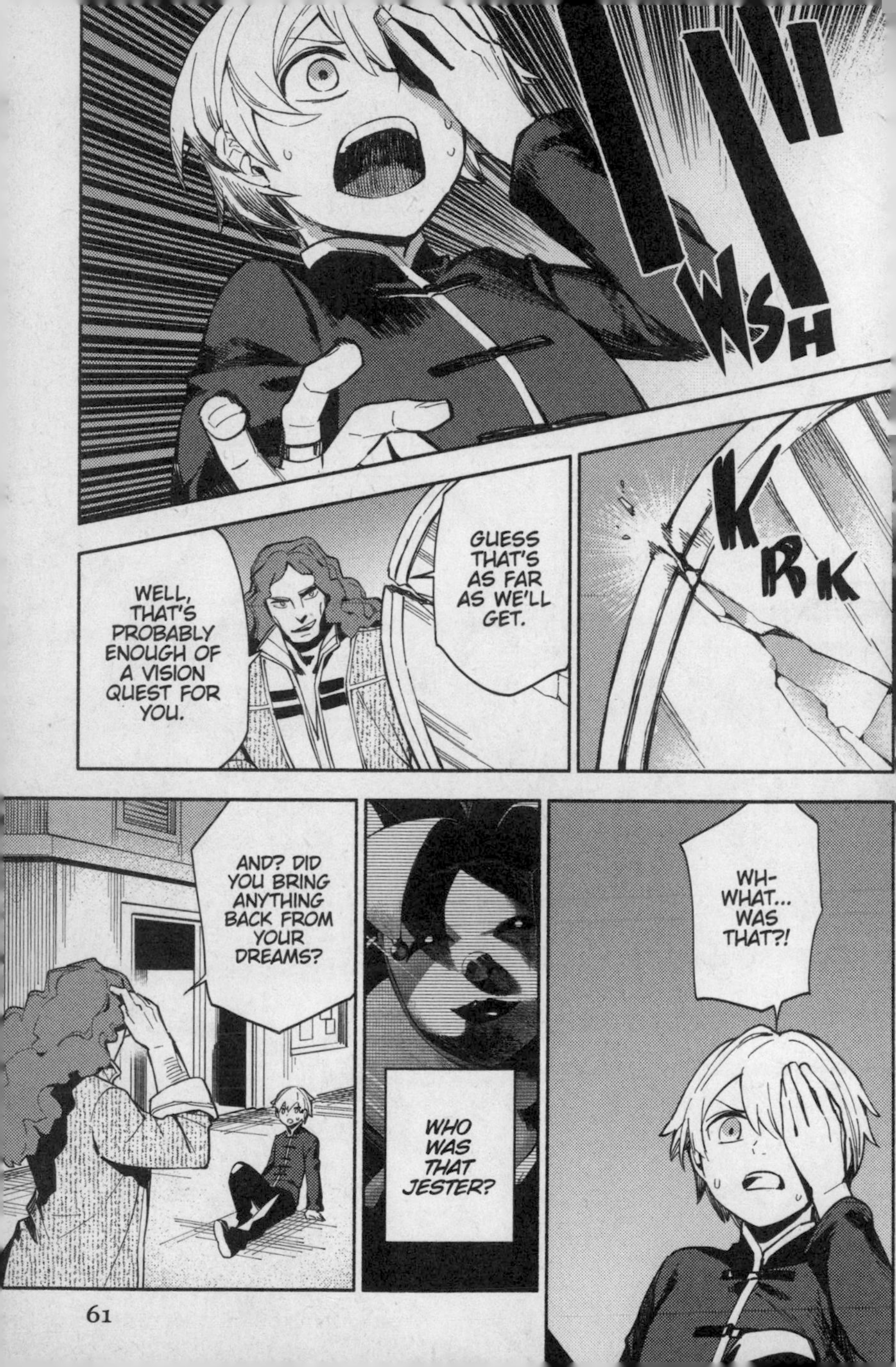
WSH
KRK
GUESS THAT'S AS FAR AS WE'LL GET.
WELL, THAT'S PROBABLY ENOUGH OF A VISION QUEST FOR YOU.
WH-WHAT... WAS THAT?!
WHO WAS THAT JESTER?
AND? DID YOU BRING ANYTHING BACK FROM YOUR DREAMS?

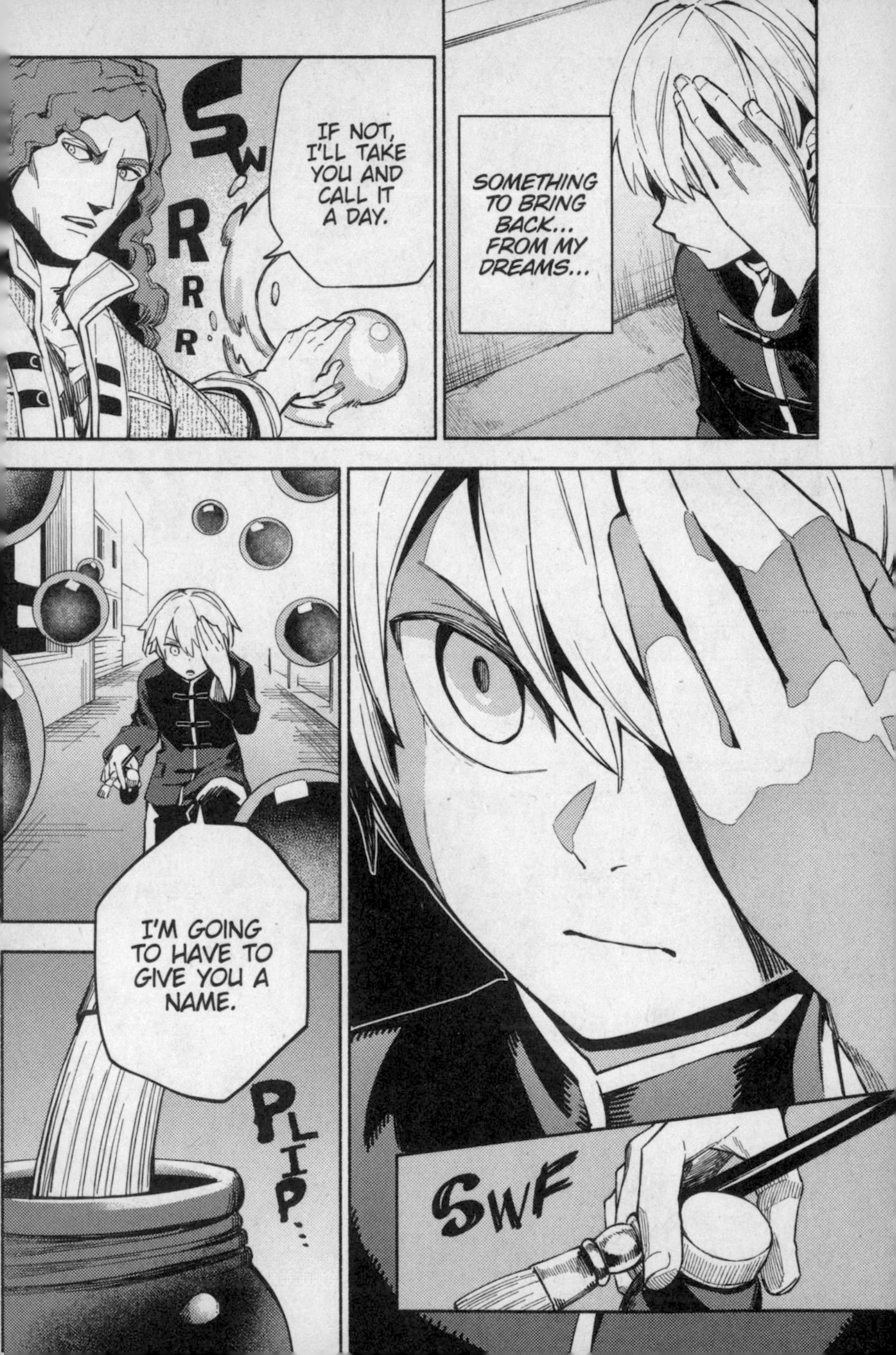
SOMETHING TO BRING BACK... FROM MY DREAMS...
SWRRRR
IF NOT, I'LL TAKE YOU AND CALL IT A DAY.
SWF
I'M GOING TO HAVE TO GIVE YOU A NAME.
PLIP...

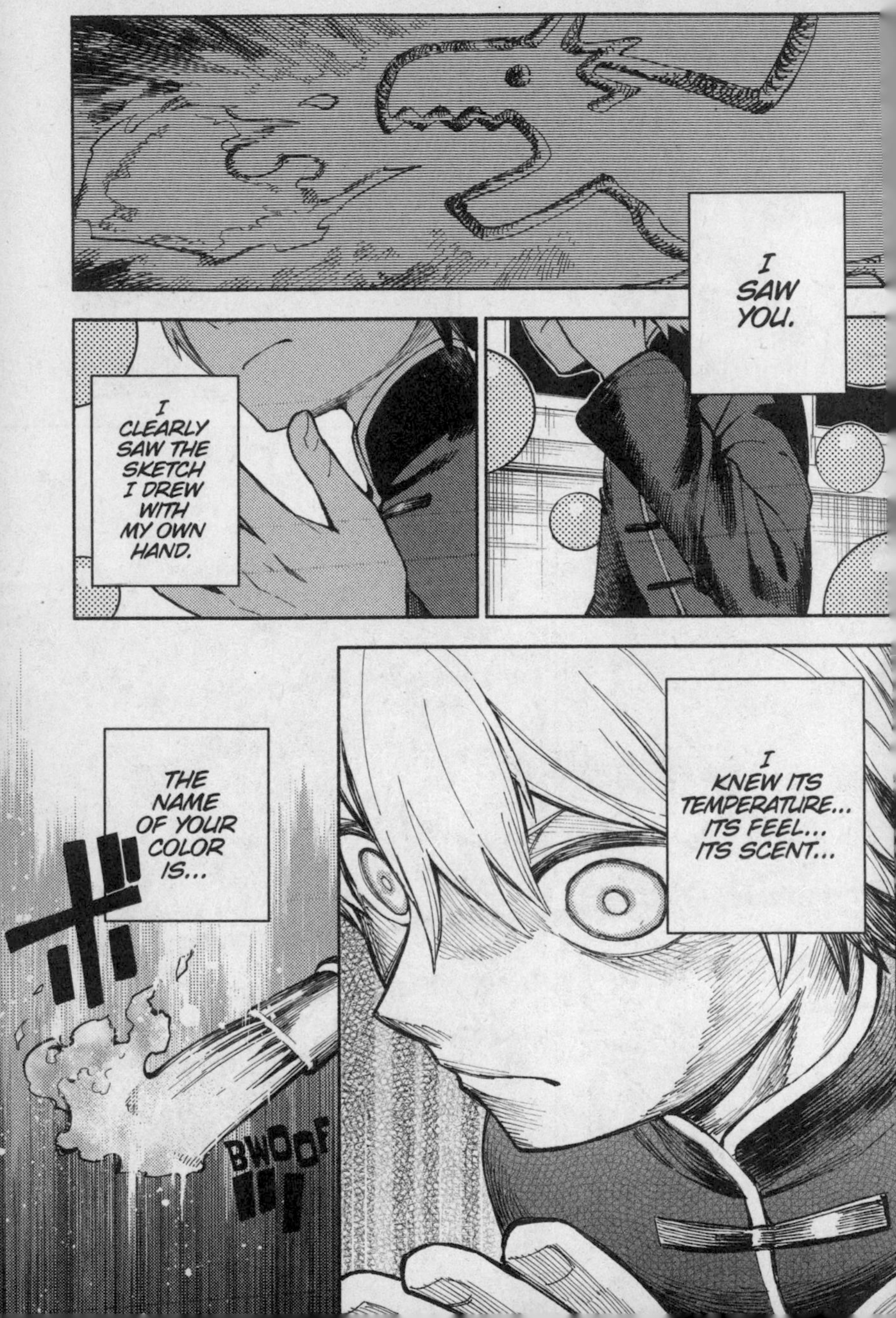
I SAW YOU.
I CLEARLY SAW THE SKETCH I DREW WITH MY OWN HAND.
I KNEW ITS TEMPERATURE... ITS FEEL... ITS SCENT...
THE NAME OF YOUR COLOR IS...
BWOOF

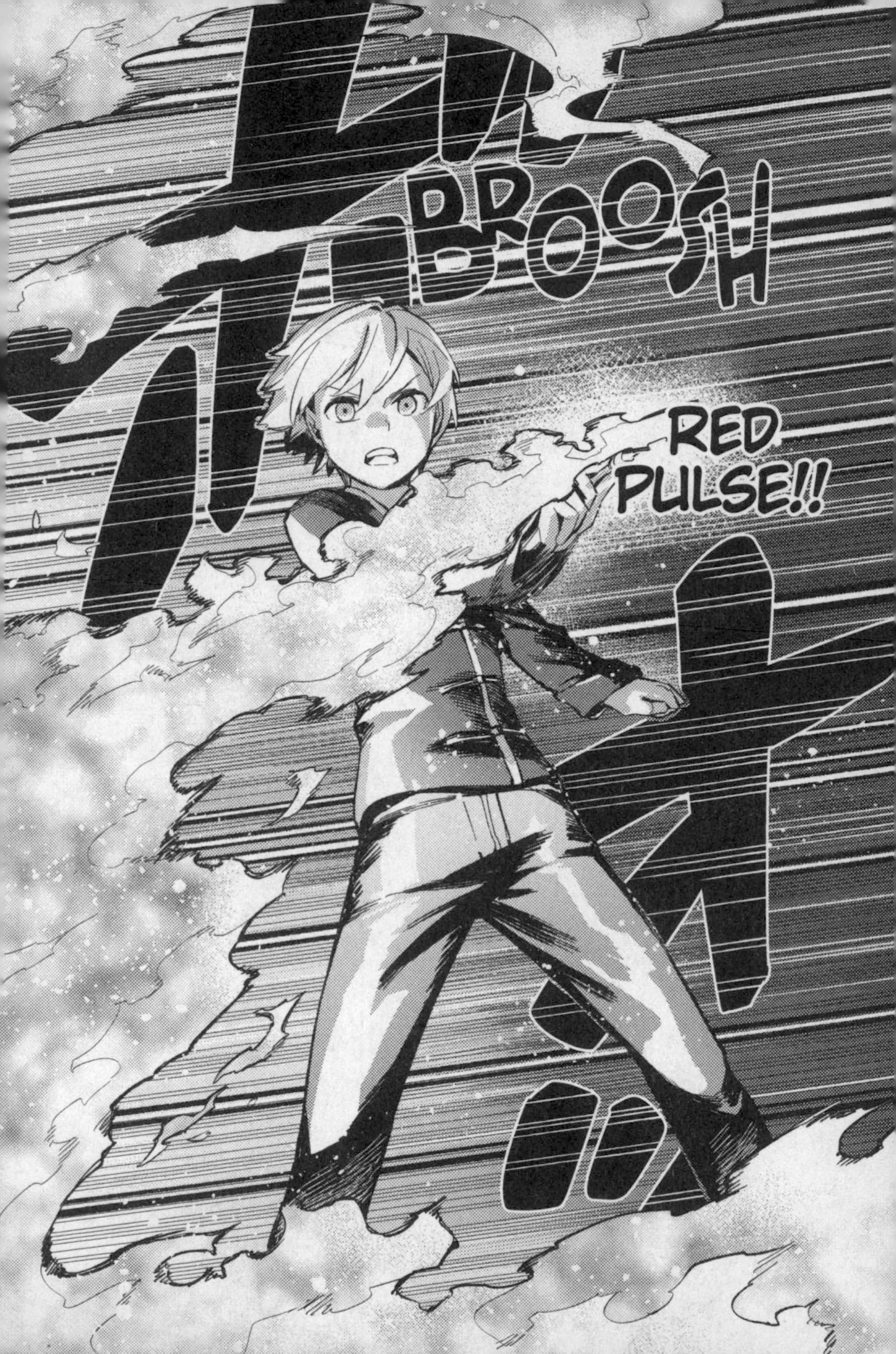
BROOSH
RED PULSE!!

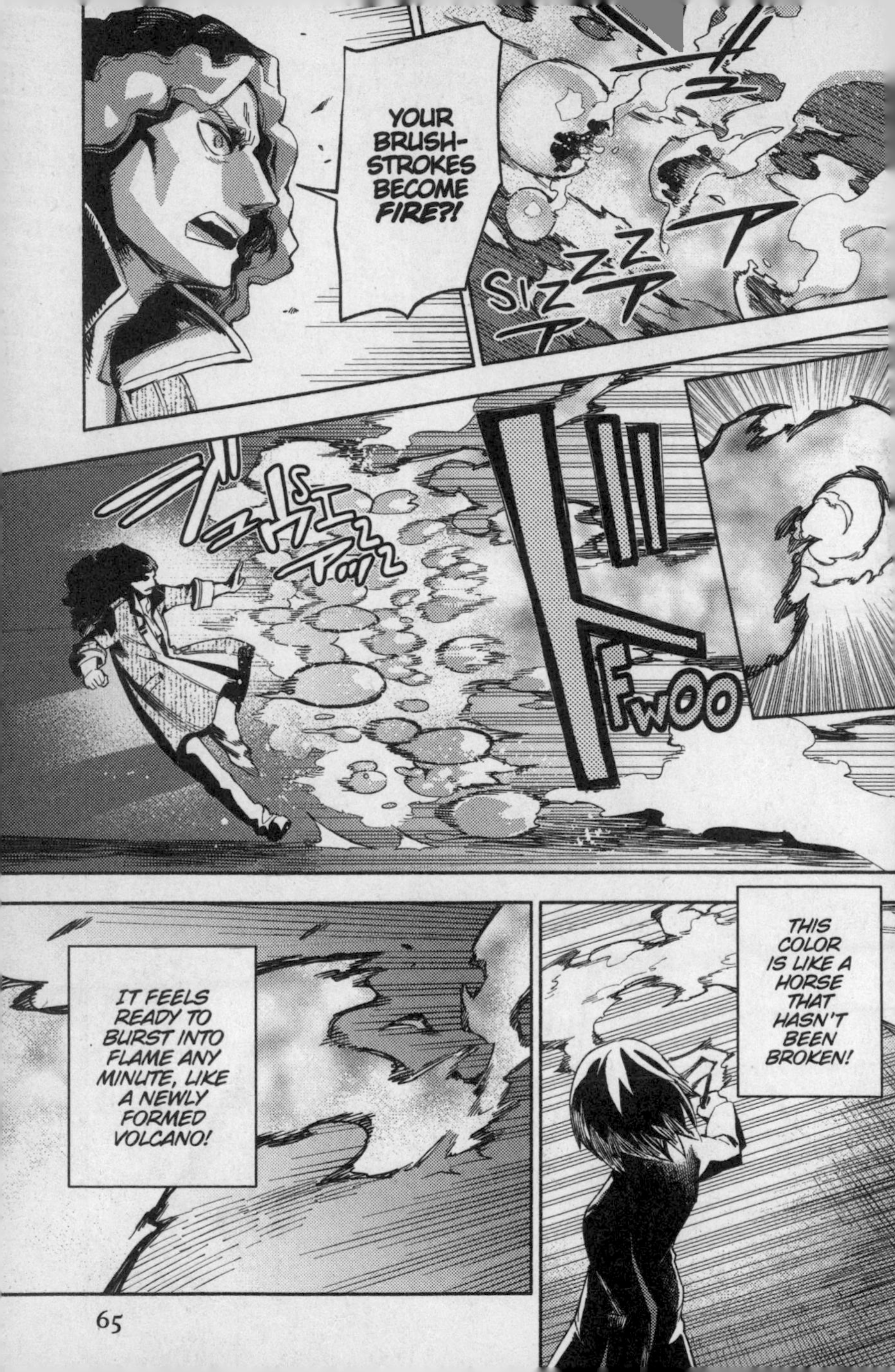
SIZZZ
YOUR BRUSH-STROKES BECOME FIRE?!
FWOO
SIZZ
THIS COLOR IS LIKE A HORSE THAT HASN'T BEEN BROKEN!
IT FEELS READY TO BURST INTO FLAME ANY MINUTE, LIKE A NEWLY FORMED VOLCANO!

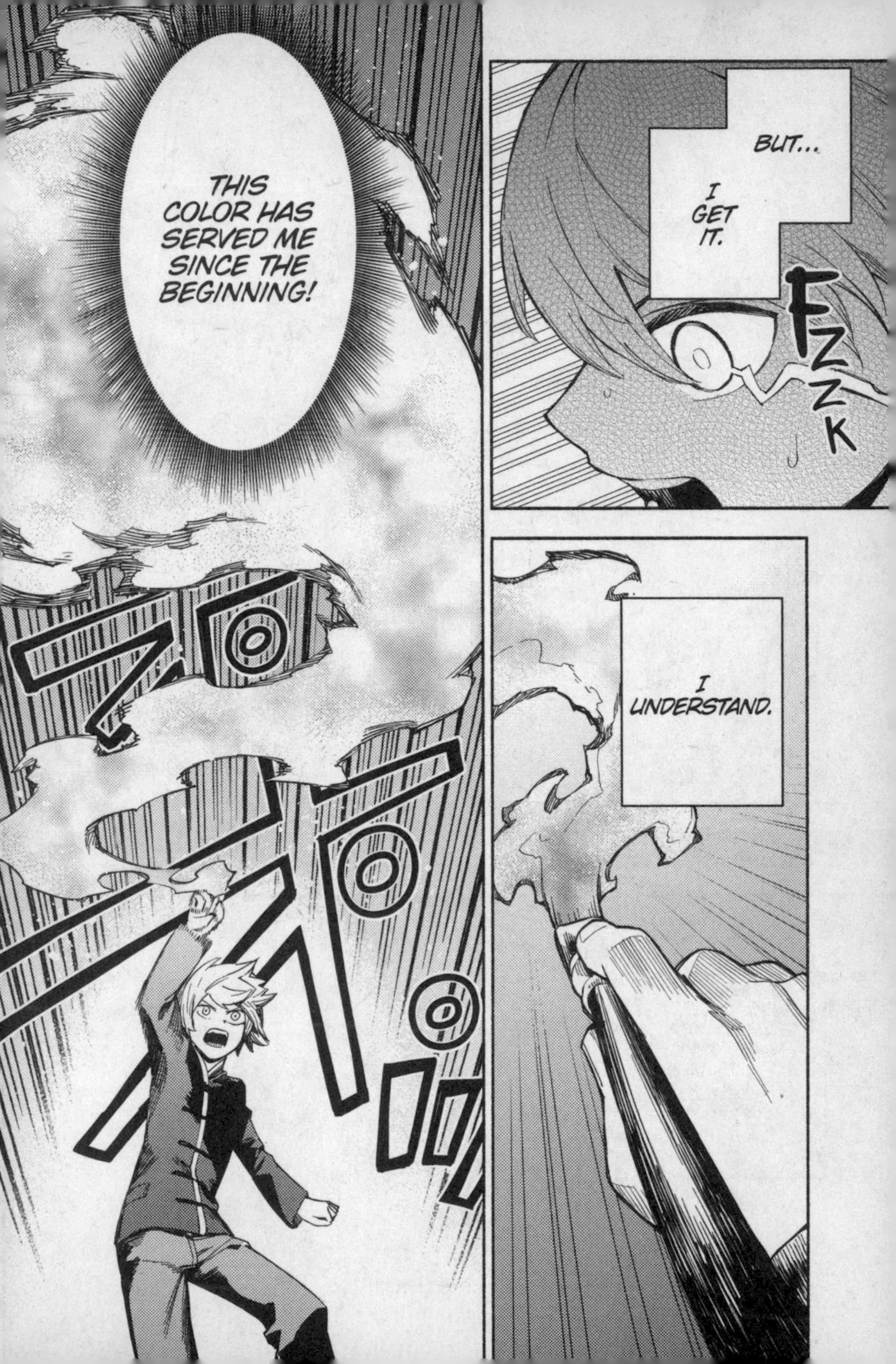
BUT...
I GET IT.
FZZK
I UNDERSTAND.
THIS COLOR HAS SERVED ME SINCE THE BEGINNING!

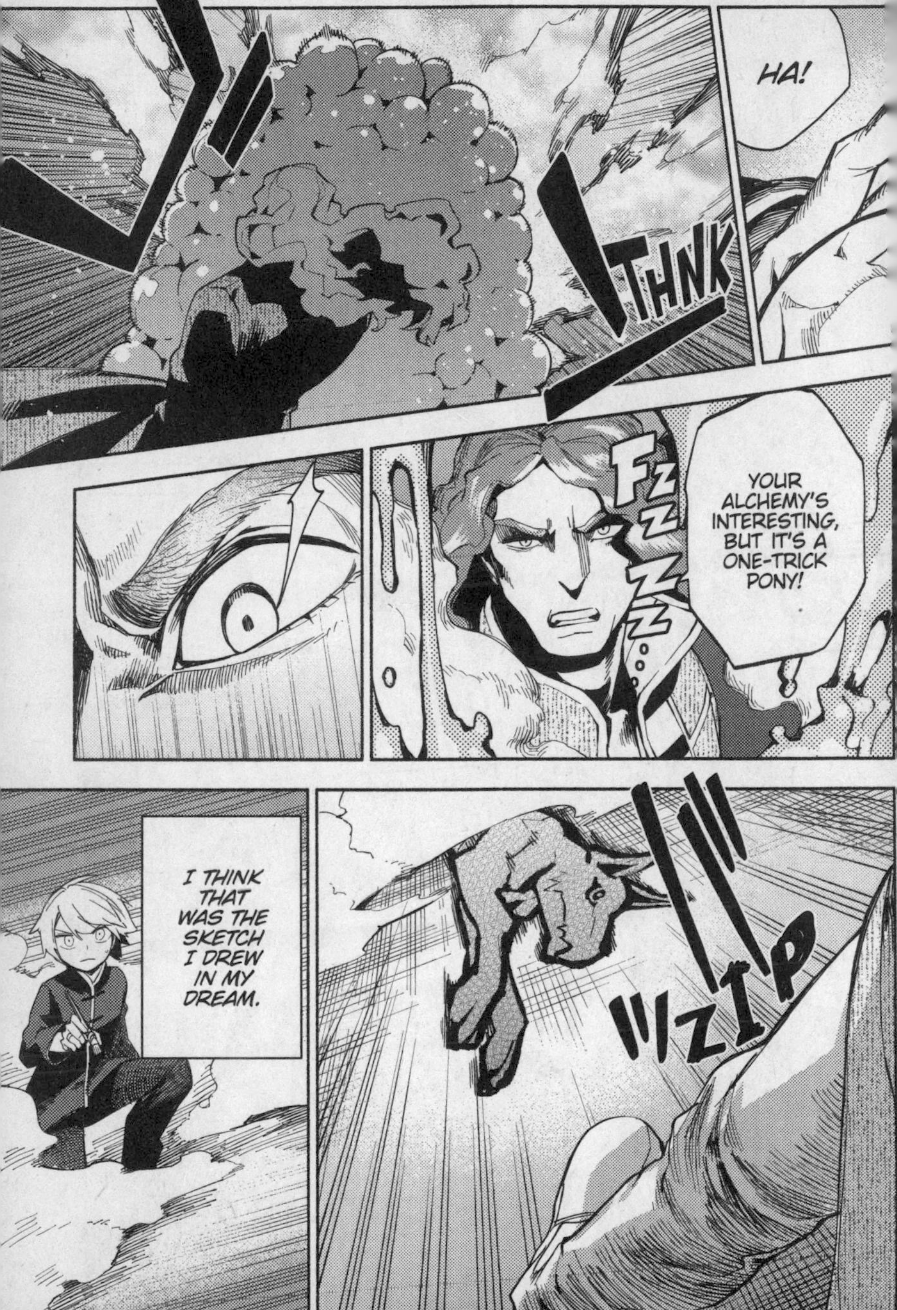
HA!
THNK
FZZZZ
YOUR ALCHEMY'S INTERESTING, BUT IT'S A ONE-TRICK PONY!
ZZIP
I THINK THAT WAS THE SKETCH I DREW IN MY DREAM.

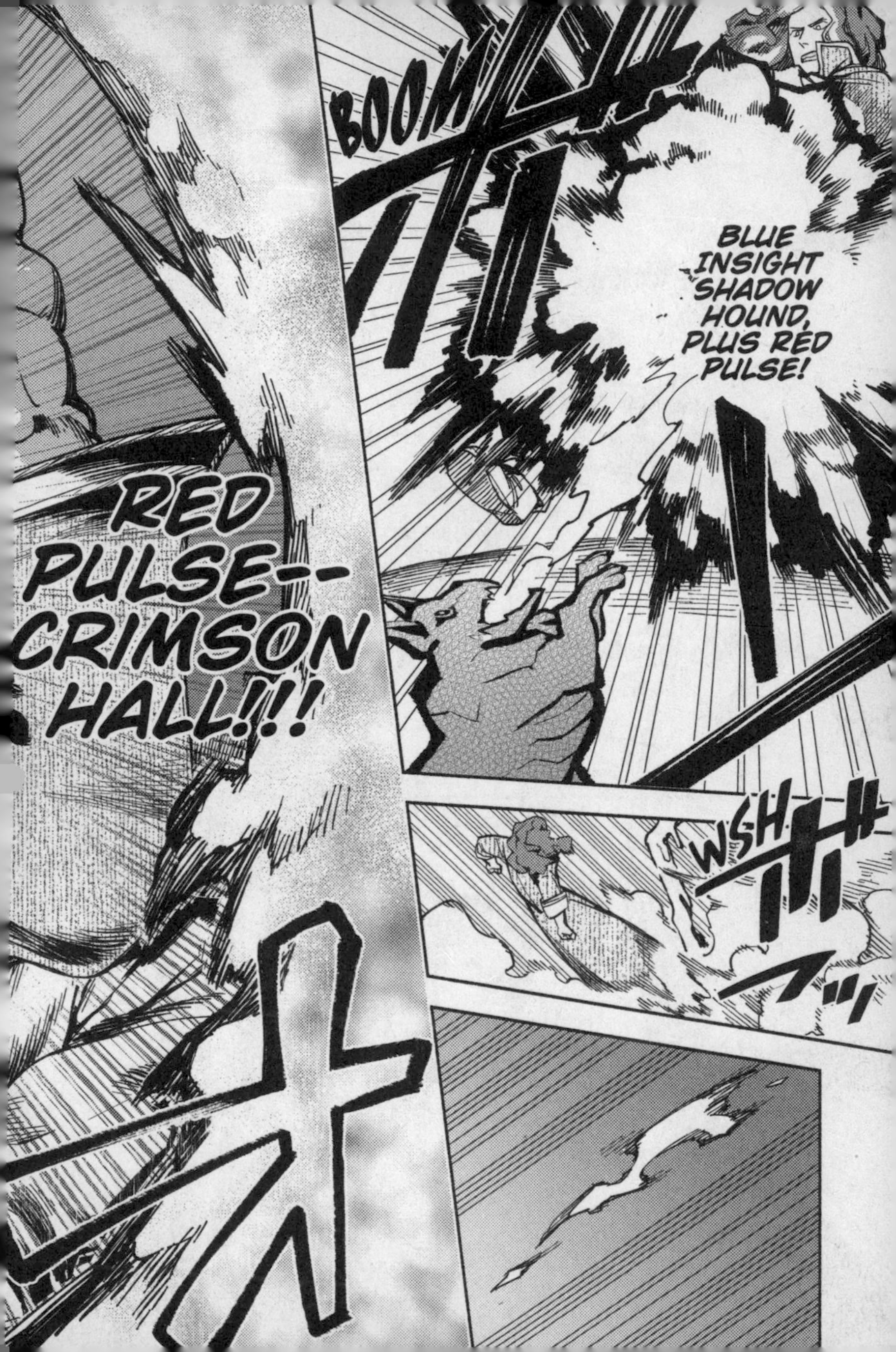
BLUE INSIGHT SHADOW HOUND, PLUS RED PULSE!
BOOM
WSH
RED PULSE--CRIMSON HALL!!!

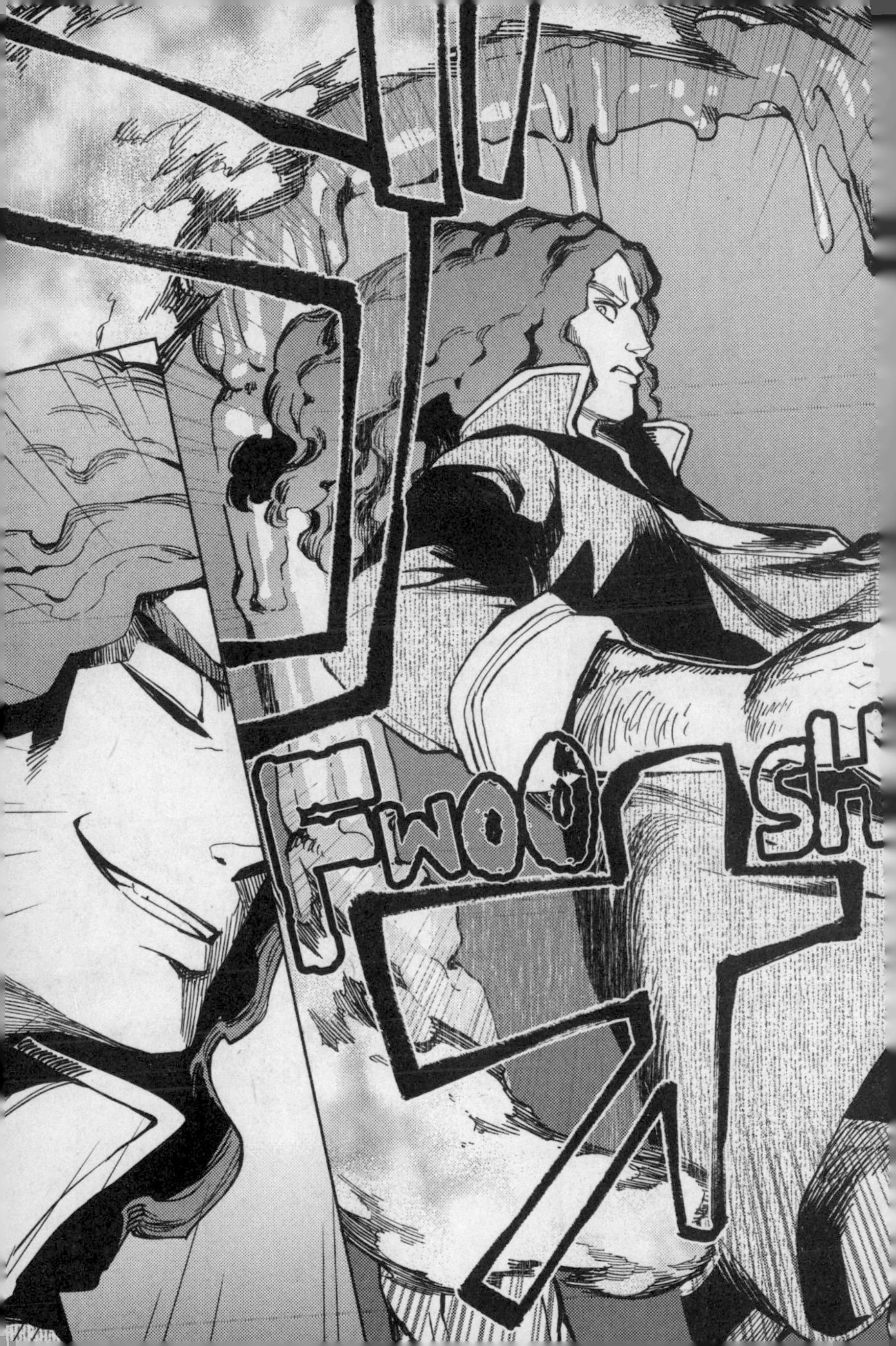
FWOO SH

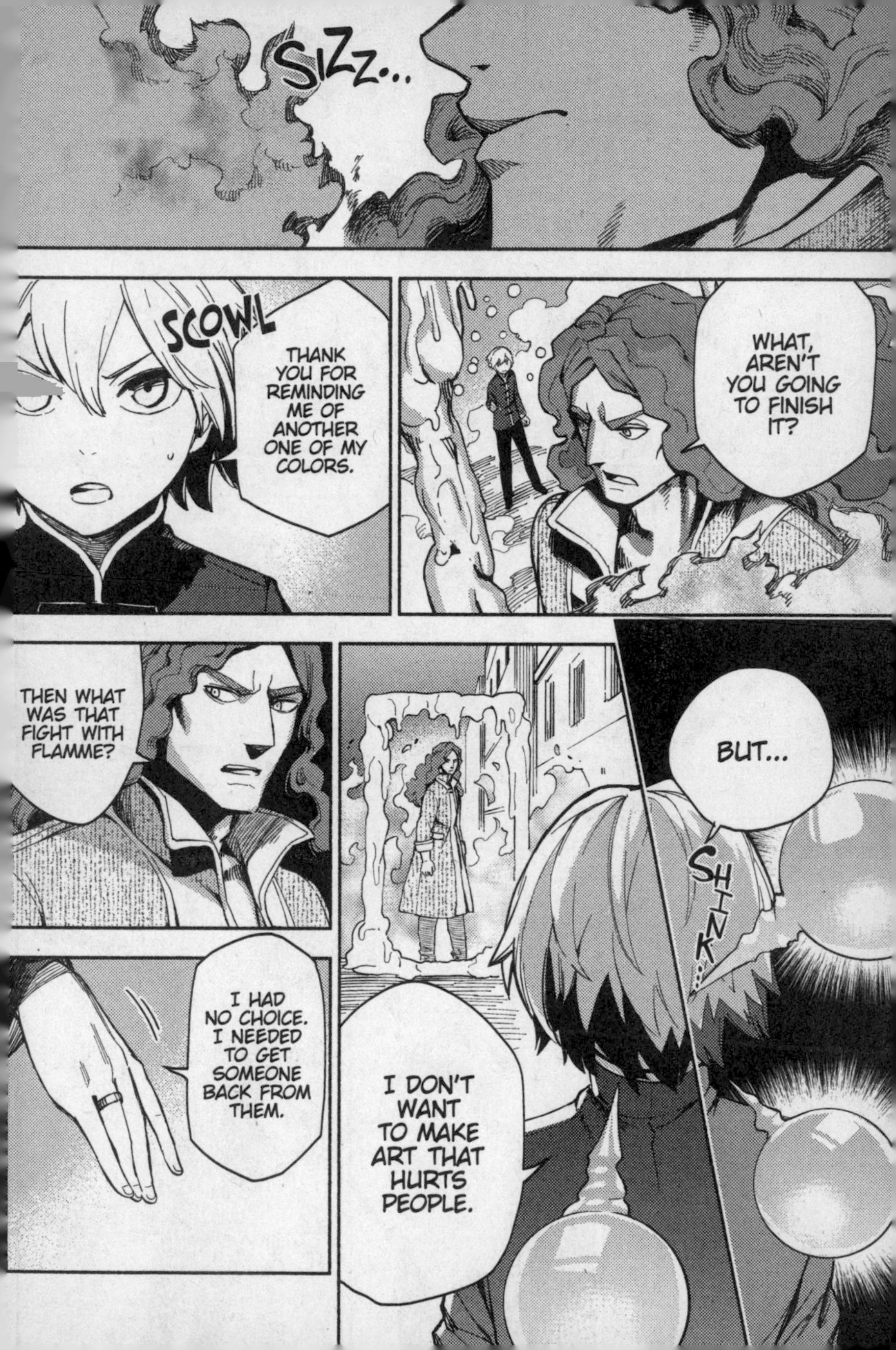
SIZZ...
WHAT, AREN'T YOU GOING TO FINISH IT?
SCOWL
THANK YOU FOR REMINDING ME OF ANOTHER ONE OF MY COLORS.
BUT...
SHINK...
I DON'T WANT TO MAKE ART THAT HURTS PEOPLE.
THEN WHAT WAS THAT FIGHT WITH FLAMME?
I HAD NO CHOICE. I NEEDED TO GET SOMEONE BACK FROM THEM.

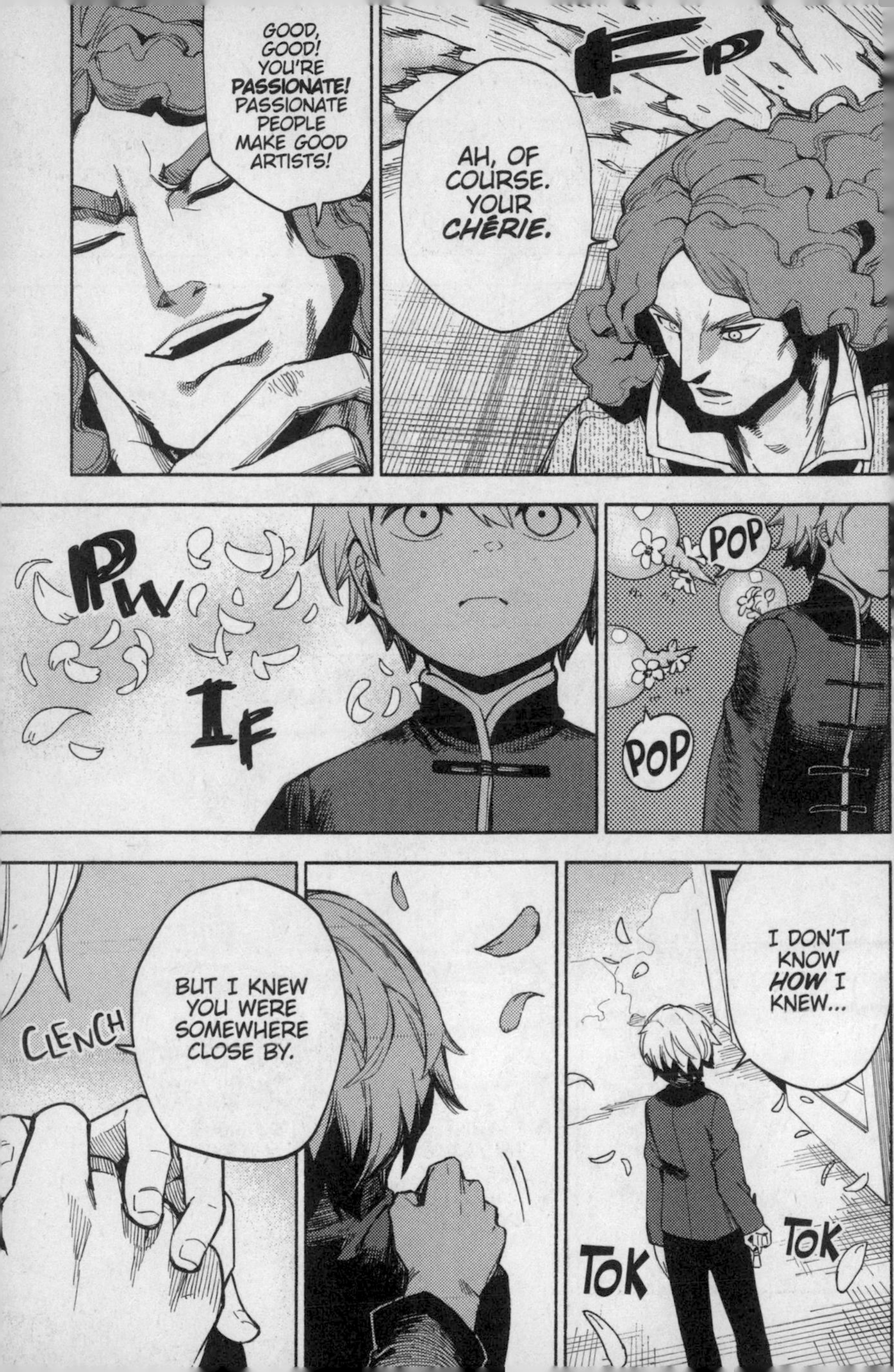
AH, OF COURSE. YOUR *CHÉRIE.*
GOOD, GOOD! YOU'RE **PASSIONATE!** PASSIONATE PEOPLE MAKE GOOD ARTISTS!
POP
POP
I DON'T KNOW *HOW* I KNEW...
TOK
TOK
BUT I KNEW YOU WERE SOMEWHERE CLOSE BY.
CLENCH

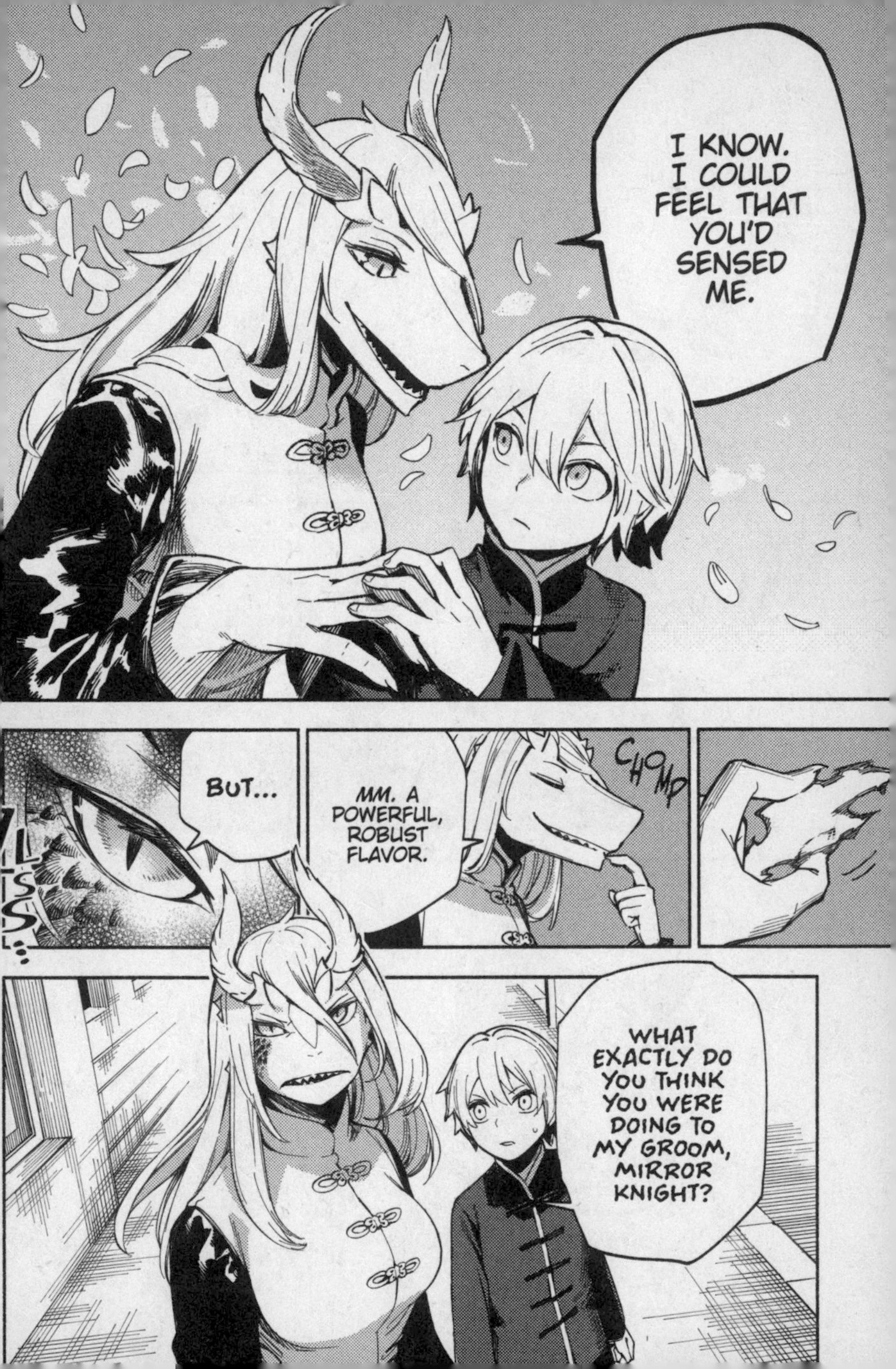
I KNOW. I COULD FEEL THAT YOU'D SENSED ME.
CHOMP
MM. A POWERFUL, ROBUST FLAVOR.
BUT...
WHAT EXACTLY DO YOU THINK YOU WERE DOING TO MY GROOM, MIRROR KNIGHT?

The Ancient
Magus' Bride
WIZARD's BLUE

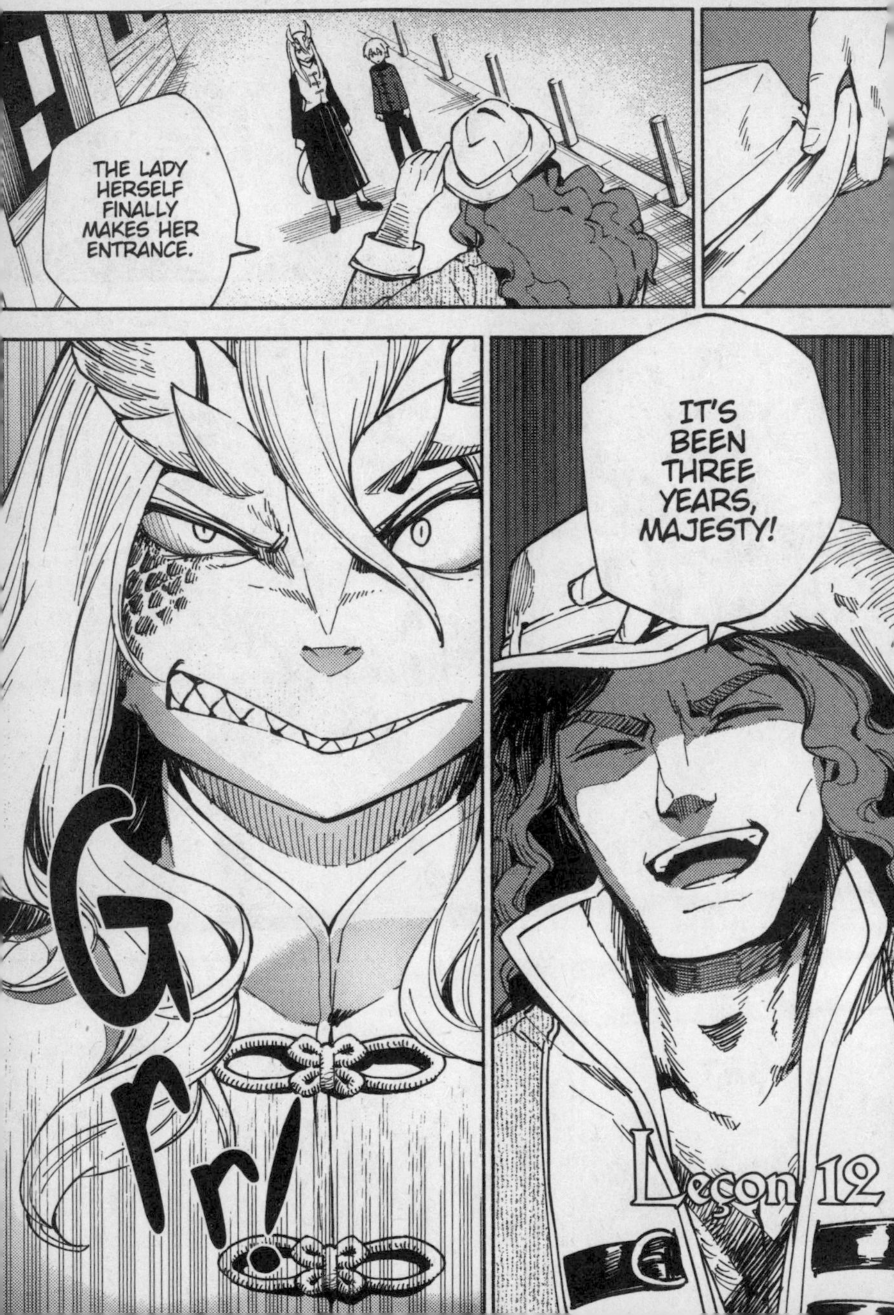
THE LADY HERSELF FINALLY MAKES HER ENTRANCE.
IT'S BEEN THREE YEARS, MAJESTY!
Leçon 12
Grr!

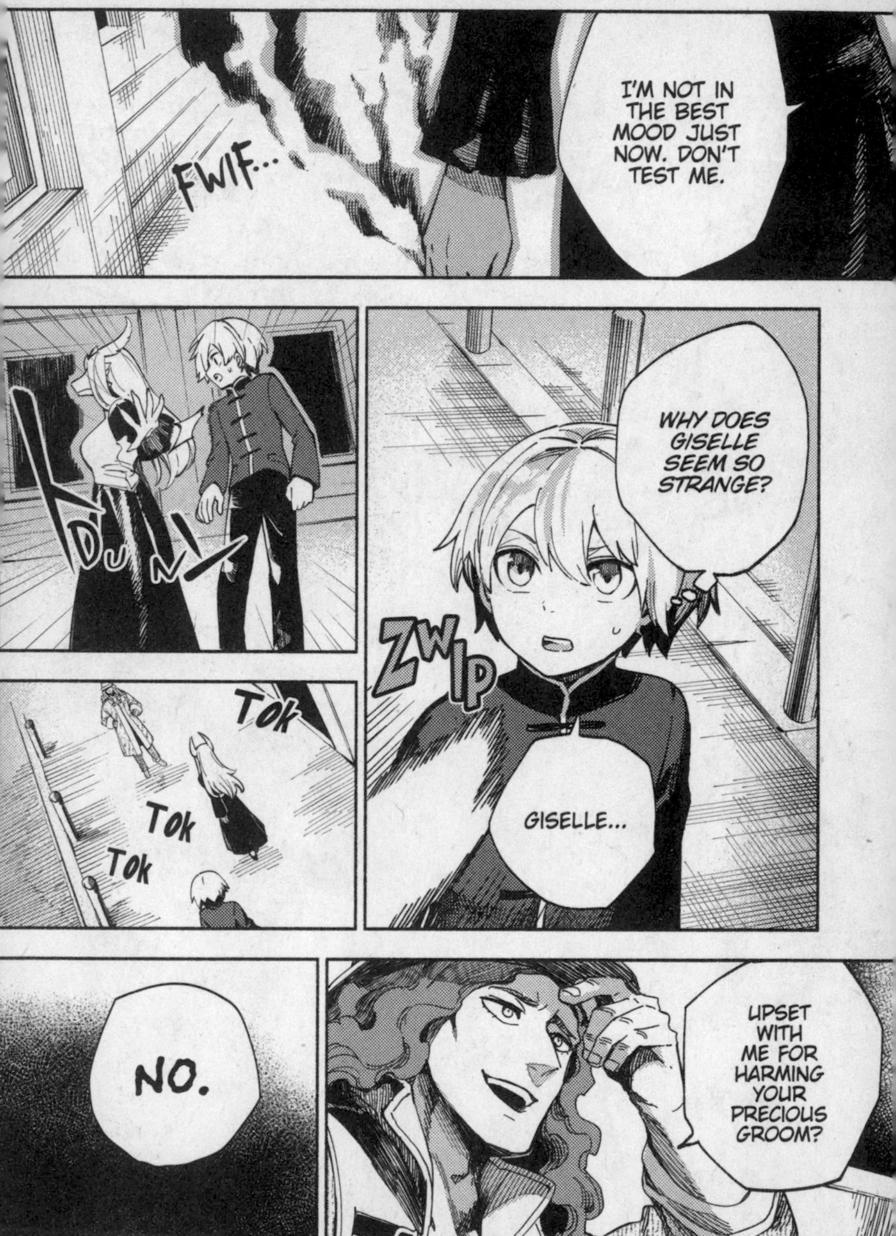
I'M NOT IN THE BEST MOOD JUST NOW. DON'T TEST ME.
FWIF...
WHY DOES GISELLE SEEM SO STRANGE?
ZWIP
GISELLE...
KDUN
TOK
TOK
TOK
UPSET WITH ME FOR HARMING YOUR PRECIOUS GROOM?
NO.

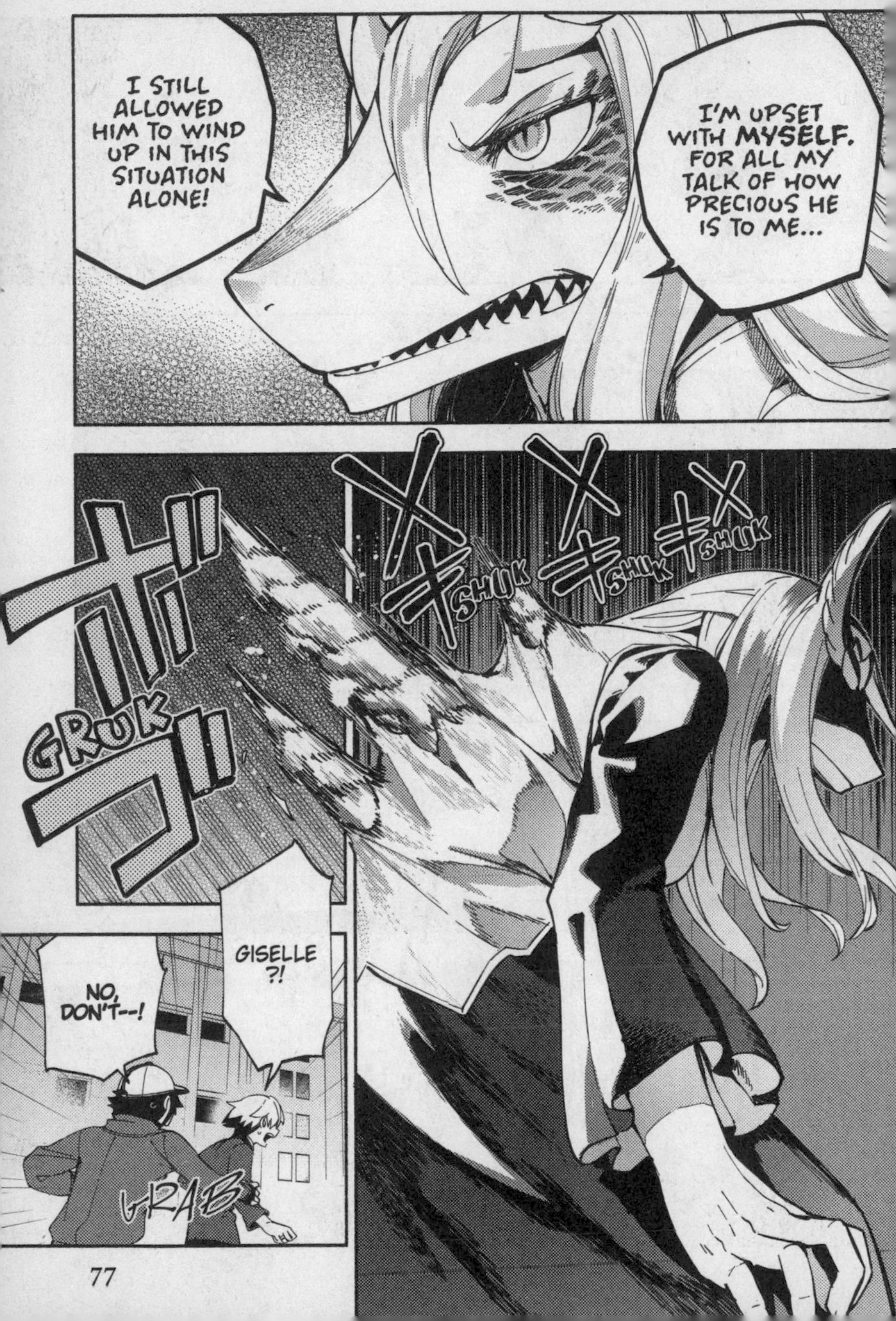
I'M UPSET WITH MYSELF. FOR ALL MY TALK OF HOW PRECIOUS HE IS TO ME...
I STILL ALLOWED HIM TO WIND UP IN THIS SITUATION ALONE!
SHUK SHUK SHUK
GRUK
GISELLE ?!
NO, DON'T--!
GRAB

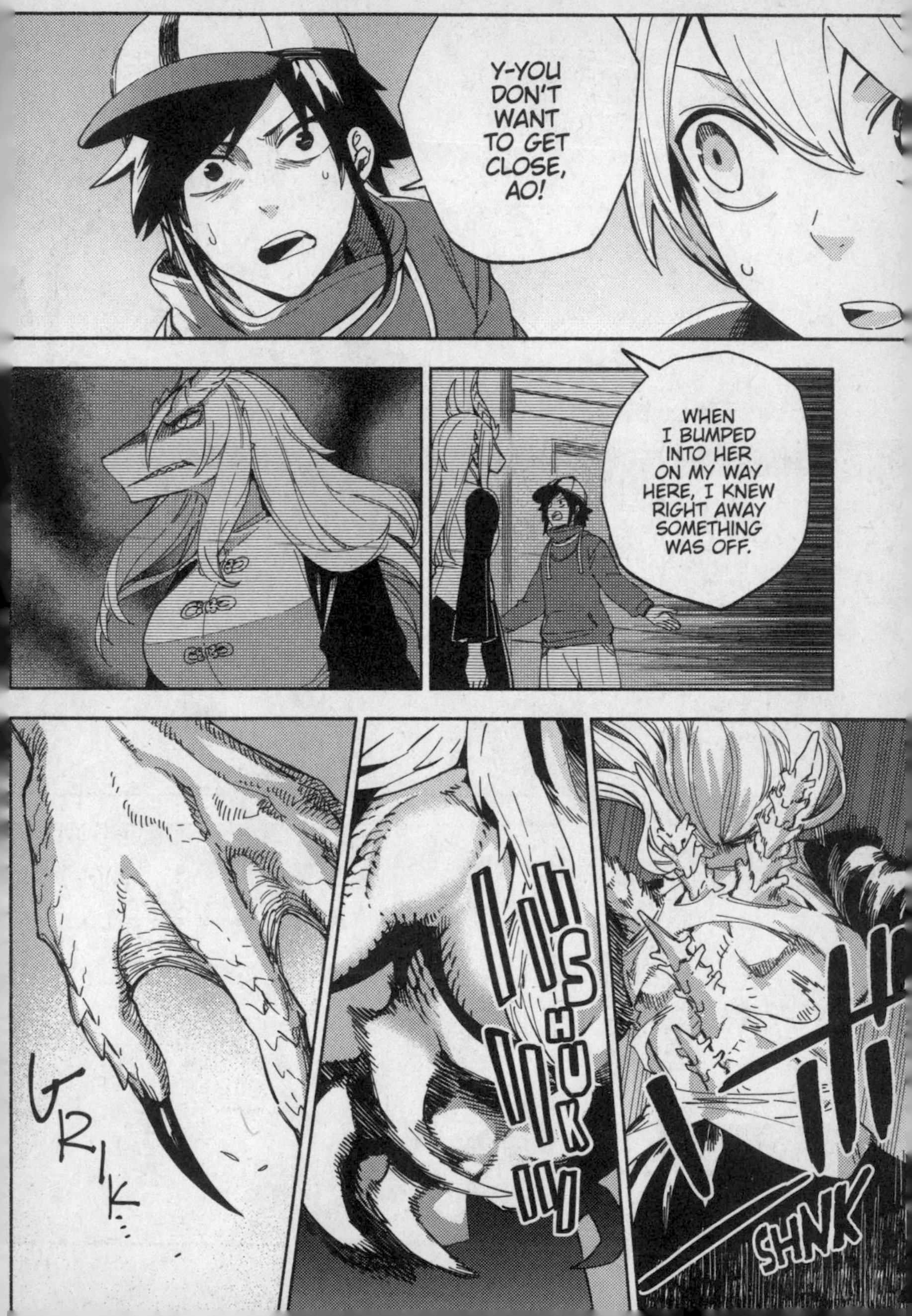
Y-YOU DON'T WANT TO GET CLOSE, AO!
WHEN I BUMPED INTO HER ON MY WAY HERE, I KNEW RIGHT AWAY SOMETHING WAS OFF.
SHNK
SHUK
GRIK...

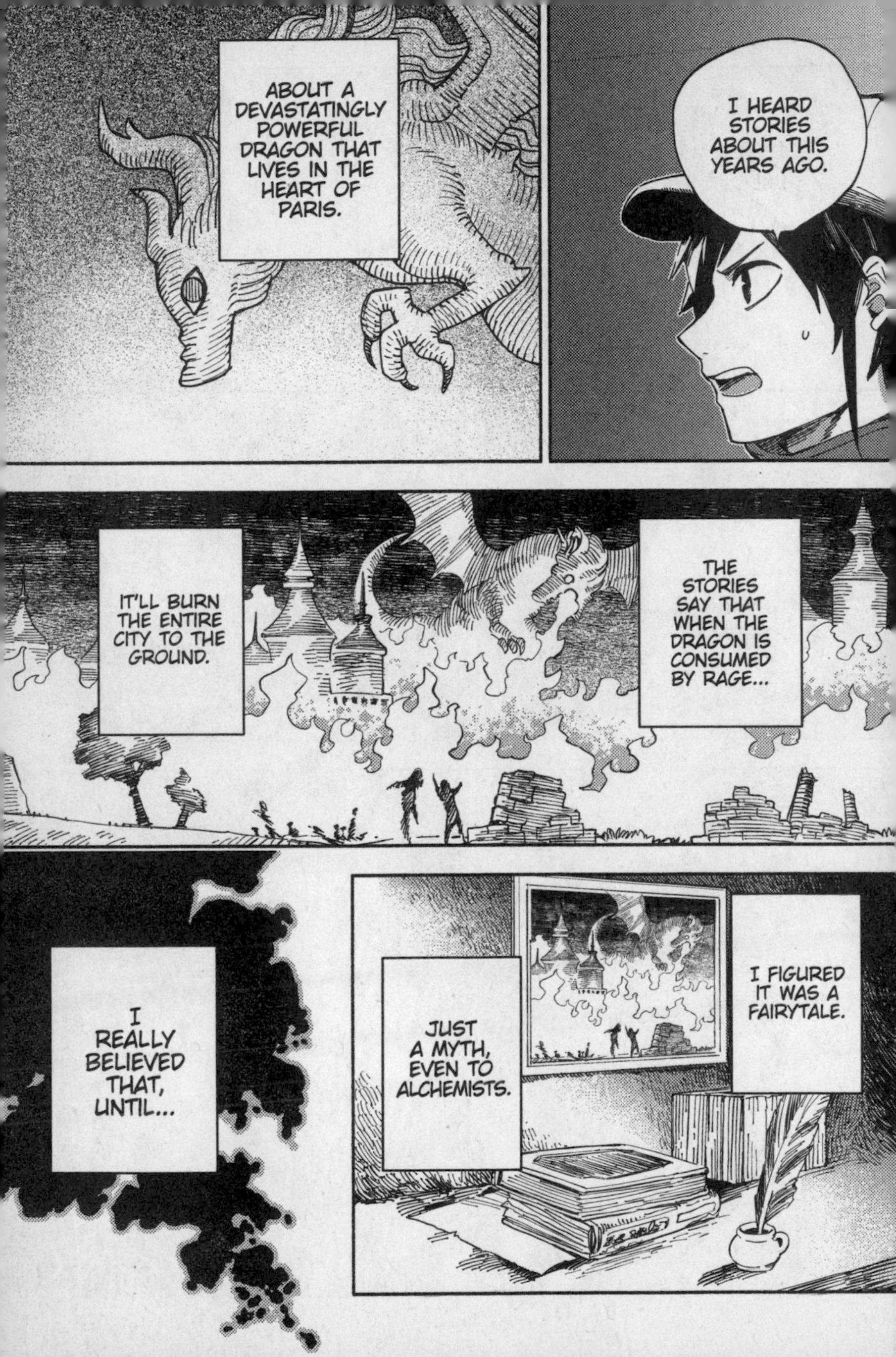
I HEARD STORIES ABOUT THIS YEARS AGO.
ABOUT A DEVASTATINGLY POWERFUL DRAGON THAT LIVES IN THE HEART OF PARIS.
THE STORIES SAY THAT WHEN THE DRAGON IS CONSUMED BY RAGE...
IT'LL BURN THE ENTIRE CITY TO THE GROUND.
I FIGURED IT WAS A FAIRYTALE.
JUST A MYTH, EVEN TO ALCHEMISTS.
I REALLY BELIEVED THAT, UNTIL...

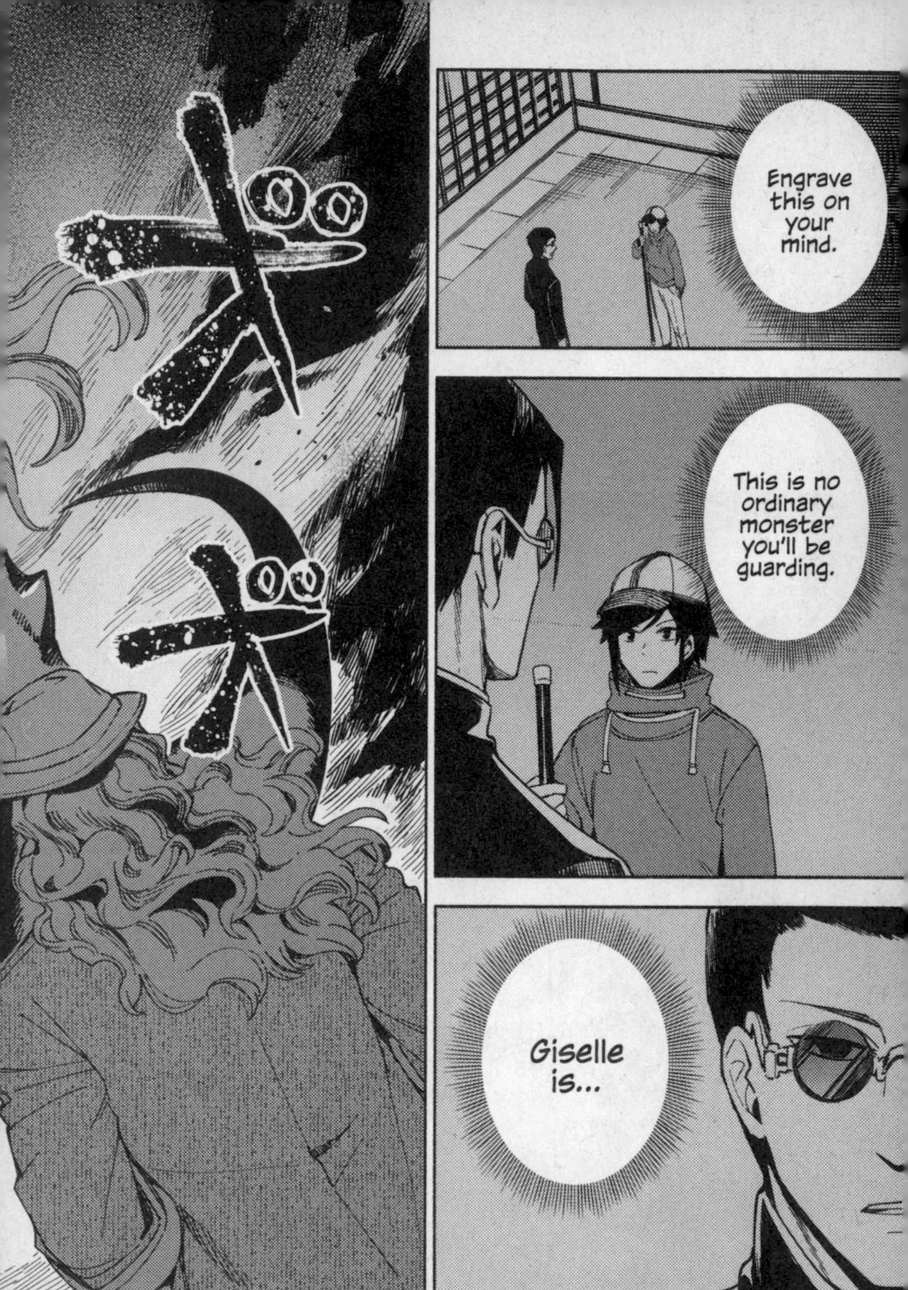
Engrave this on your mind.
This is no ordinary monster you'll be guarding.
Giselle is...

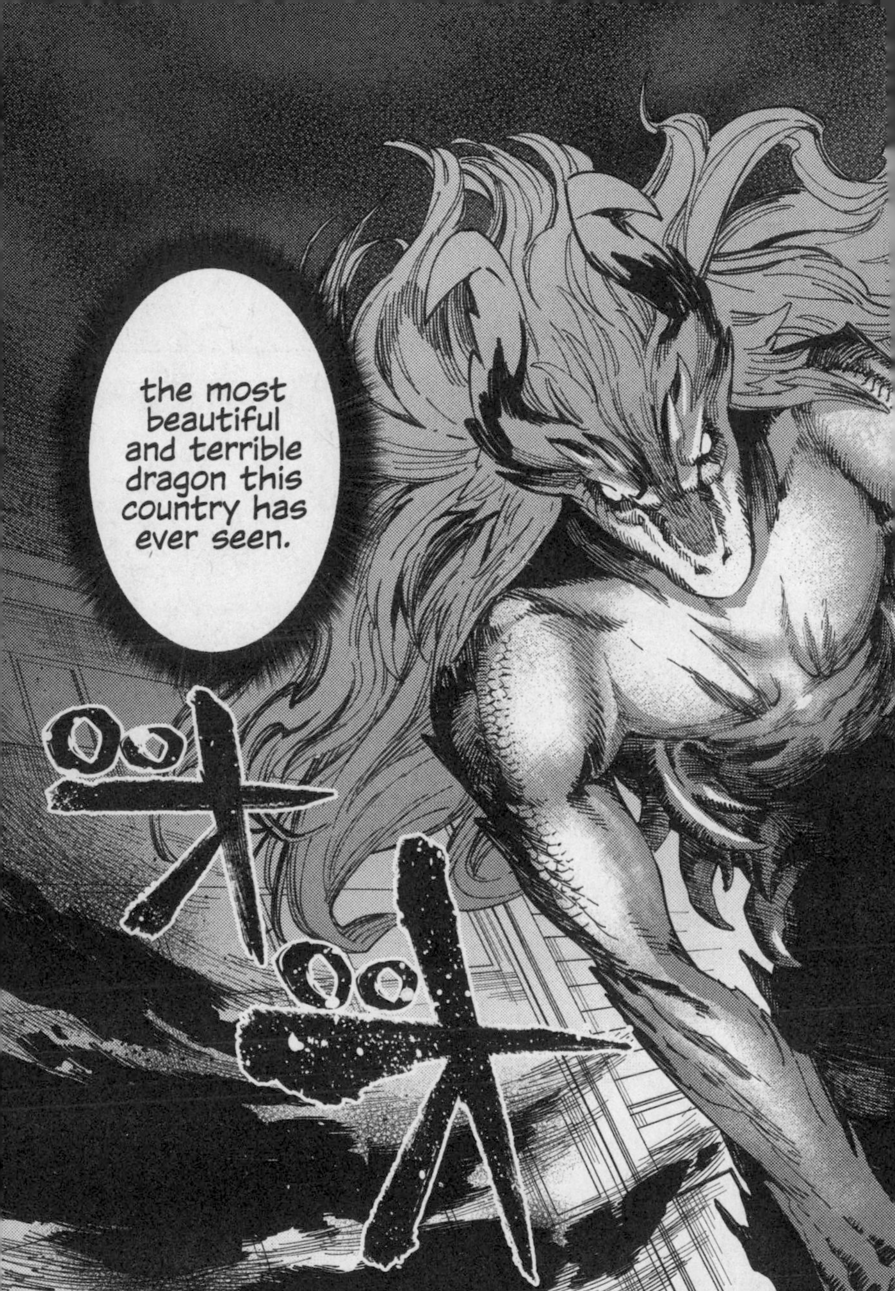
the most beautiful and terrible dragon this country has ever seen.

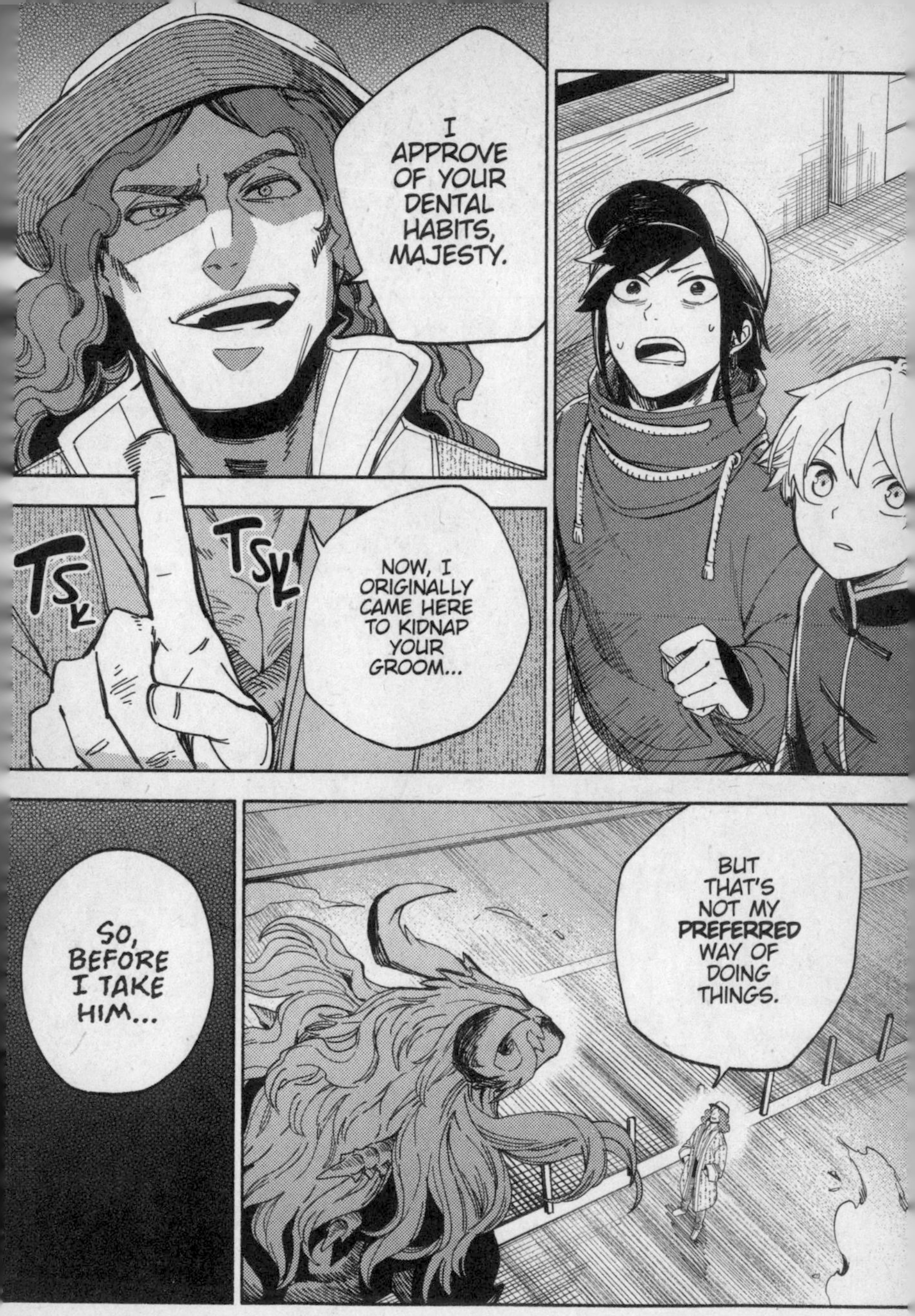
I APPROVE OF YOUR DENTAL HABITS, MAJESTY.
TSK
TSK
NOW, I ORIGINALLY CAME HERE TO KIDNAP YOUR GROOM...
BUT THAT'S NOT MY **PREFERRED** WAY OF DOING THINGS.
SO, BEFORE I TAKE HIM...

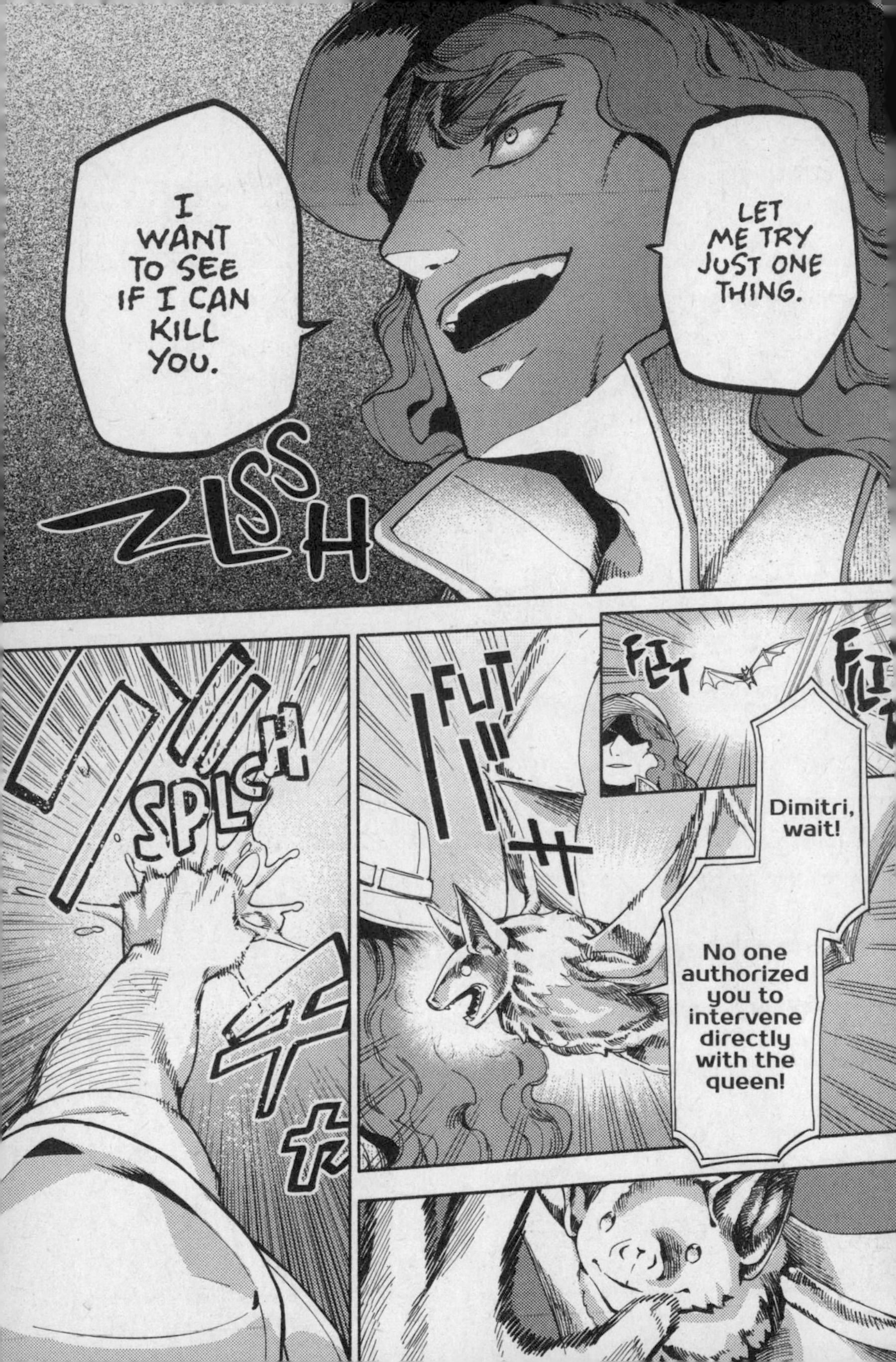

LET ME TRY JUST ONE THING.
I WANT TO SEE IF I CAN KILL YOU.
ZLSSH
FLIT
FLIT
Dimitri, wait!
No one authorized you to intervene directly with the queen!
FLIT
SPLCH

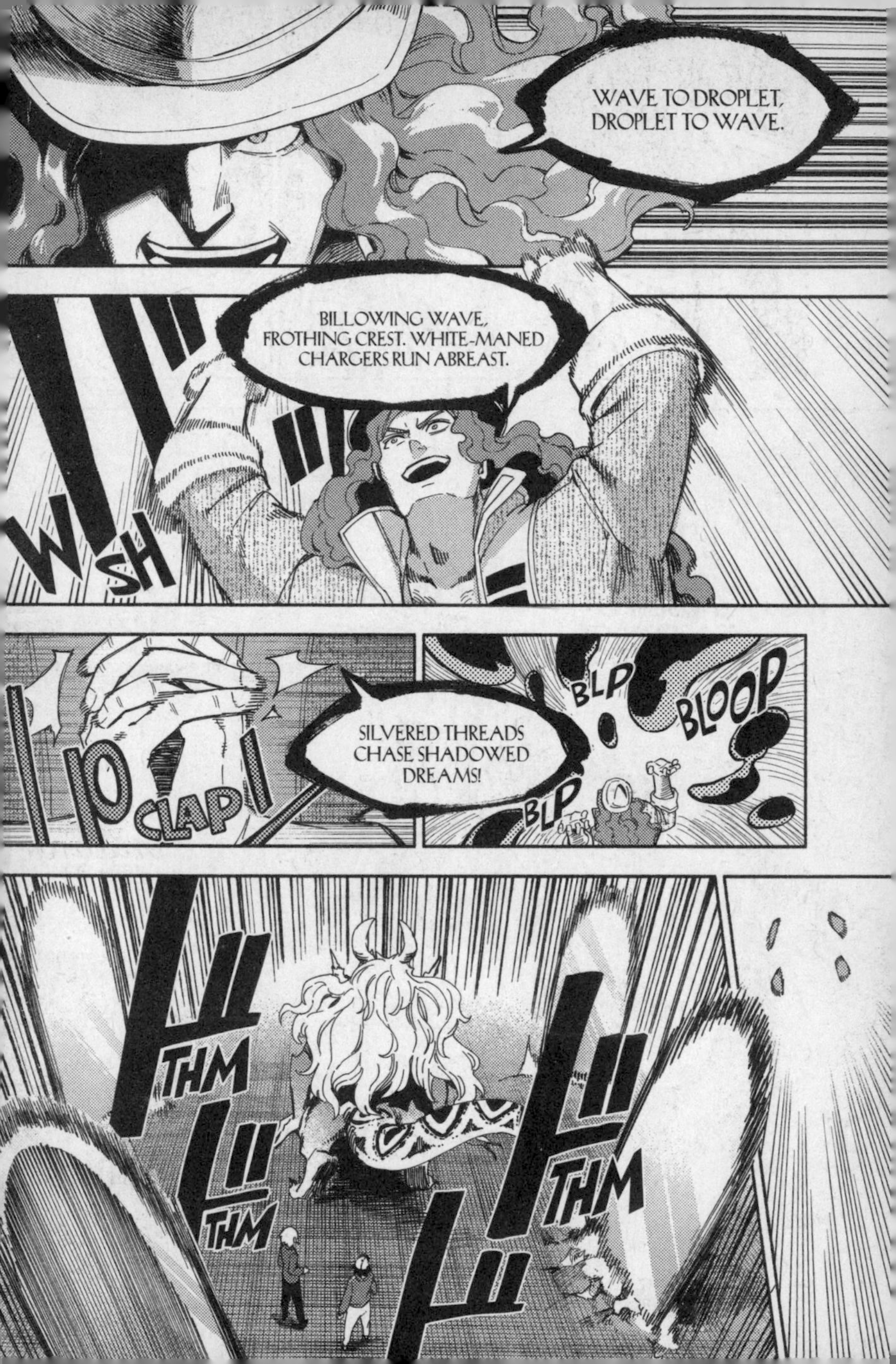
WAVE TO DROPLET, DROPLET TO WAVE.
BILLOWING WAVE, FROTHING CREST. WHITE-MANED CHARGERS RUN ABREAST.
WSH
BLP
BLOOP
BLP
SILVERED THREADS CHASE SHADOWED DREAMS!
CLAP
THM
THM
THM
THM

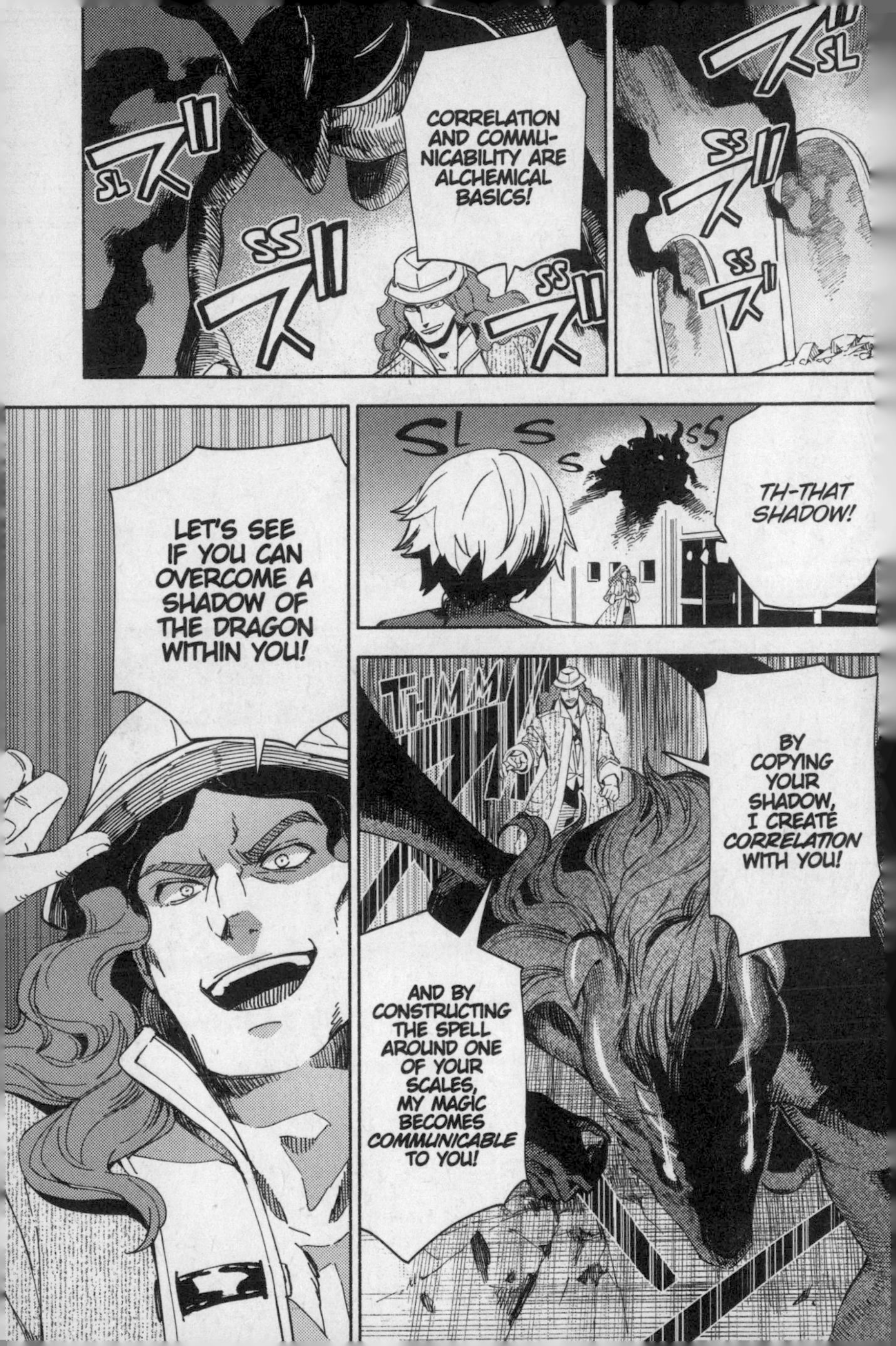
SL
SS
SS
CORRELATION AND COMMUNICABILITY ARE ALCHEMICAL BASICS!
SL
SS
SS
TH-THAT SHADOW!
SS
SL S S
BY COPYING YOUR SHADOW, I CREATE CORRELATION WITH YOU!
THMM
AND BY CONSTRUCTING THE SPELL AROUND ONE OF YOUR SCALES, MY MAGIC BECOMES COMMUNICABLE TO YOU!
LET'S SEE IF YOU CAN OVERCOME A SHADOW OF THE DRAGON WITHIN YOU!

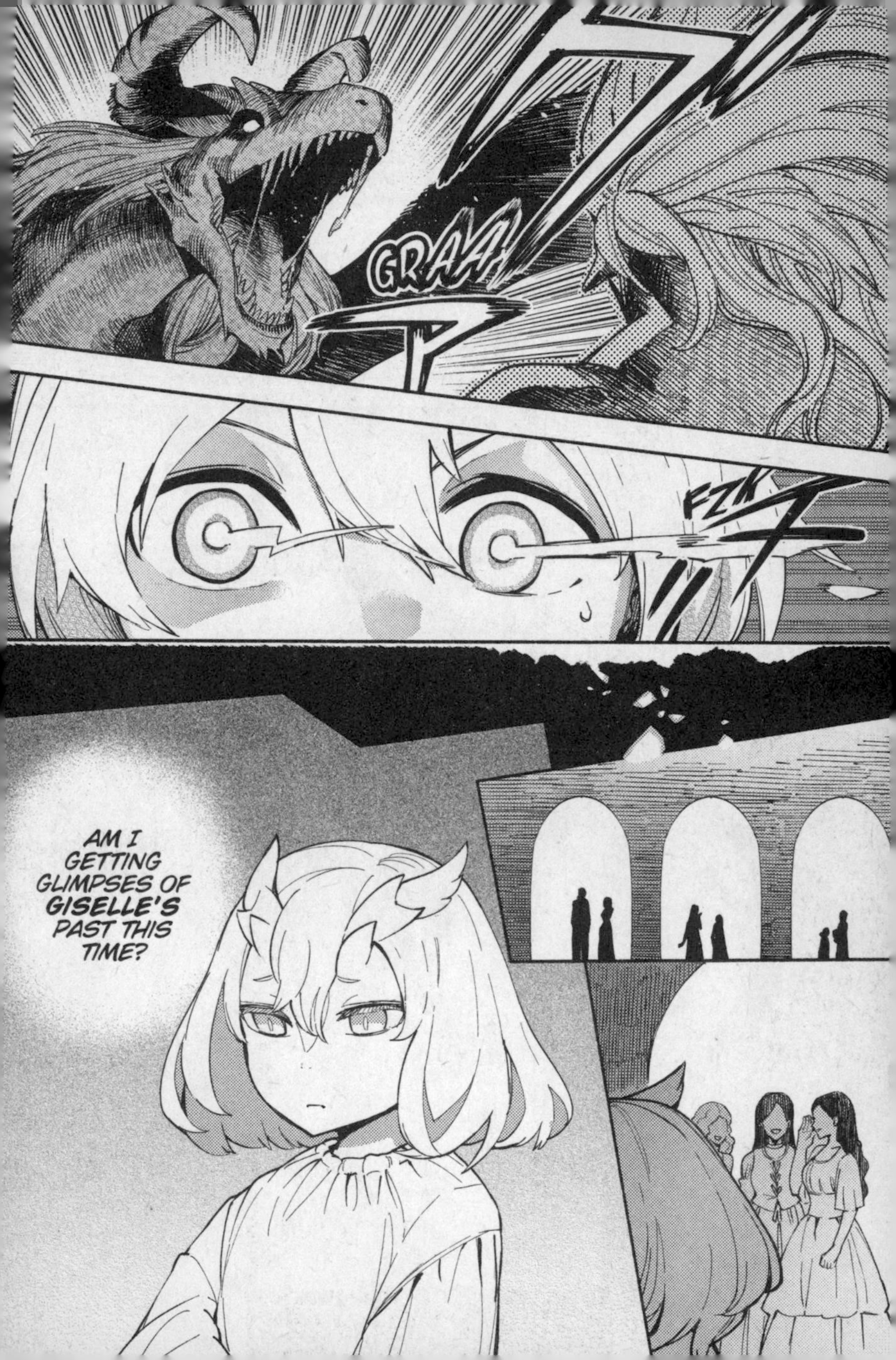
GRAAA!
FZK
AM I GETTING GLIMPSES OF GISELLE'S PAST THIS TIME?

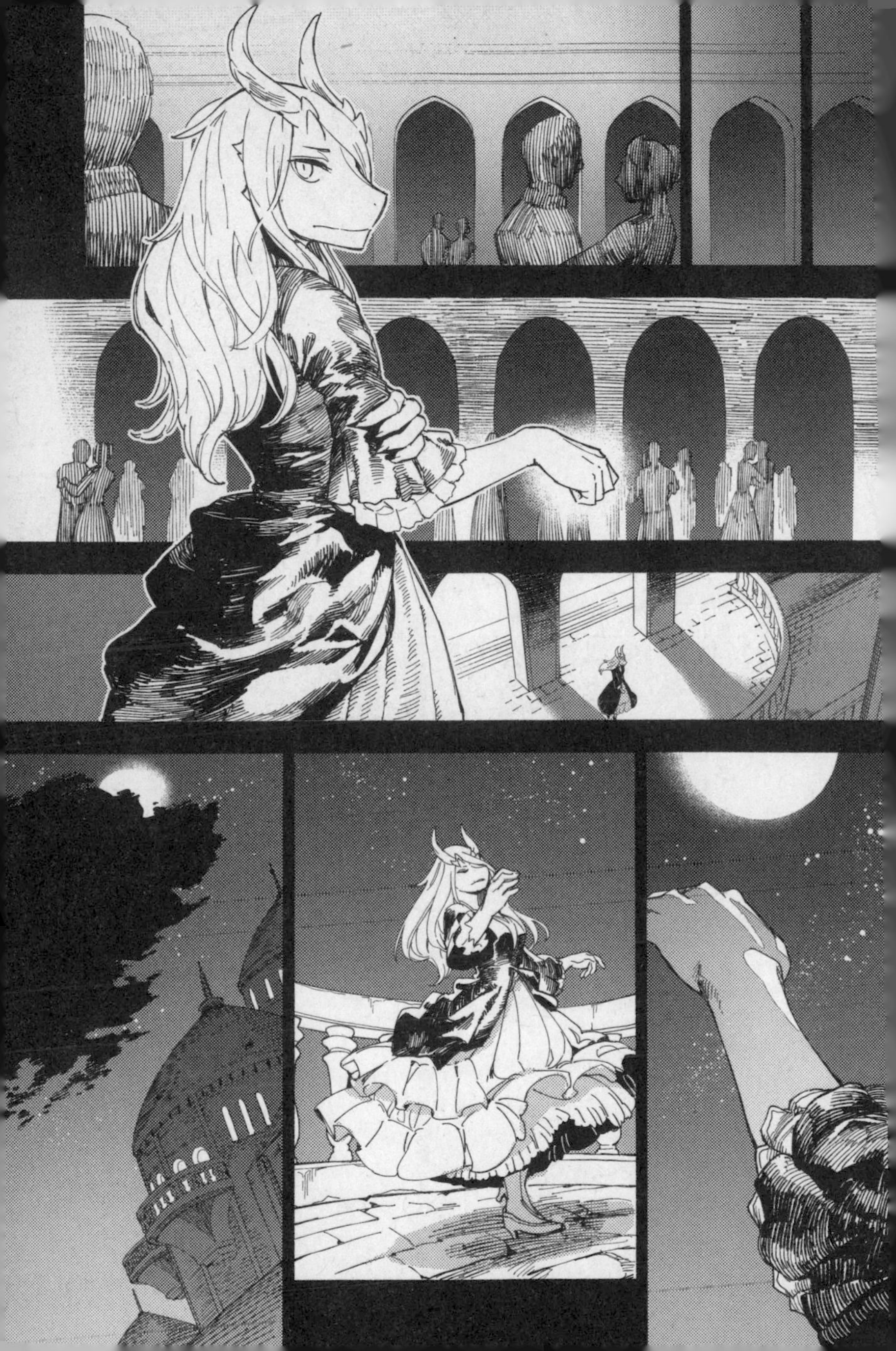

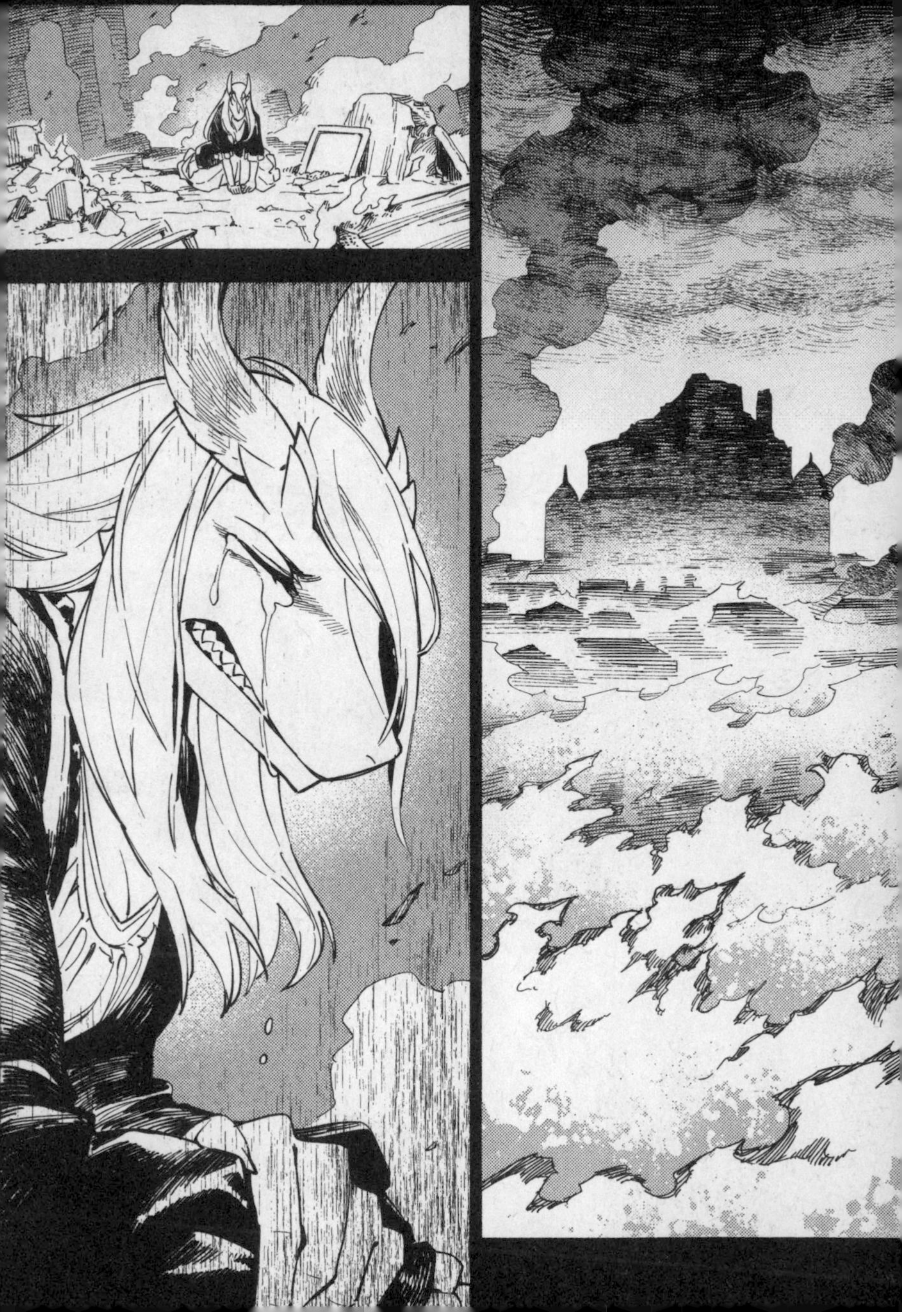

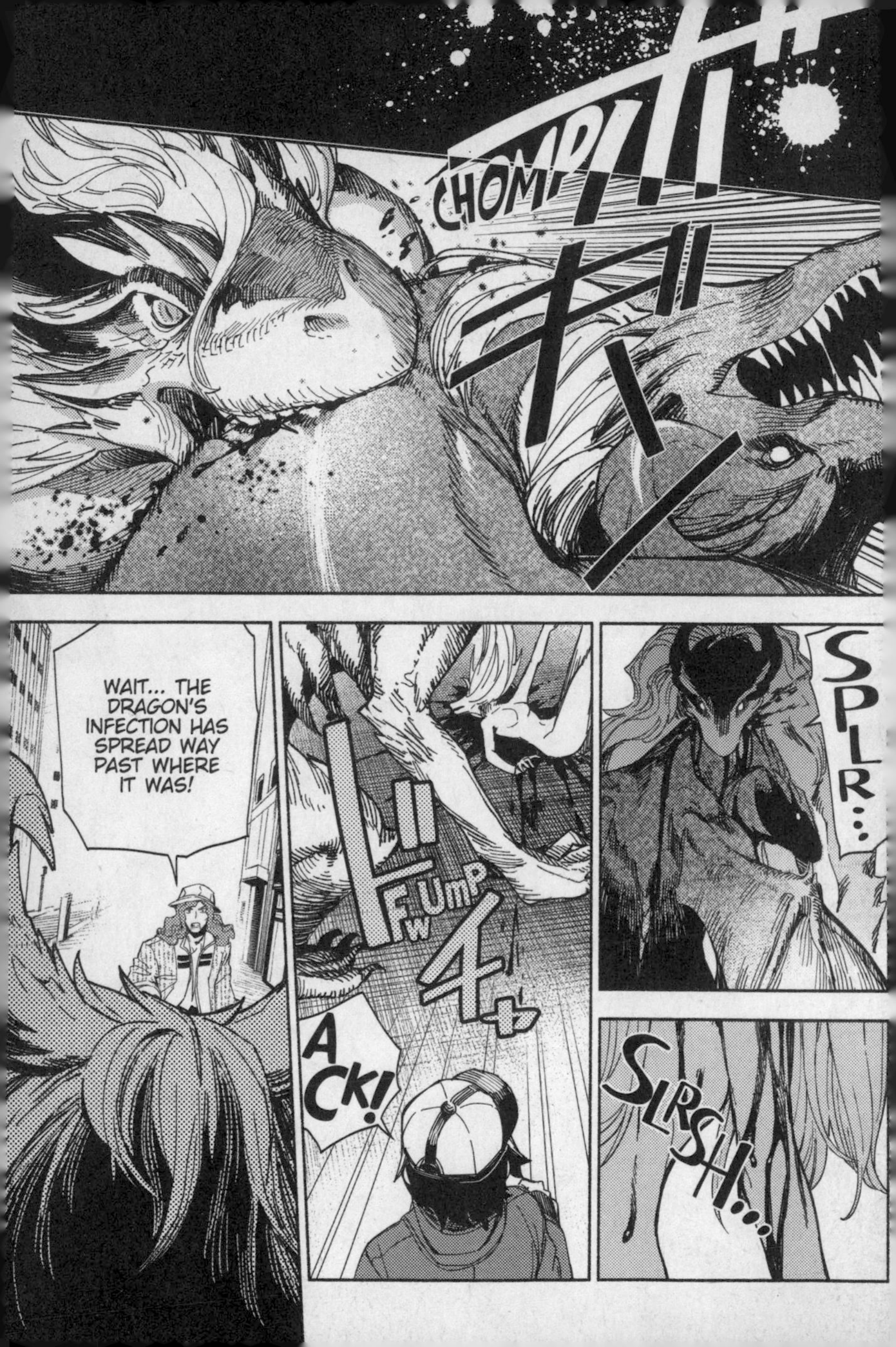
CHOMP!!!
SPLR...
SLRSH...
FWUMP
ACK!
WAIT... THE DRAGON'S INFECTION HAS SPREAD WAY PAST WHERE IT WAS!

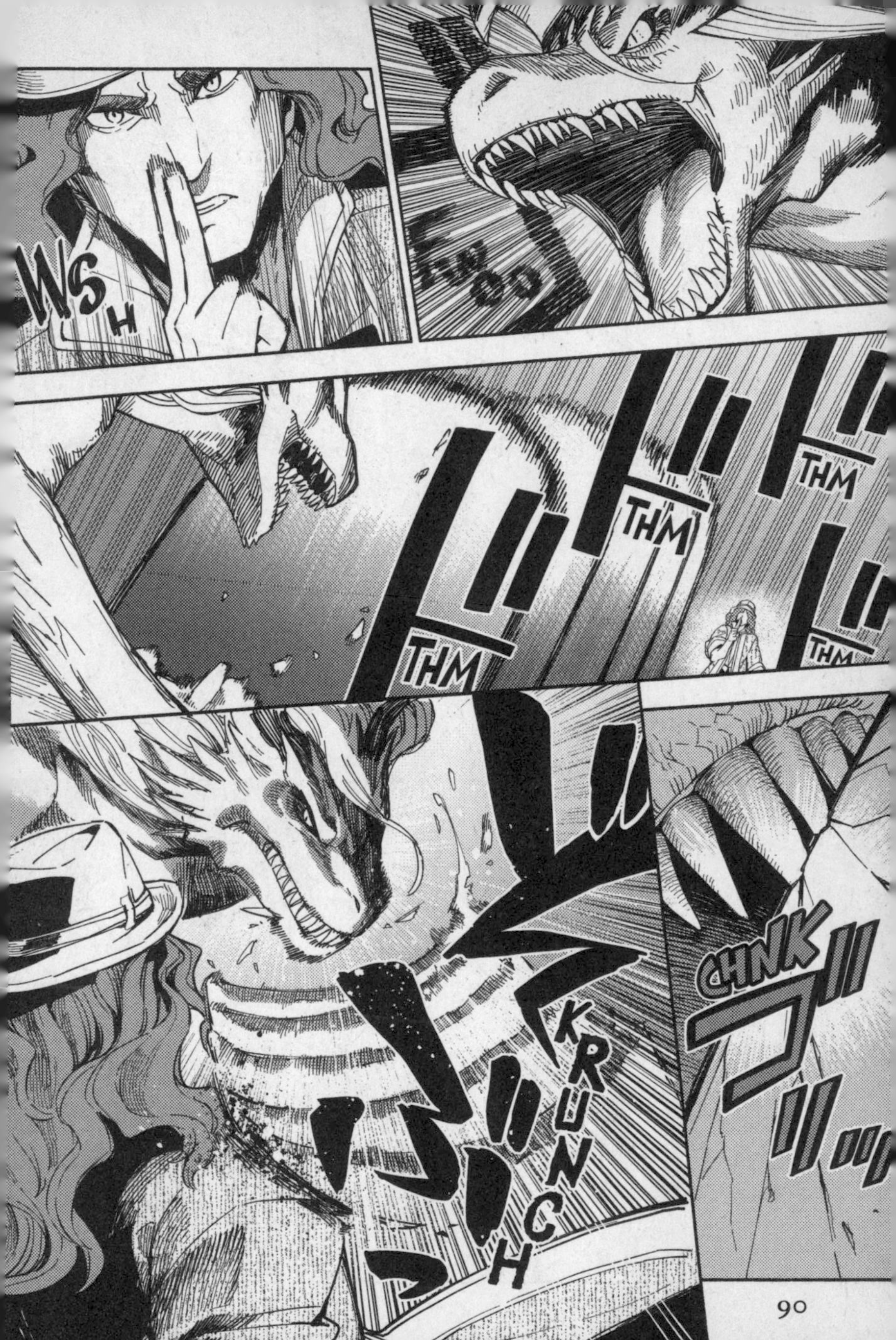
WSH
THM
THM
THM
THM
CHNK
KRUNCH

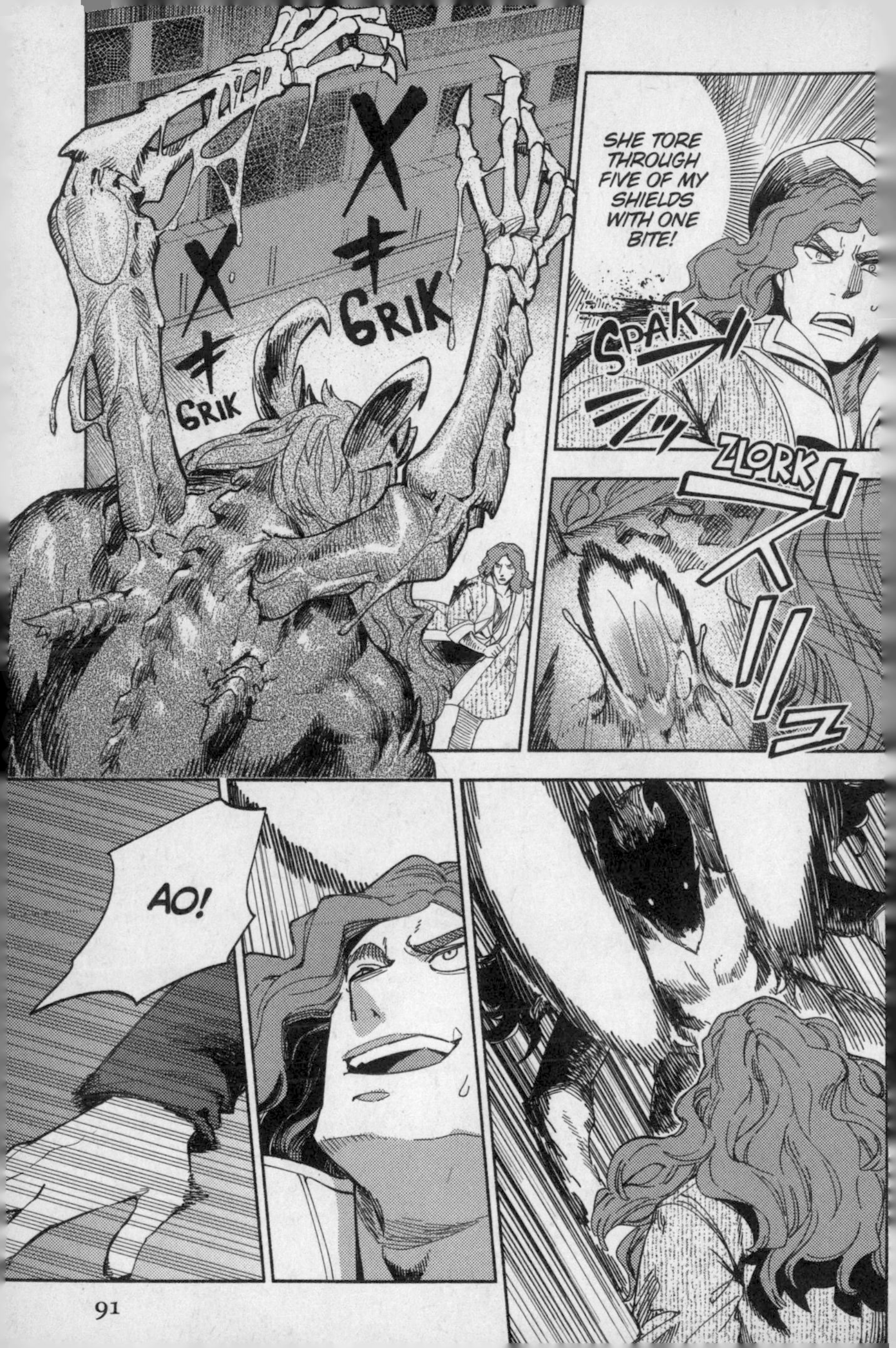
SHE TORE THROUGH FIVE OF MY SHIELDS WITH ONE BITE!
SPAK
ZLORK
GRIK
GRIK
AO!

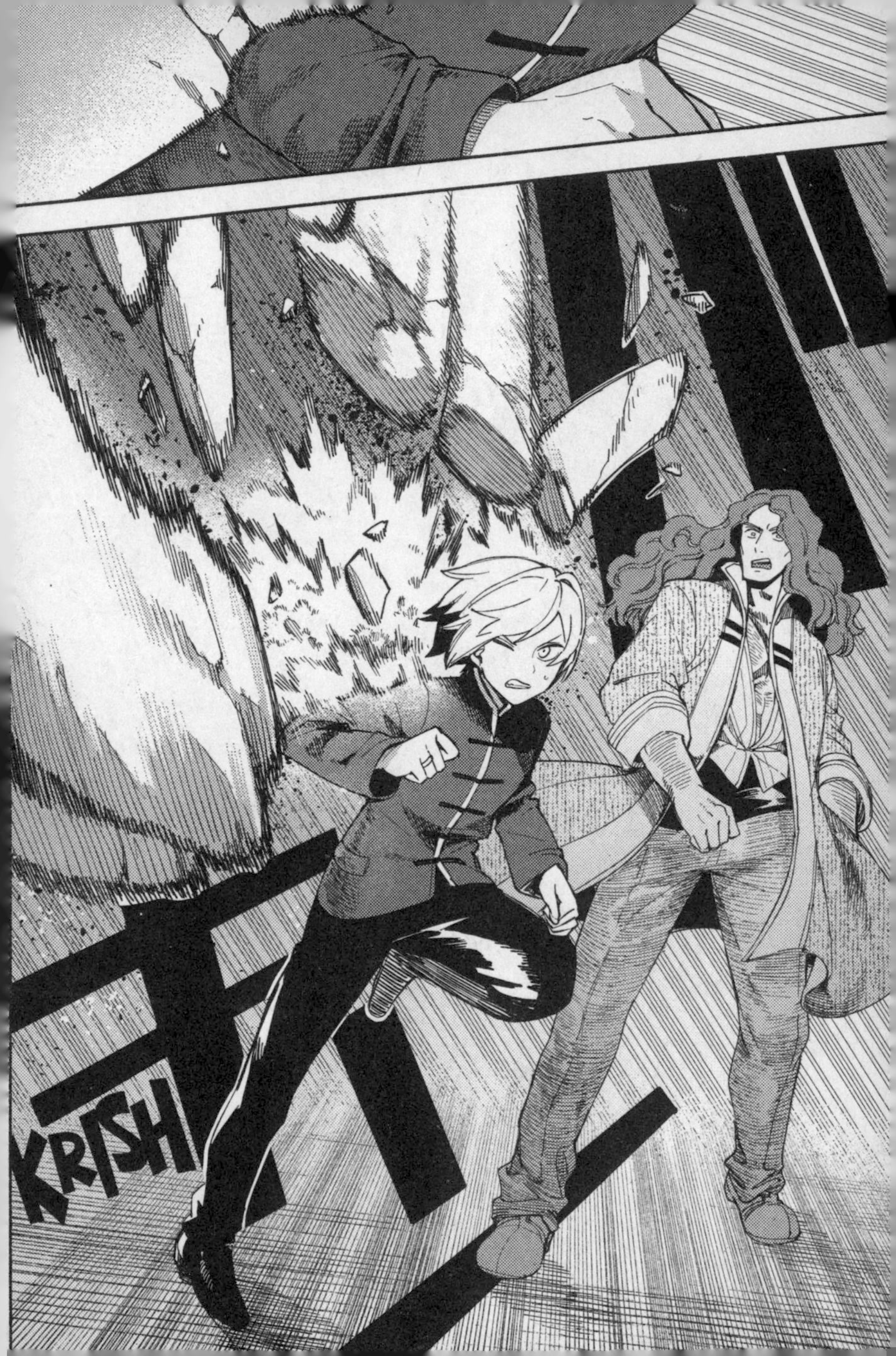
KRTSH

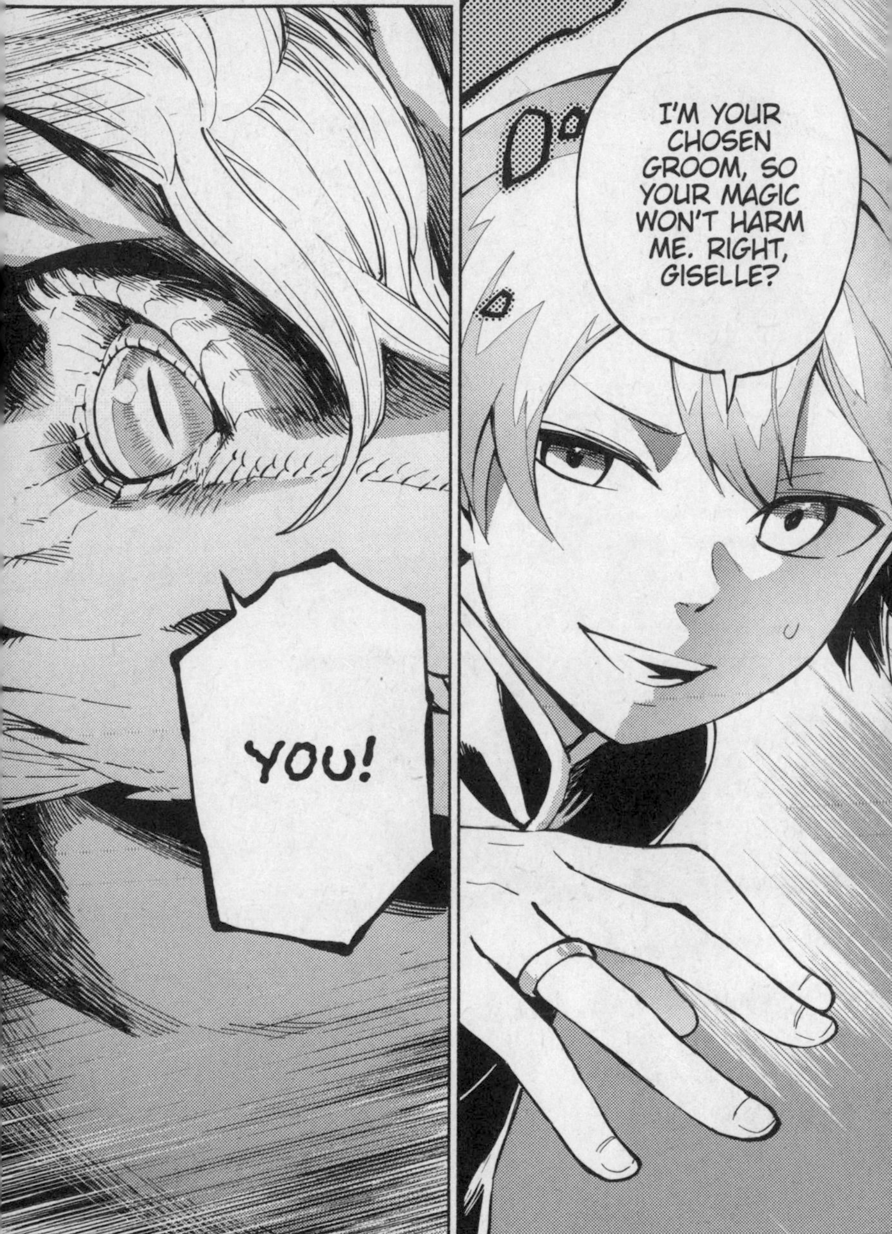
I'M YOUR CHOSEN GROOM, SO YOUR MAGIC WON'T HARM ME. RIGHT, GISELLE?
YOU!

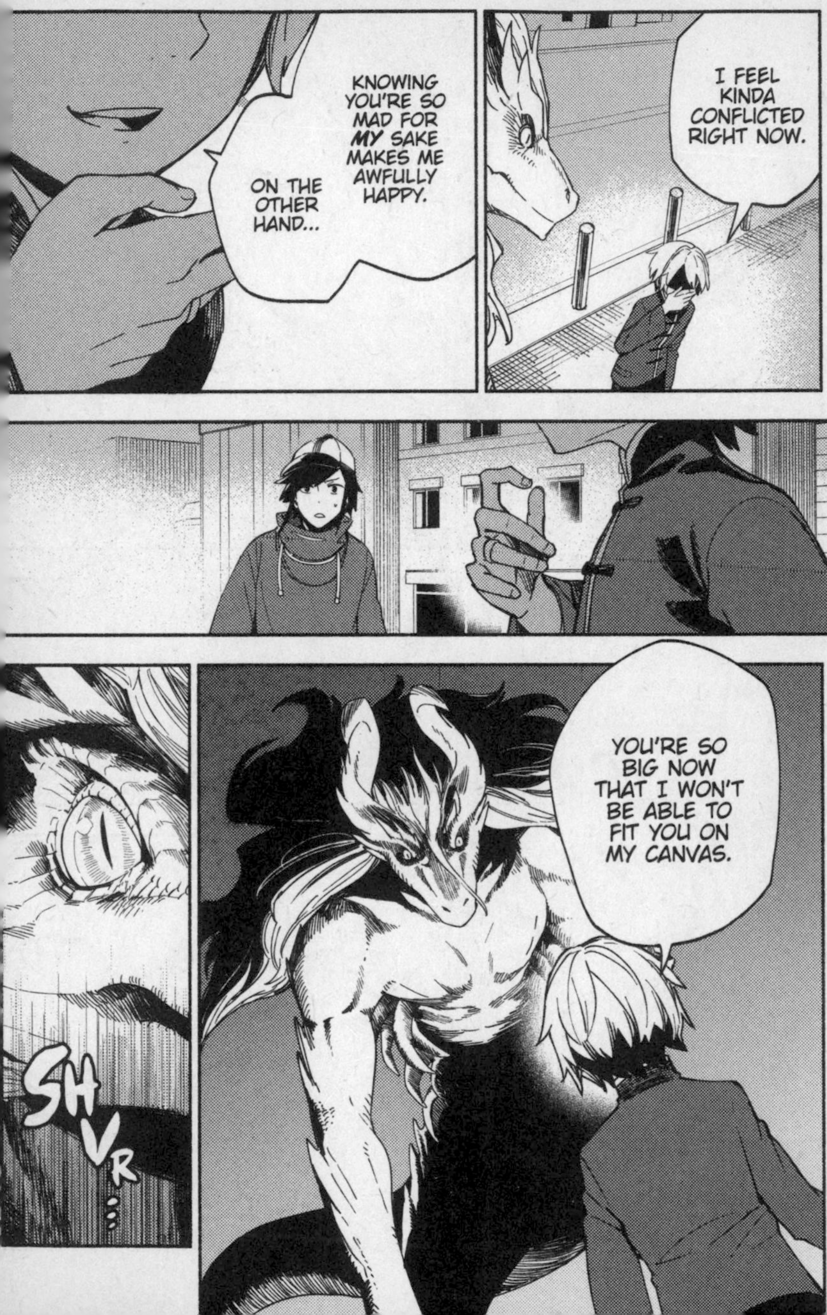
I FEEL KINDA CONFLICTED RIGHT NOW.
KNOWING YOU'RE SO MAD FOR *MY* SAKE MAKES ME AWFULLY HAPPY.
ON THE OTHER HAND...
YOU'RE SO BIG NOW THAT I WON'T BE ABLE TO FIT YOU ON MY CANVAS.
SHVR...

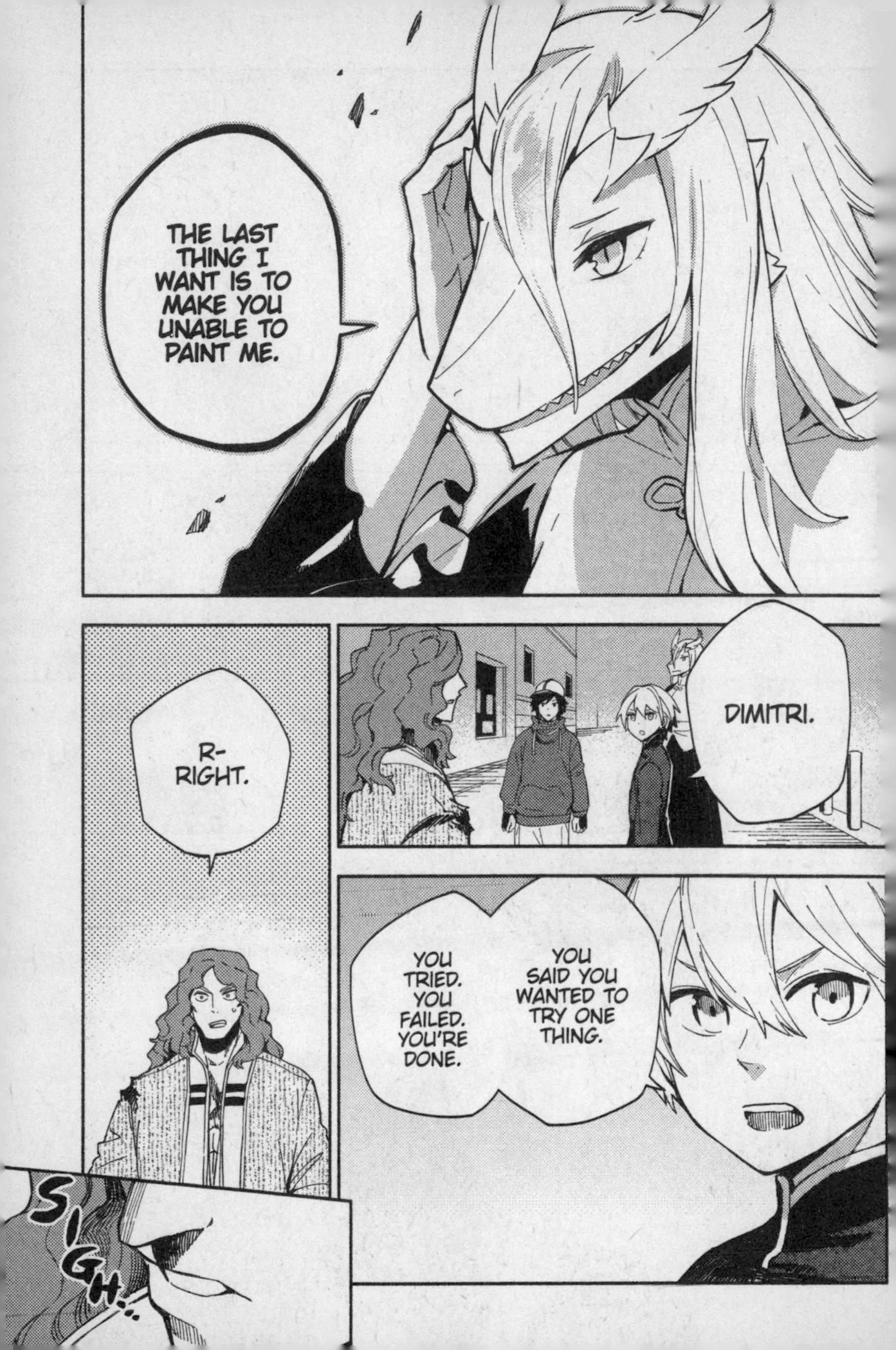
THE LAST THING I WANT IS TO MAKE YOU UNABLE TO PAINT ME.
DIMITRI.
YOU SAID YOU WANTED TO TRY ONE THING.
YOU TRIED. YOU FAILED. YOU'RE DONE.
R- RIGHT.
SIGH...

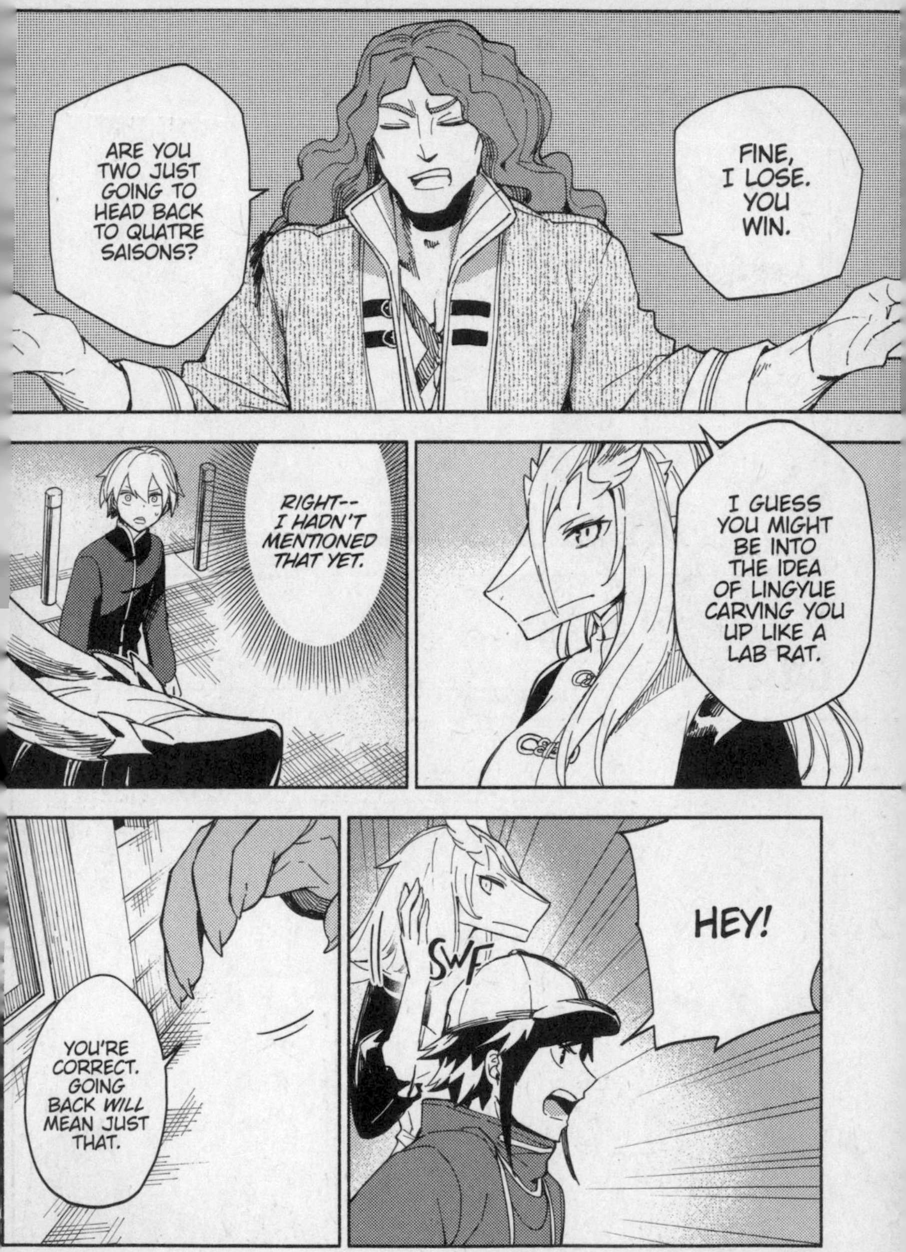
FINE, I LOSE. YOU WIN.
ARE YOU TWO JUST GOING TO HEAD BACK TO QUATRE SAISONS?
I GUESS YOU MIGHT BE INTO THE IDEA OF LINGYUE CARVING YOU UP LIKE A LAB RAT.
RIGHT-- I HADN'T MENTIONED THAT YET.
HEY!
SWF
YOU'RE CORRECT. GOING BACK *WILL* MEAN JUST THAT.

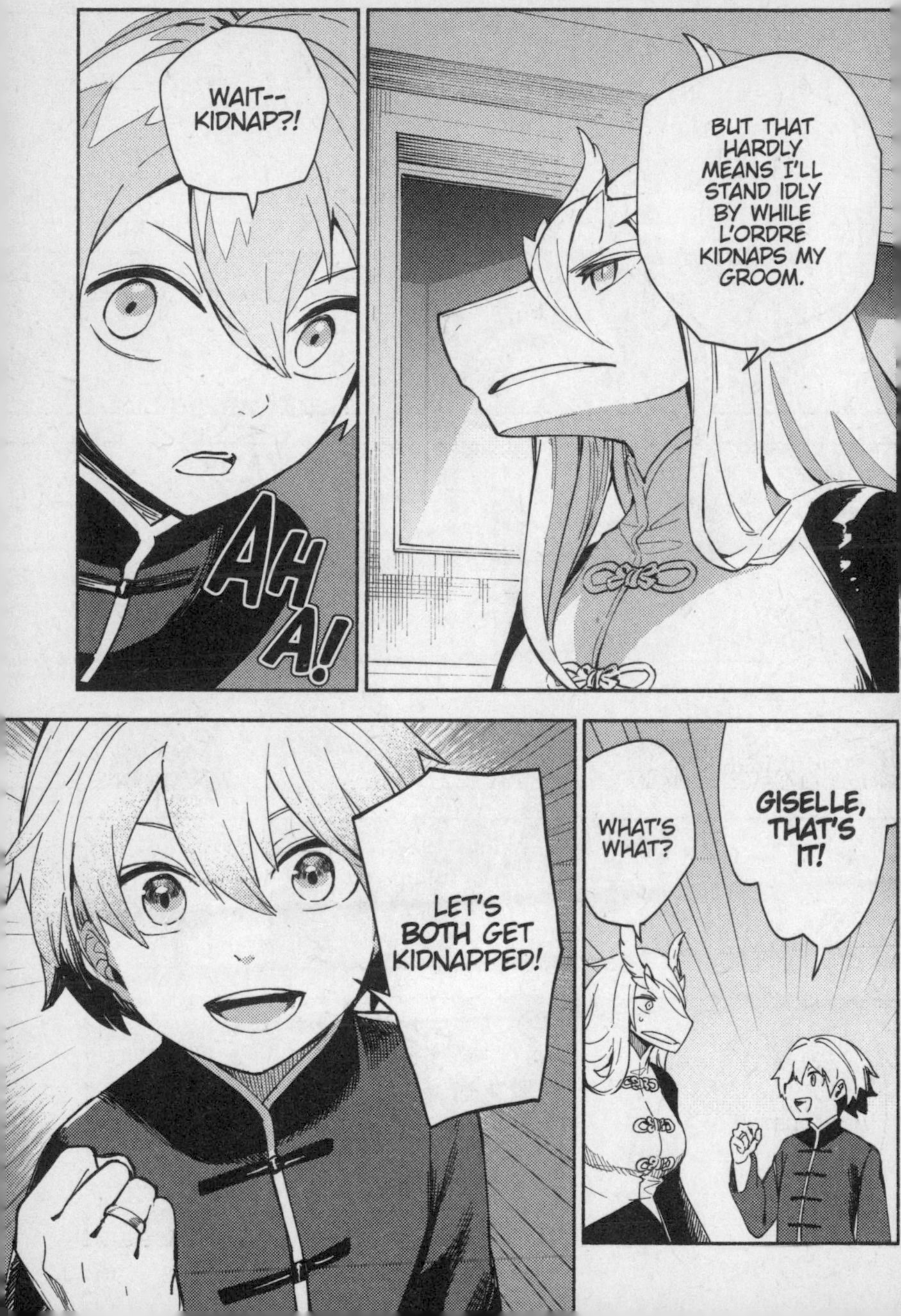
BUT THAT HARDLY MEANS I'LL STAND IDLY BY WHILE L'ORDRE KIDNAPS MY GROOM.
WAIT-- KIDNAP?!
AHA!
GISELLE, THAT'S IT!
WHAT'S WHAT?
LET'S BOTH GET KIDNAPPED!

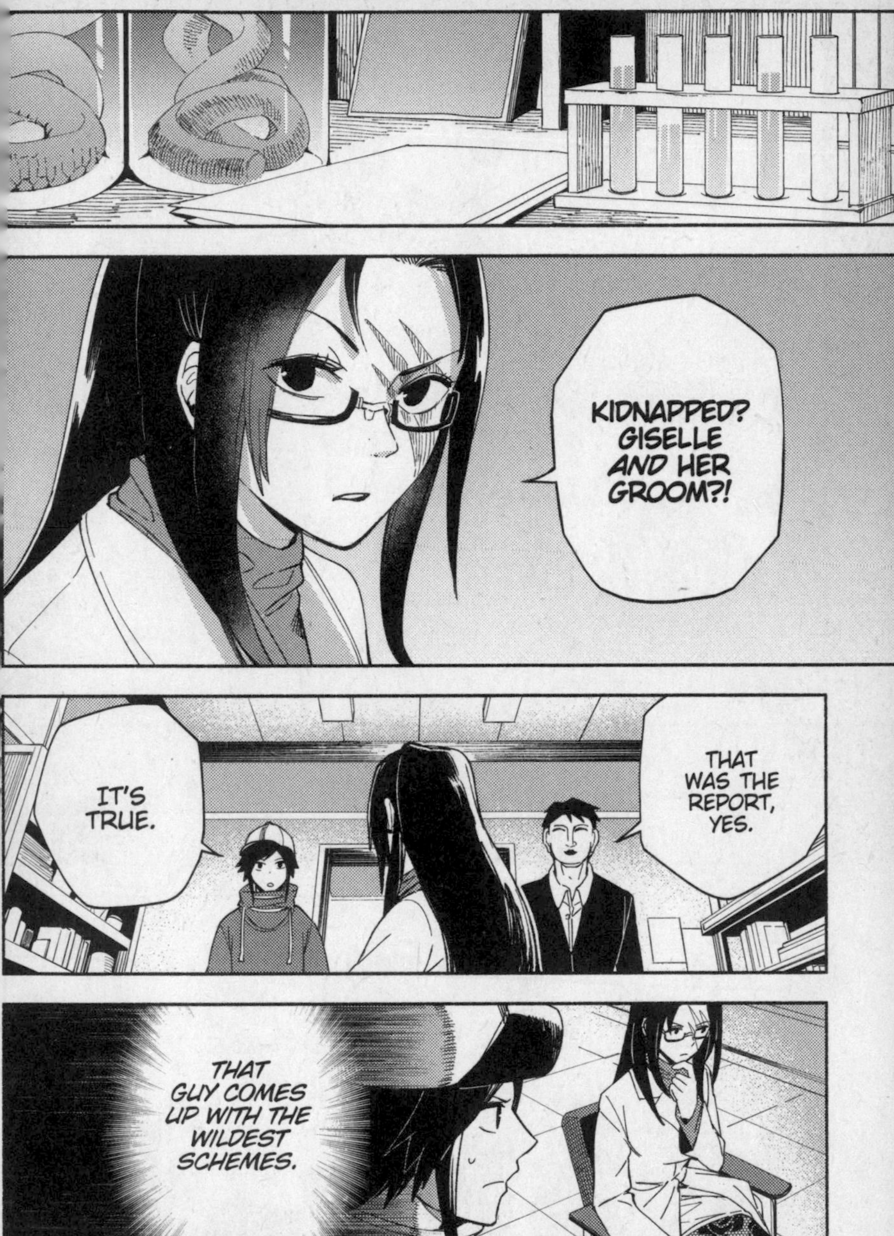
KIDNAPPED? GISELLE AND HER GROOM?!
THAT WAS THE REPORT, YES.
IT'S TRUE.
THAT GUY COMES UP WITH THE WILDEST SCHEMES.

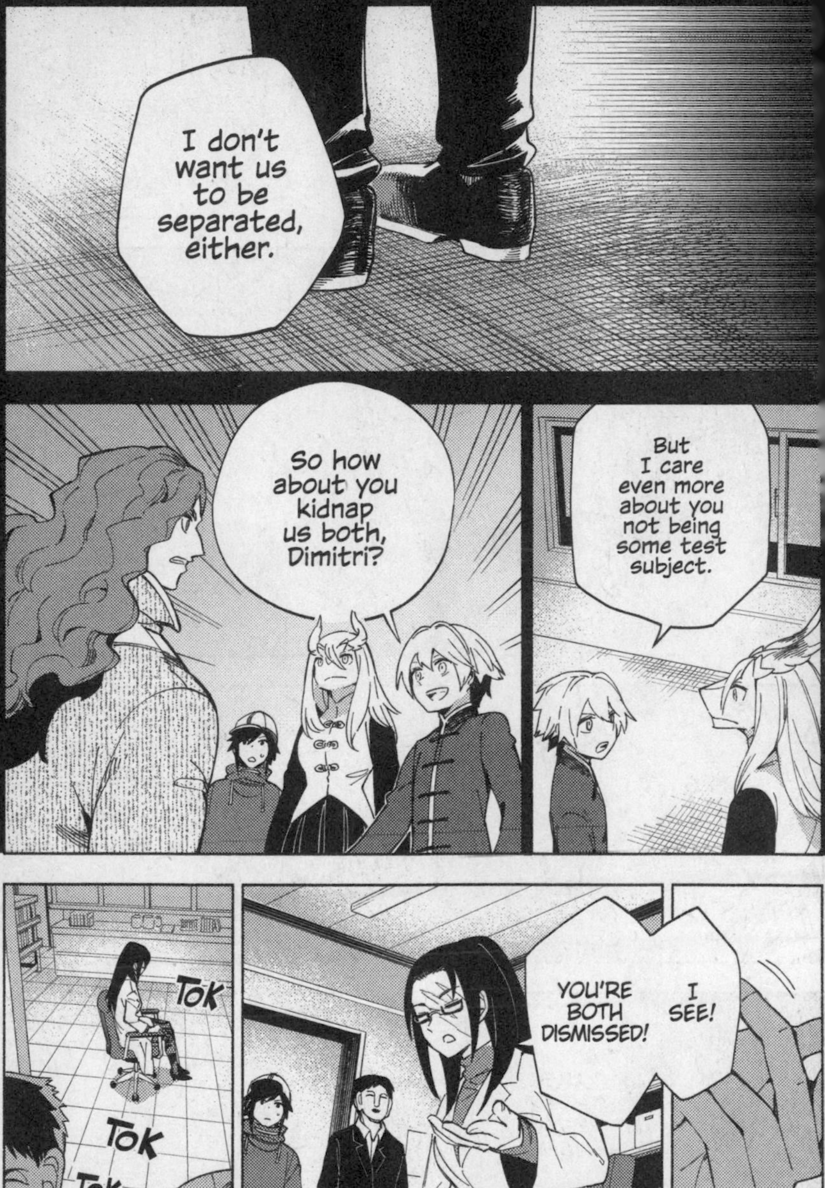
I don't want us to be separated, either.
But I care even more about you not being some test subject.
So how about you kidnap us both, Dimitri?
I SEE!
YOU'RE BOTH DISMISSED!
TOK
TOK
TOK

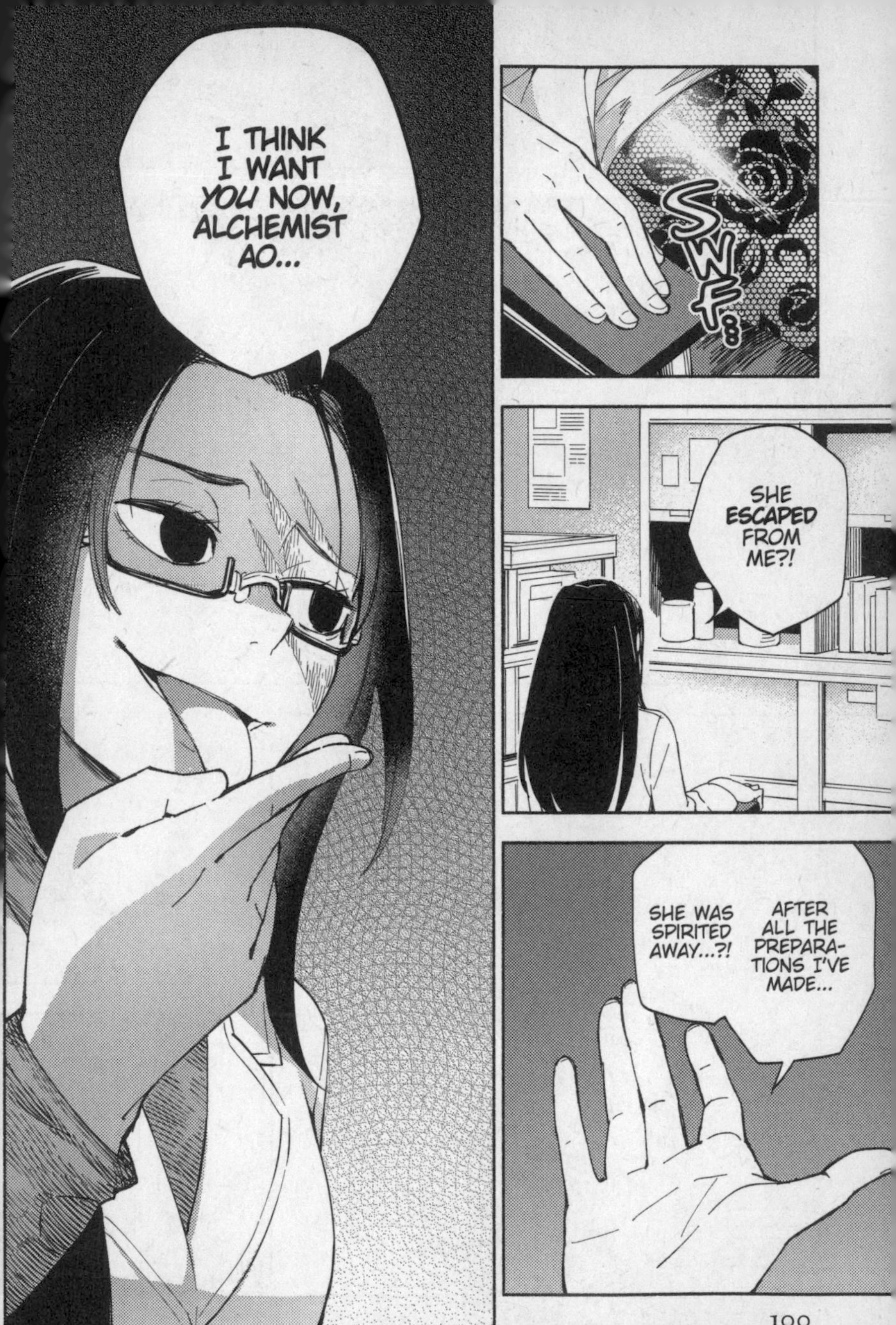
SWF
SHE ESCAPED FROM ME?!
AFTER ALL THE PREPARATIONS I'VE MADE...
SHE WAS SPIRITED AWAY...?!
I THINK I WANT *YOU* NOW, ALCHEMIST AO...

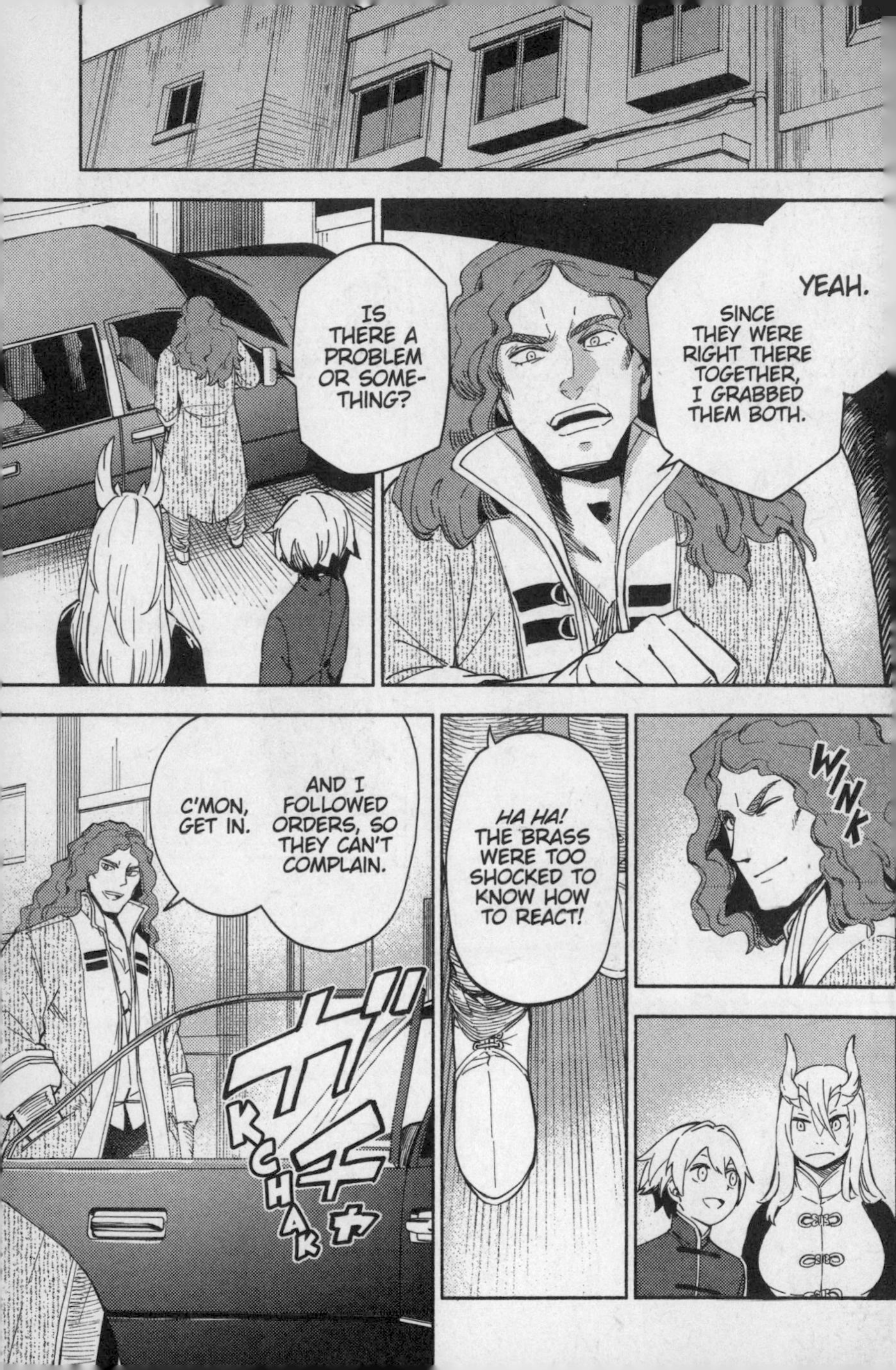
YEAH.
SINCE THEY WERE RIGHT THERE TOGETHER, I GRABBED THEM BOTH.
IS THERE A PROBLEM OR SOME-THING?
WINK
HA HA! THE BRASS WERE TOO SHOCKED TO KNOW HOW TO REACT!
AND I FOLLOWED ORDERS, SO THEY CAN'T COMPLAIN.
C'MON, GET IN.
ガチャ
KCHAK

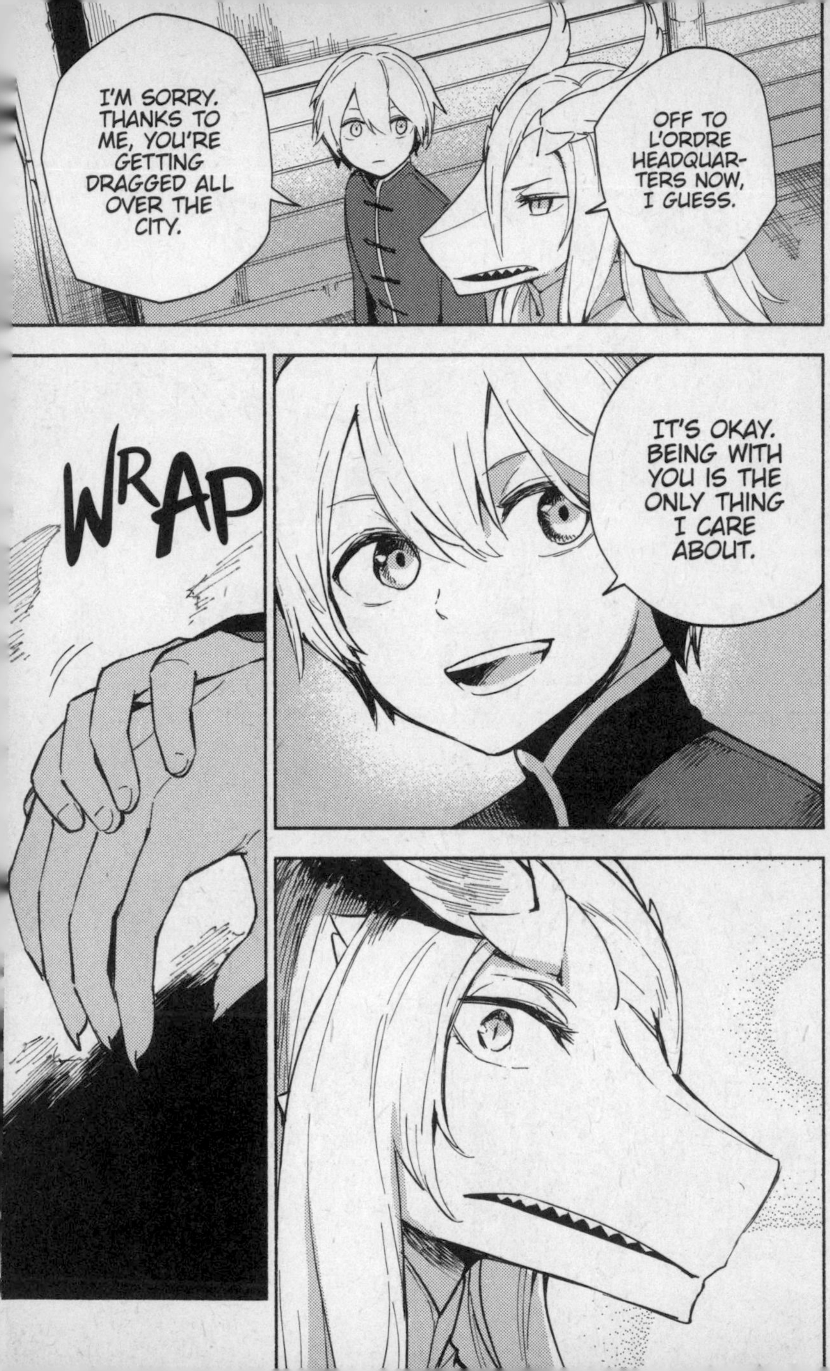
OFF TO L'ORDRE HEADQUARTERS NOW, I GUESS.
I'M SORRY. THANKS TO ME, YOU'RE GETTING DRAGGED ALL OVER THE CITY.
IT'S OKAY. BEING WITH YOU IS THE ONLY THING I CARE ABOUT.
WRAP

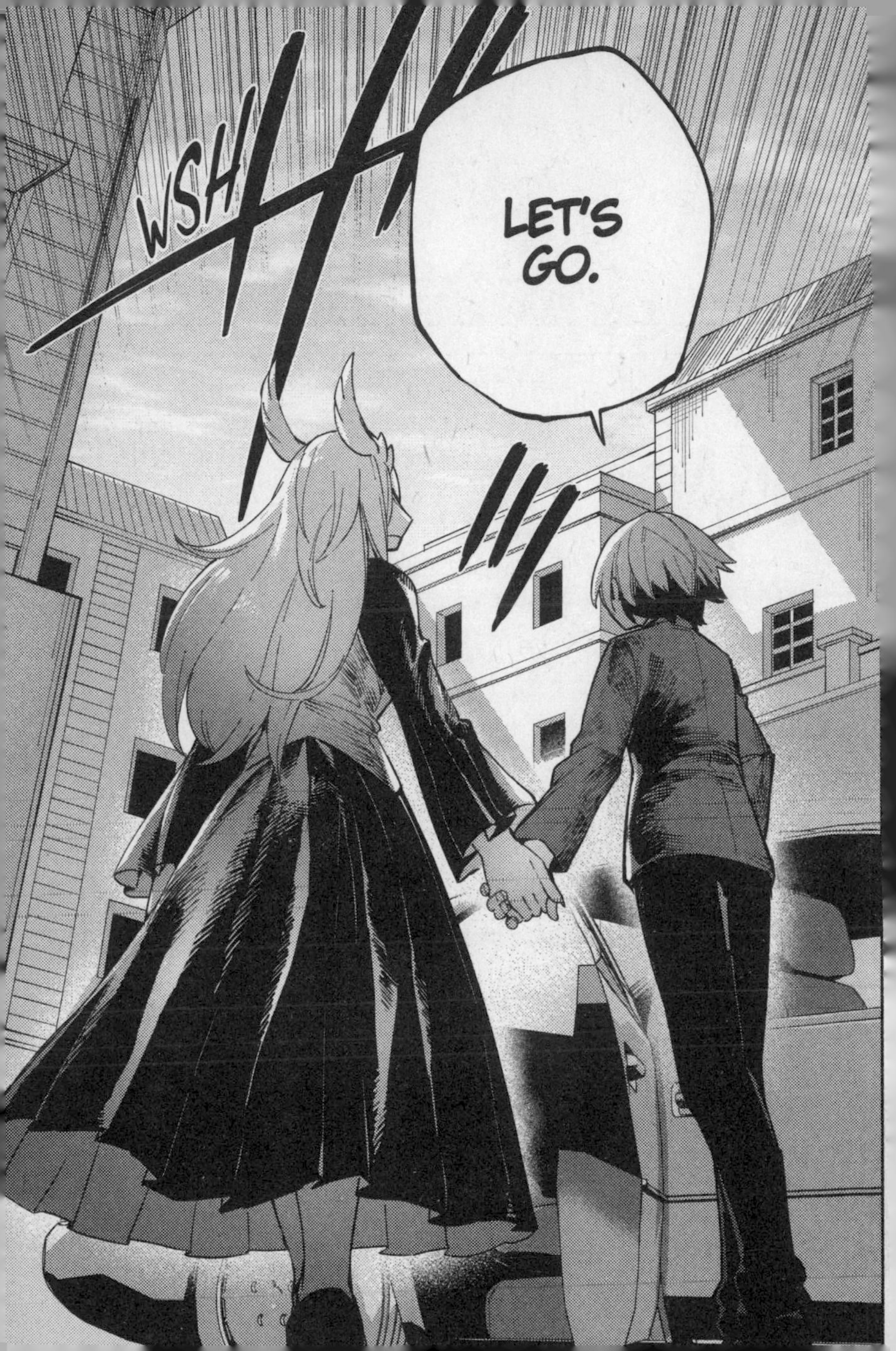
WSH
LET'S GO.

The Ancient Magus' Bride

WIZARD's BLUE

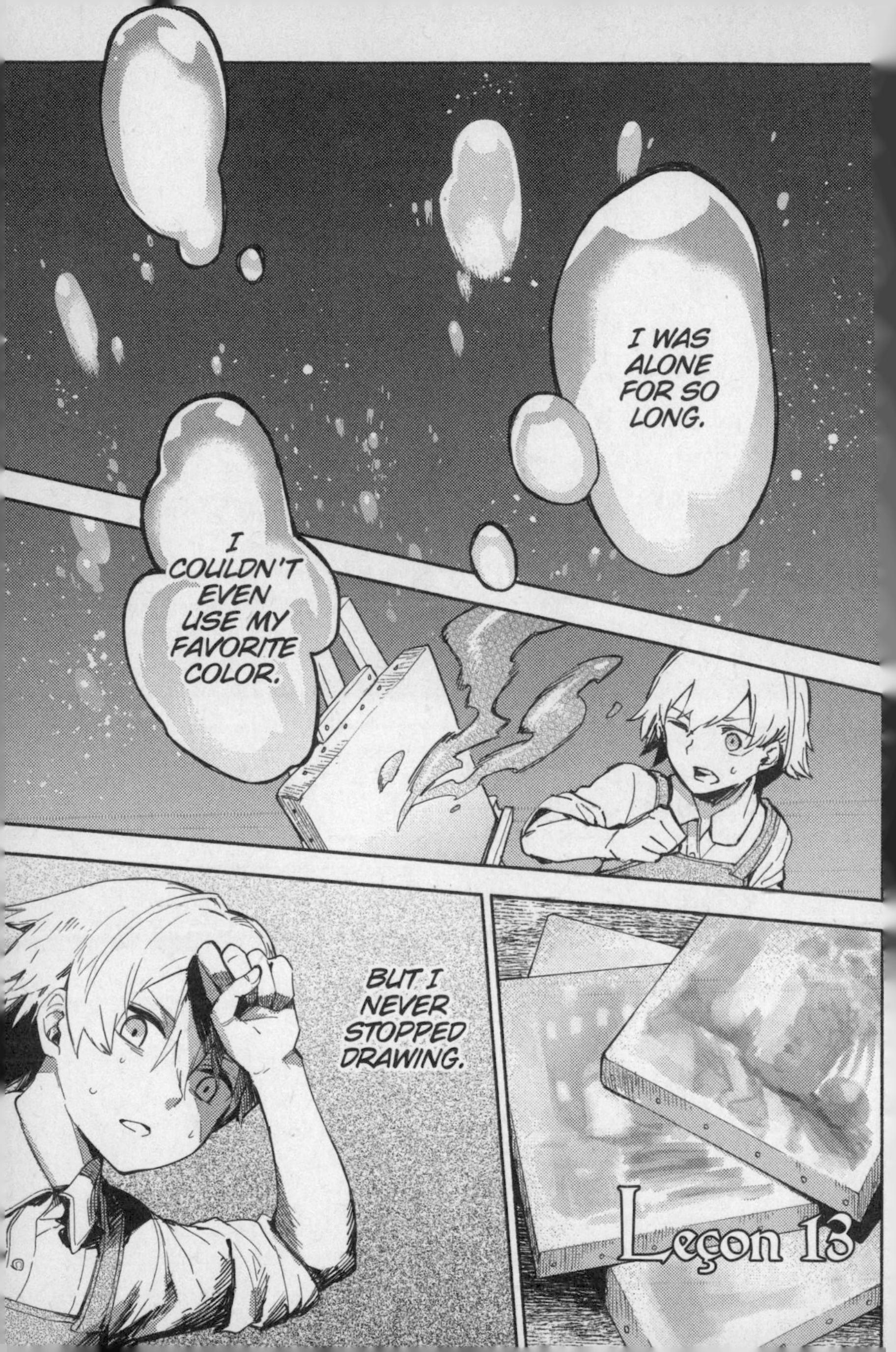
I WAS ALONE FOR SO LONG.
I COULDN'T EVEN USE MY FAVORITE COLOR.
Leçon 13
BUT I NEVER STOPPED DRAWING.

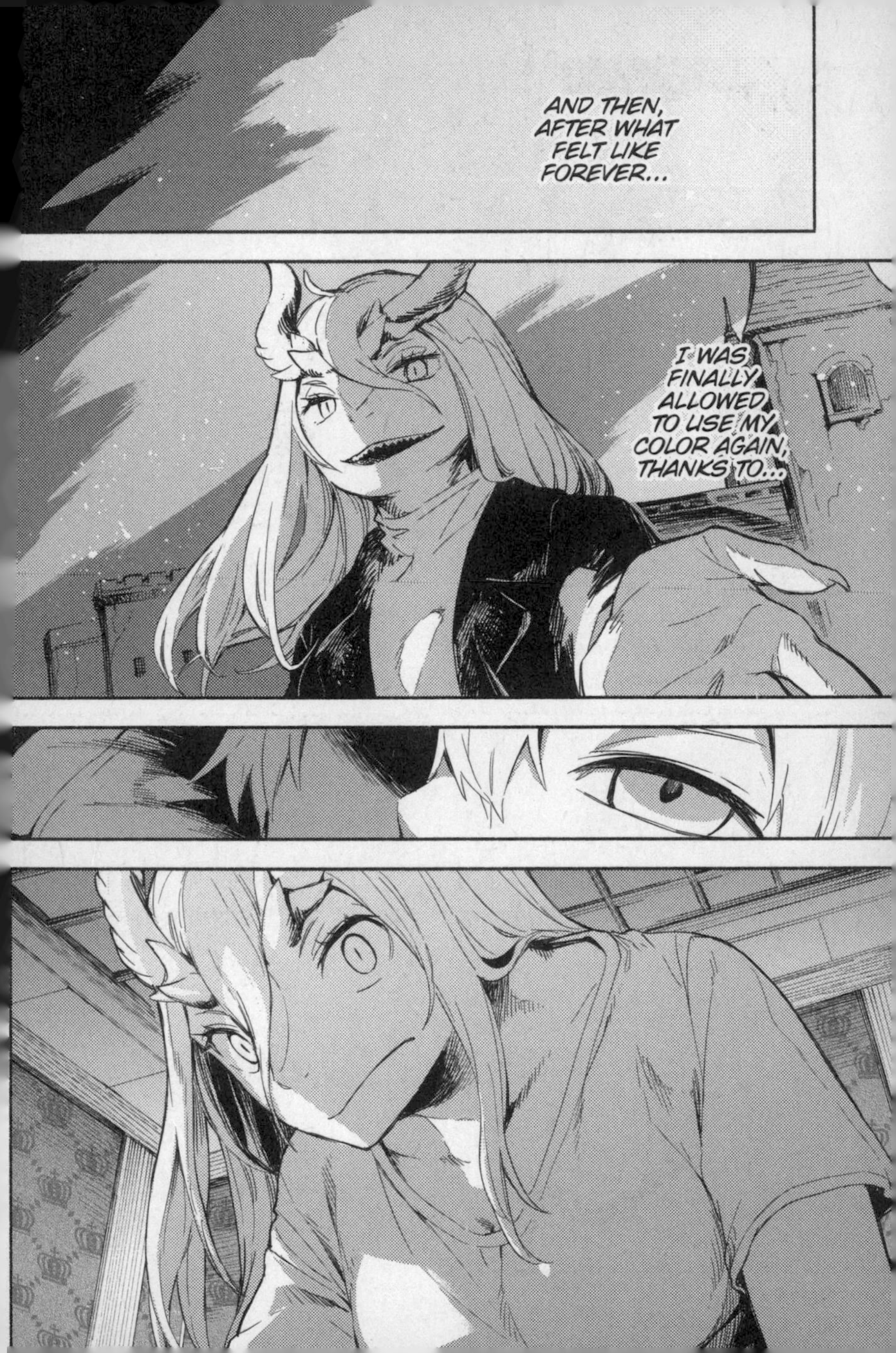
AND THEN, AFTER WHAT FELT LIKE FOREVER...
I WAS FINALLY ALLOWED TO USE MY COLOR AGAIN, THANKS TO...

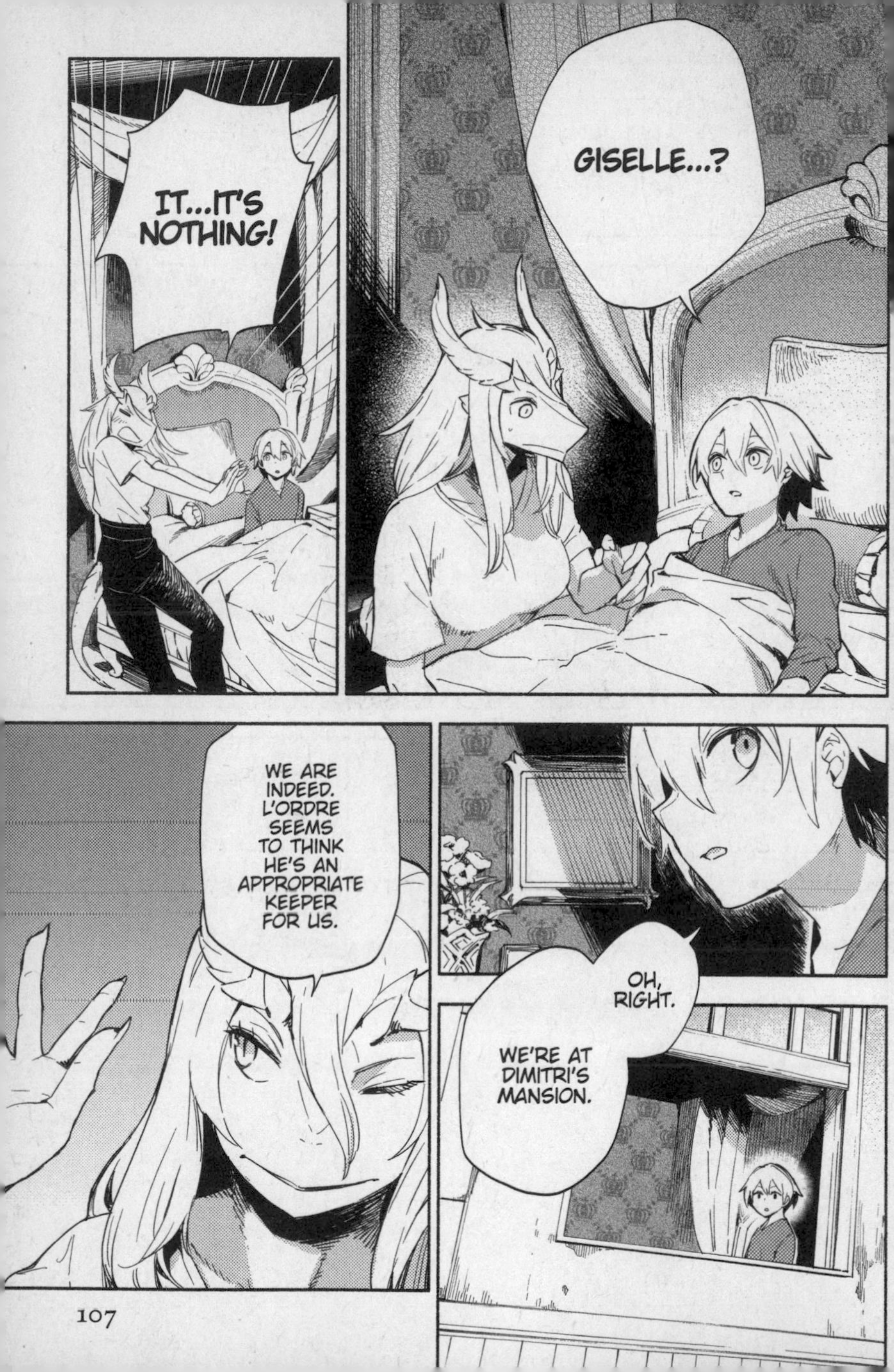
GISELLE...?
IT...IT'S NOTHING!
OH, RIGHT.
WE'RE AT DIMITRI'S MANSION.
WE ARE INDEED. L'ORDRE SEEMS TO THINK HE'S AN APPROPRIATE KEEPER FOR US.

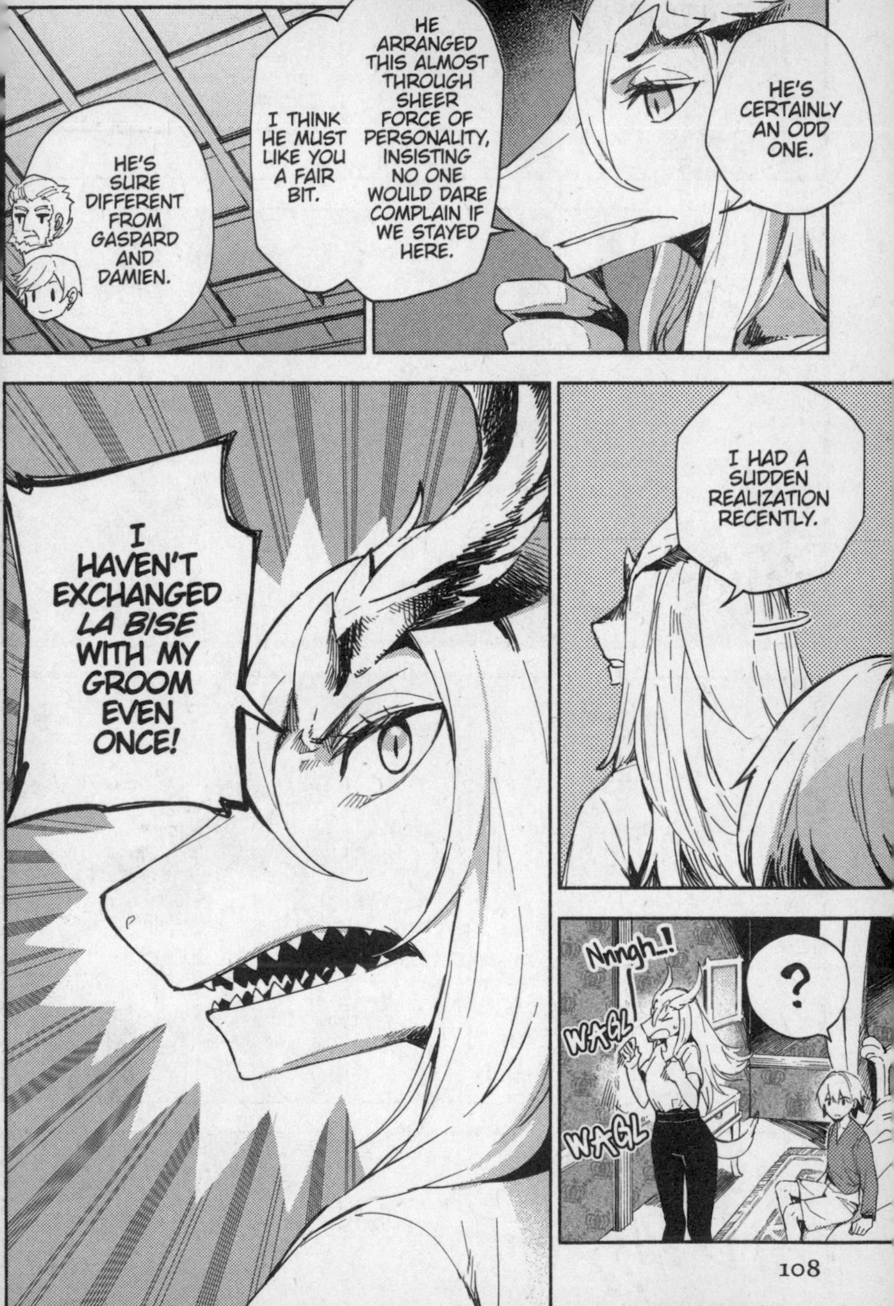
HE'S CERTAINLY AN ODD ONE.
HE ARRANGED THIS ALMOST THROUGH SHEER FORCE OF PERSONALITY, INSISTING NO ONE WOULD DARE COMPLAIN IF WE STAYED HERE.
I THINK HE MUST LIKE YOU A FAIR BIT.
HE'S SURE DIFFERENT FROM GASPARD AND DAMIEN.
I HAD A SUDDEN REALIZATION RECENTLY.
?
Nnngh..!
WAGL
WAGL
I HAVEN'T EXCHANGED *LA BISE* WITH MY GROOM EVEN ONCE!

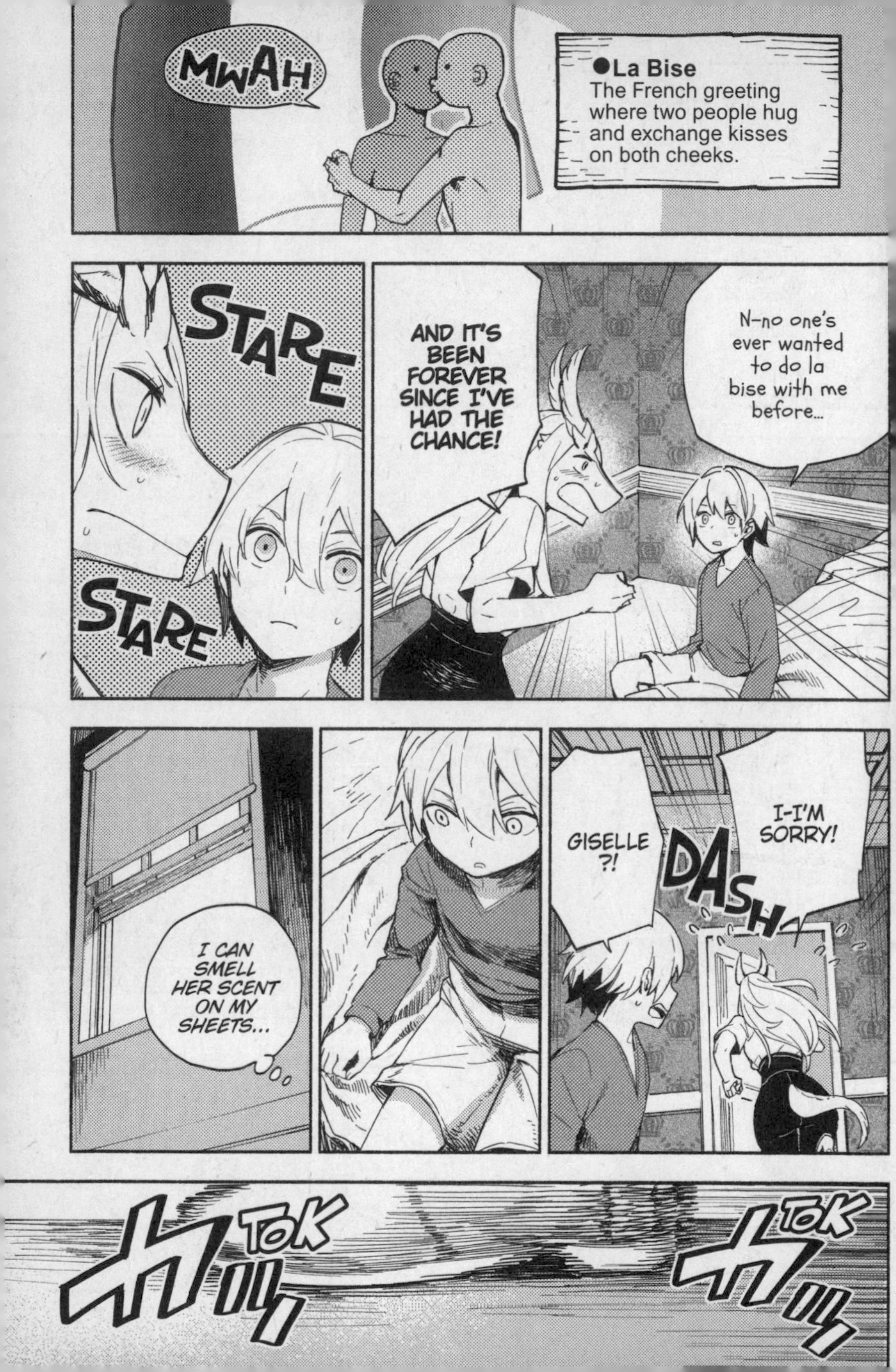
●La Bise
The French greeting where two people hug and exchange kisses on both cheeks.
MWAH
N-no one's ever wanted to do la bise with me before...
AND IT'S BEEN FOREVER SINCE I'VE HAD THE CHANCE!
STARE
STARE
I-I'M SORRY!
GISELLE ?!
DASH
I CAN SMELL HER SCENT ON MY SHEETS...
TOK
TOK

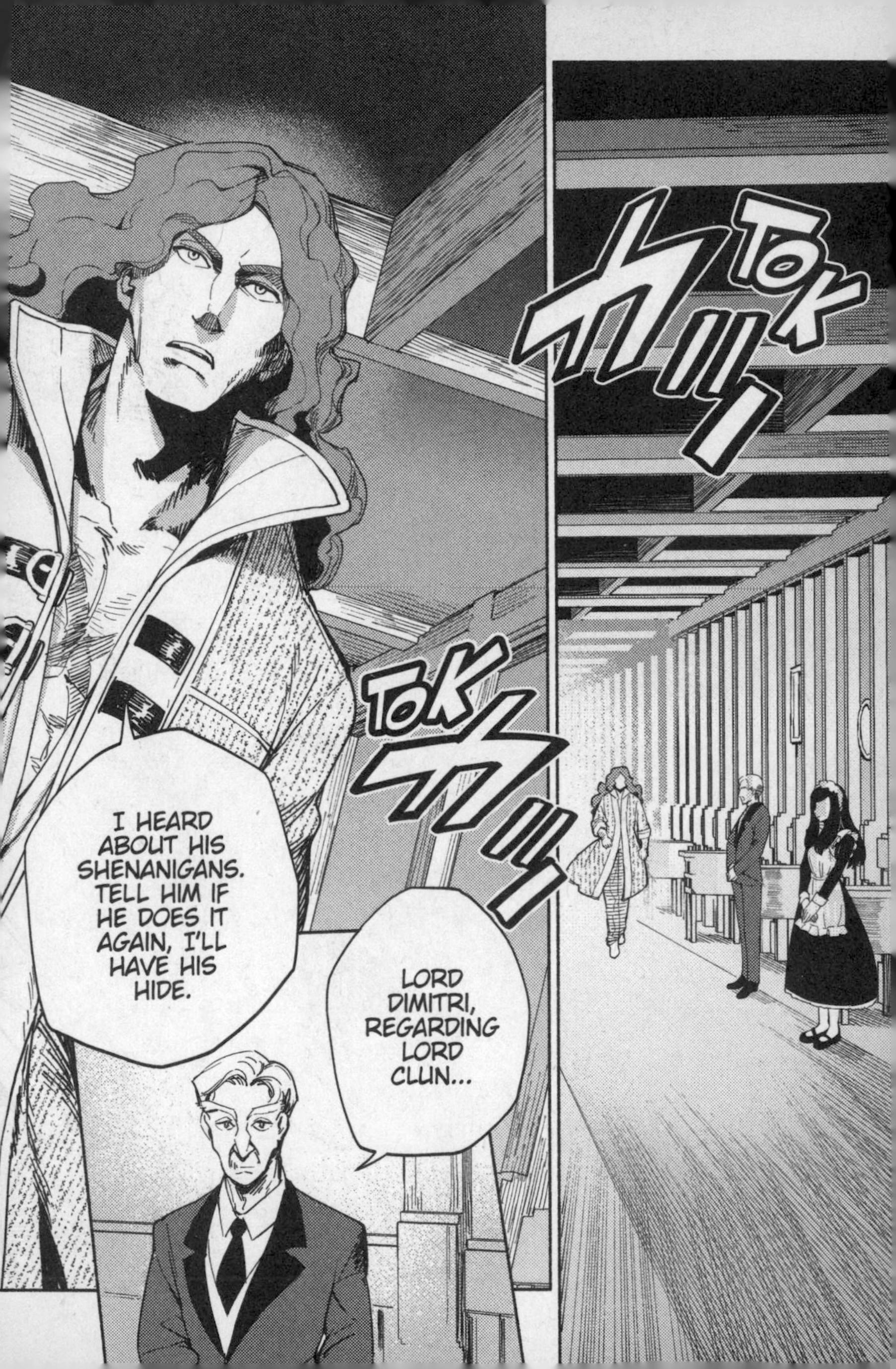
TOK
TOK
LORD DIMITRI, REGARDING LORD CLUN...
I HEARD ABOUT HIS SHENANIGANS. TELL HIM IF HE DOES IT AGAIN, I'LL HAVE HIS HIDE.

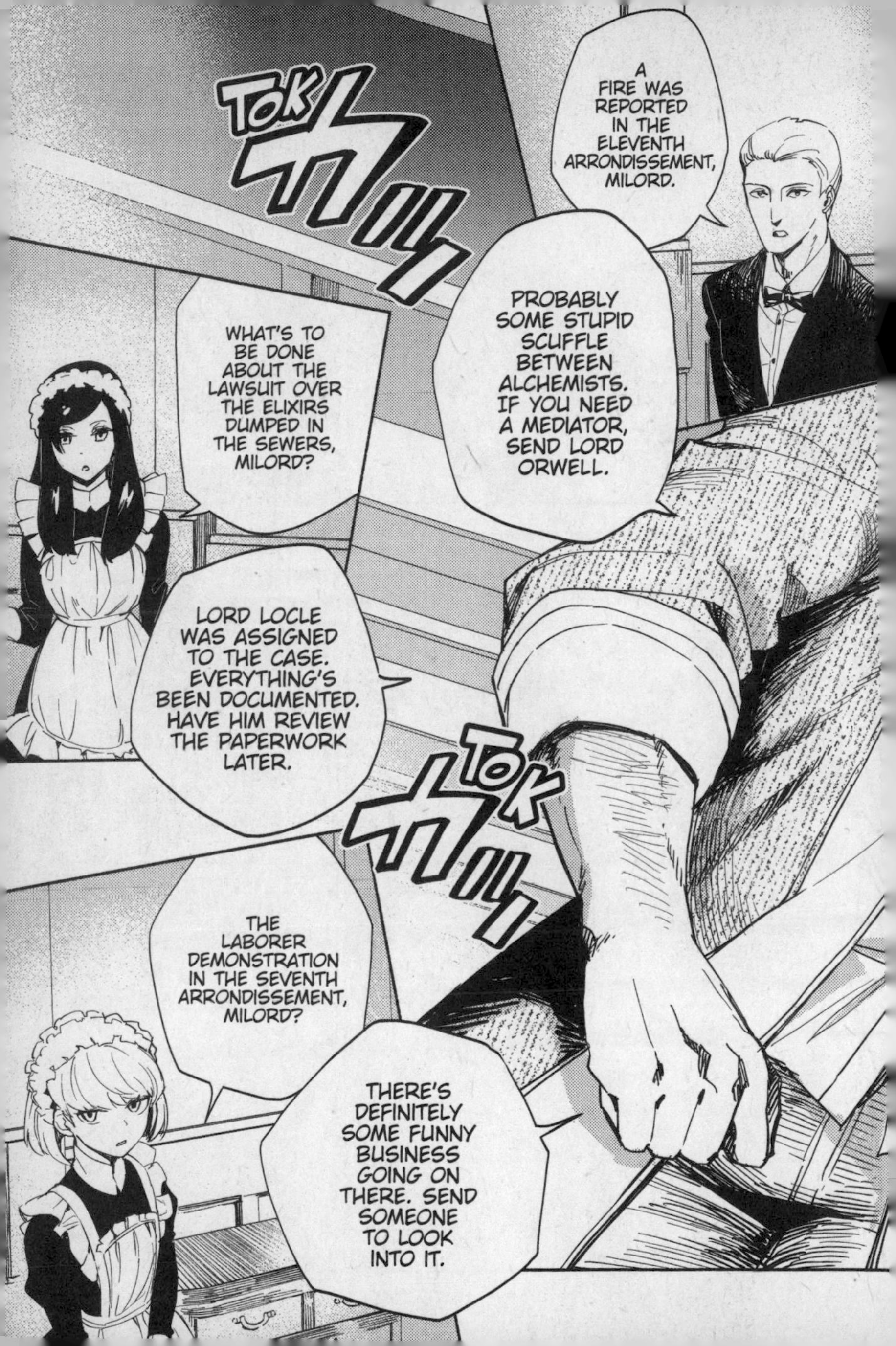
TOK
A FIRE WAS REPORTED IN THE ELEVENTH ARRONDISSEMENT, MILORD.
PROBABLY SOME STUPID SCUFFLE BETWEEN ALCHEMISTS. IF YOU NEED A MEDIATOR, SEND LORD ORWELL.
WHAT'S TO BE DONE ABOUT THE LAWSUIT OVER THE ELIXIRS DUMPED IN THE SEWERS, MILORD?
LORD LOCLE WAS ASSIGNED TO THE CASE. EVERYTHING'S BEEN DOCUMENTED. HAVE HIM REVIEW THE PAPERWORK LATER.
TOK
THE LABORER DEMONSTRATION IN THE SEVENTH ARRONDISSEMENT, MILORD?
THERE'S DEFINITELY SOME FUNNY BUSINESS GOING ON THERE. SEND SOMEONE TO LOOK INTO IT.

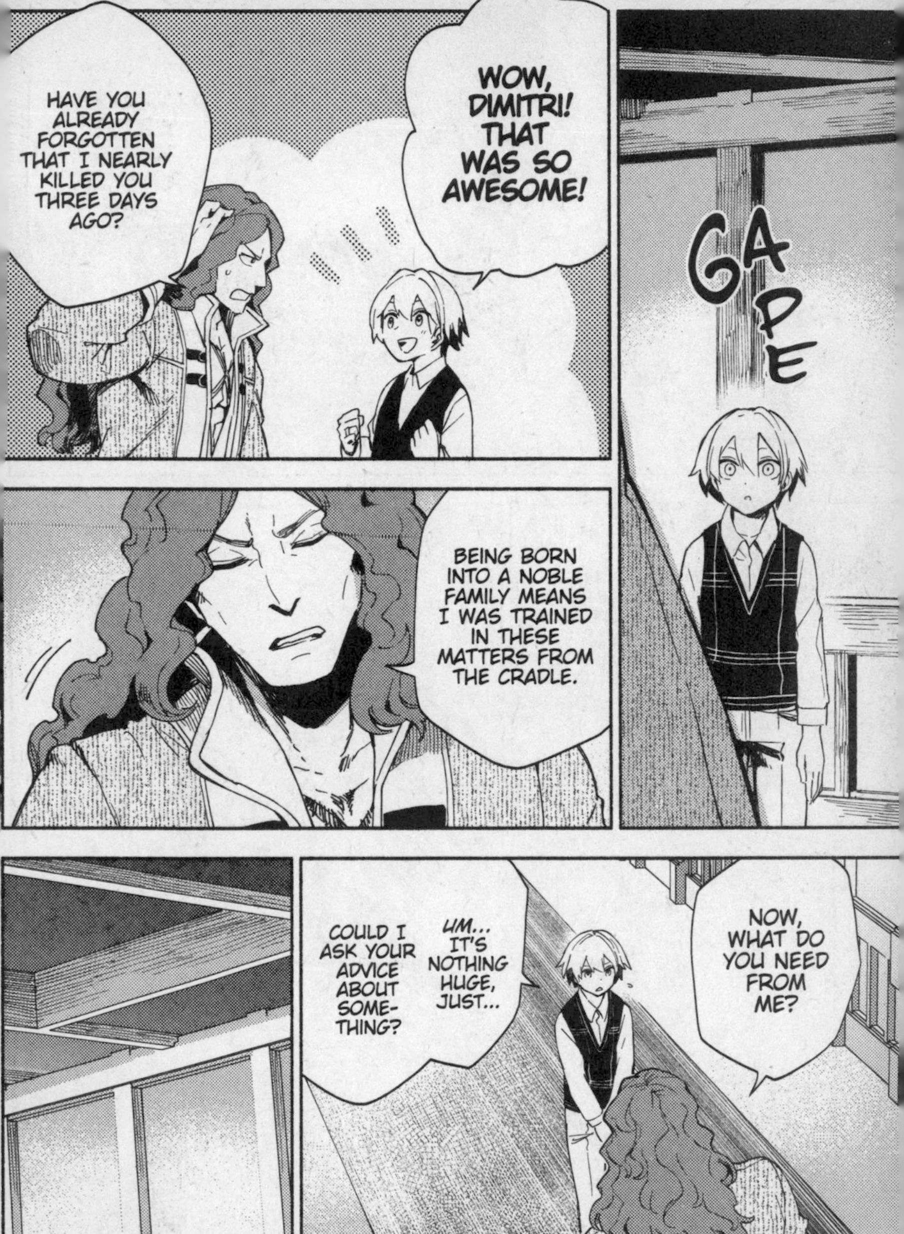
GAPE
WOW, DIMITRI! THAT WAS SO AWESOME!
HAVE YOU ALREADY FORGOTTEN THAT I NEARLY KILLED YOU THREE DAYS AGO?
BEING BORN INTO A NOBLE FAMILY MEANS I WAS TRAINED IN THESE MATTERS FROM THE CRADLE.
NOW, WHAT DO YOU NEED FROM ME?
UM... IT'S NOTHING HUGE, JUST...
COULD I ASK YOUR ADVICE ABOUT SOME-THING?

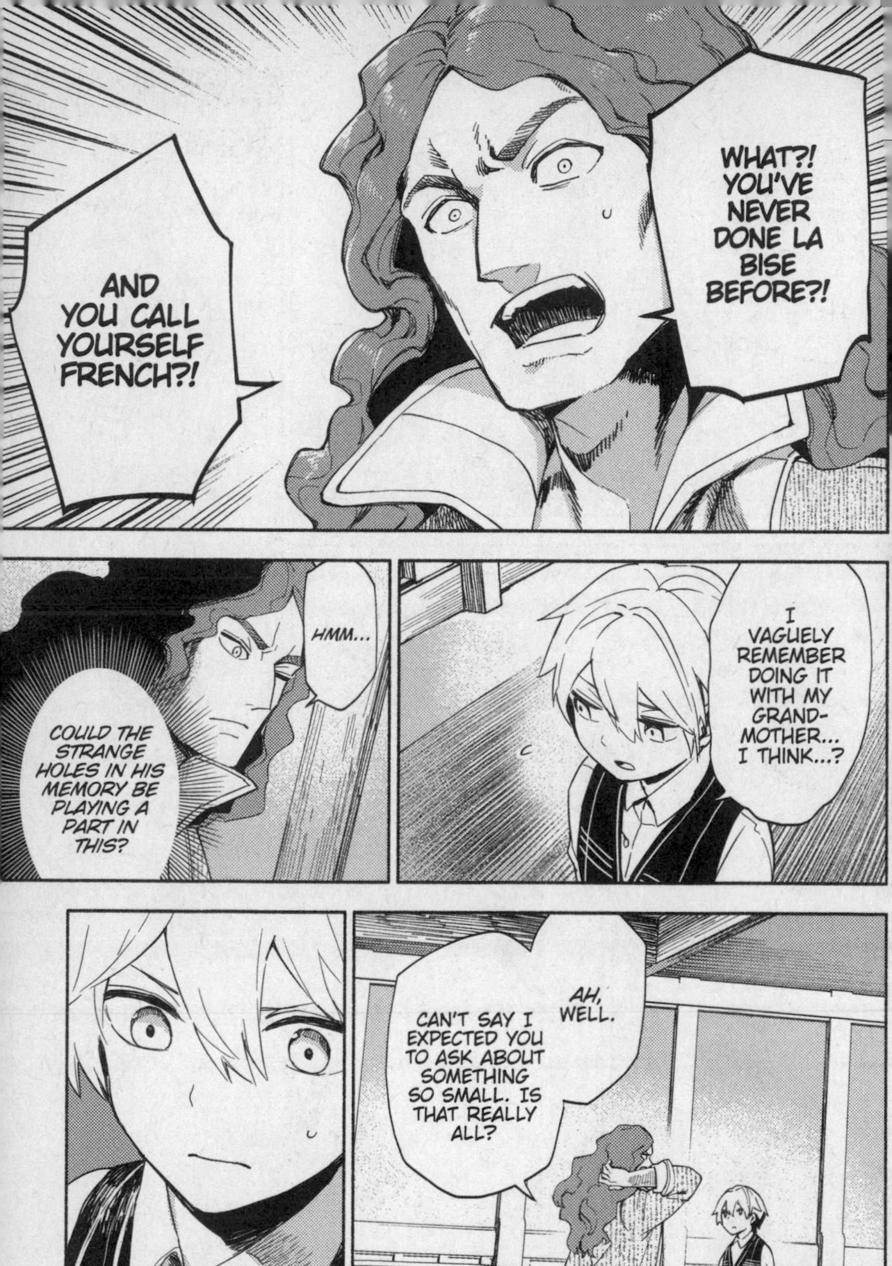
WHAT?! YOU'VE NEVER DONE LA BISE BEFORE?!
AND YOU CALL YOURSELF FRENCH?!
I VAGUELY REMEMBER DOING IT WITH MY GRAND-MOTHER... I THINK...?
HMM...
COULD THE STRANGE HOLES IN HIS MEMORY BE PLAYING A PART IN THIS?
AH, WELL.
CAN'T SAY I EXPECTED YOU TO ASK ABOUT SOMETHING SO SMALL. IS THAT REALLY ALL?

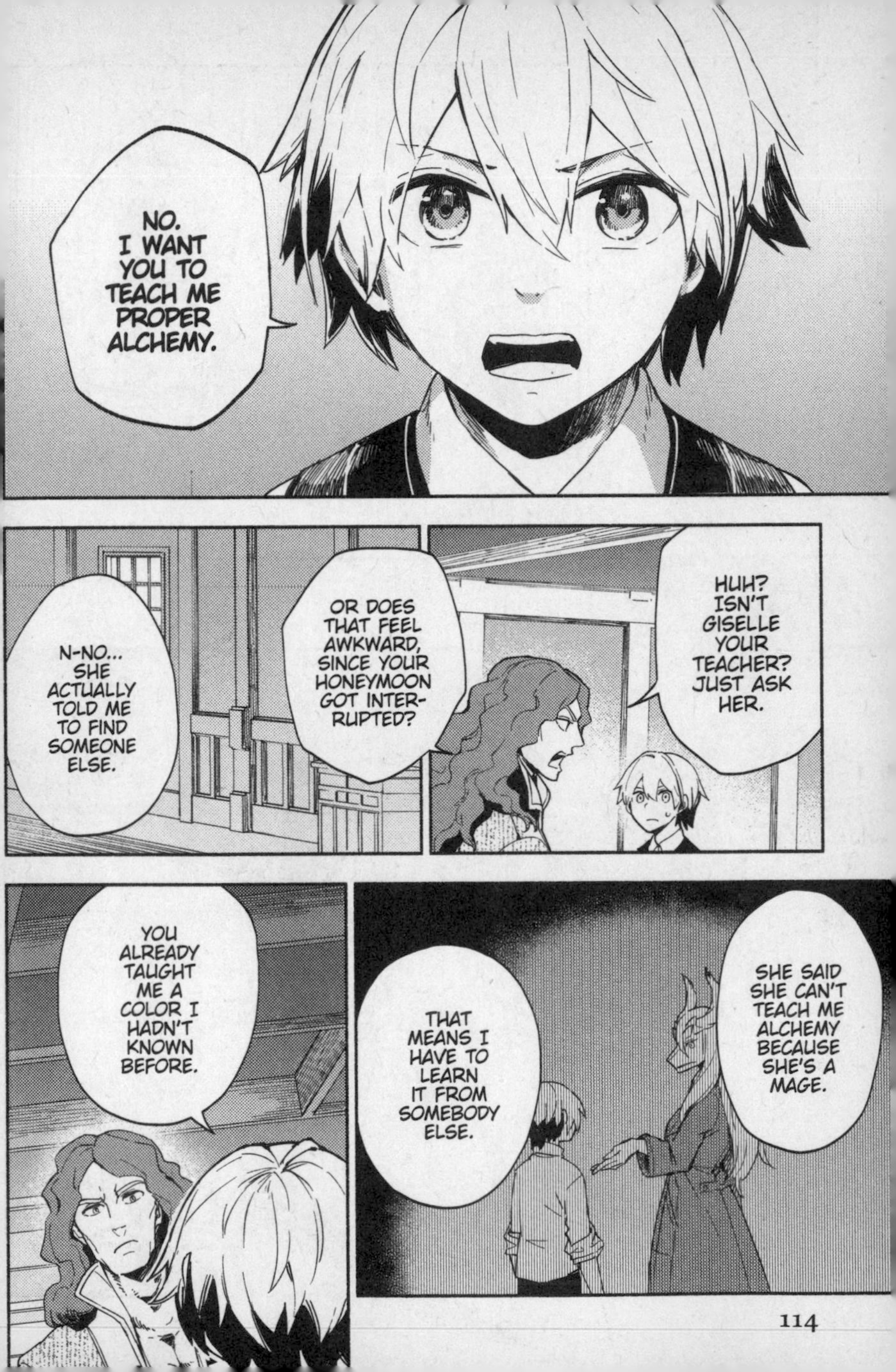
NO. I WANT YOU TO TEACH ME PROPER ALCHEMY.
HUH? ISN'T GISELLE YOUR TEACHER? JUST ASK HER.
OR DOES THAT FEEL AWKWARD, SINCE YOUR HONEYMOON GOT INTER-RUPTED?
N-NO... SHE ACTUALLY TOLD ME TO FIND SOMEONE ELSE.
SHE SAID SHE CAN'T TEACH ME ALCHEMY BECAUSE SHE'S A MAGE.
THAT MEANS I HAVE TO LEARN IT FROM SOMEBODY ELSE.
YOU ALREADY TAUGHT ME A COLOR I HADN'T KNOWN BEFORE.

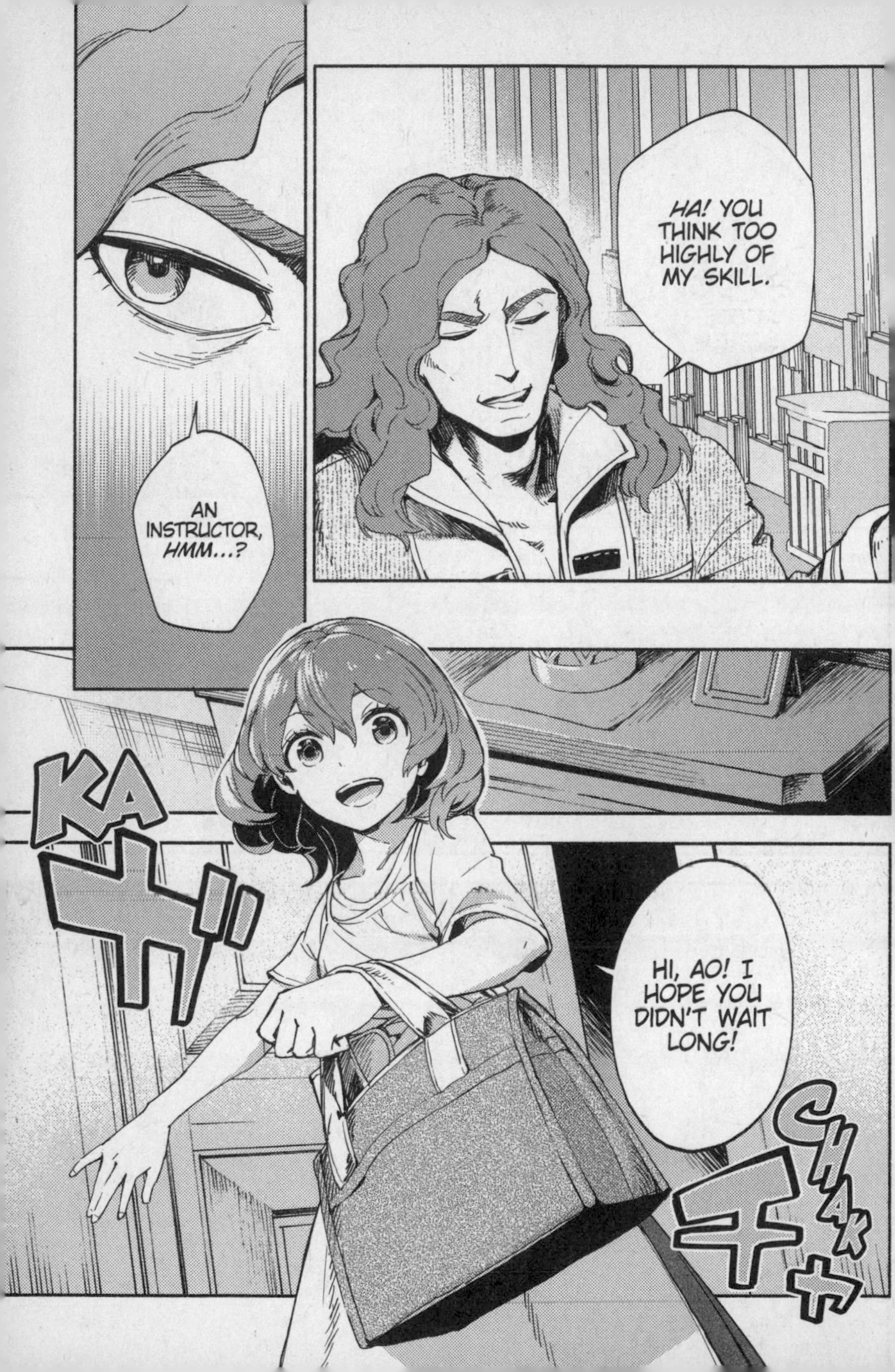
HA! YOU THINK TOO HIGHLY OF MY SKILL.
AN INSTRUCTOR, HMM...?
HI, AO! I HOPE YOU DIDN'T WAIT LONG!
KA
CHAK

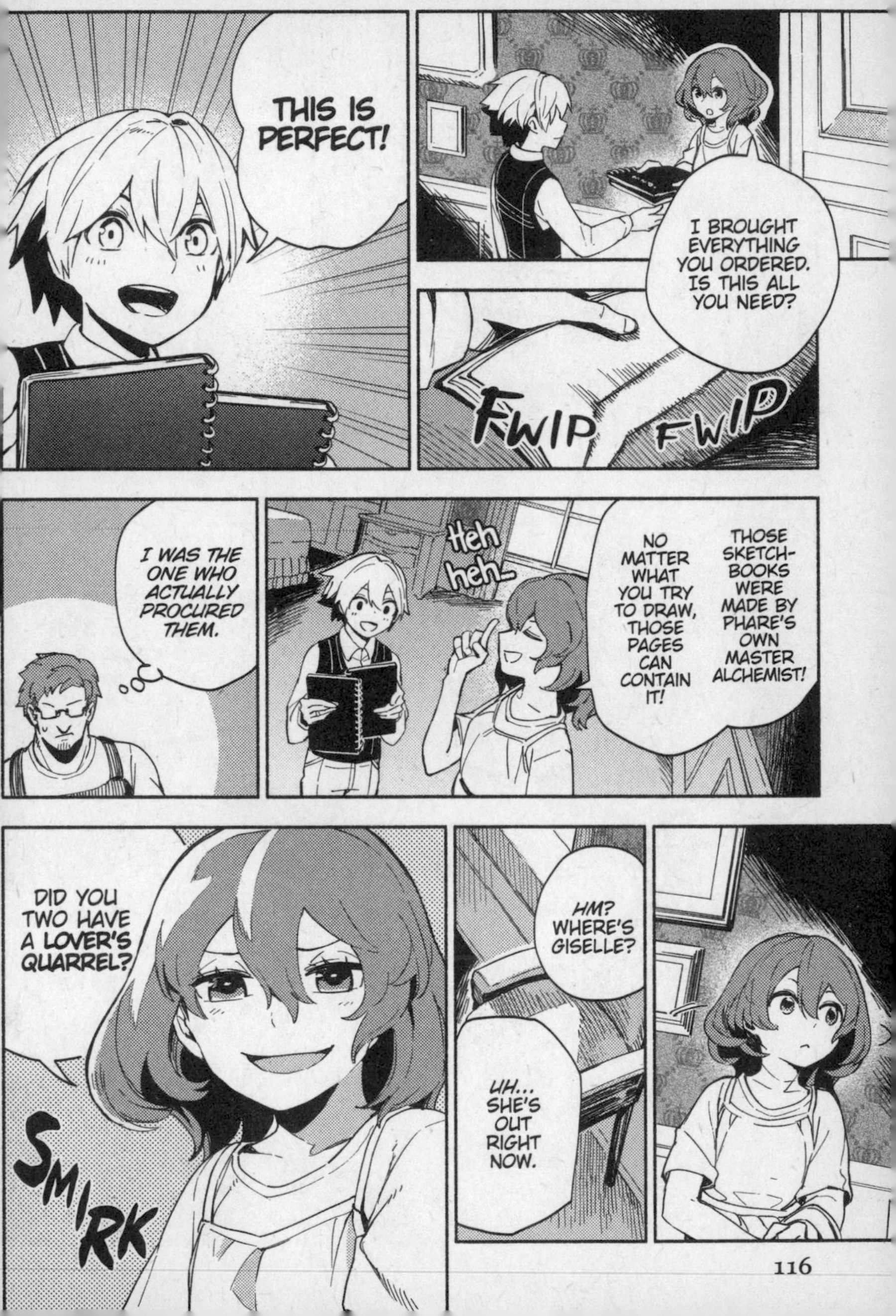
I BROUGHT EVERYTHING YOU ORDERED. IS THIS ALL YOU NEED?
FWIP
FWIP
THIS IS PERFECT!
THOSE SKETCH-BOOKS WERE MADE BY PHARE'S OWN MASTER ALCHEMIST!
NO MATTER WHAT YOU TRY TO DRAW, THOSE PAGES CAN CONTAIN IT!
Heh heh...
I WAS THE ONE WHO ACTUALLY PROCURED THEM.
HM? WHERE'S GISELLE?
UH... SHE'S OUT RIGHT NOW.
DID YOU TWO HAVE A LOVER'S QUARREL?
SMIRK

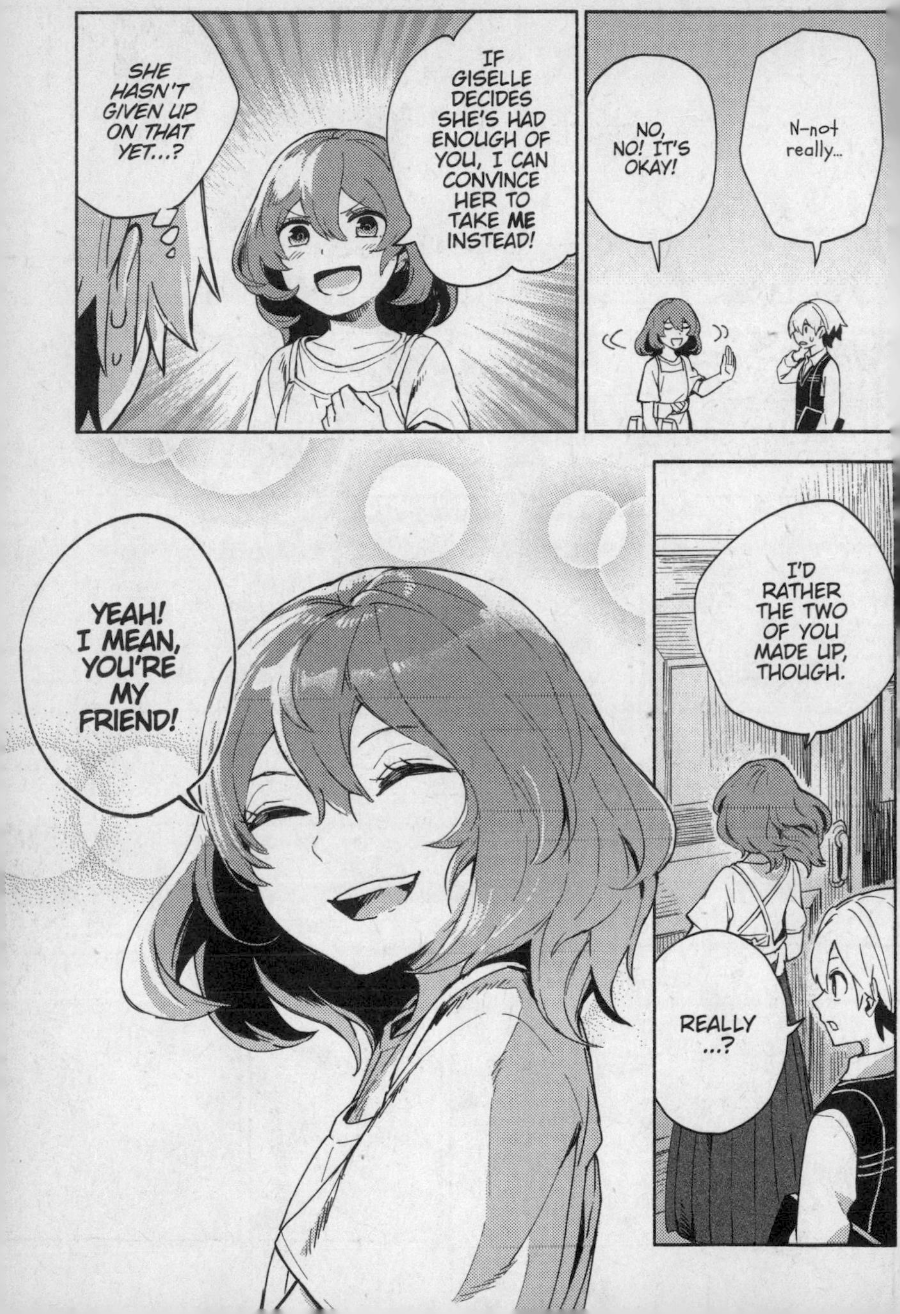
N-not really...
NO, NO! IT'S OKAY!
IF GISELLE DECIDES SHE'S HAD ENOUGH OF YOU, I CAN CONVINCE HER TO TAKE ME INSTEAD!
SHE HASN'T GIVEN UP ON THAT YET...?
I'D RATHER THE TWO OF YOU MADE UP, THOUGH.
REALLY ...?
YEAH! I MEAN, YOU'RE MY FRIEND!

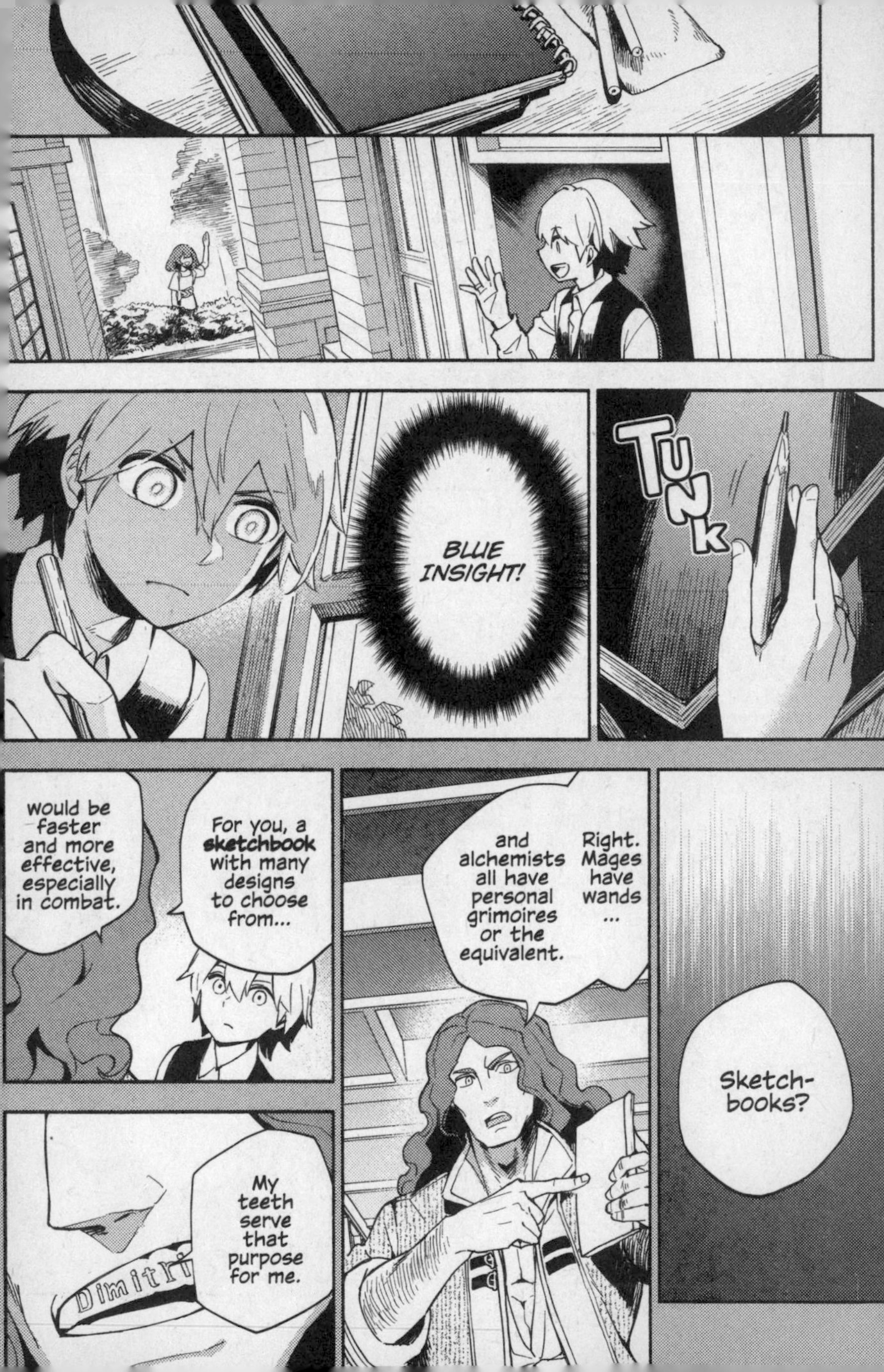
TUNK
BLUE INSIGHT!
Sketch-books?
Right. Mages have wands...
and alchemists all have personal grimoires or the equivalent.
For you, a **sketchbook** with many designs to choose from...
would be faster and more effective, especially in combat.
My teeth serve that purpose for me.
Dimitri

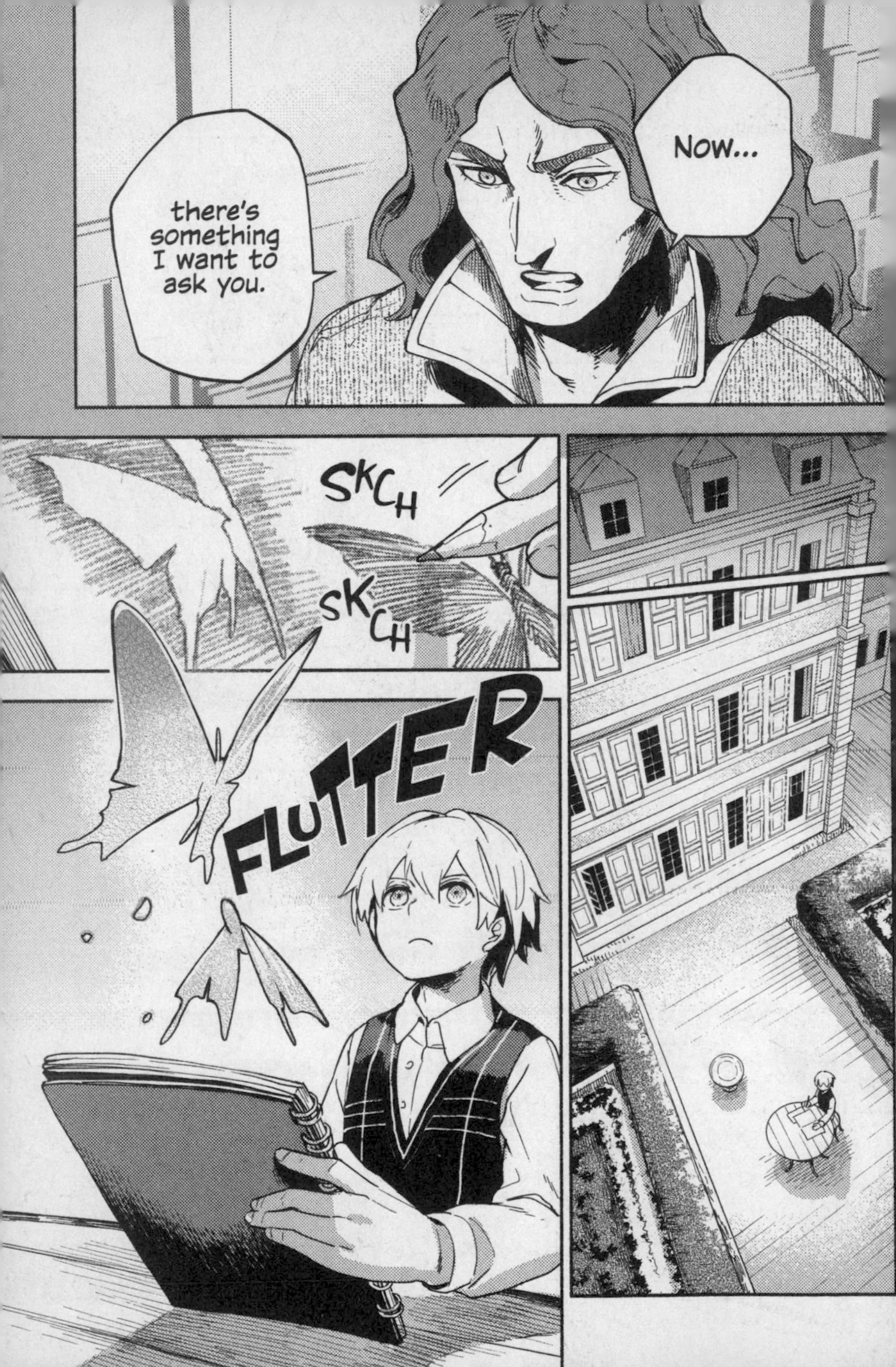
NOW...
there's something I want to ask you.
SKCH
SKCH
FLUTTER

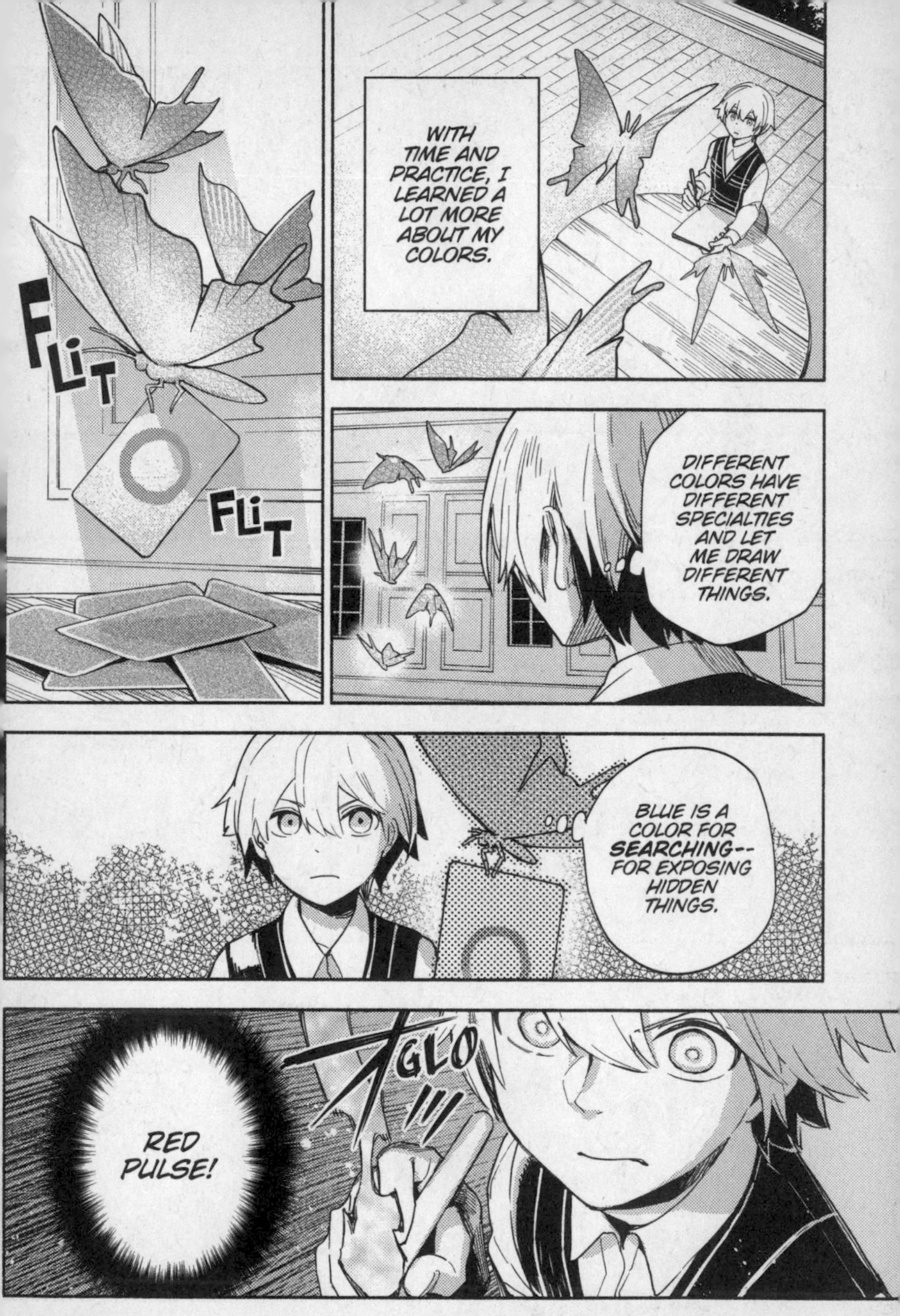
WITH TIME AND PRACTICE, I LEARNED A LOT MORE ABOUT MY COLORS.
DIFFERENT COLORS HAVE DIFFERENT SPECIALTIES AND LET ME DRAW DIFFERENT THINGS.
FLIT
FLIT
BLUE IS A COLOR FOR SEARCHING-- FOR EXPOSING HIDDEN THINGS.
GLO!!!
RED PULSE!

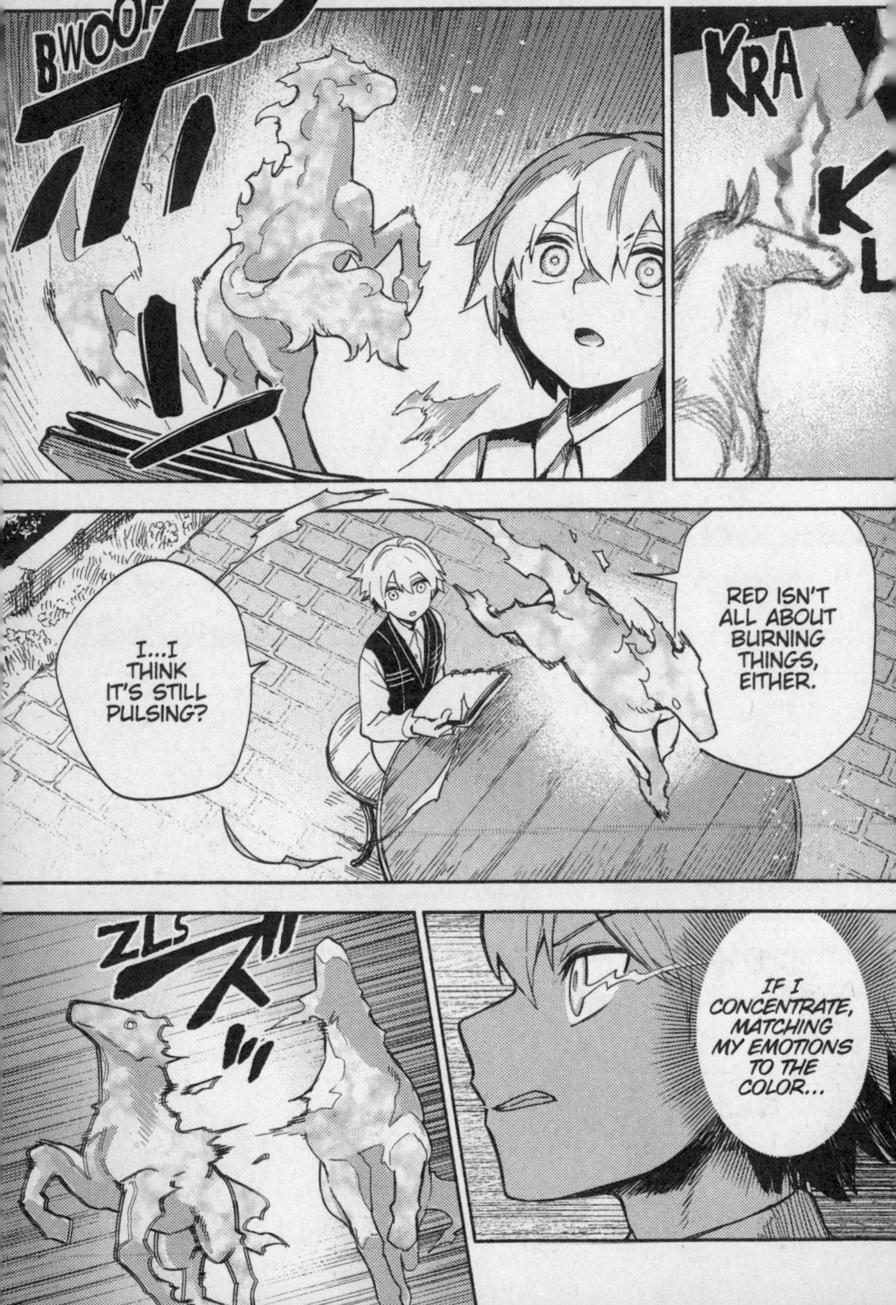
KRA
KL
BWOOF
RED ISN'T ALL ABOUT BURNING THINGS, EITHER.
I...I THINK IT'S STILL PULSING?
IF I CONCENTRATE, MATCHING MY EMOTIONS TO THE COLOR...
ZLS

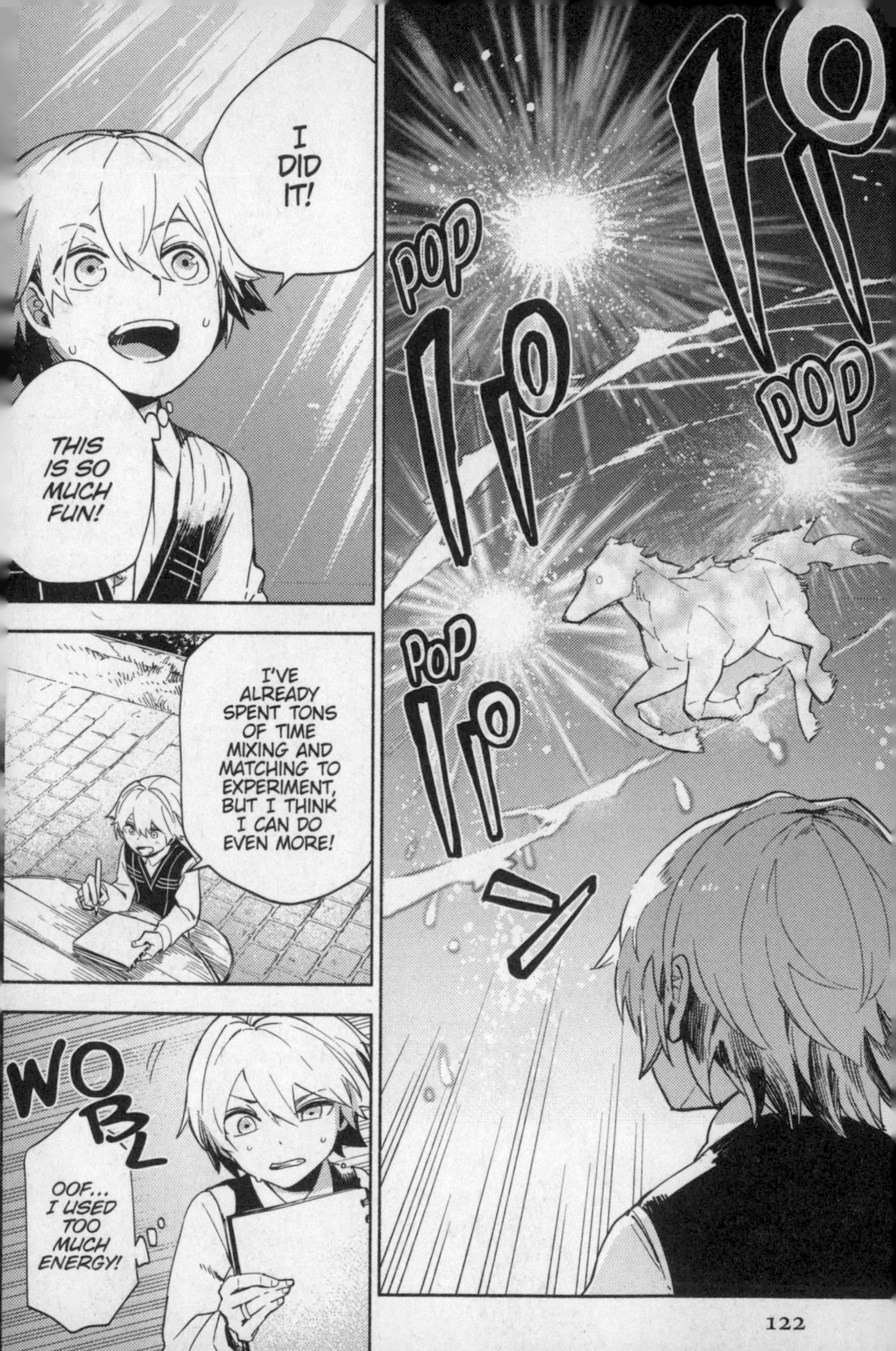
pop
pop
PoP
I DID IT!
THIS IS SO MUCH FUN!
I'VE ALREADY SPENT TONS OF TIME MIXING AND MATCHING TO EXPERIMENT, BUT I THINK I CAN DO EVEN MORE!
WOBL
OOF... I USED TOO MUCH ENERGY!

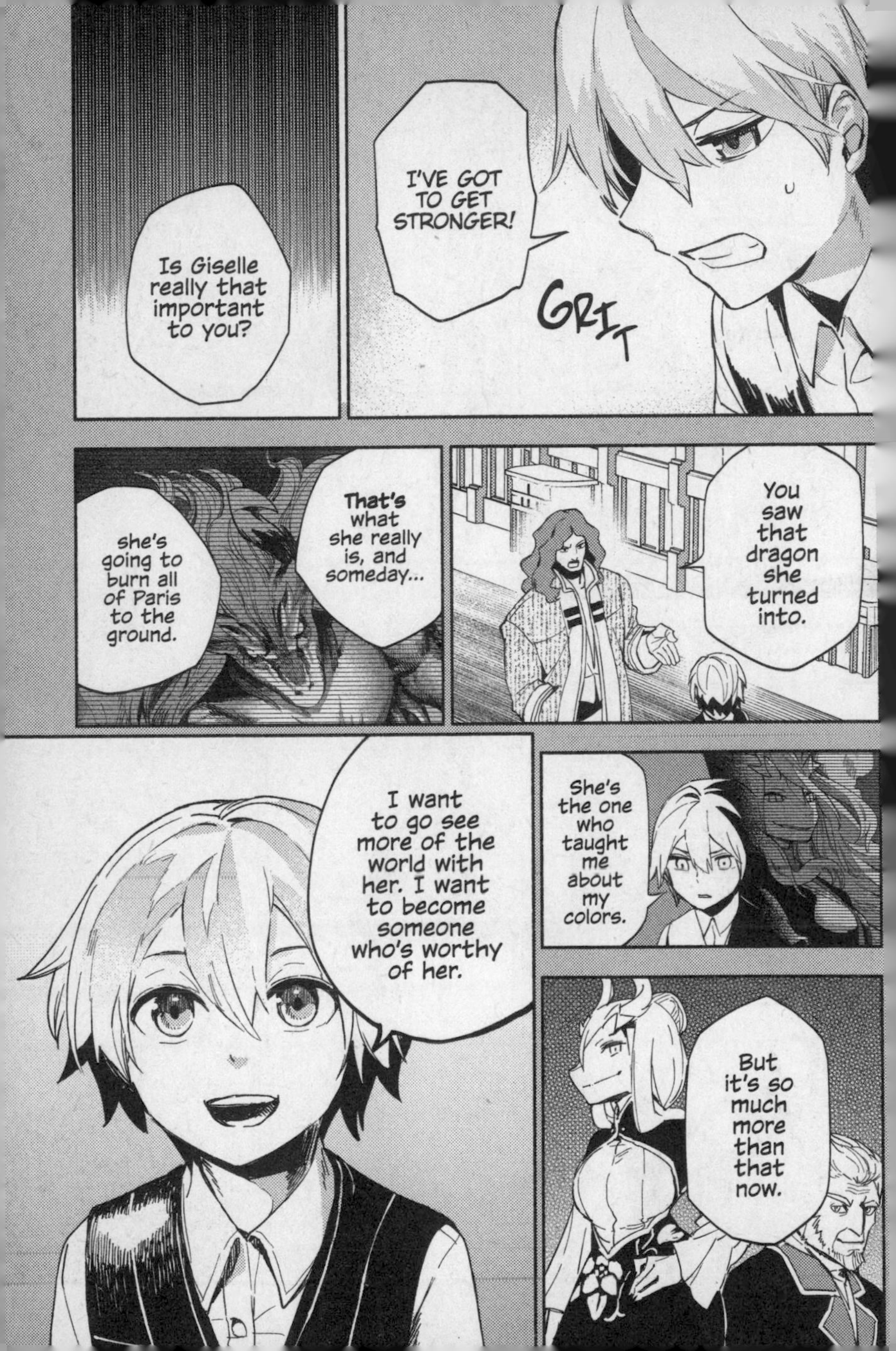
I'VE GOT TO GET STRONGER!
GRIT
Is Giselle really that important to you?
You saw that dragon she turned into.
That's what she really is, and someday...
she's going to burn all of Paris to the ground.
She's the one who taught me about my colors.
But it's so much more than that now.
I want to go see more of the world with her. I want to become someone who's worthy of her.

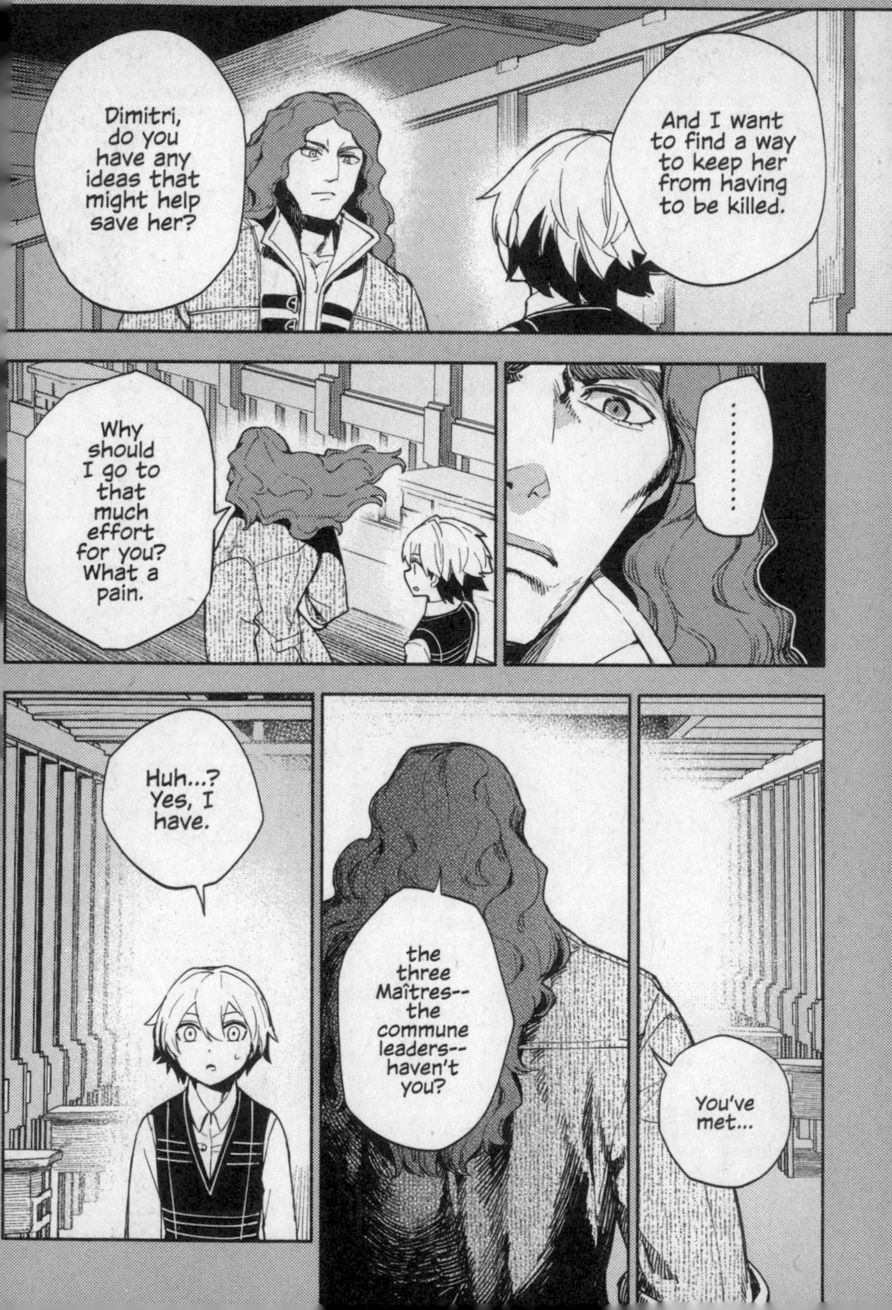
And I want to find a way to keep her from having to be killed.
Dimitri, do you have any ideas that might help save her?
....
Why should I go to that much effort for you? What a pain.
You've met...
the three Maîtres--the commune leaders--haven't you?
Huh...? Yes, I have.

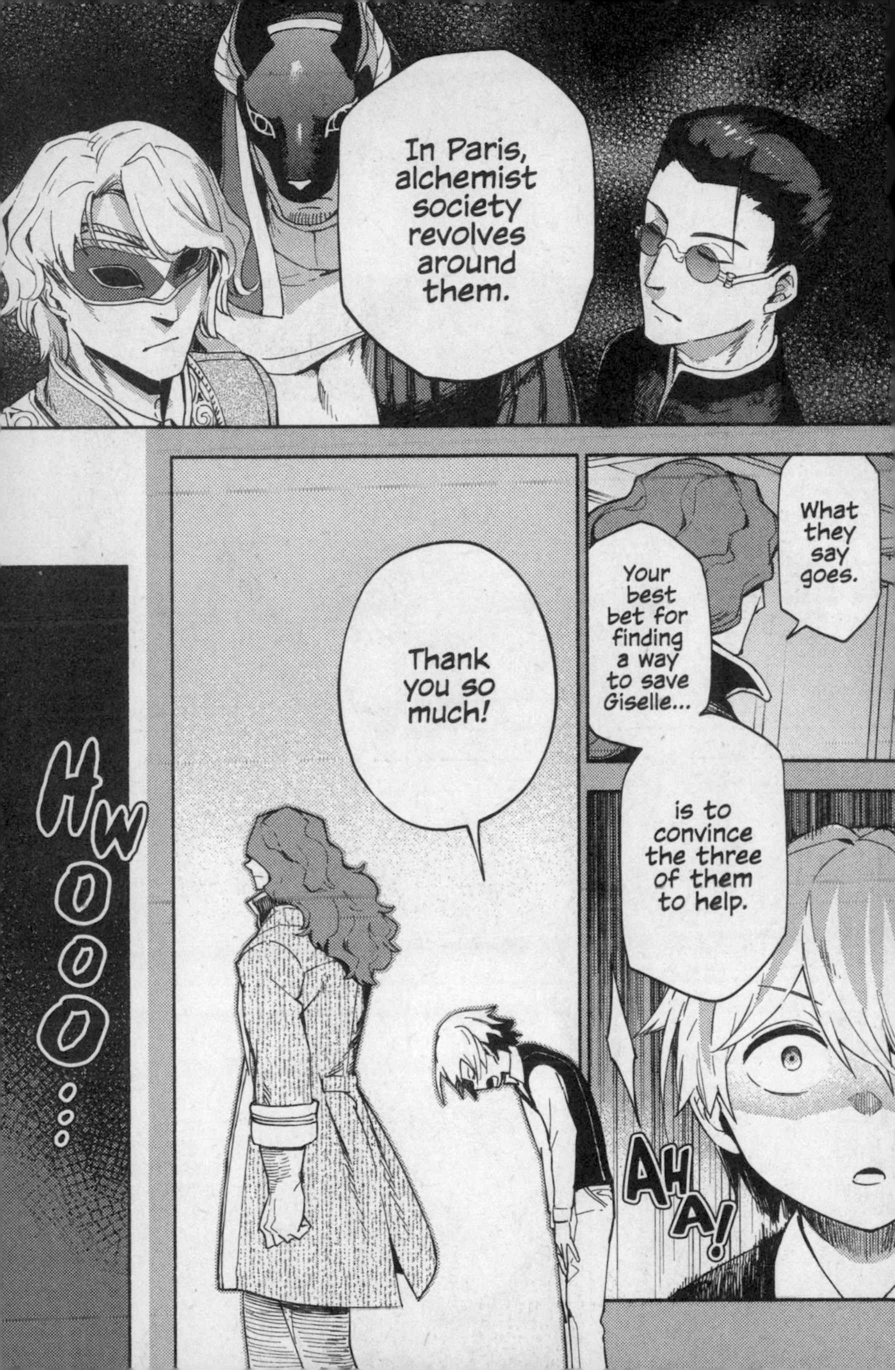
In Paris, alchemist society revolves around them.
What they say goes.
Your best bet for finding a way to save Giselle...
is to convince the three of them to help.
AHA!
Thank you so much!
HWOOOO...

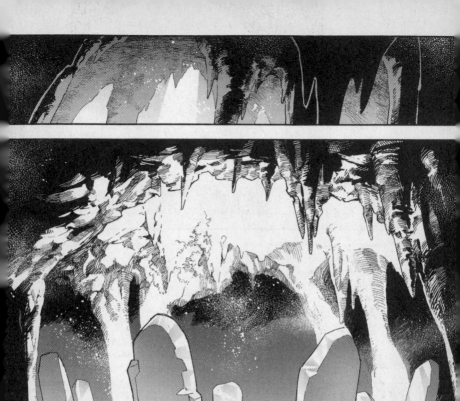

I'M ASKING YOU TO RETURN GISELLE TO QUATRE SAISONS.

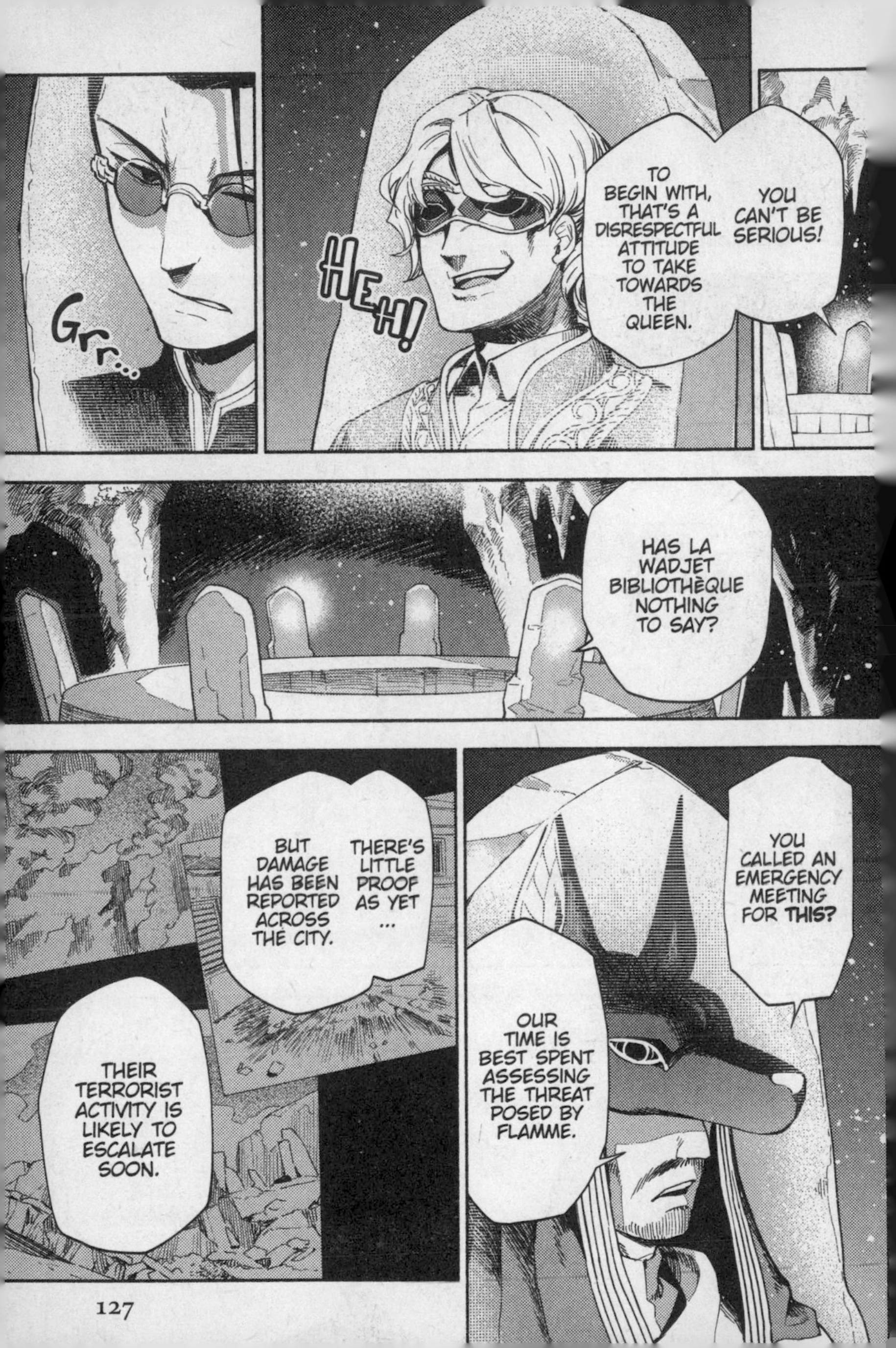
YOU CAN'T BE SERIOUS!
TO BEGIN WITH, THAT'S A DISRESPECTFUL ATTITUDE TO TAKE TOWARDS THE QUEEN.
HEH!
Grr...
HAS LA WADJET BIBLIOTHÈQUE NOTHING TO SAY?
YOU CALLED AN EMERGENCY MEETING FOR THIS?
OUR TIME IS BEST SPENT ASSESSING THE THREAT POSED BY FLAMME.
THERE'S LITTLE PROOF AS YET ...
BUT DAMAGE HAS BEEN REPORTED ACROSS THE CITY.
THEIR TERRORIST ACTIVITY IS LIKELY TO ESCALATE SOON.

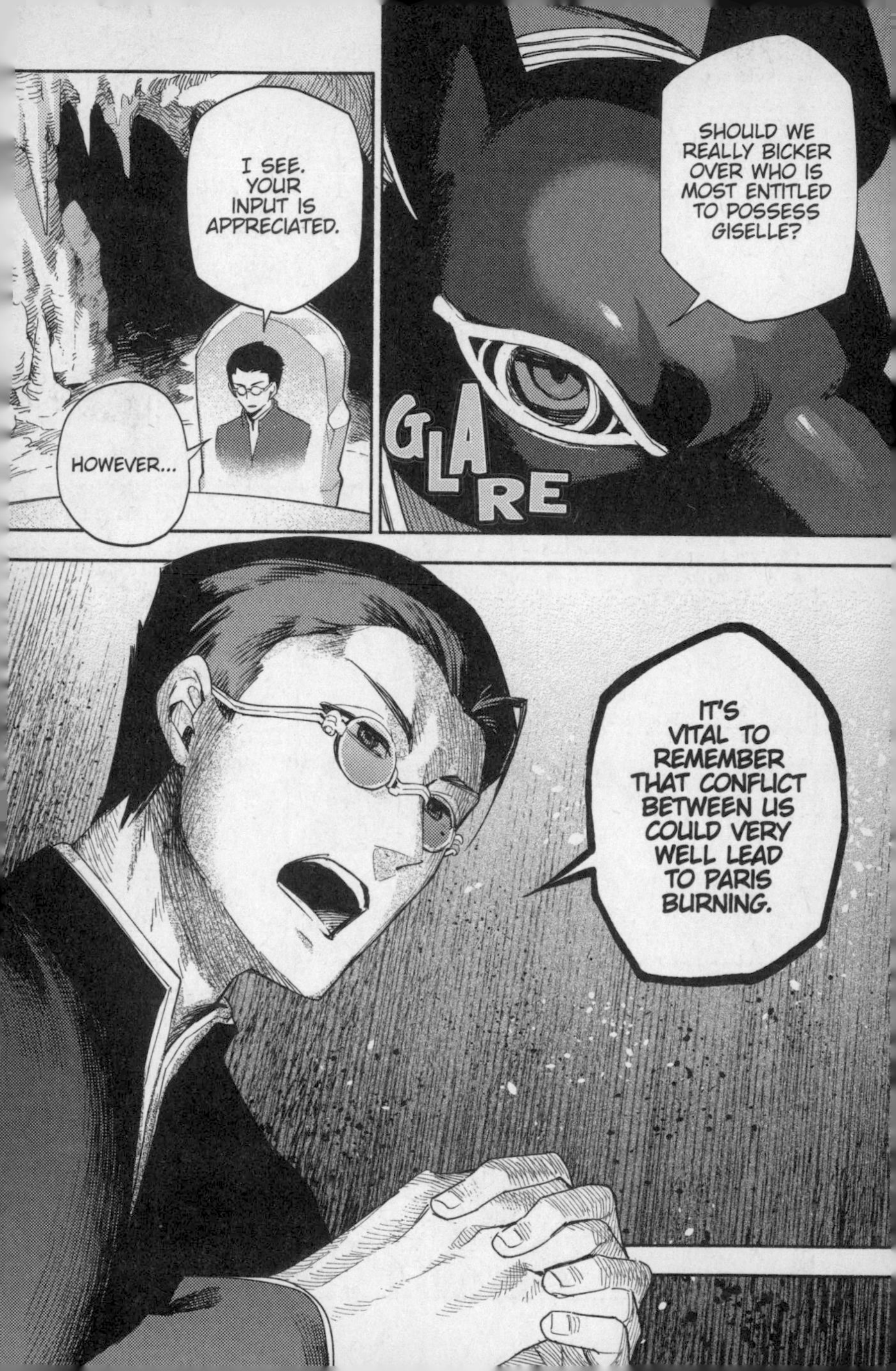
SHOULD WE REALLY BICKER OVER WHO IS MOST ENTITLED TO POSSESS GISELLE?
GLARE
I SEE. YOUR INPUT IS APPRECIATED.
HOWEVER...
IT'S VITAL TO REMEMBER THAT CONFLICT BETWEEN US COULD VERY WELL LEAD TO PARIS BURNING.

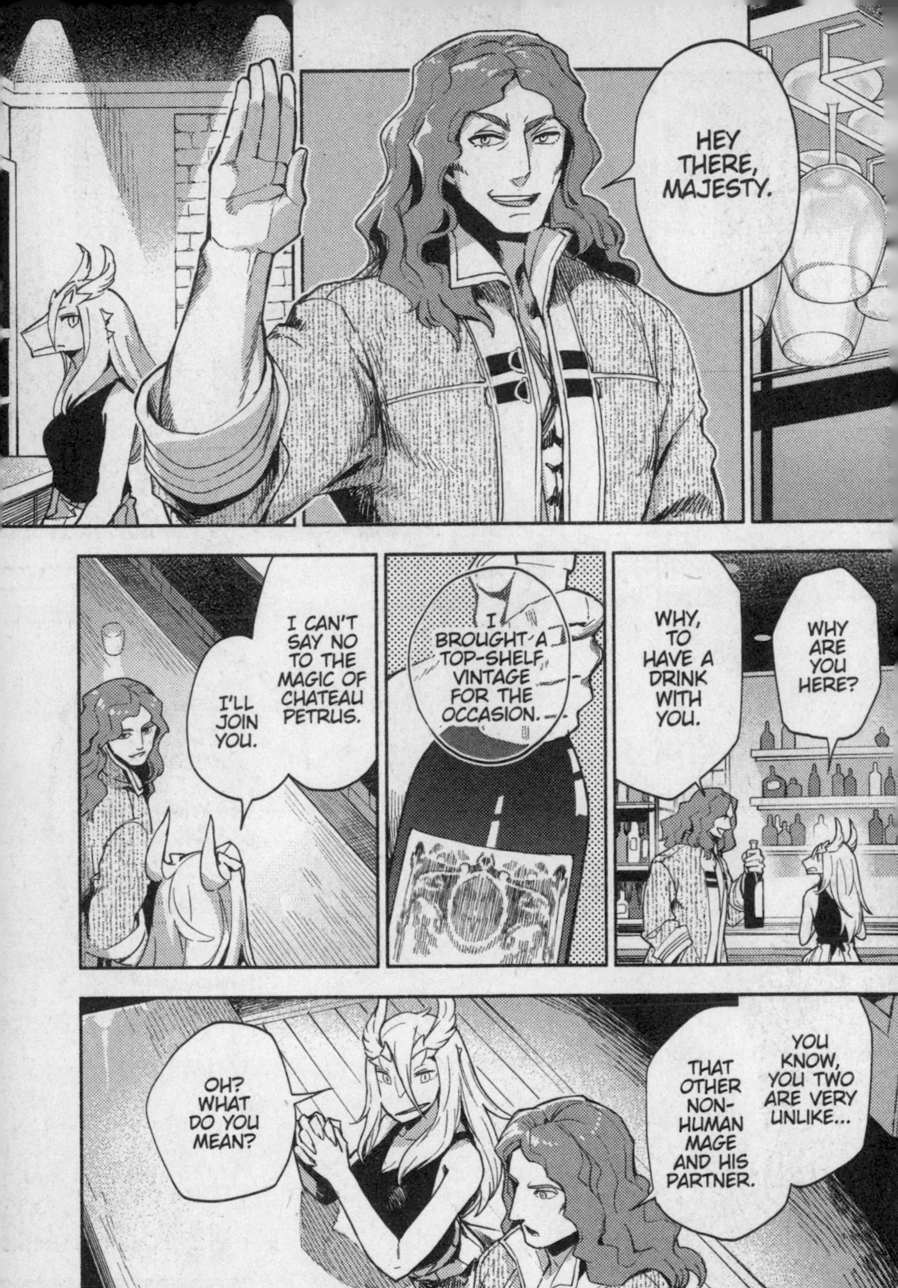
HEY THERE, MAJESTY.
WHY ARE YOU HERE?
WHY, TO HAVE A DRINK WITH YOU.
I BROUGHT A TOP-SHELF VINTAGE FOR THE OCCASION.
I CAN'T SAY NO TO THE MAGIC OF CHATEAU PETRUS.
I'LL JOIN YOU.
YOU KNOW, YOU TWO ARE VERY UNLIKE...
THAT OTHER NON-HUMAN MAGE AND HIS PARTNER.
OH? WHAT DO YOU MEAN?

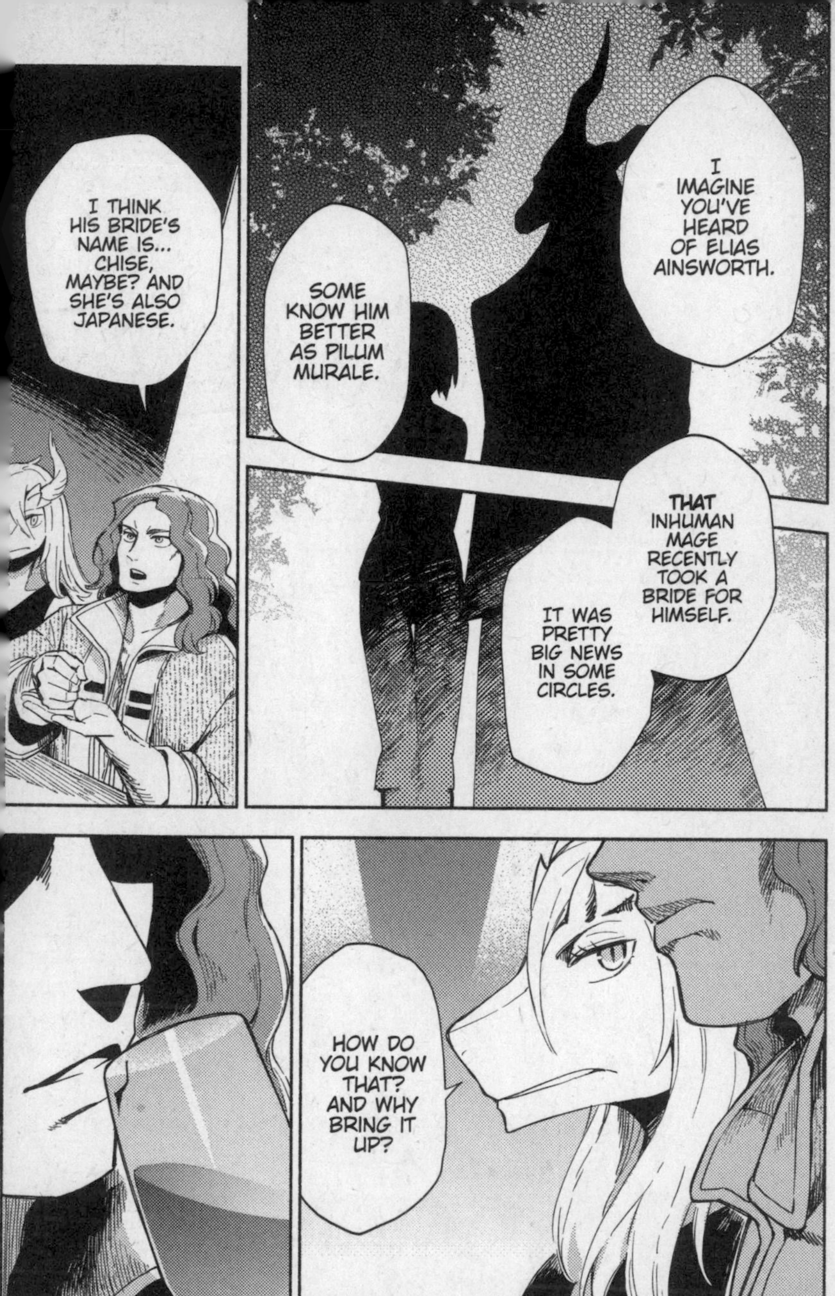
I IMAGINE YOU'VE HEARD OF ELIAS AINSWORTH.
SOME KNOW HIM BETTER AS PILUM MURALE.
THAT INHUMAN MAGE RECENTLY TOOK A BRIDE FOR HIMSELF.
IT WAS PRETTY BIG NEWS IN SOME CIRCLES.
I THINK HIS BRIDE'S NAME IS... CHISE, MAYBE? AND SHE'S ALSO JAPANESE.
HOW DO YOU KNOW THAT? AND WHY BRING IT UP?

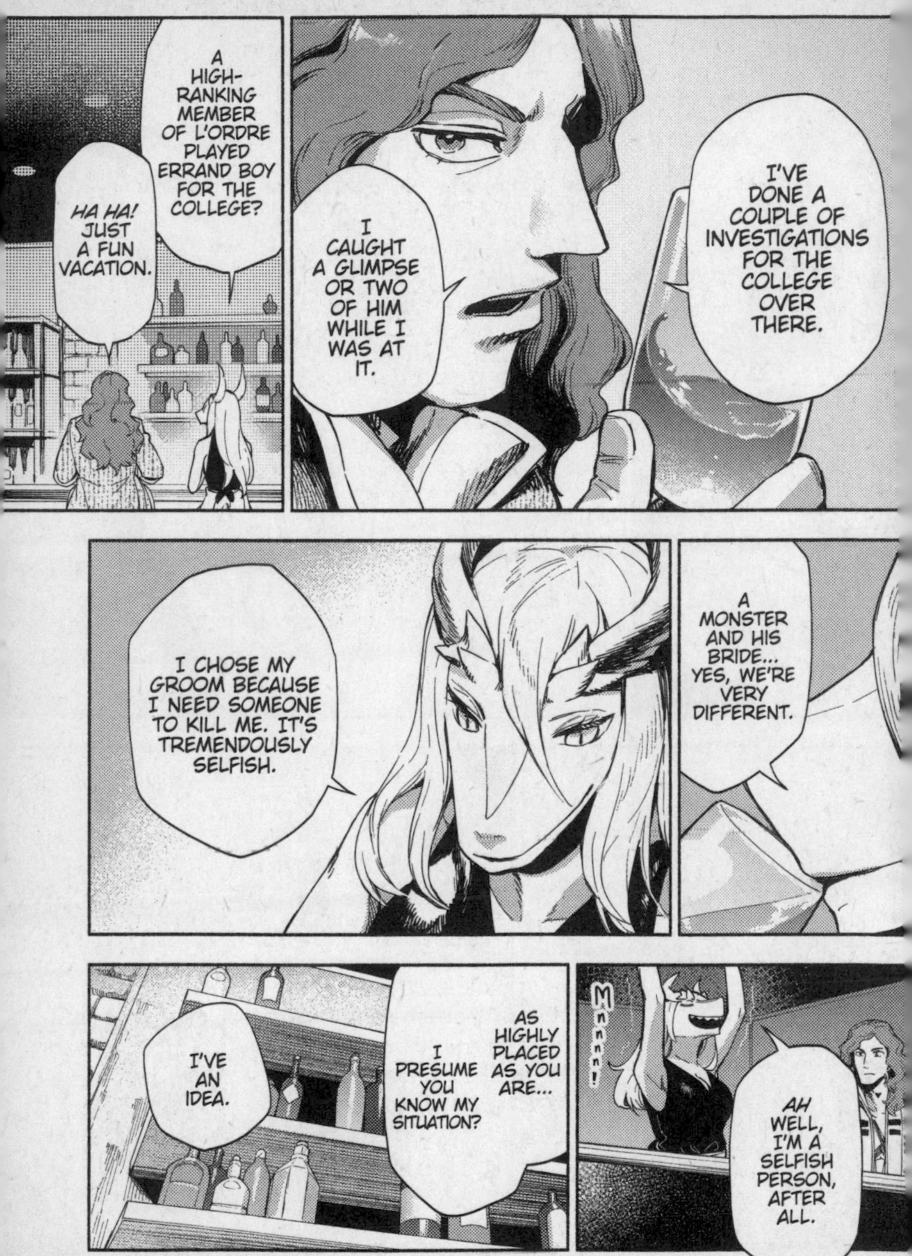
I'VE DONE A COUPLE OF INVESTIGATIONS FOR THE COLLEGE OVER THERE.
I CAUGHT A GLIMPSE OR TWO OF HIM WHILE I WAS AT IT.
A HIGH-RANKING MEMBER OF L'ORDRE PLAYED ERRAND BOY FOR THE COLLEGE?
HA HA! JUST A FUN VACATION.
A MONSTER AND HIS BRIDE... YES, WE'RE VERY DIFFERENT.
I CHOSE MY GROOM BECAUSE I NEED SOMEONE TO KILL ME. IT'S TREMENDOUSLY SELFISH.
Mnnnn!
AH WELL, I'M A SELFISH PERSON, AFTER ALL.
AS HIGHLY PLACED AS YOU ARE...
I PRESUME YOU KNOW MY SITUATION?
I'VE AN IDEA.

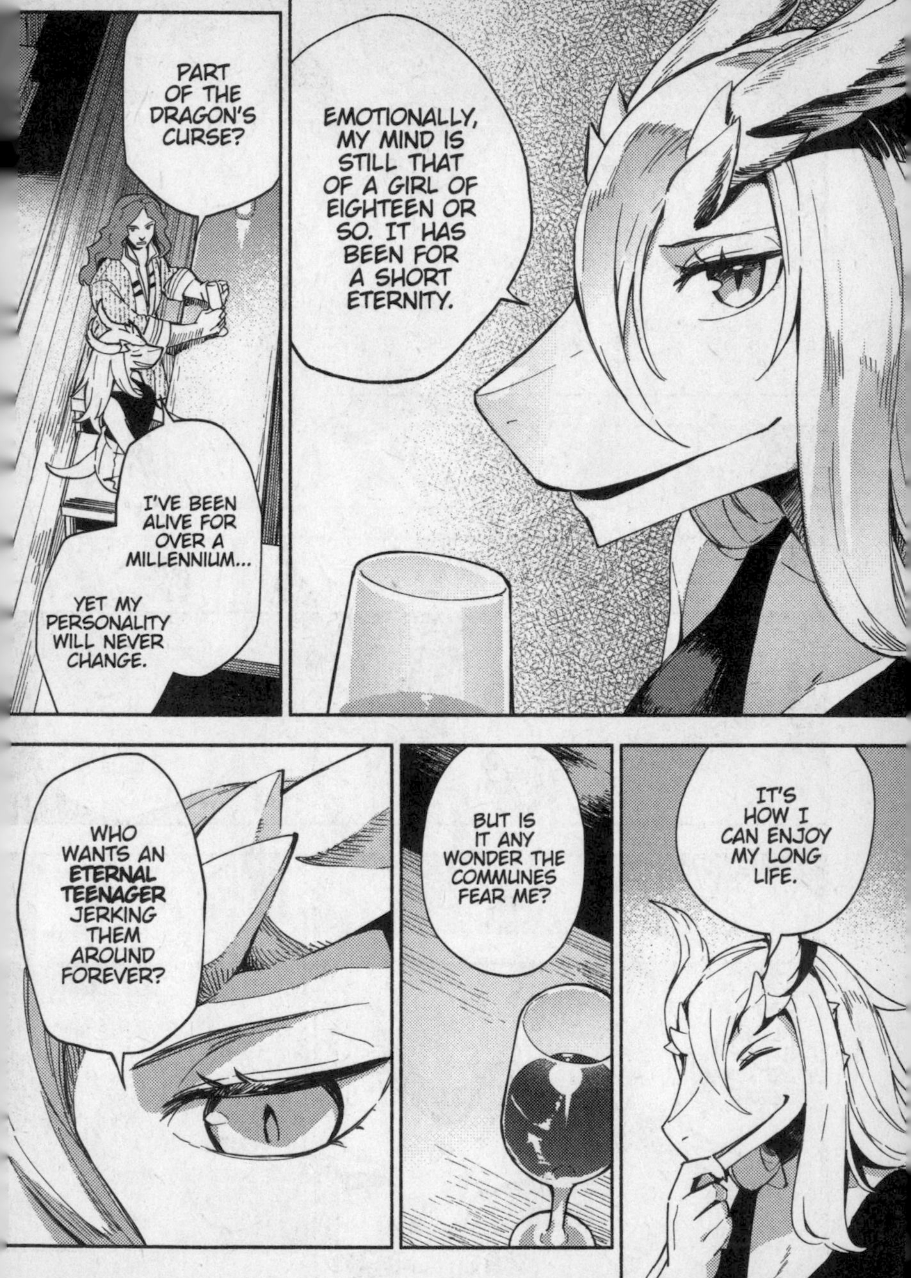
EMOTIONALLY, MY MIND IS STILL THAT OF A GIRL OF EIGHTEEN OR SO. IT HAS BEEN FOR A SHORT ETERNITY.
PART OF THE DRAGON'S CURSE?
I'VE BEEN ALIVE FOR OVER A MILLENNIUM...
YET MY PERSONALITY WILL NEVER CHANGE.
IT'S HOW I CAN ENJOY MY LONG LIFE.
BUT IS IT ANY WONDER THE COMMUNES FEAR ME?
WHO WANTS AN **ETERNAL TEENAGER** JERKING THEM AROUND FOREVER?

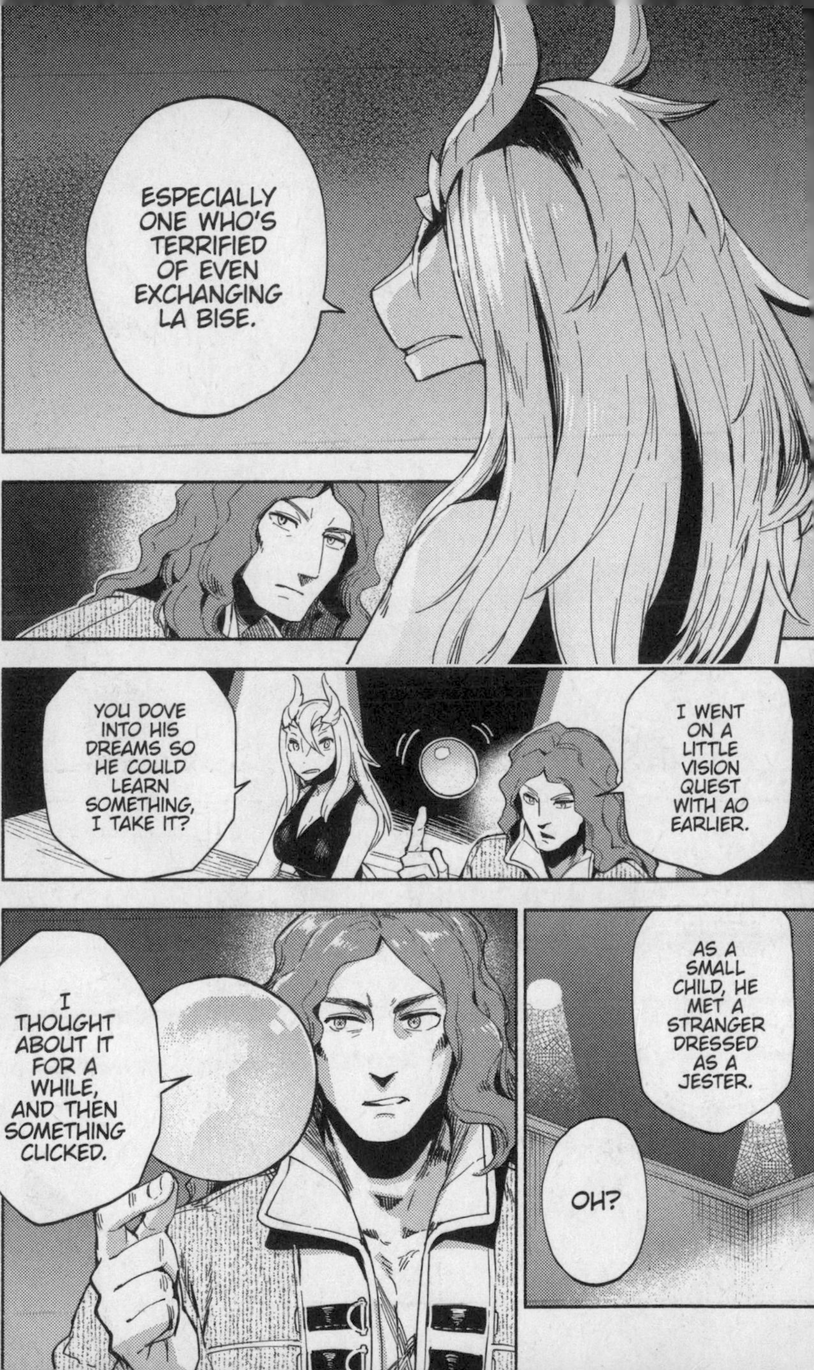
ESPECIALLY ONE WHO'S TERRIFIED OF EVEN EXCHANGING LA BISE.
I WENT ON A LITTLE VISION QUEST WITH AO EARLIER.
YOU DOVE INTO HIS DREAMS SO HE COULD LEARN SOMETHING, I TAKE IT?
AS A SMALL CHILD, HE MET A STRANGER DRESSED AS A JESTER.
OH?
I THOUGHT ABOUT IT FOR A WHILE, AND THEN SOMETHING CLICKED.

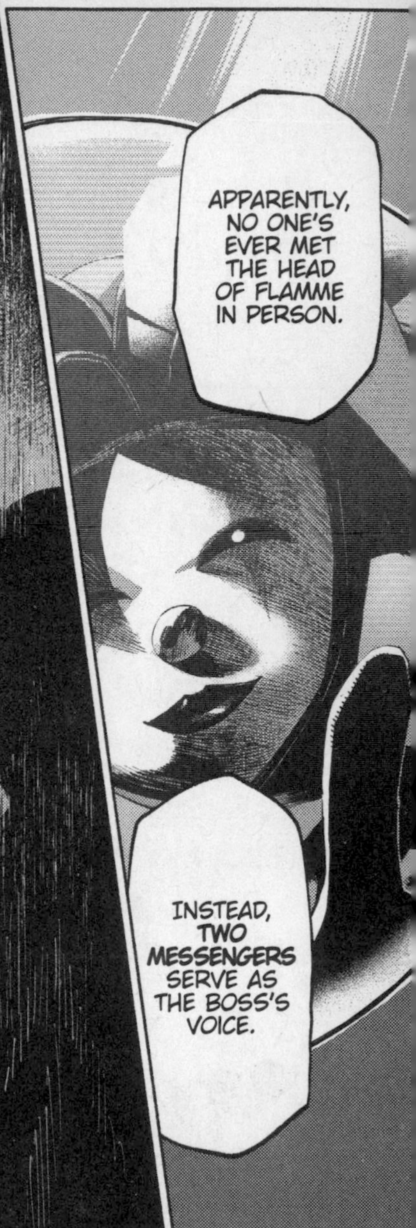
APPARENTLY, NO ONE'S EVER MET THE HEAD OF FLAMME IN PERSON.
INSTEAD, TWO MESSENGERS SERVE AS THE BOSS'S VOICE.

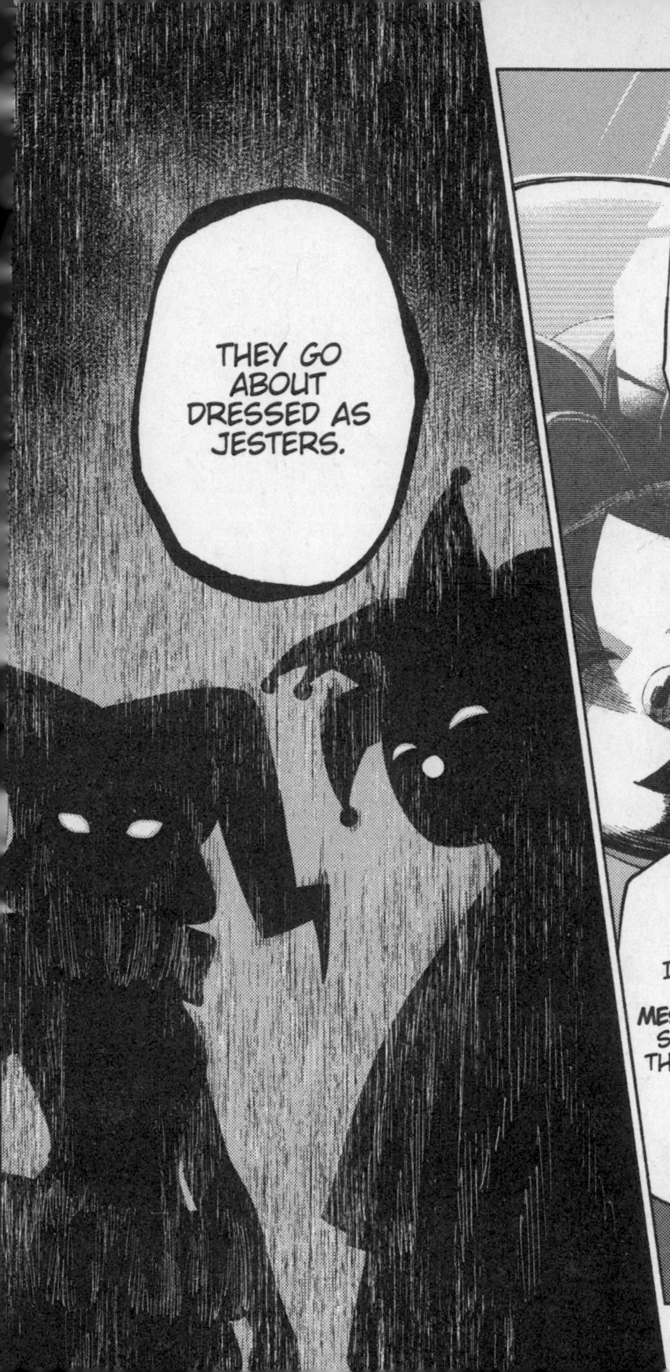
THEY GO ABOUT DRESSED AS JESTERS.

The Ancient Magus' Bride

WIZARD's BLUE

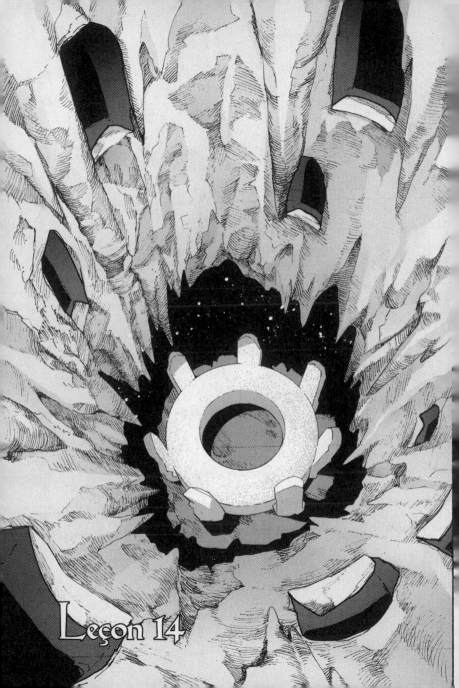

Leçon 14

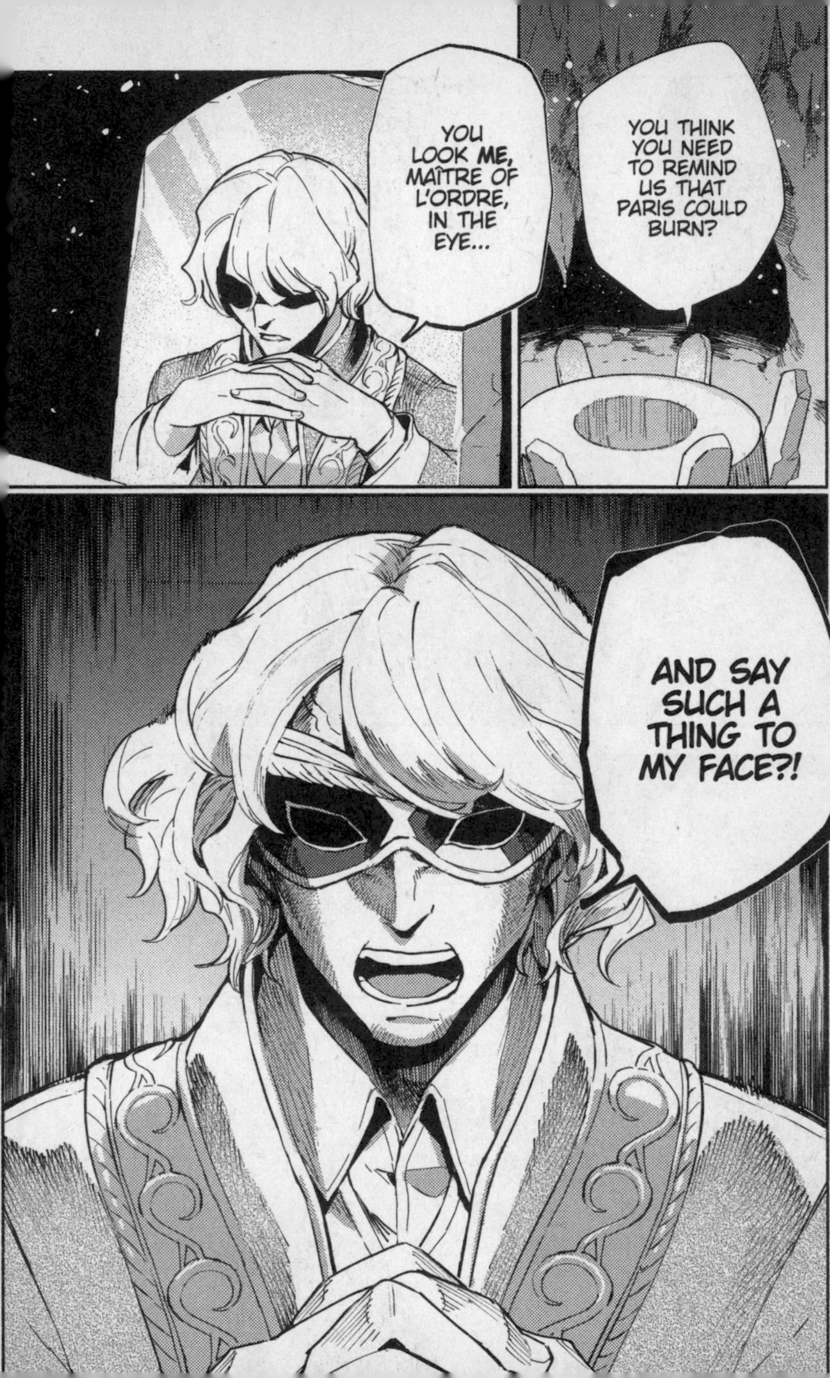
YOU THINK YOU NEED TO REMIND US THAT PARIS COULD BURN?
YOU LOOK ME, MAÎTRE OF L'ORDRE, IN THE EYE...
AND SAY SUCH A THING TO MY FACE?!

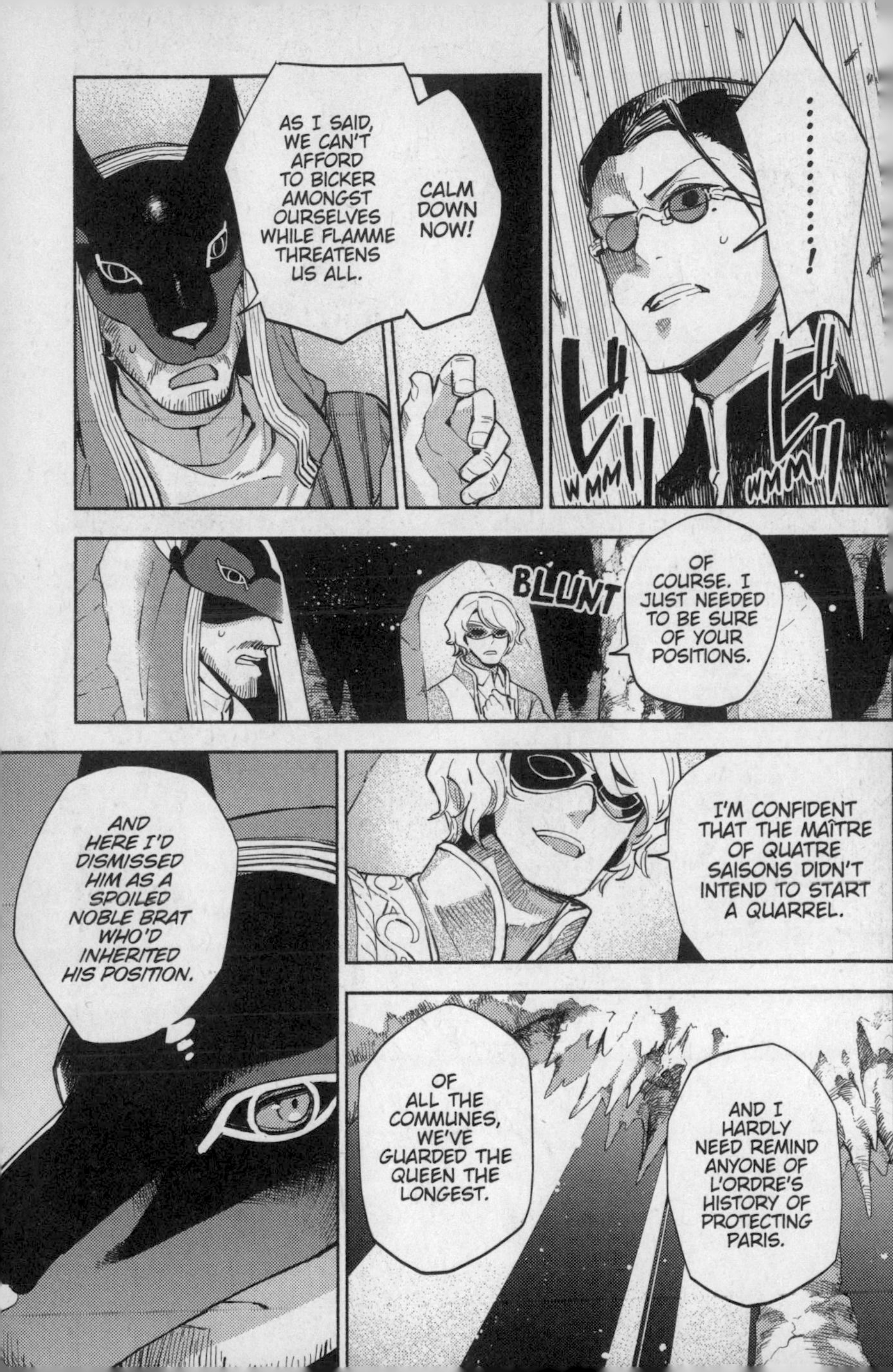
......!
ビビ WMM
ビビ WMM
CALM DOWN NOW!
AS I SAID, WE CAN'T AFFORD TO BICKER AMONGST OURSELVES WHILE FLAMME THREATENS US ALL.
BLUNT
OF COURSE. I JUST NEEDED TO BE SURE OF YOUR POSITIONS.
I'M CONFIDENT THAT THE MAÎTRE OF QUATRE SAISONS DIDN'T INTEND TO START A QUARREL.
AND I HARDLY NEED REMIND ANYONE OF L'ORDRE'S HISTORY OF PROTECTING PARIS.
OF ALL THE COMMUNES, WE'VE GUARDED THE QUEEN THE LONGEST.
AND HERE I'D DISMISSED HIM AS A SPOILED NOBLE BRAT WHO'D INHERITED HIS POSITION.

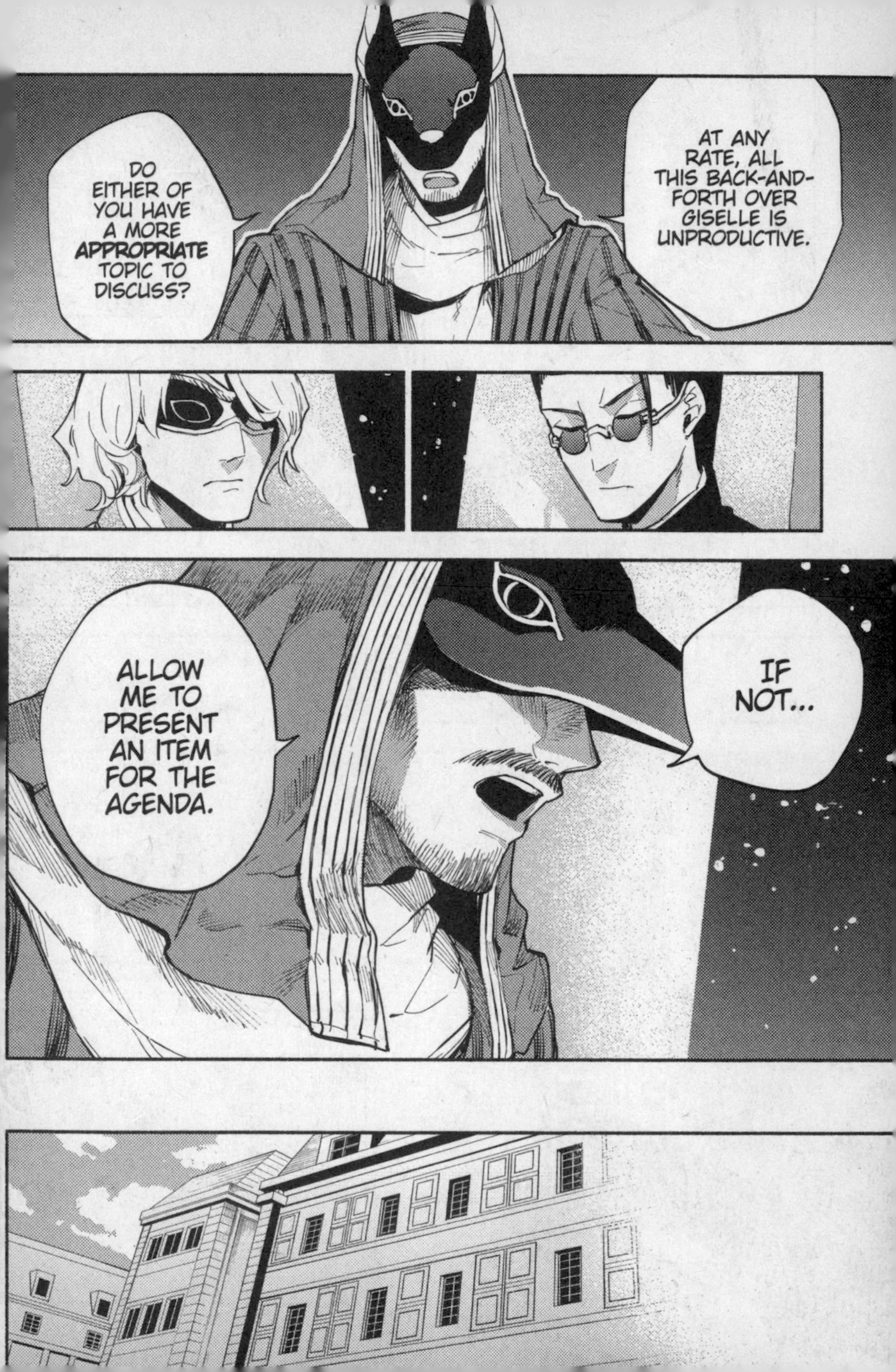
AT ANY RATE, ALL THIS BACK-AND-FORTH OVER GISELLE IS UNPRODUCTIVE.
DO EITHER OF YOU HAVE A MORE **APPROPRIATE** TOPIC TO DISCUSS?
IF NOT...
ALLOW ME TO PRESENT AN ITEM FOR THE AGENDA.

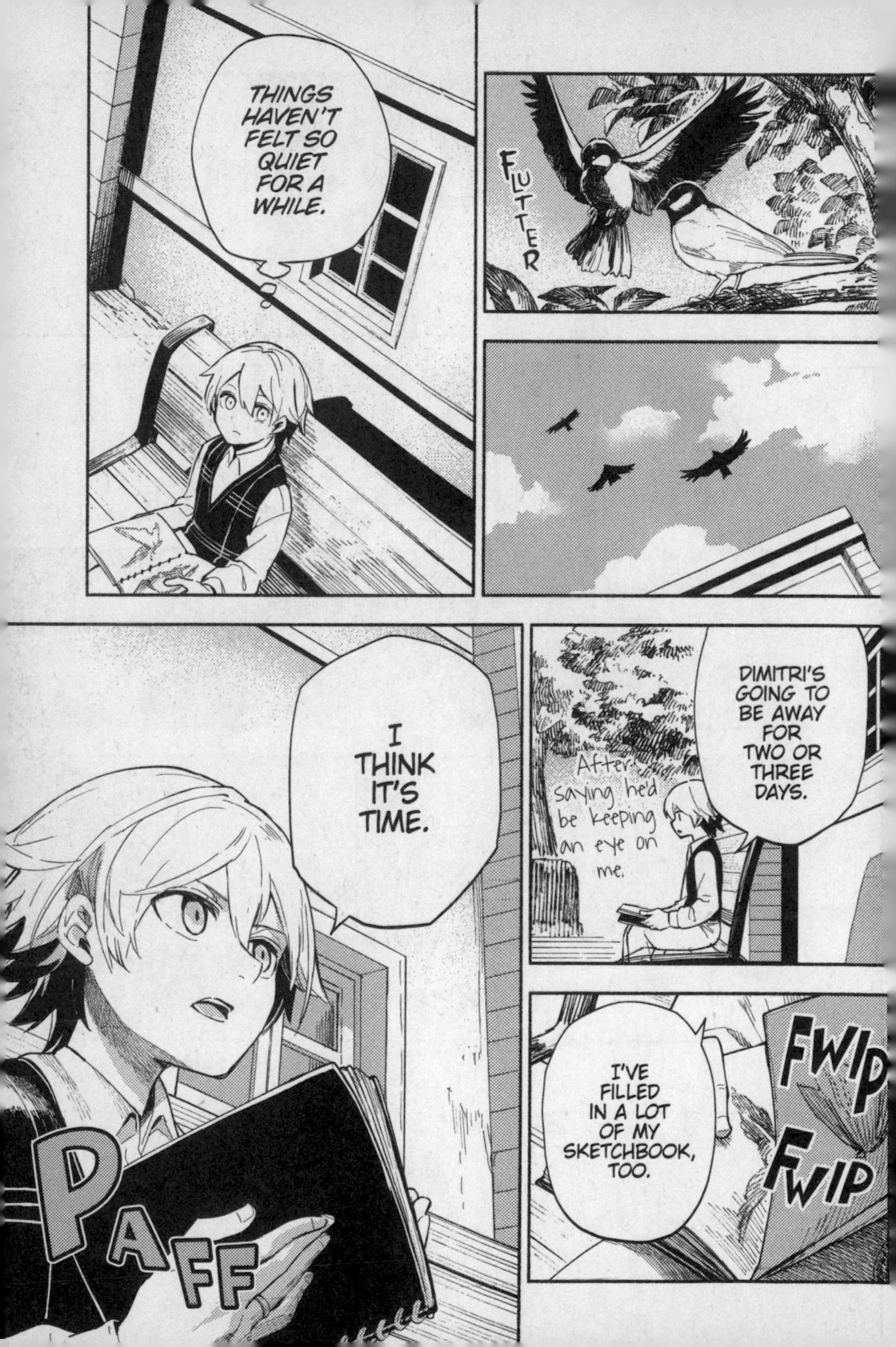
FLUTTER
THINGS HAVEN'T FELT SO QUIET FOR A WHILE.
DIMITRI'S GOING TO BE AWAY FOR TWO OR THREE DAYS.
After saying he'd be keeping an eye on me.
FWIP FWIP
I'VE FILLED IN A LOT OF MY SKETCHBOOK, TOO.
I THINK IT'S TIME.
PAFF

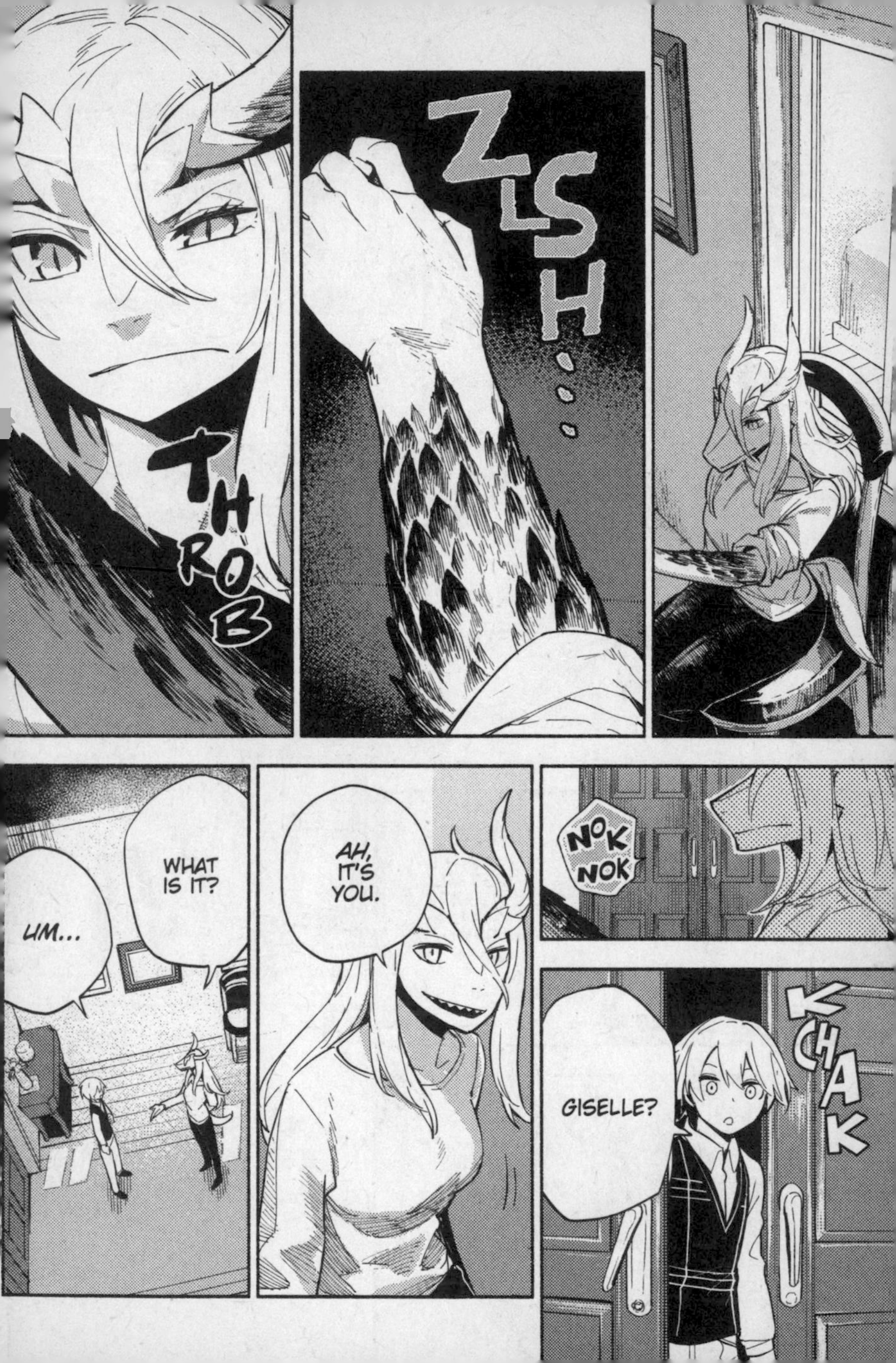
ZLSH...
THROB
NOK NOK
KCHAK
GISELLE?
AH, IT'S YOU.
WHAT IS IT?
UM...

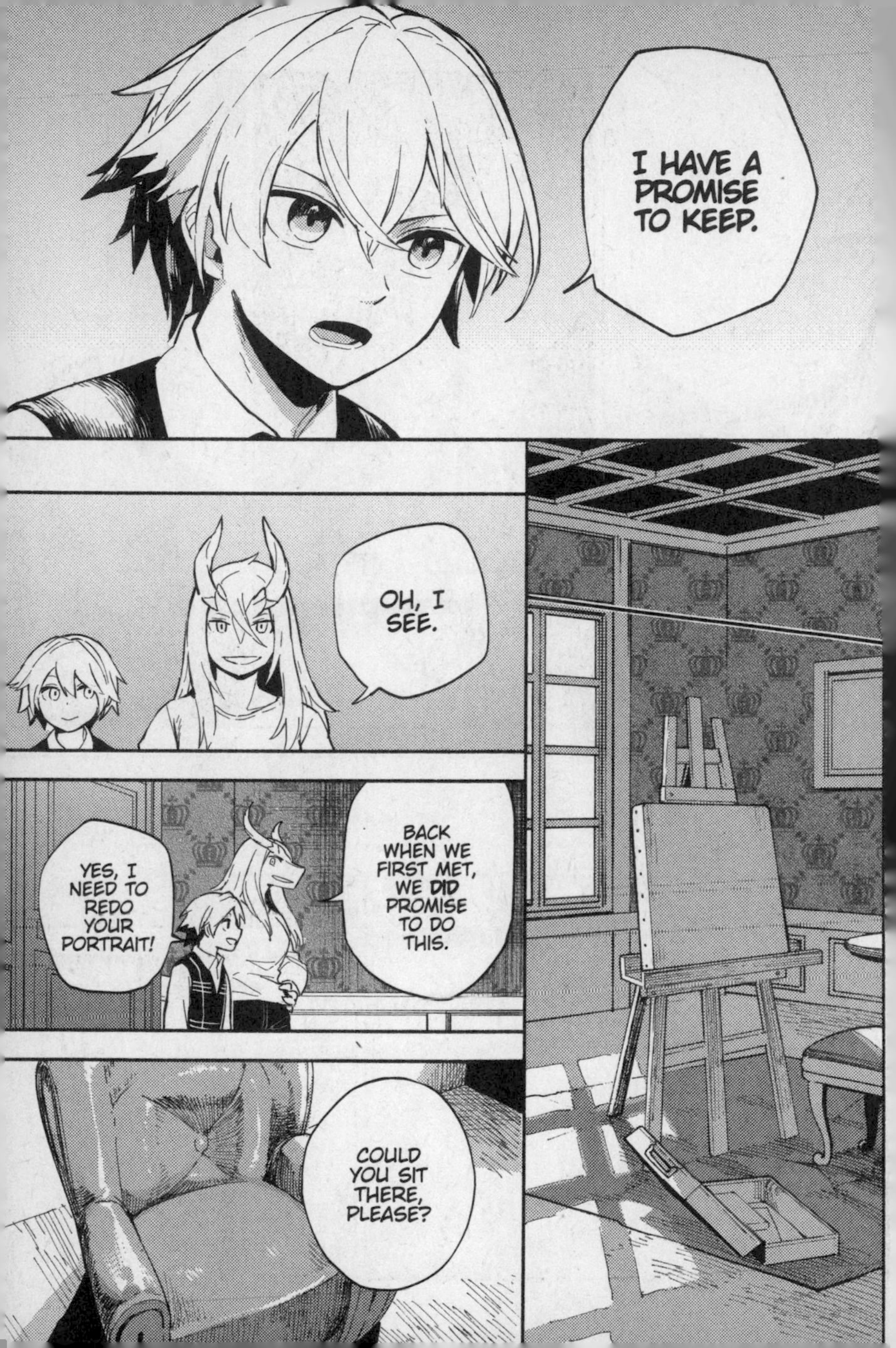
I HAVE A PROMISE TO KEEP.
OH, I SEE.
BACK WHEN WE FIRST MET, WE **DID** PROMISE TO DO THIS.
YES, I NEED TO REDO YOUR PORTRAIT!
COULD YOU SIT THERE, PLEASE?

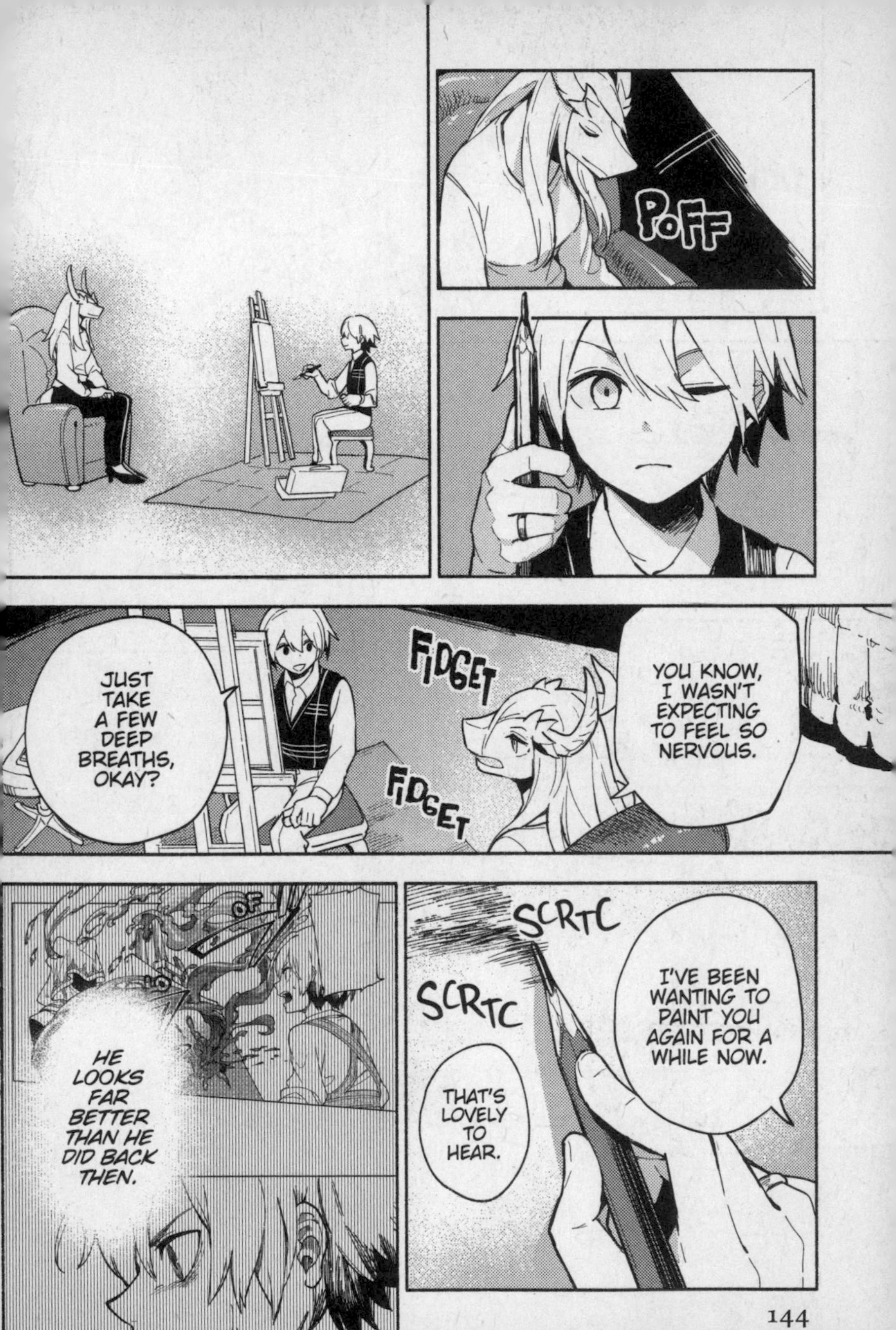
POFF
YOU KNOW, I WASN'T EXPECTING TO FEEL SO NERVOUS.
FIDGET
FIDGET
JUST TAKE A FEW DEEP BREATHS, OKAY?
SCRTC
I'VE BEEN WANTING TO PAINT YOU AGAIN FOR A WHILE NOW.
SCRTC
THAT'S LOVELY TO HEAR.
HE LOOKS FAR BETTER THAN HE DID BACK THEN.

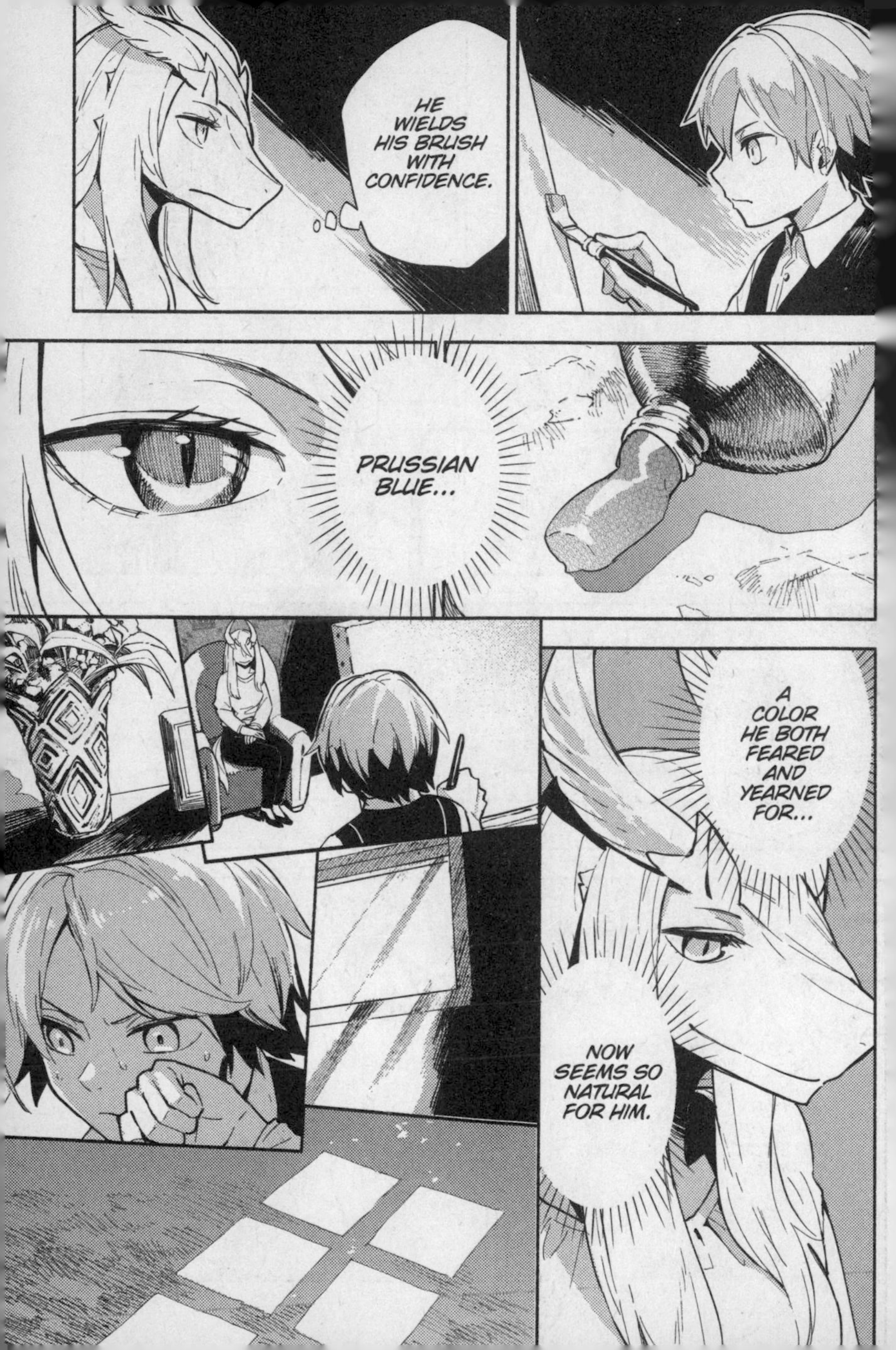
HE WIELDS HIS BRUSH WITH CONFIDENCE.
PRUSSIAN BLUE...
A COLOR HE BOTH FEARED AND YEARNED FOR...
NOW SEEMS SO NATURAL FOR HIM.

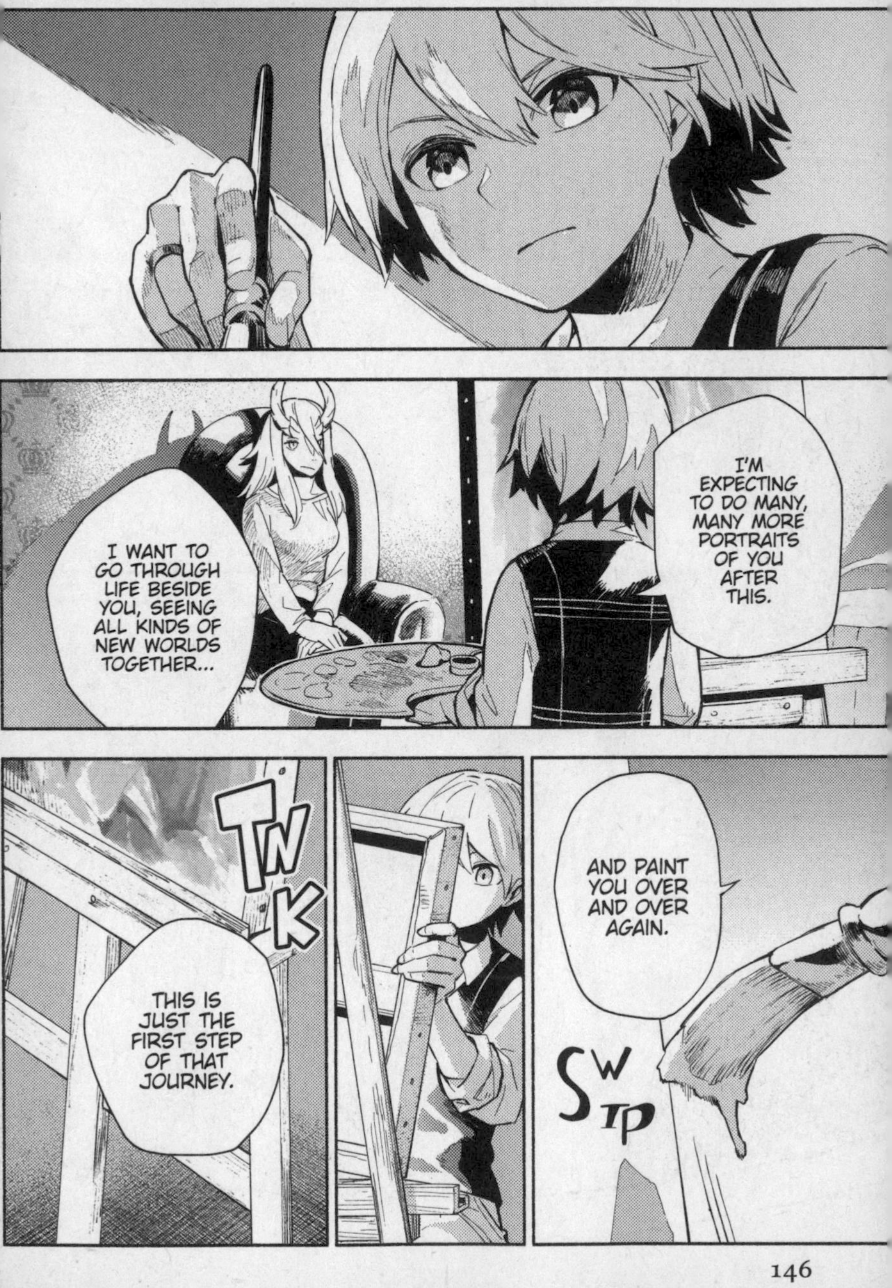
I'M EXPECTING TO DO MANY, MANY MORE PORTRAITS OF YOU AFTER THIS.
I WANT TO GO THROUGH LIFE BESIDE YOU, SEEING ALL KINDS OF NEW WORLDS TOGETHER...
AND PAINT YOU OVER AND OVER AGAIN.
SWTP
TNK
THIS IS JUST THE FIRST STEP OF THAT JOURNEY.

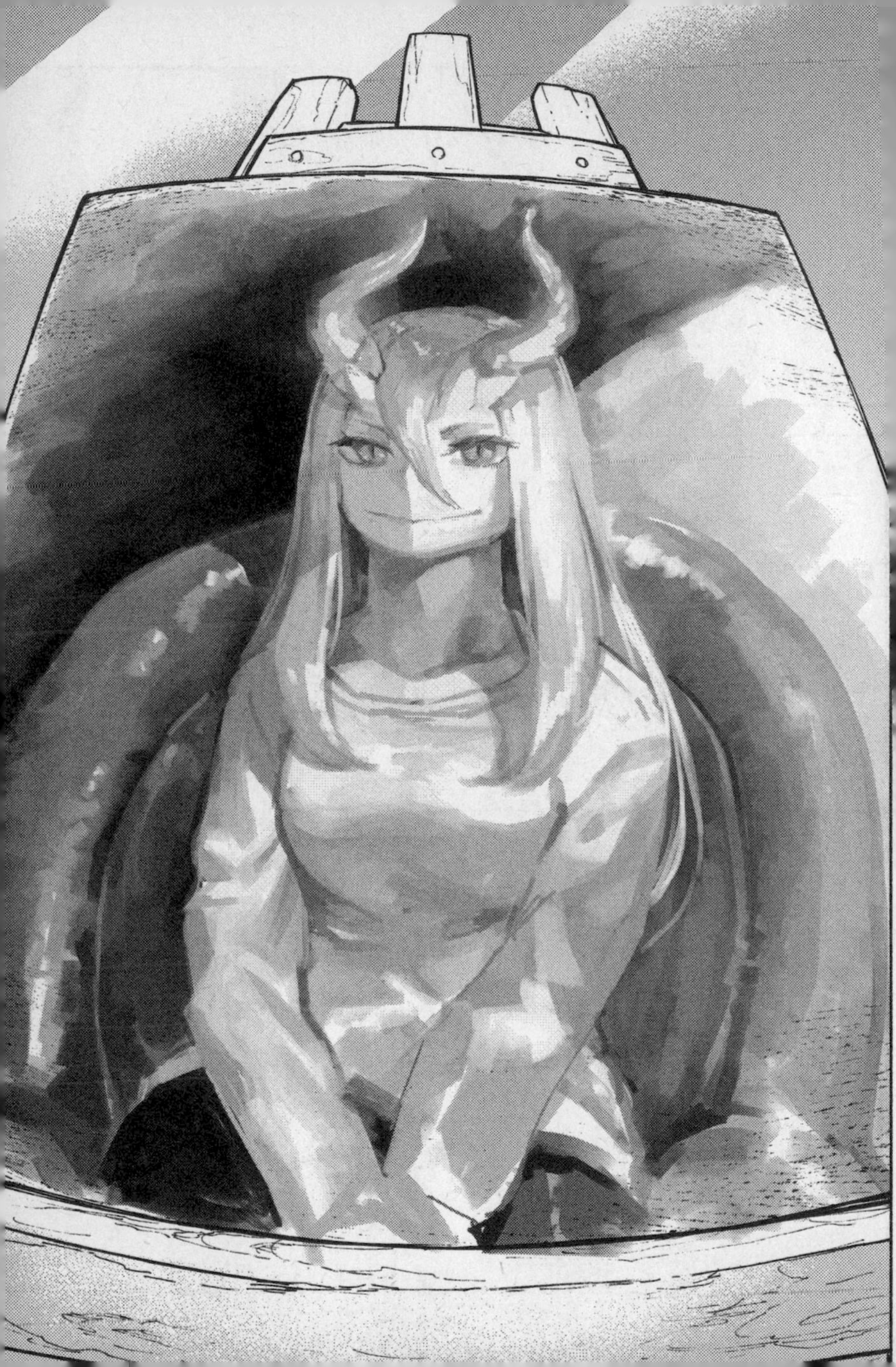

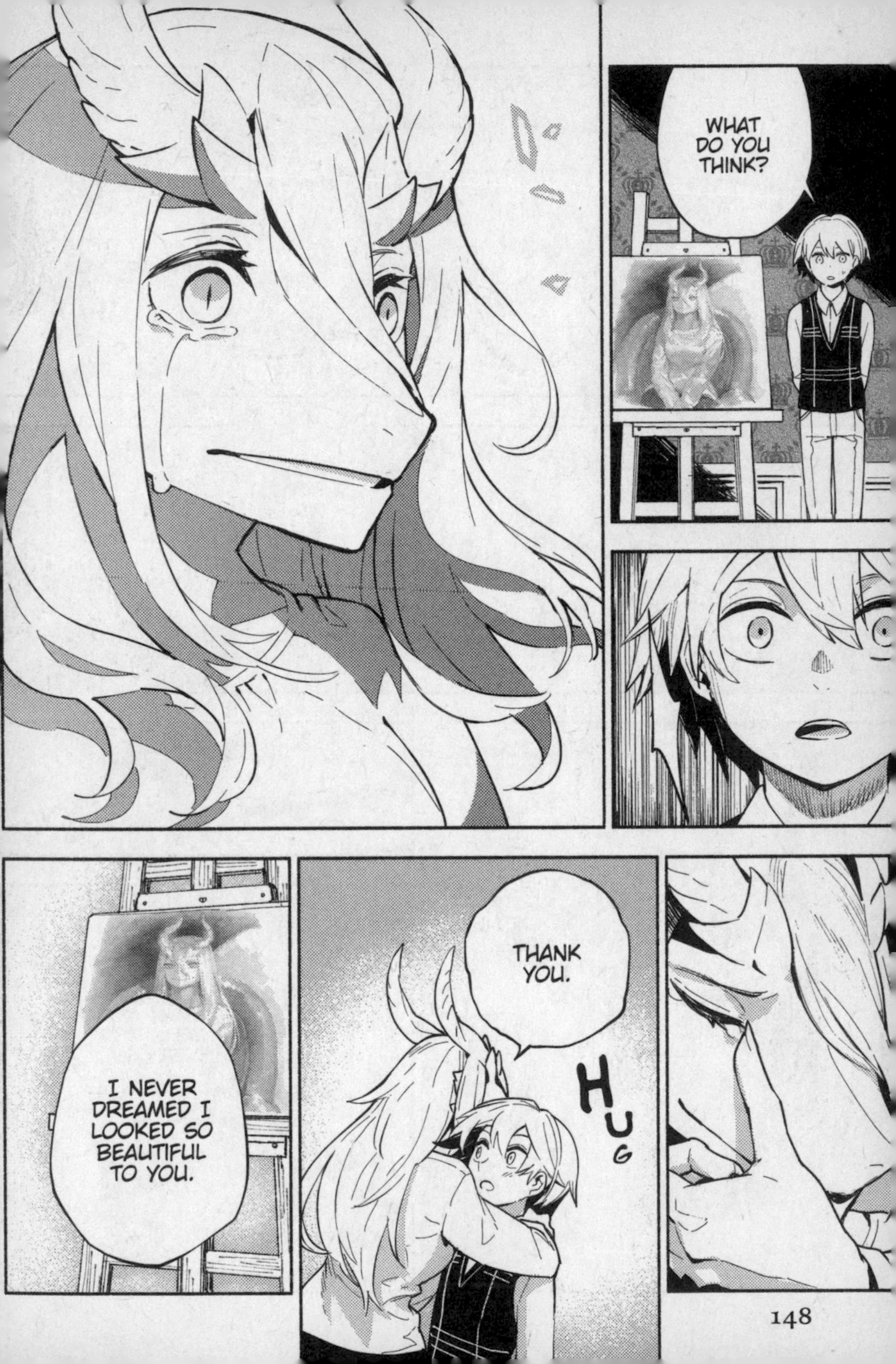
WHAT DO YOU THINK?
THANK YOU.
HUG
I NEVER DREAMED I LOOKED SO BEAUTIFUL TO YOU.

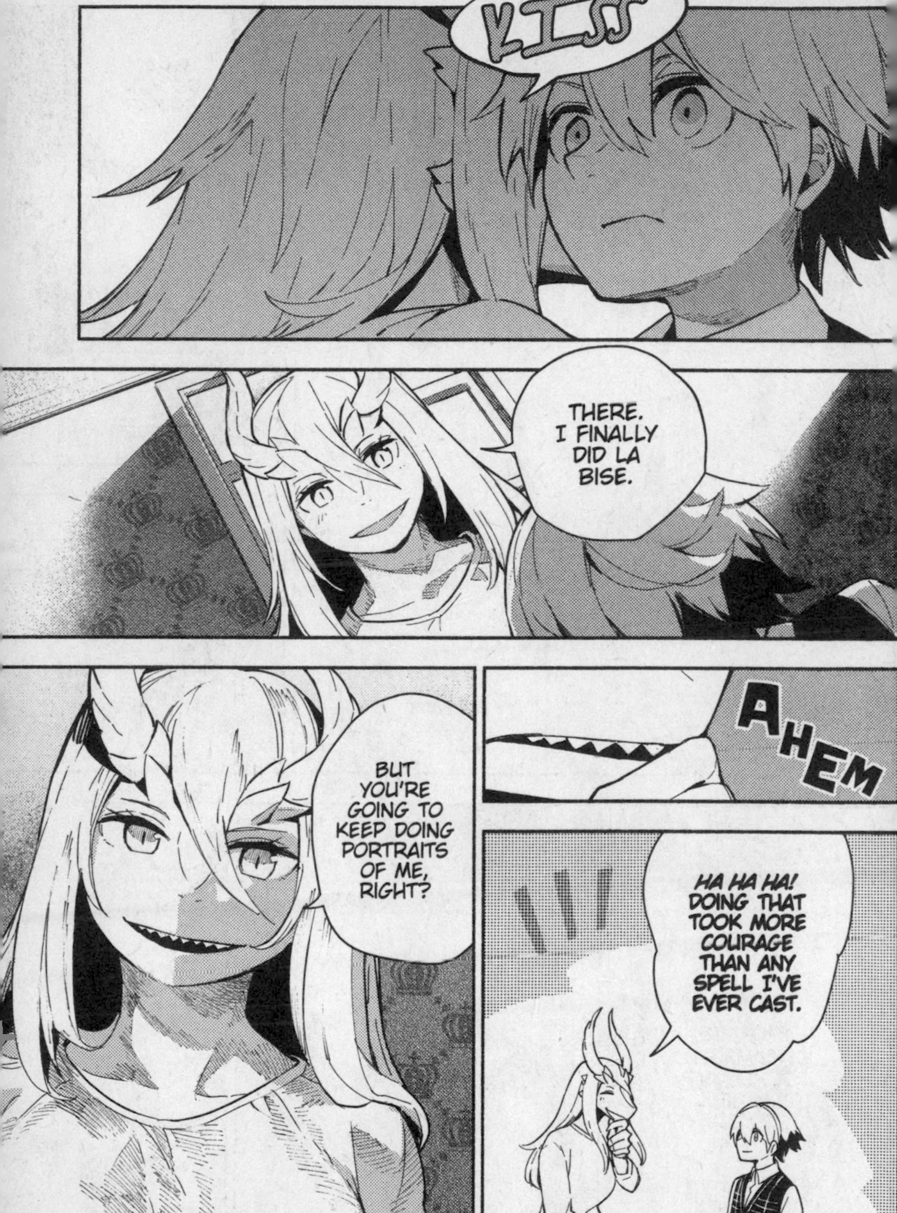
KISS
THERE. I FINALLY DID LA BISE.
AHEM
HA HA HA! DOING THAT TOOK MORE COURAGE THAN ANY SPELL I'VE EVER CAST.
BUT YOU'RE GOING TO KEEP DOING PORTRAITS OF ME, RIGHT?

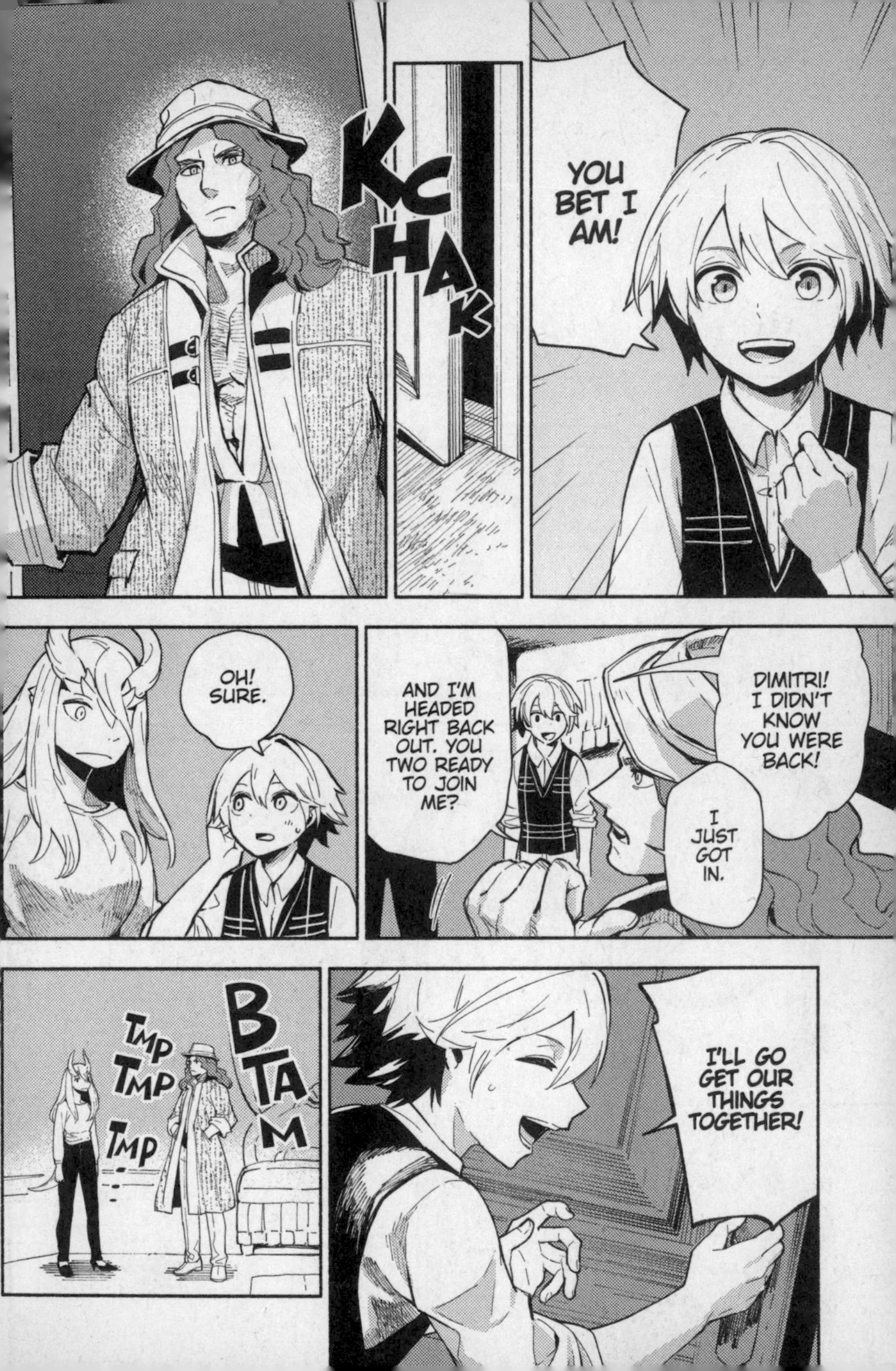
YOU BET I AM!
KCHAK
DIMITRI! I DIDN'T KNOW YOU WERE BACK!
I JUST GOT IN.
AND I'M HEADED RIGHT BACK OUT. YOU TWO READY TO JOIN ME?
OH! SURE.
I'LL GO GET OUR THINGS TOGETHER!
BTAM
TMP TMP
TMP

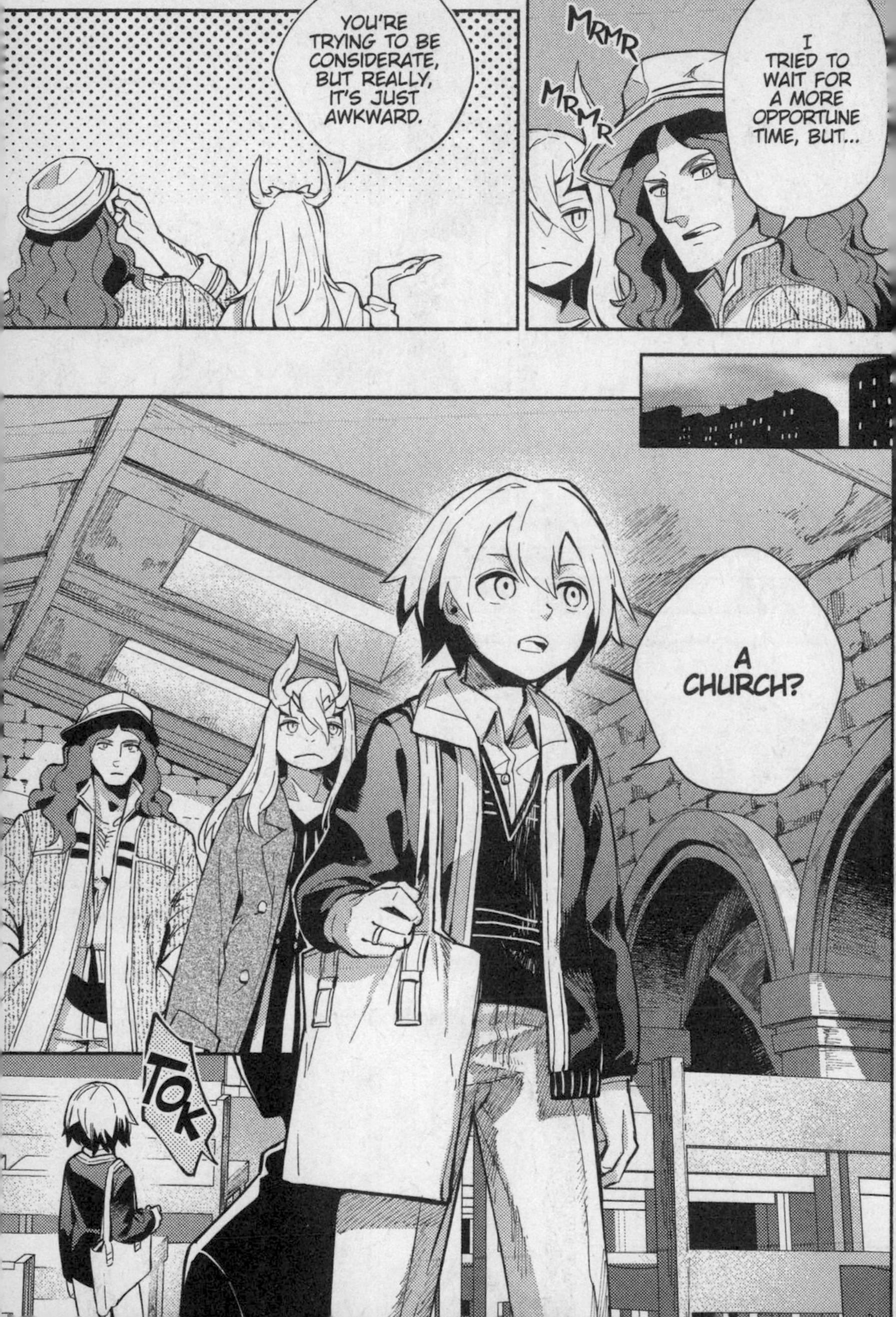
MRMR
MRMR
I TRIED TO WAIT FOR A MORE OPPORTUNE TIME, BUT...
YOU'RE TRYING TO BE CONSIDERATE, BUT REALLY, IT'S JUST AWKWARD.
A CHURCH?
TOK

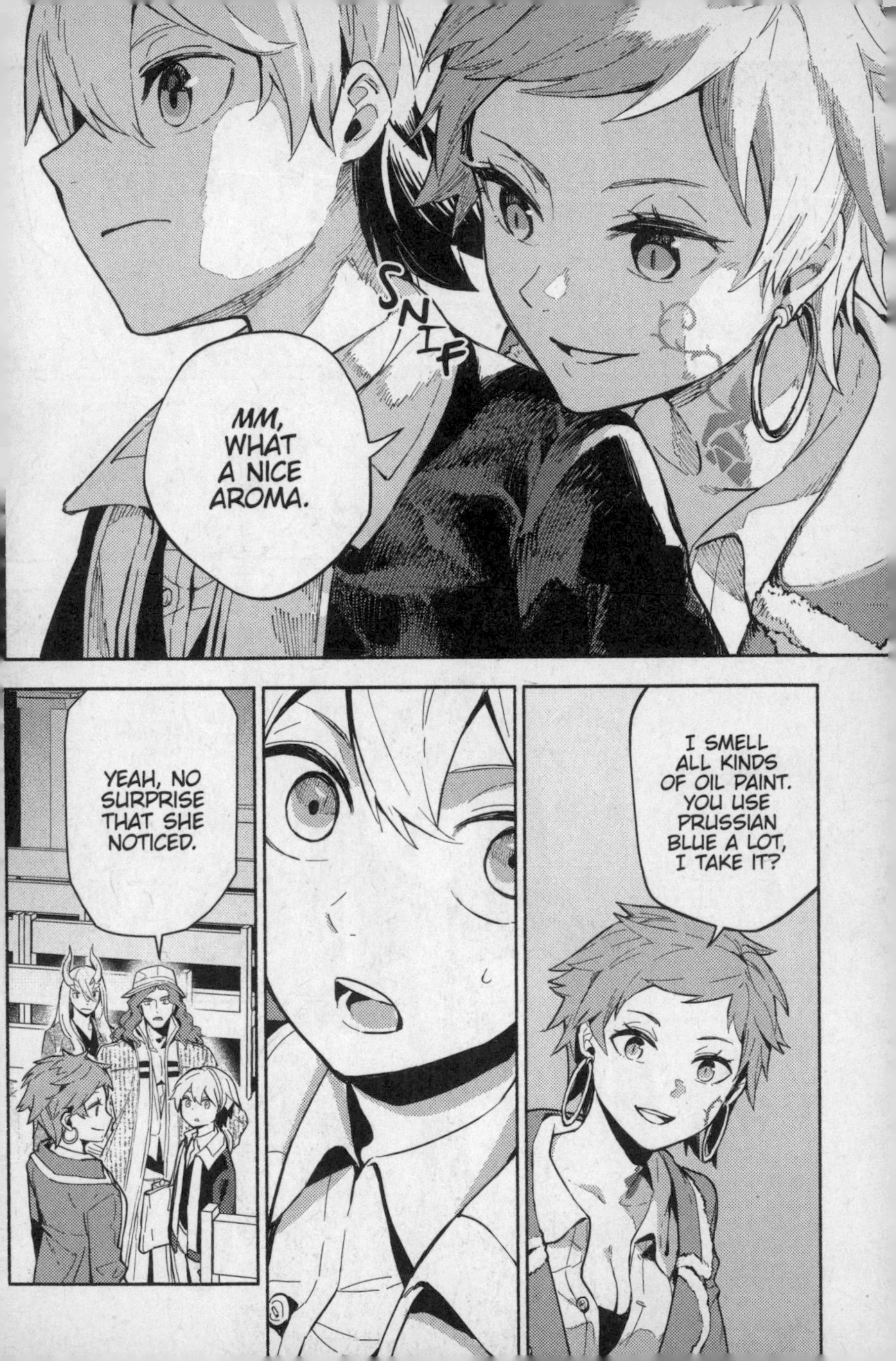
SNIF
MM, WHAT A NICE AROMA.
I SMELL ALL KINDS OF OIL PAINT. YOU USE PRUSSIAN BLUE A LOT, I TAKE IT?
YEAH, NO SURPRISE THAT SHE NOTICED.

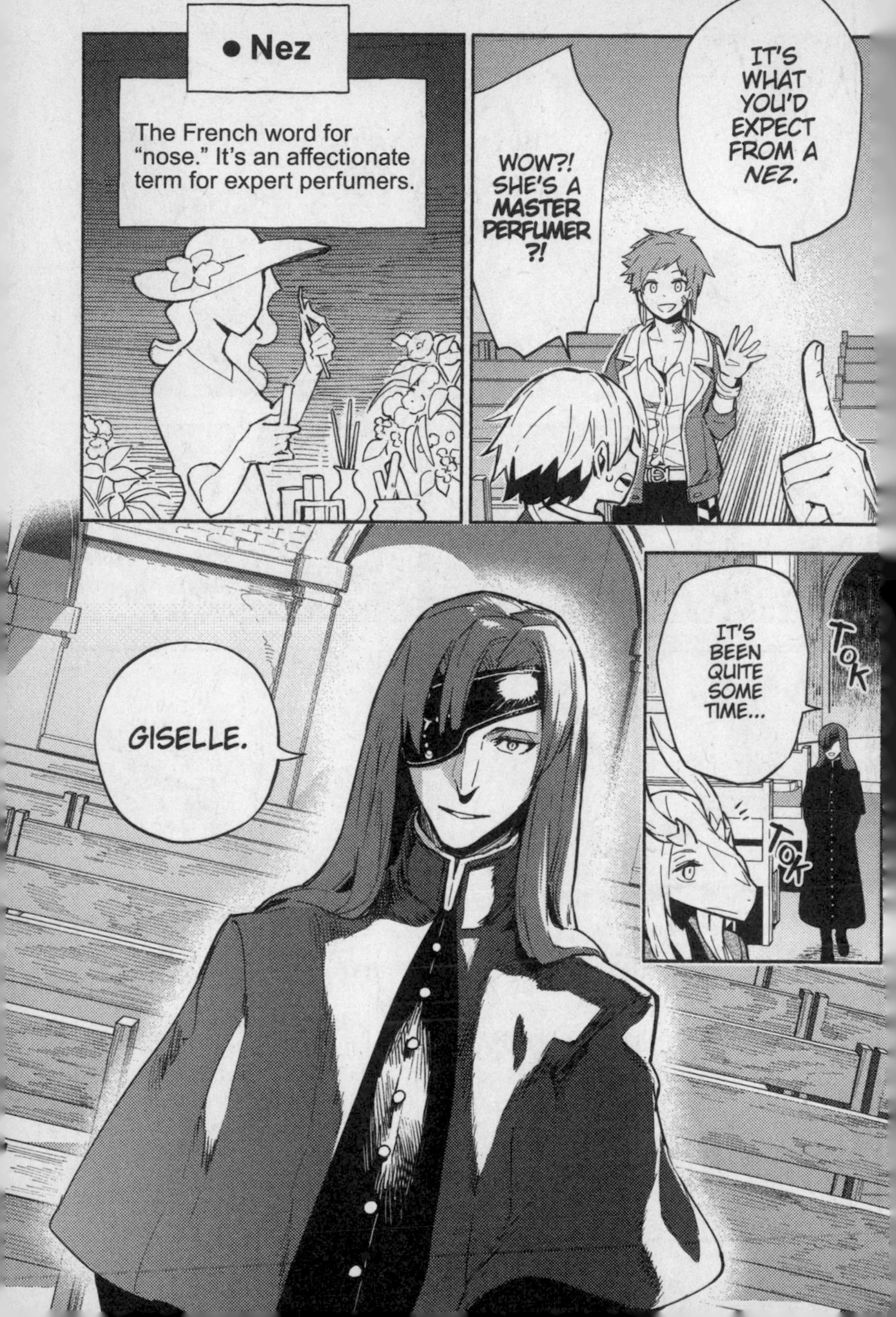
IT'S WHAT YOU'D EXPECT FROM A NEZ.
WOW?! SHE'S A MASTER PERFUMER?!
● Nez
The French word for "nose." It's an affectionate term for expert perfumers.
TOK
IT'S BEEN QUITE SOME TIME...
TOK
GISELLE.

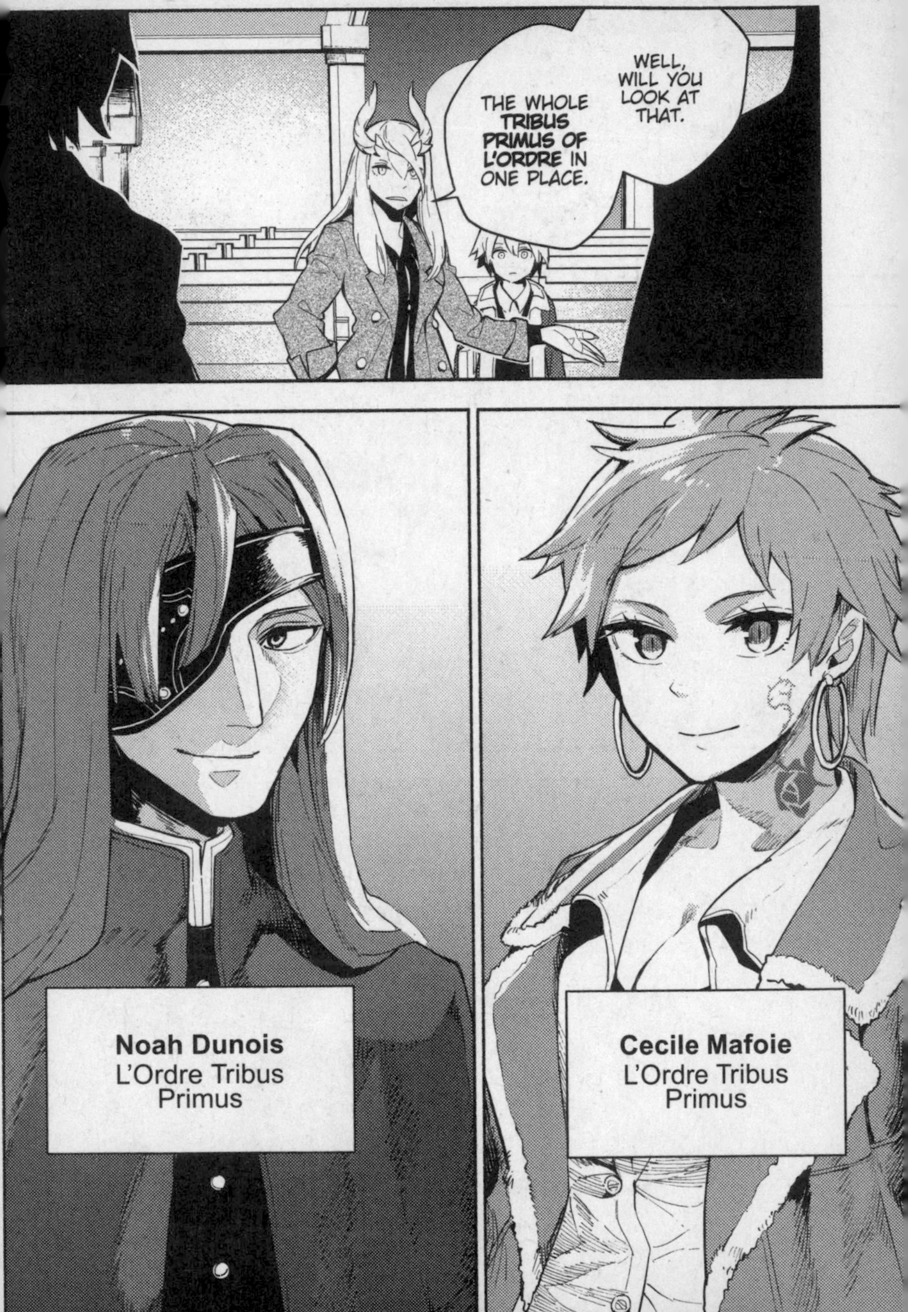
WELL, WILL YOU LOOK AT THAT.
THE WHOLE TRIBUS PRIMUS OF L'ORDRE IN ONE PLACE.
Cecile Mafoie
L'Ordre Tribus Primus
Noah Dunois
L'Ordre Tribus Primus

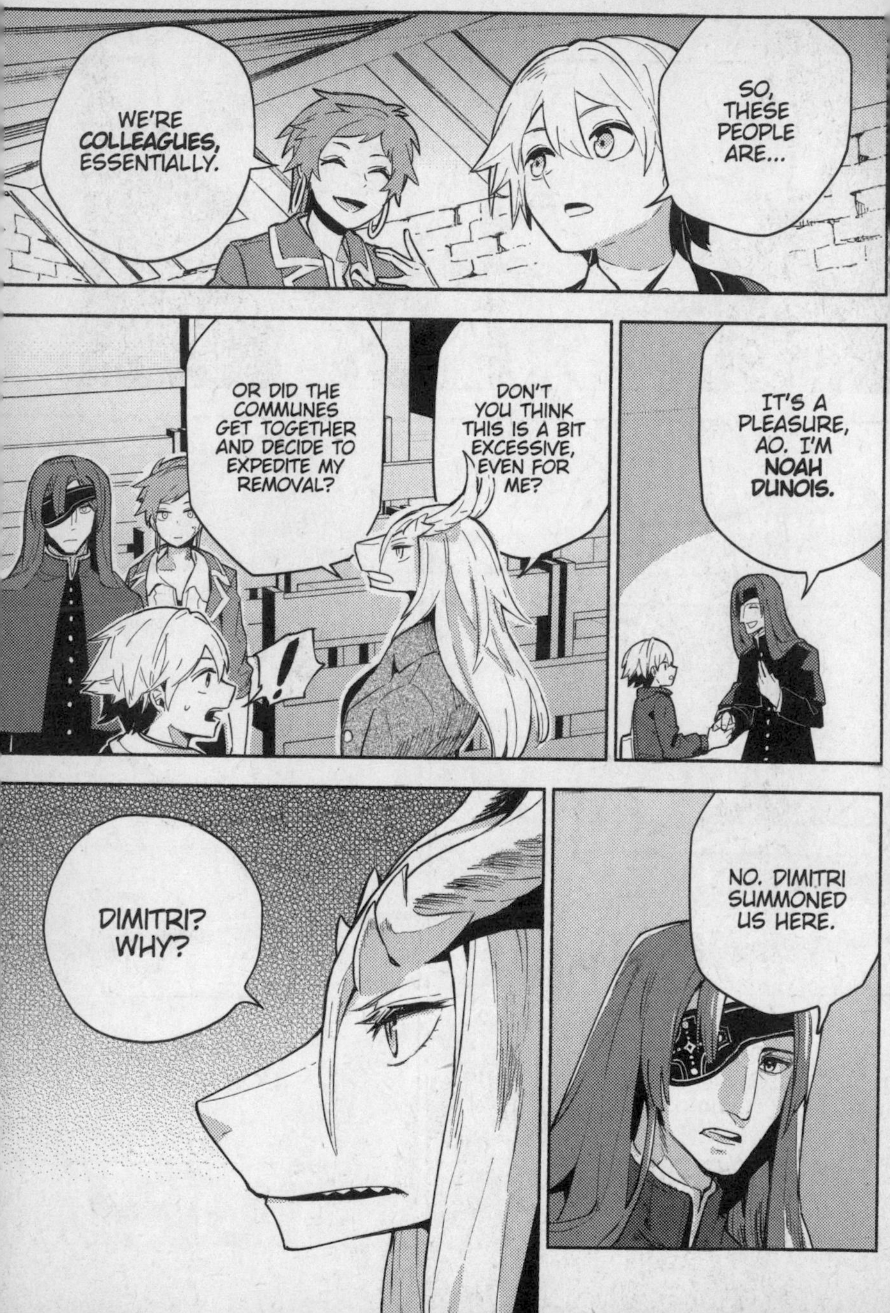
SO, THESE PEOPLE ARE...
WE'RE COLLEAGUES, ESSENTIALLY.
IT'S A PLEASURE, AO. I'M NOAH DUNOIS.
DON'T YOU THINK THIS IS A BIT EXCESSIVE, EVEN FOR ME?
OR DID THE COMMUNES GET TOGETHER AND DECIDE TO EXPEDITE MY REMOVAL?
NO. DIMITRI SUMMONED US HERE.
DIMITRI? WHY?

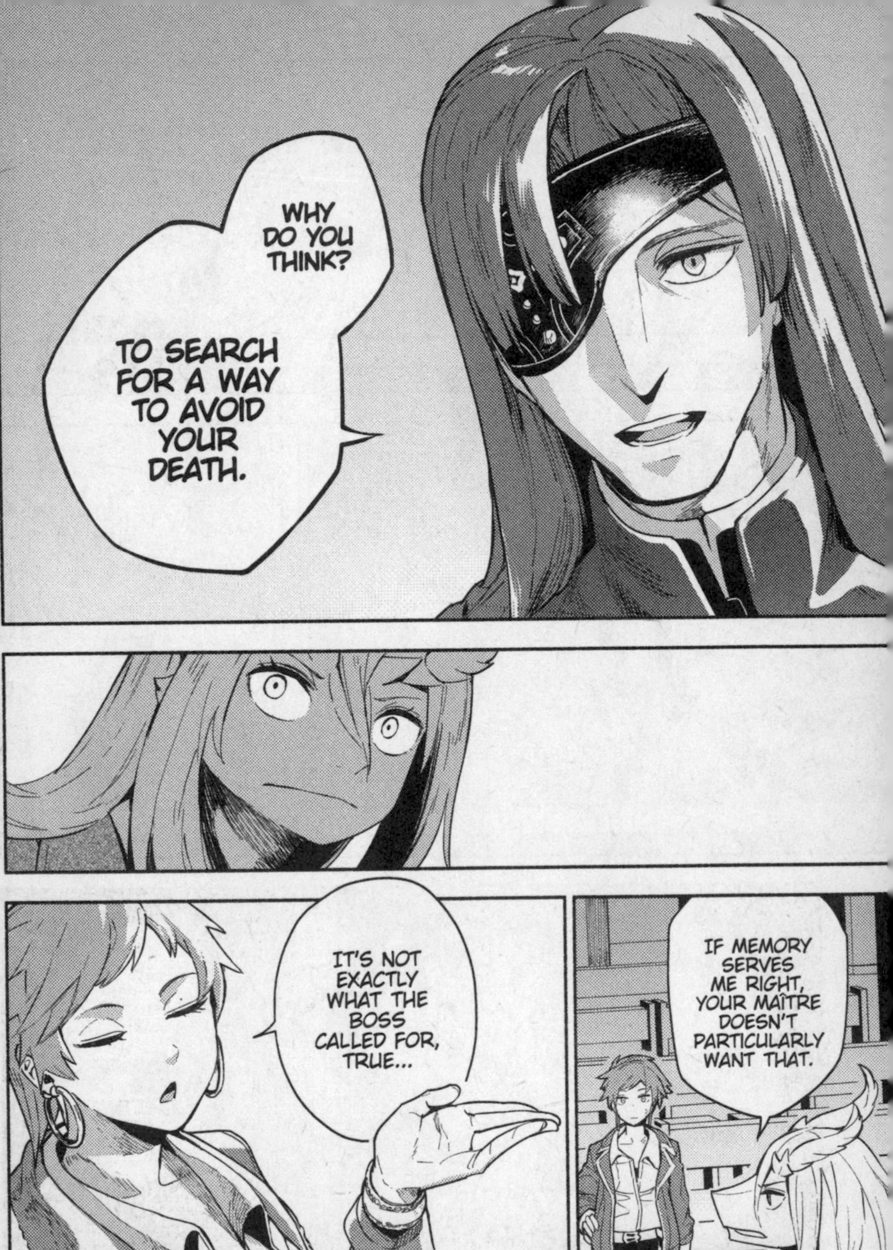
WHY DO YOU THINK?
TO SEARCH FOR A WAY TO AVOID YOUR DEATH.
IF MEMORY SERVES ME RIGHT, YOUR MAÎTRE DOESN'T PARTICULARLY WANT THAT.
IT'S NOT EXACTLY WHAT THE BOSS CALLED FOR, TRUE...

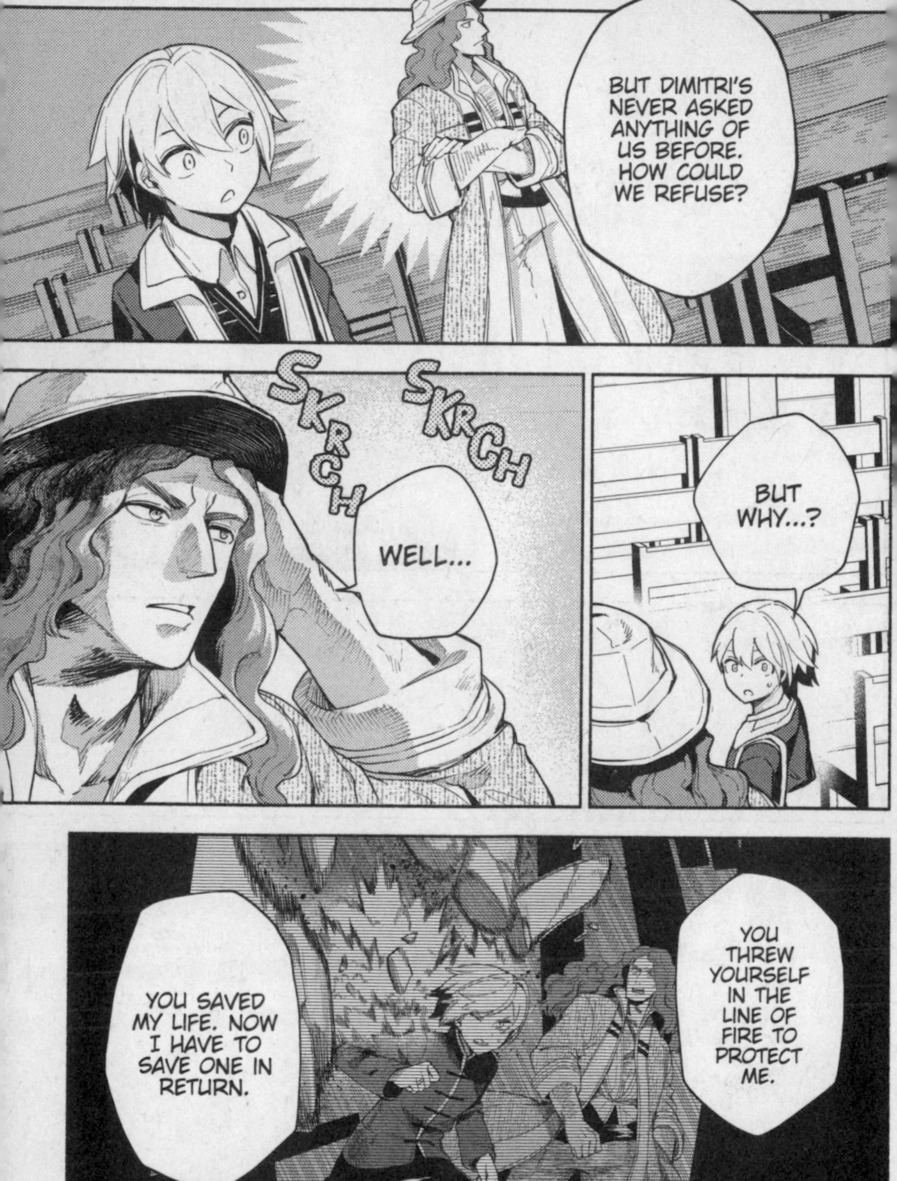
BUT DIMITRI'S NEVER ASKED ANYTHING OF US BEFORE. HOW COULD WE REFUSE?
BUT WHY...?
SKRCH
SKRCH
WELL...
YOU THREW YOURSELF IN THE LINE OF FIRE TO PROTECT ME.
YOU SAVED MY LIFE. NOW I HAVE TO SAVE ONE IN RETURN.

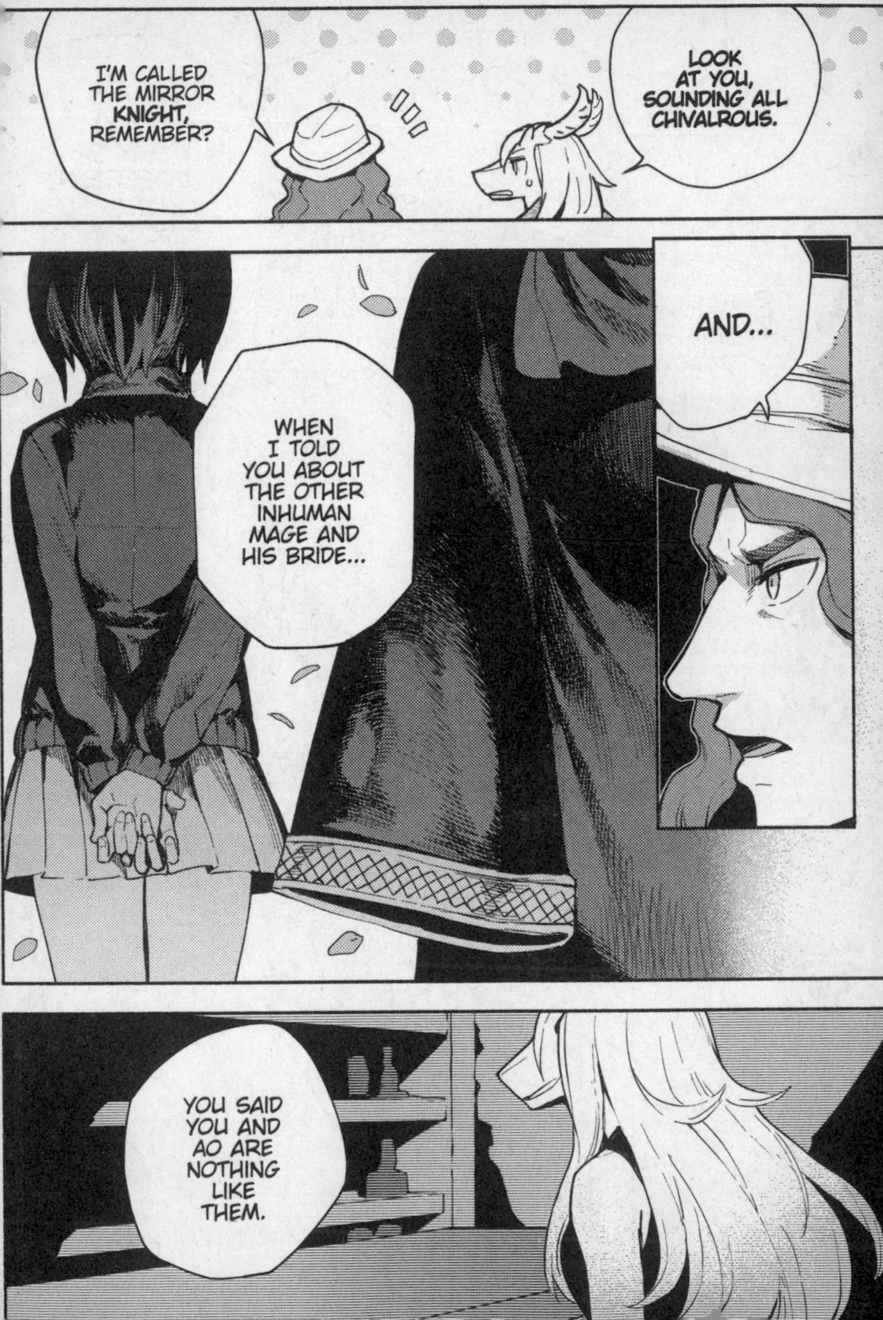
LOOK AT YOU, SOUNDING ALL CHIVALROUS.
I'M CALLED THE MIRROR KNIGHT, REMEMBER?
AND...
WHEN I TOLD YOU ABOUT THE OTHER INHUMAN MAGE AND HIS BRIDE...
YOU SAID YOU AND AO ARE NOTHING LIKE THEM.

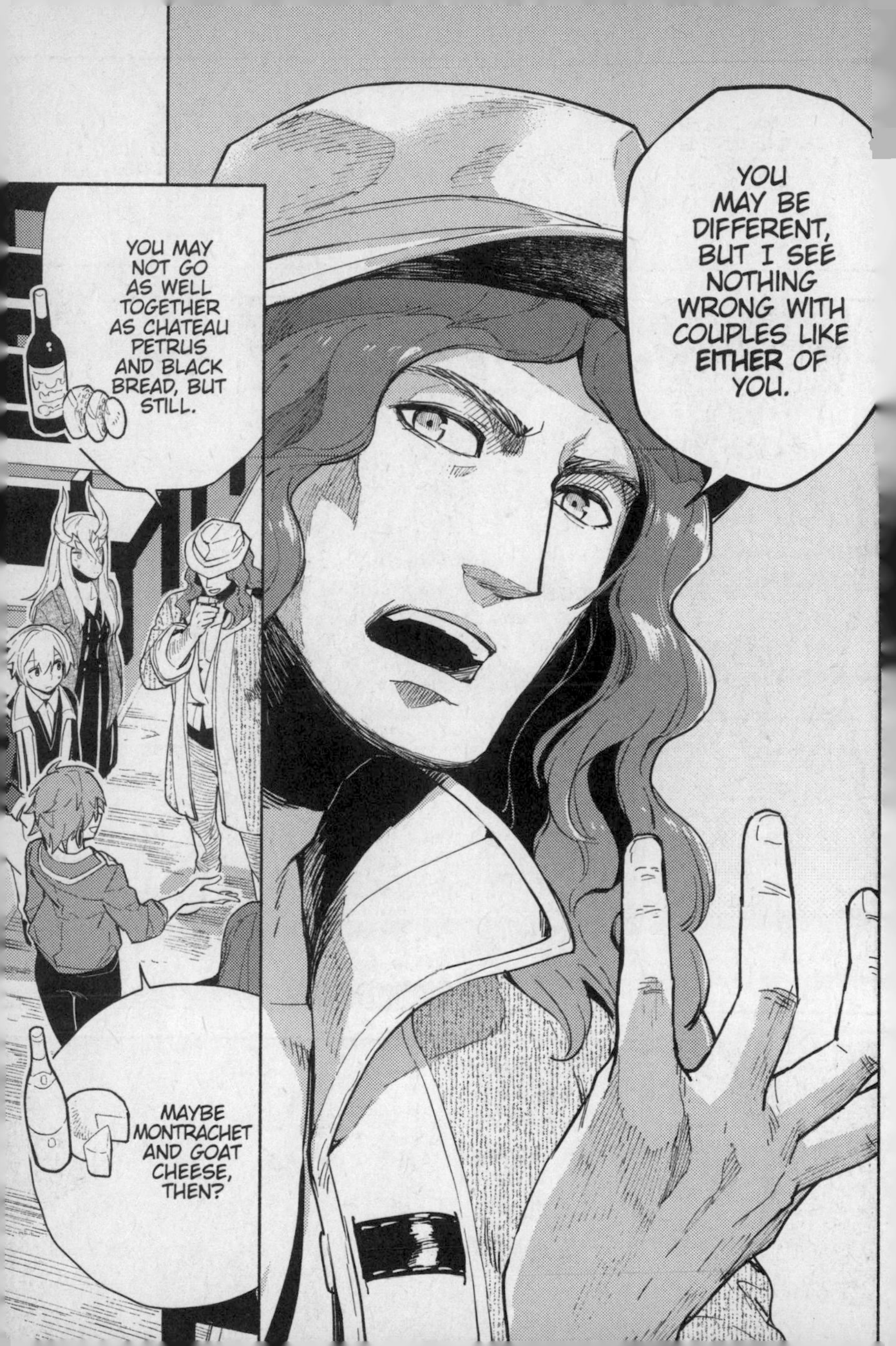
YOU MAY BE DIFFERENT, BUT I SEE NOTHING WRONG WITH COUPLES LIKE EITHER OF YOU.
YOU MAY NOT GO AS WELL TOGETHER AS CHATEAU PETRUS AND BLACK BREAD, BUT STILL.
MAYBE MONTRACHET AND GOAT CHEESE, THEN?

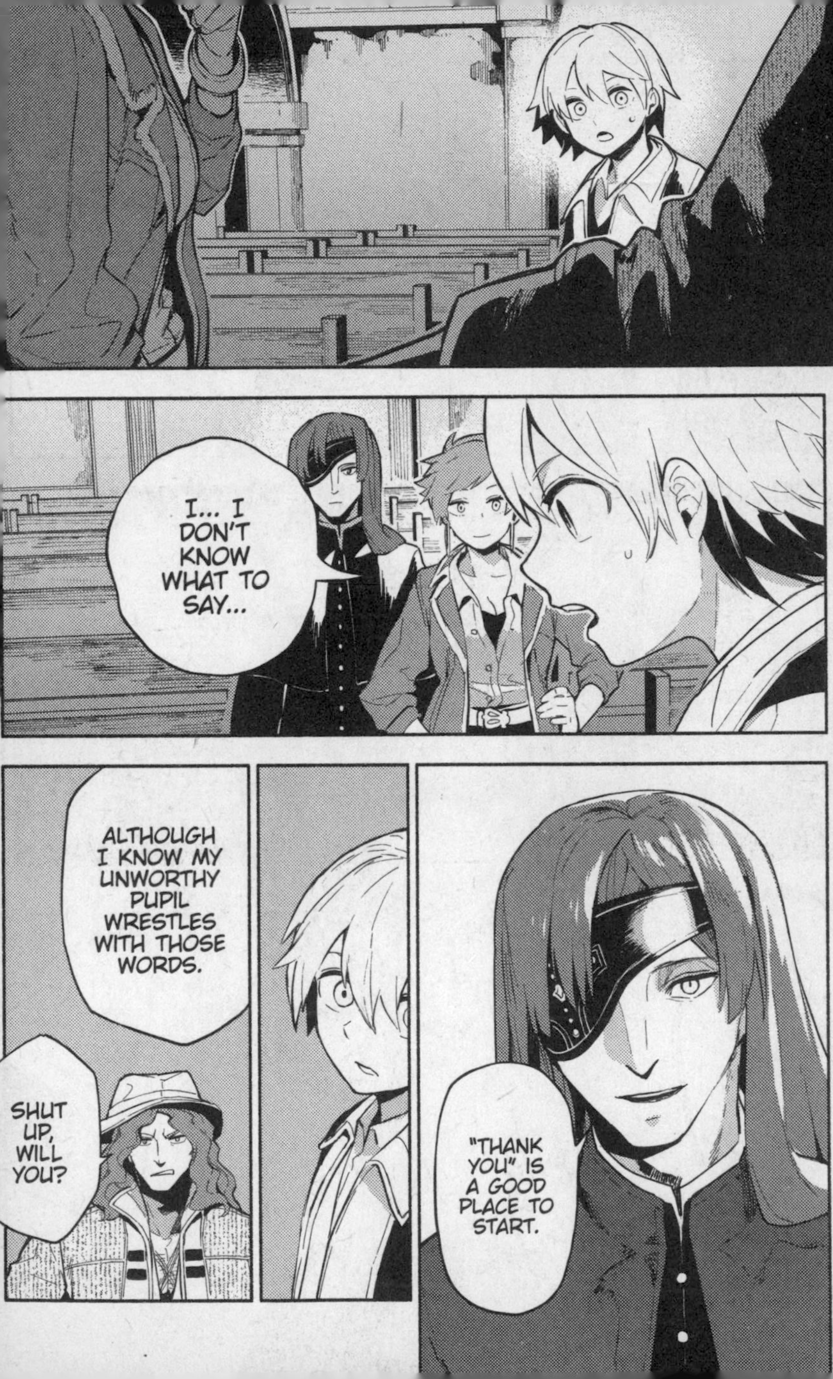
I... I DON'T KNOW WHAT TO SAY...
"THANK YOU" IS A GOOD PLACE TO START.
ALTHOUGH I KNOW MY UNWORTHY PUPIL WRESTLES WITH THOSE WORDS.
SHUT UP, WILL YOU?

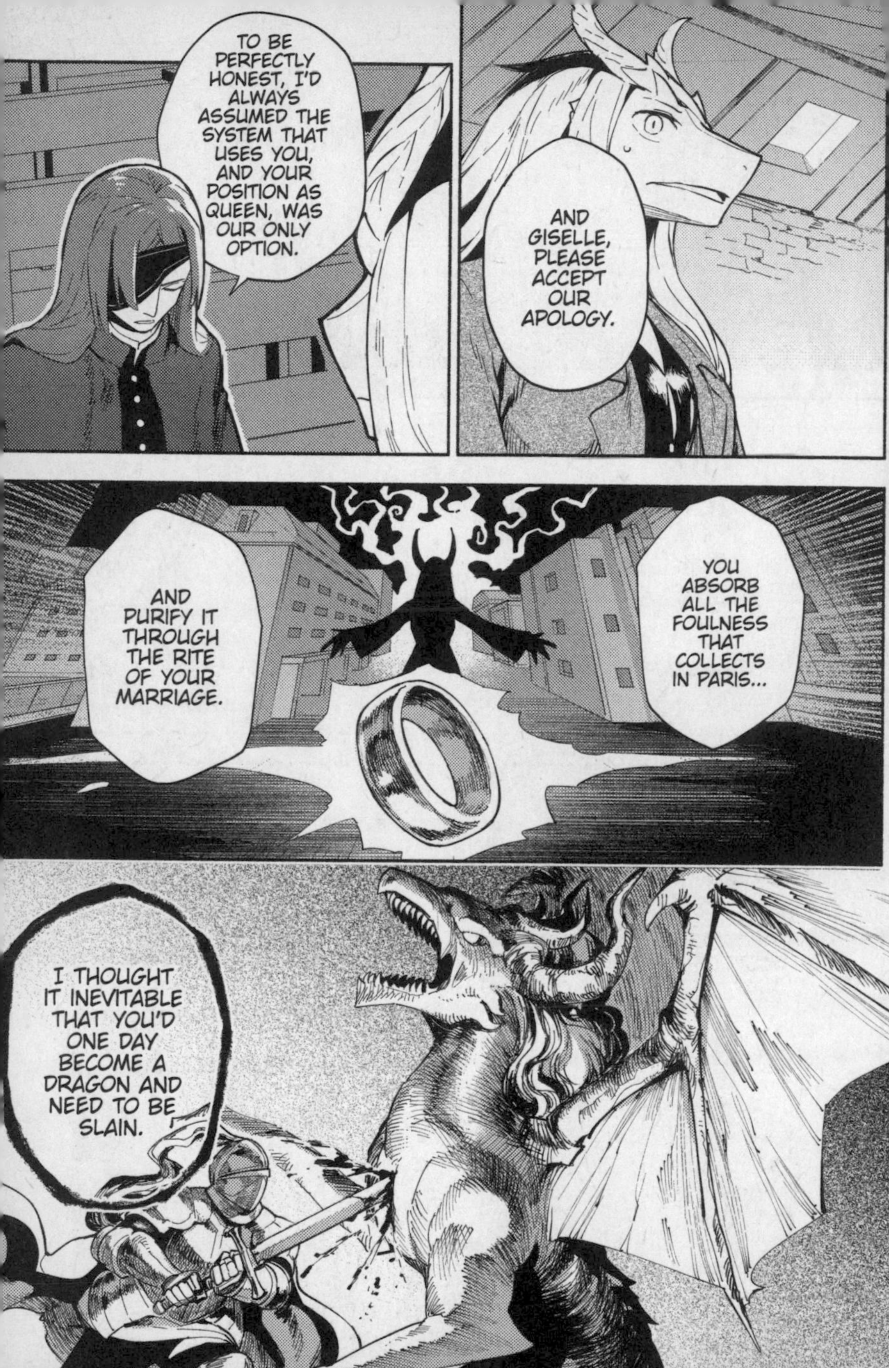
AND GISELLE, PLEASE ACCEPT OUR APOLOGY.
TO BE PERFECTLY HONEST, I'D ALWAYS ASSUMED THE SYSTEM THAT USES YOU, AND YOUR POSITION AS QUEEN, WAS OUR ONLY OPTION.
YOU ABSORB ALL THE FOULNESS THAT COLLECTS IN PARIS...
AND PURIFY IT THROUGH THE RITE OF YOUR MARRIAGE.
I THOUGHT IT INEVITABLE THAT YOU'D ONE DAY BECOME A DRAGON AND NEED TO BE SLAIN.

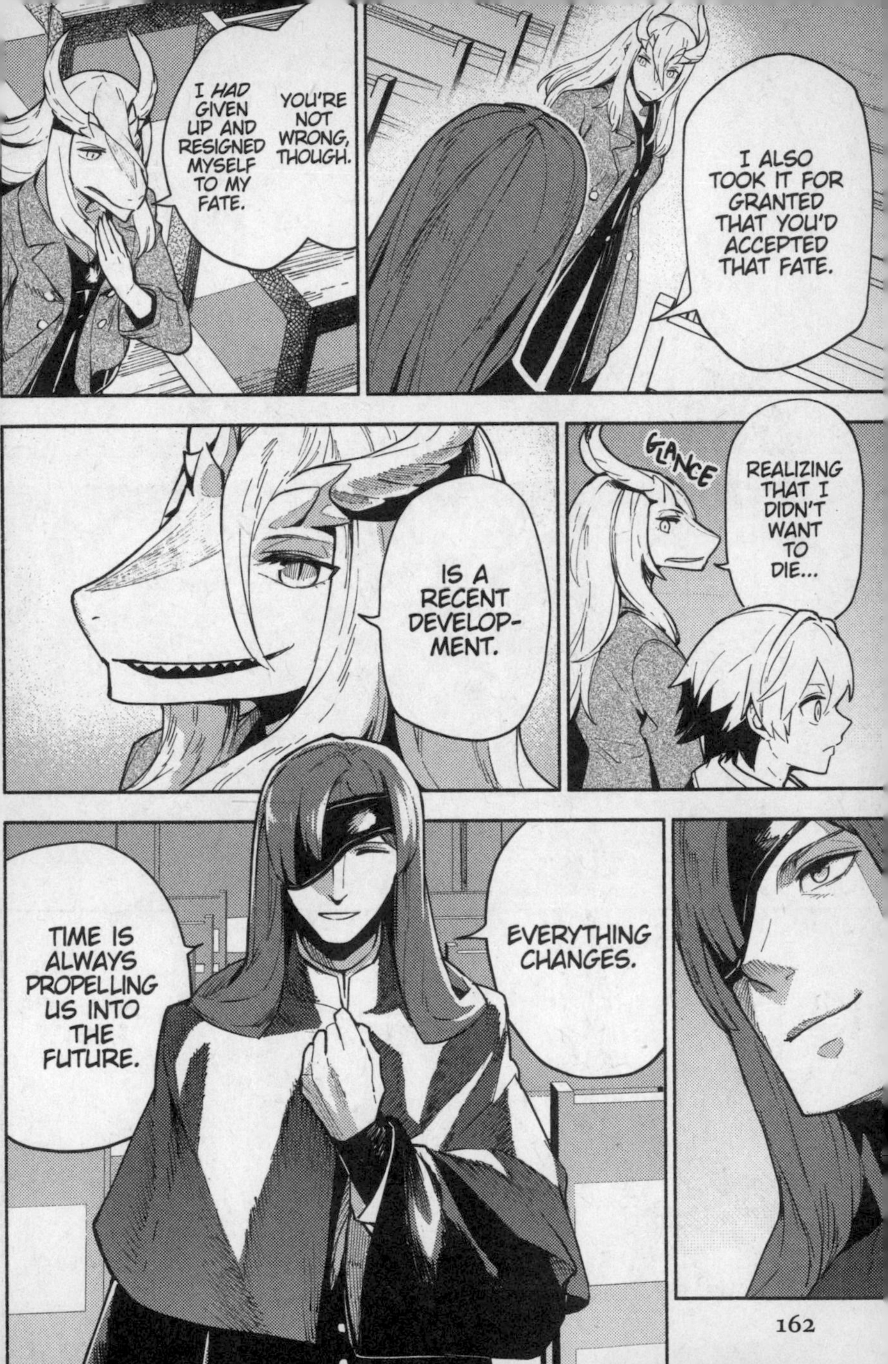
I ALSO TOOK IT FOR GRANTED THAT YOU'D ACCEPTED THAT FATE.
YOU'RE NOT WRONG, THOUGH.
I *HAD* GIVEN UP AND RESIGNED MYSELF TO MY FATE.
GLANCE
REALIZING THAT I DIDN'T WANT TO DIE...
IS A RECENT DEVELOPMENT.
EVERYTHING CHANGES.
TIME IS ALWAYS PROPELLING US INTO THE FUTURE.

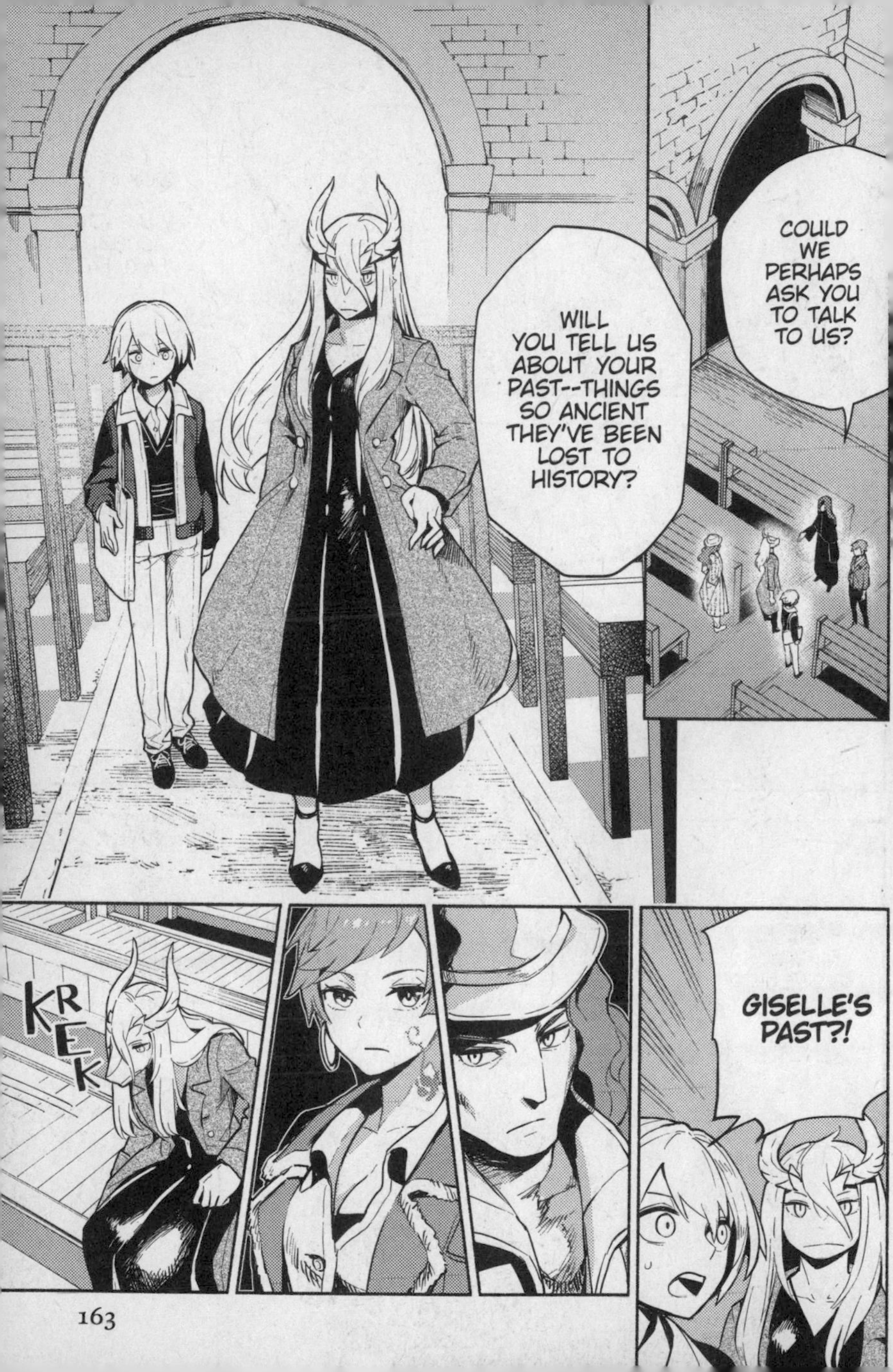
COULD WE PERHAPS ASK YOU TO TALK TO US?
WILL YOU TELL US ABOUT YOUR PAST--THINGS SO ANCIENT THEY'VE BEEN LOST TO HISTORY?
GISELLE'S PAST?!
KREK

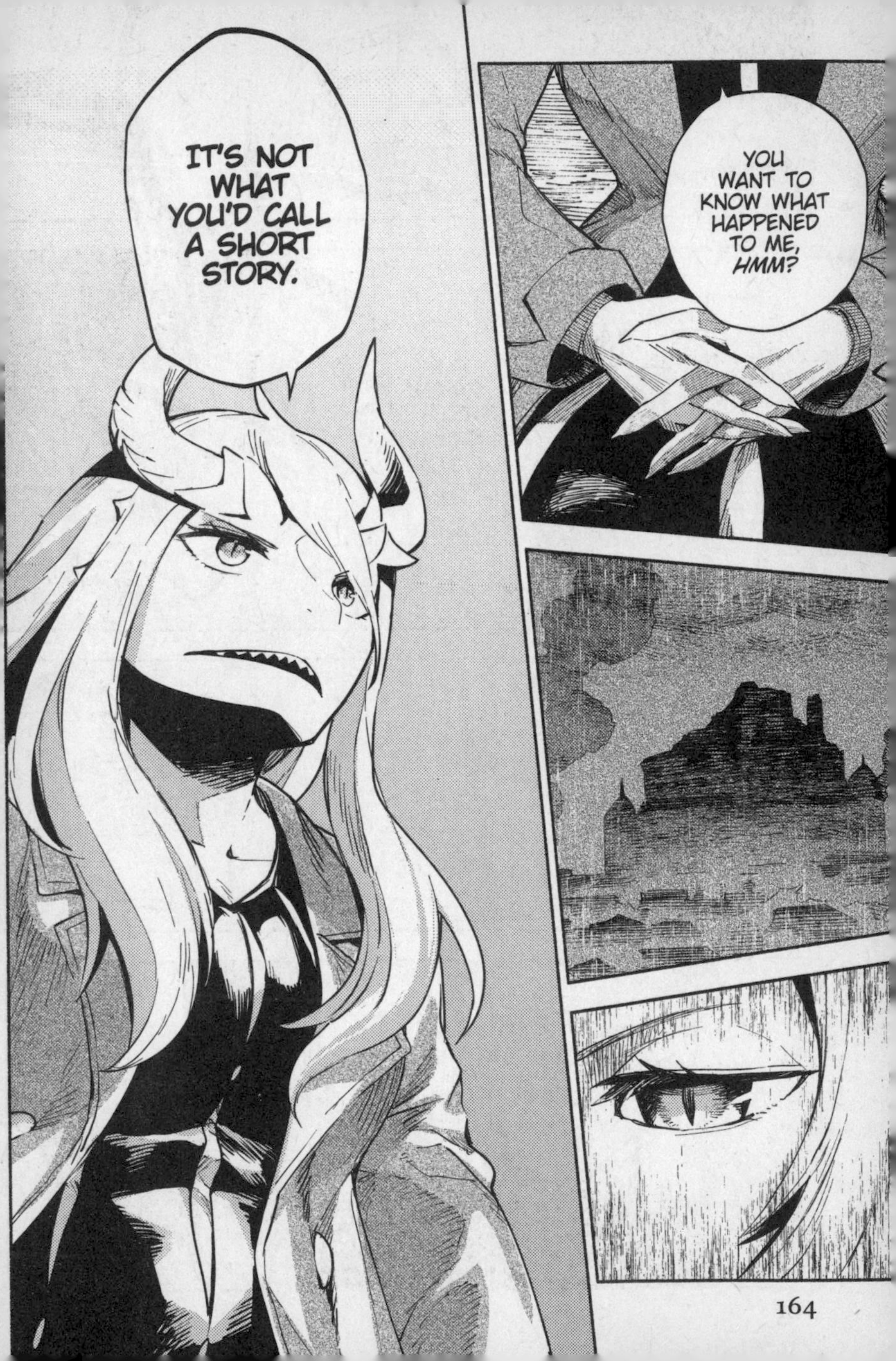
YOU WANT TO KNOW WHAT HAPPENED TO ME, *HMM?*
IT'S NOT WHAT YOU'D CALL A SHORT STORY.

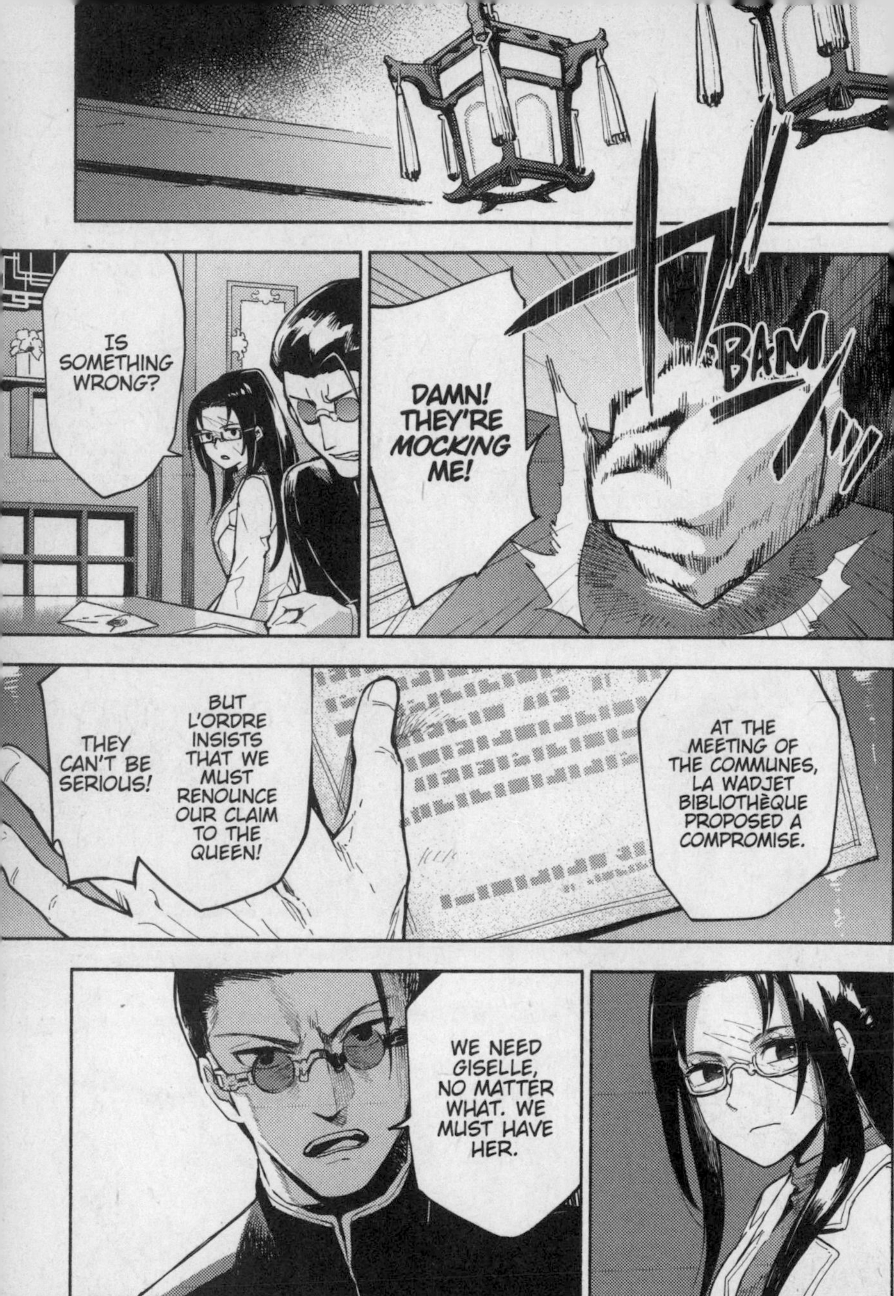
BAM
DAMN! THEY'RE MOCKING ME!
IS SOMETHING WRONG?
AT THE MEETING OF THE COMMUNES, LA WADJET BIBLIOTHÈQUE PROPOSED A COMPROMISE.
BUT L'ORDRE INSISTS THAT WE MUST RENOUNCE OUR CLAIM TO THE QUEEN!
THEY CAN'T BE SERIOUS!
WE NEED GISELLE, NO MATTER WHAT. WE MUST HAVE HER.

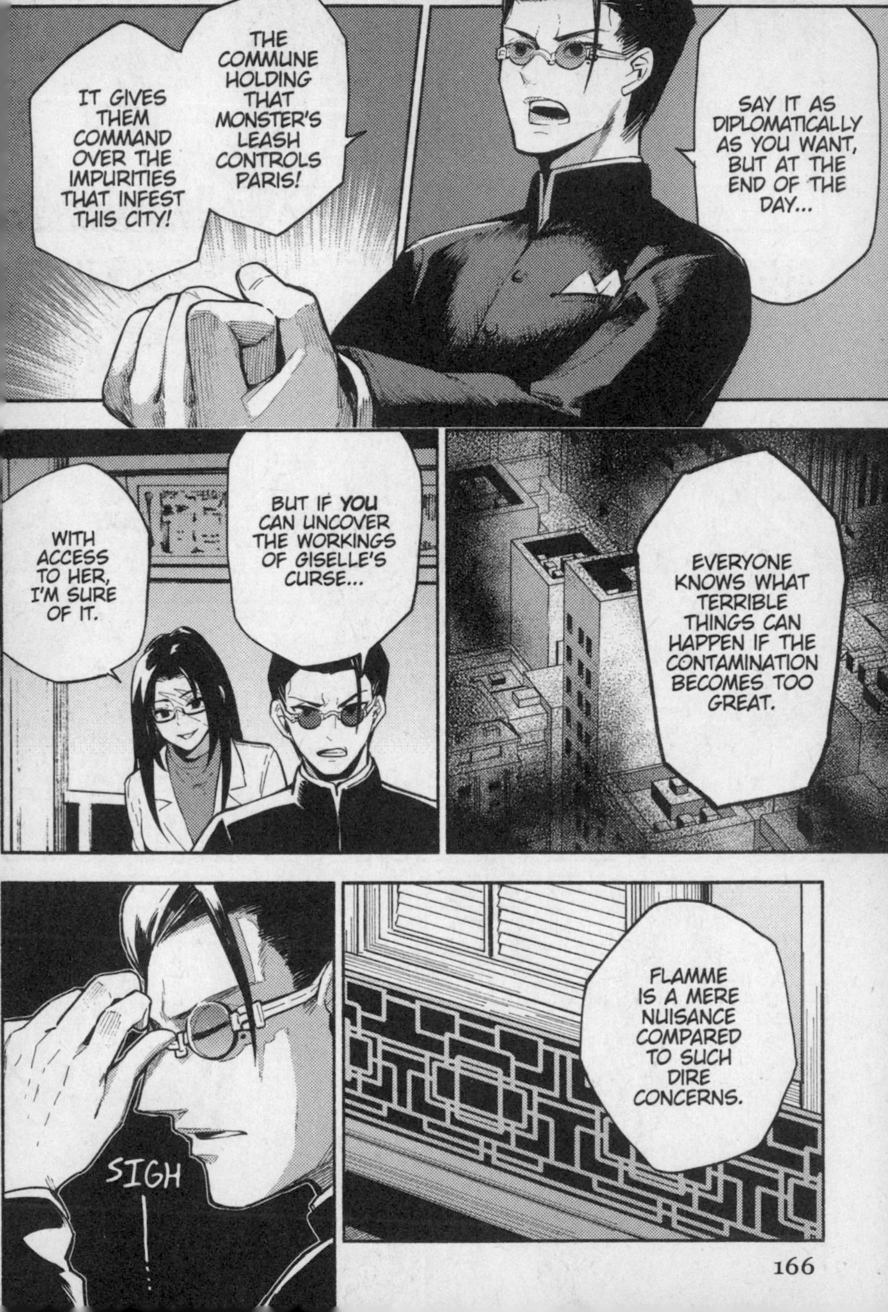
SAY IT AS DIPLOMATICALLY AS YOU WANT, BUT AT THE END OF THE DAY...
THE COMMUNE HOLDING THAT MONSTER'S LEASH CONTROLS PARIS!
IT GIVES THEM COMMAND OVER THE IMPURITIES THAT INFEST THIS CITY!
EVERYONE KNOWS WHAT TERRIBLE THINGS CAN HAPPEN IF THE CONTAMINATION BECOMES TOO GREAT.
BUT IF YOU CAN UNCOVER THE WORKINGS OF GISELLE'S CURSE...
WITH ACCESS TO HER, I'M SURE OF IT.
FLAMME IS A MERE NUISANCE COMPARED TO SUCH DIRE CONCERNS.
SIGH

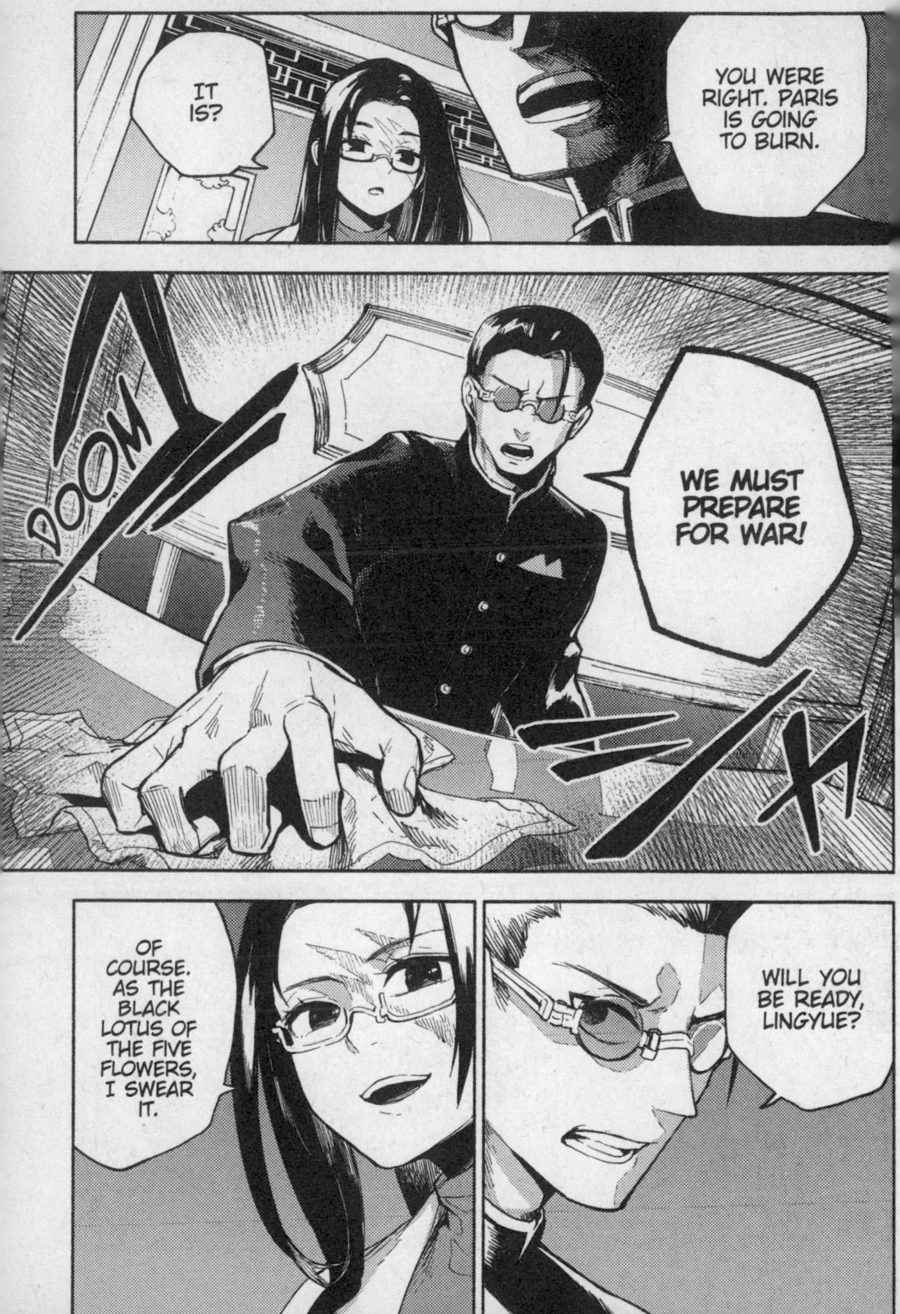
YOU WERE RIGHT. PARIS IS GOING TO BURN.
IT IS?
WE MUST PREPARE FOR WAR!
DOOM
WILL YOU BE READY, LINGYUE?
OF COURSE. AS THE BLACK LOTUS OF THE FIVE FLOWERS, I SWEAR IT.

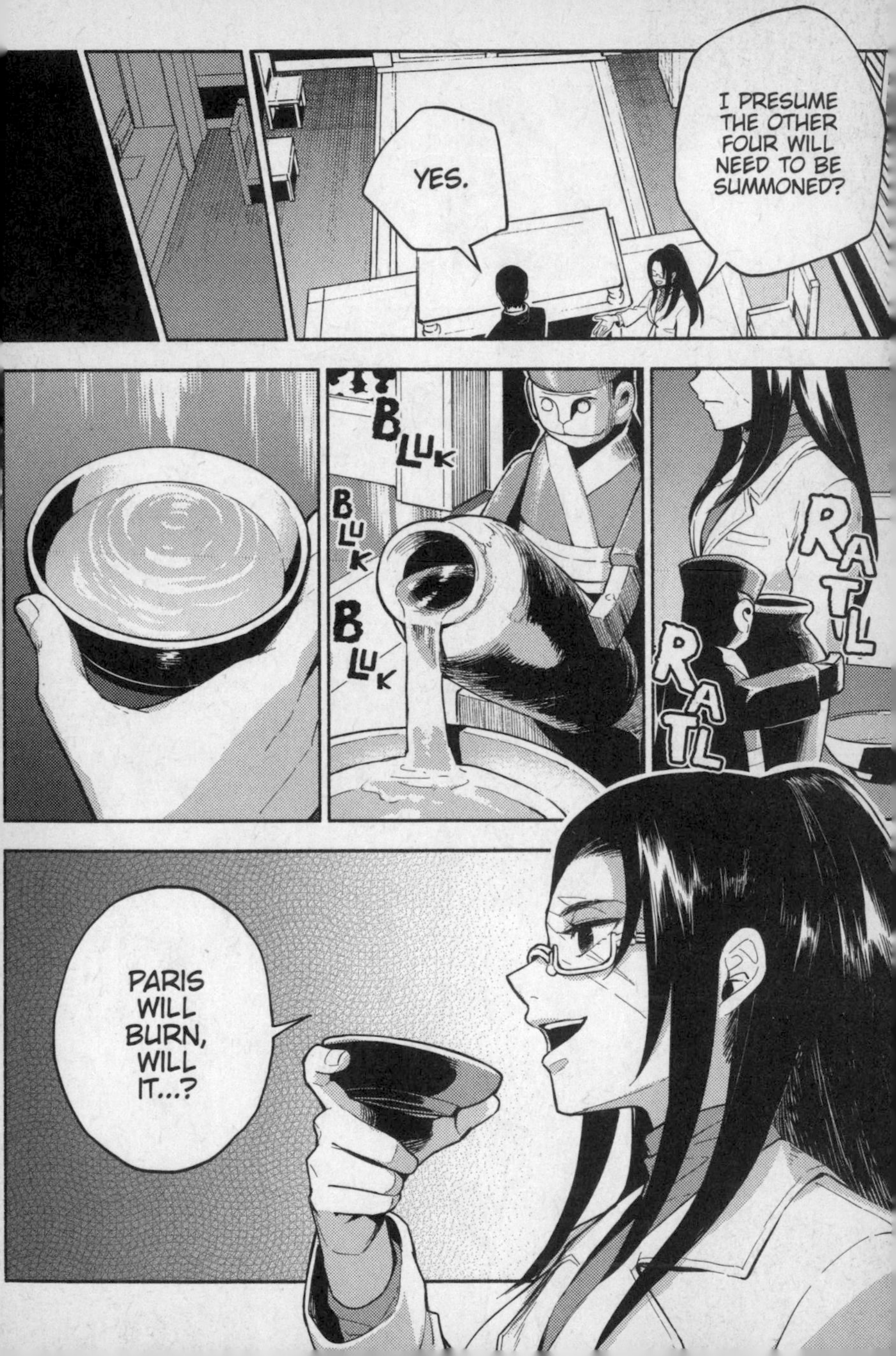
I PRESUME THE OTHER FOUR WILL NEED TO BE SUMMONED?
YES.
RATTL
RATTL
BLUK
BLUK
BLUK
PARIS WILL BURN, WILL IT...?

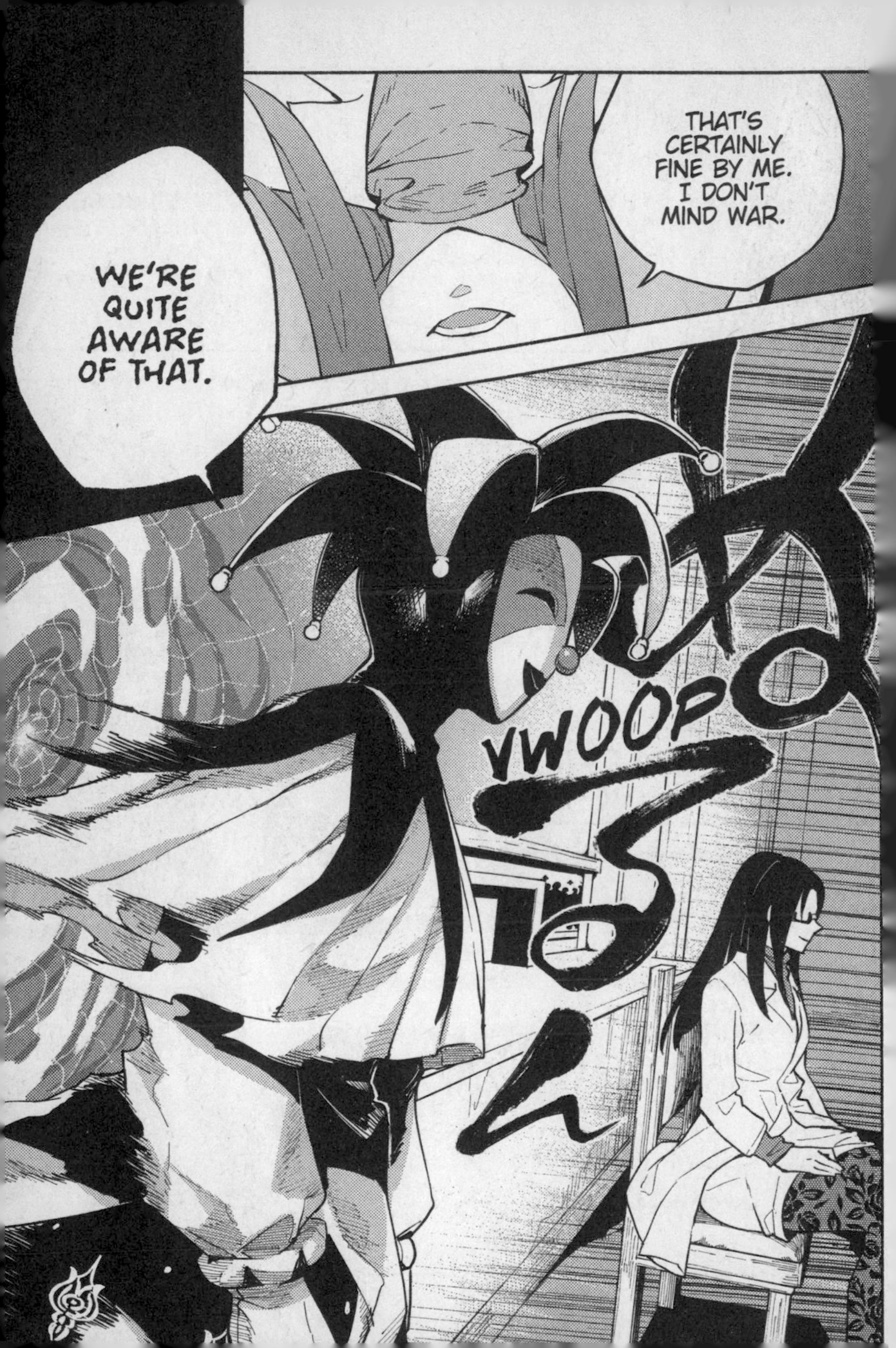
THAT'S CERTAINLY FINE BY ME. I DON'T MIND WAR.
WE'RE QUITE AWARE OF THAT.
VWOOP

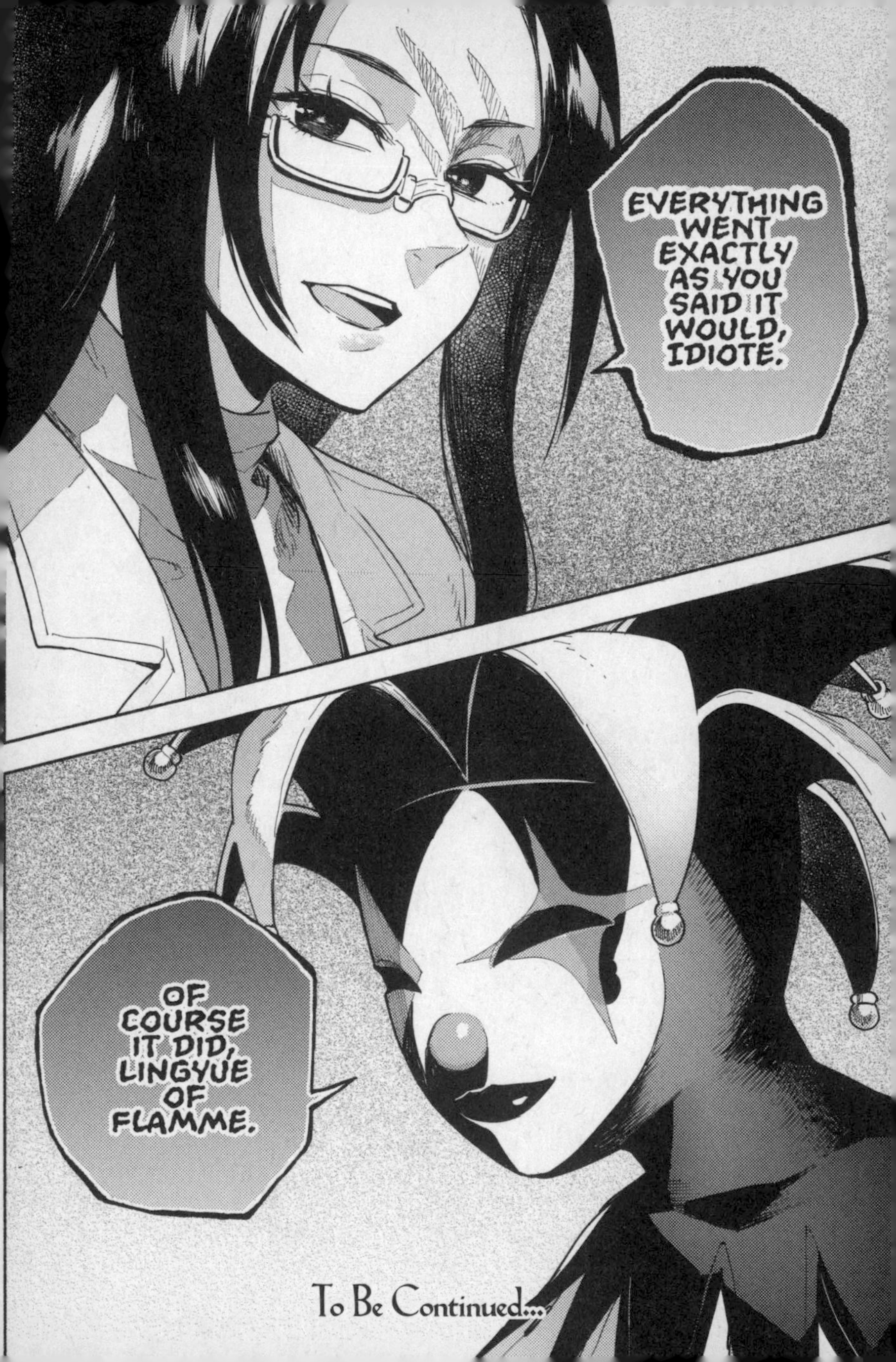
EVERYTHING WENT EXACTLY AS YOU SAID IT WOULD, IDIOTE.
OF COURSE IT DID, LINGYUE OF FLAMME.
To Be Continued...

Wizard's Blue

Afterword

Presenting Volume 3 of *Wizard's Blue!*
The world has changed quite a bit since
we last met in Volume 2. It's almost as if
the colors that comprise it have shifted.
As I write this, in the summer of 2020, we
are still trapped in confusion. The virus
is invisible and frightening. Many
tragedies have occurred.
I believe that at times like these, the
need for stories becomes even clearer.
They make you happy. They excite you. I
hope the energy from this story gives you
the strength to keep going tomorrow. That
thought's always on my mind as I work on
Giselle and Ao's worlds, as well as new
characters like Dimitri and Lingyue.

I've been thinking about Giselle's past
since the inception of this story, and in the
next volume, we finally reach it. Those
scenes I've wanted to see for so long have
finally been brought to life by Tsukumo's
art! You can see them for yourself first on
the Manga Door app. When I got to read
them, I was smiling the whole time. My
thanks again to Yamazaki-san's generous
oversight, to my ever-helpful editor S-san,
and of course, to all of you.

August 2020
Penned while watching the anime
Deca-Dence.

三田 誠
Sanda Makoto

Understanding Tsukumo in Six Panels or Less!

Trials Arc

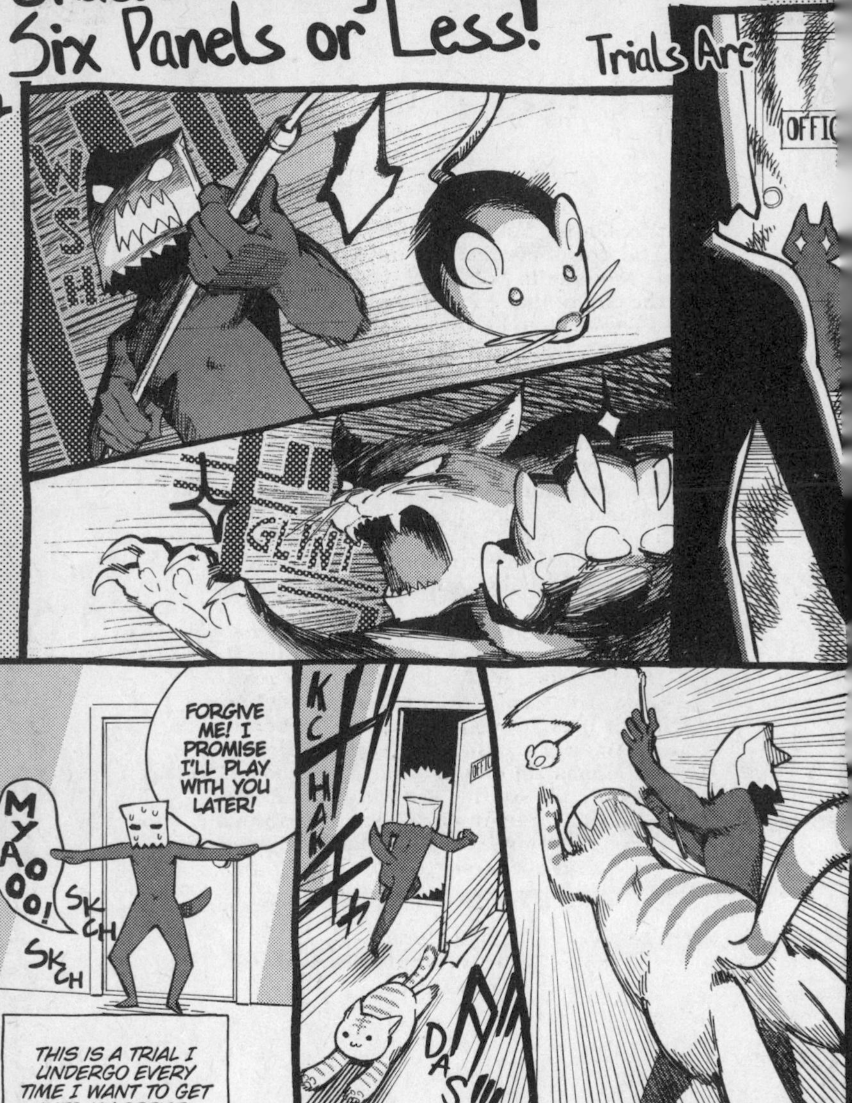
WSH
GLINT
KCHAK
DASH!!!
FORGIVE ME! I PROMISE I'LL PLAY WITH YOU LATER!
MYAOOO!
SKCH
SKCH
THIS IS A TRIAL I UNDERGO EVERY TIME I WANT TO GET INTO MY OFFICE.

Thank you very much for purchasing Volume 3!

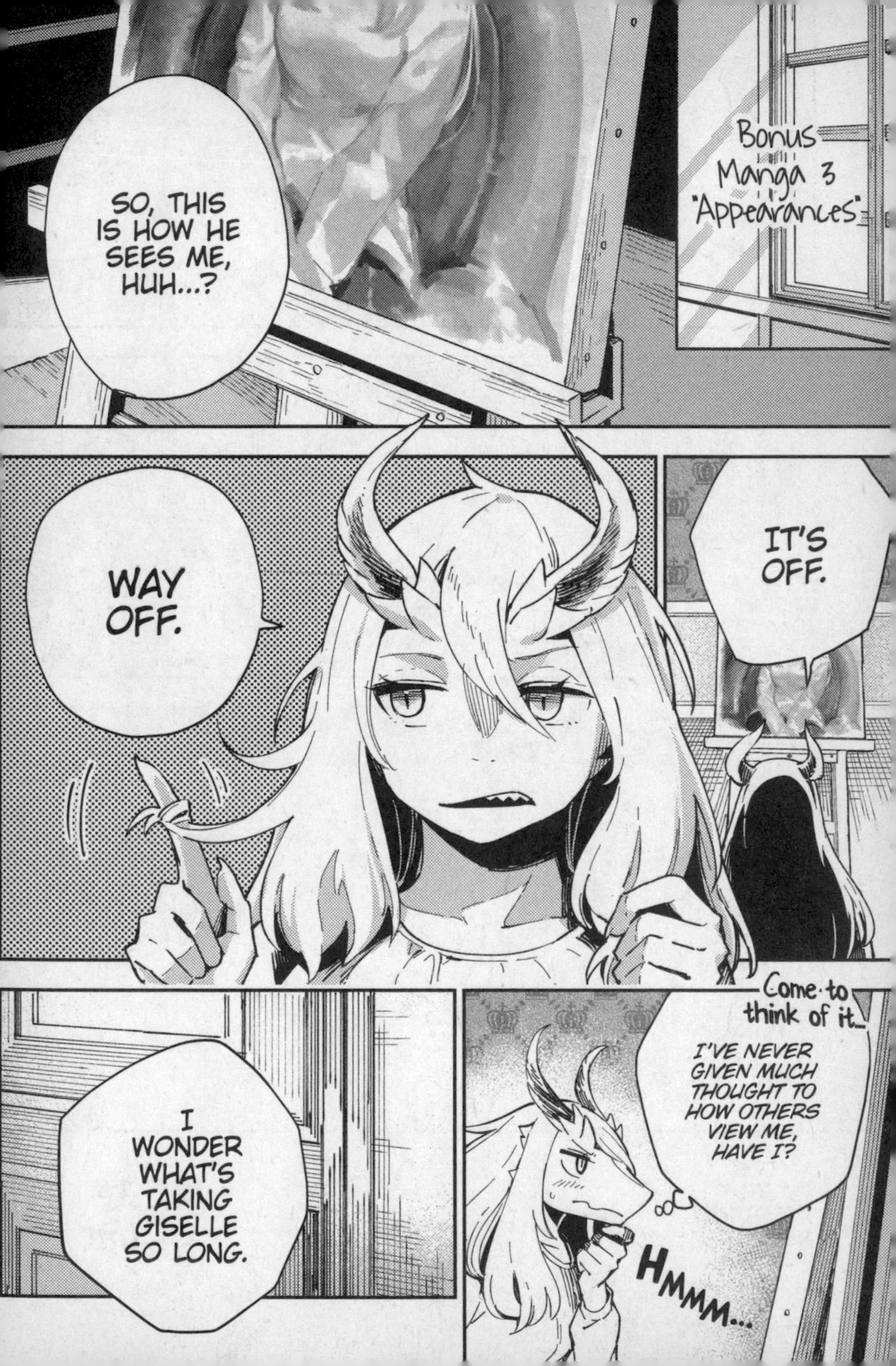
Bonus Manga 3 "Appearances"
SO, THIS IS HOW HE SEES ME, HUH...?
IT'S OFF.
WAY OFF.
Come to think of it...
I'VE NEVER GIVEN MUCH THOUGHT TO HOW OTHERS VIEW ME, HAVE I?
HMMM...
I WONDER WHAT'S TAKING GISELLE SO LONG.

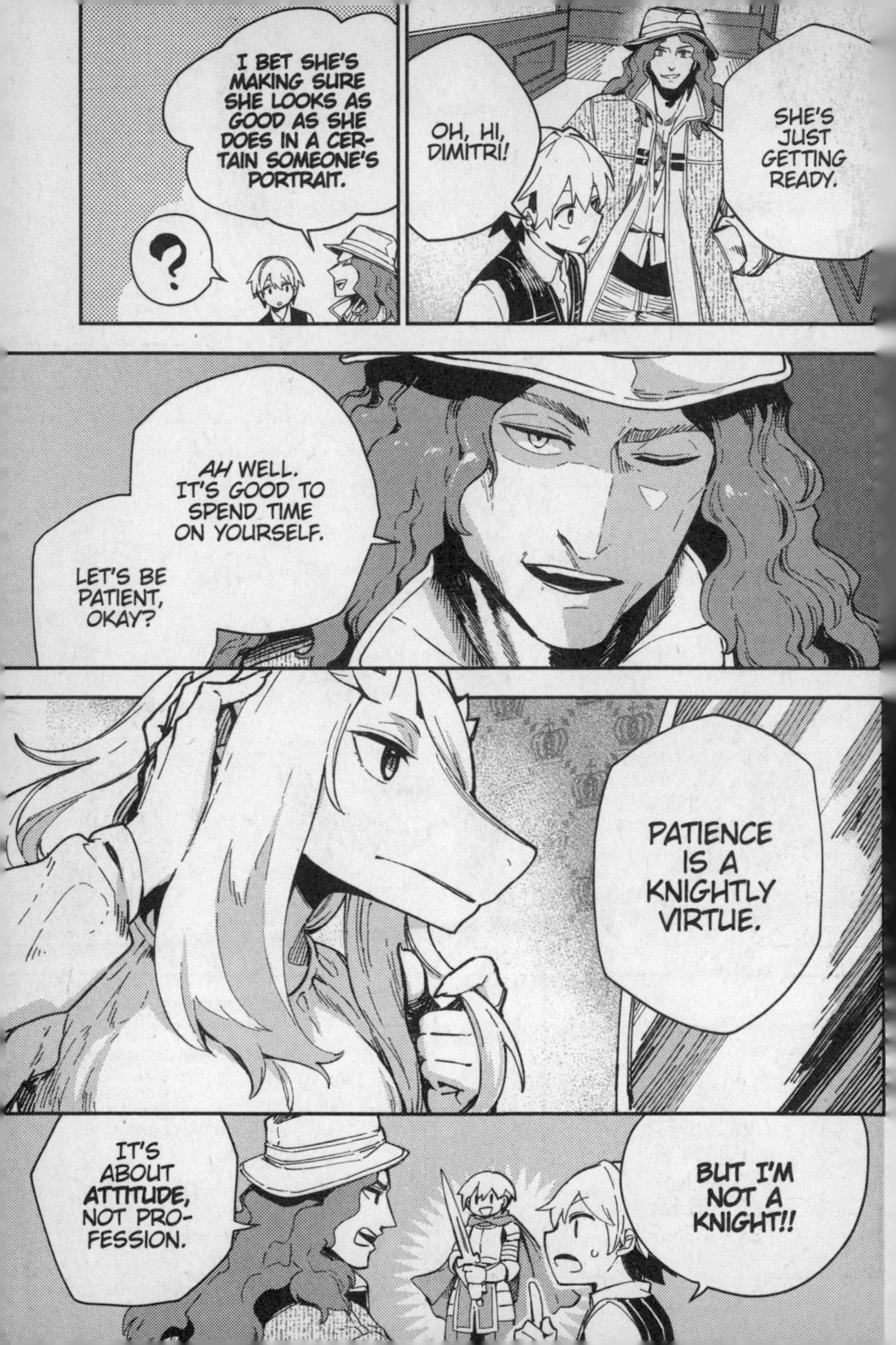
SHE'S JUST GETTING READY.
OH, HI, DIMITRI!
I BET SHE'S MAKING SURE SHE LOOKS AS GOOD AS SHE DOES IN A CER-TAIN SOMEONE'S PORTRAIT.
?
AH WELL. IT'S GOOD TO SPEND TIME ON YOURSELF.
LET'S BE PATIENT, OKAY?
PATIENCE IS A KNIGHTLY VIRTUE.
BUT I'M NOT A KNIGHT!!
IT'S ABOUT ATTITUDE, NOT PRO-FESSION.

Bonus Four-Panel Manga Part 4

Once Upon a Time...

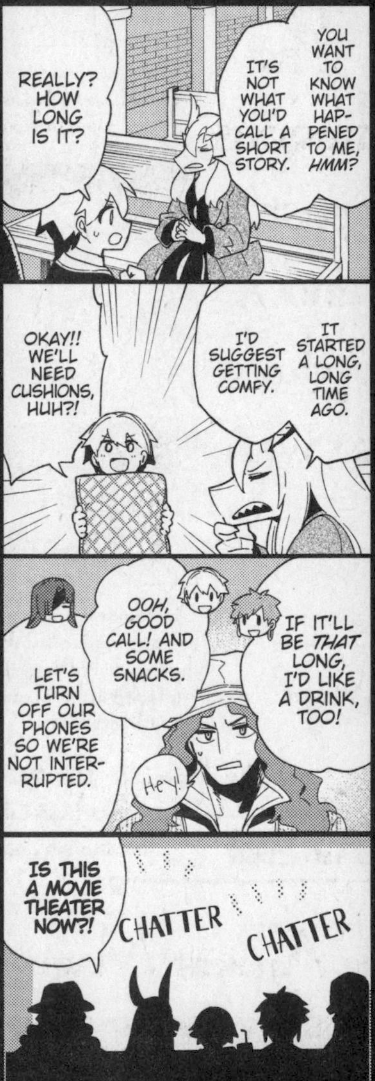
YOU WANT TO KNOW WHAT HAPPENED TO ME, *HMM?*
IT'S NOT WHAT YOU'D CALL A SHORT STORY.
REALLY? HOW LONG IS IT?
IT STARTED A LONG, LONG TIME AGO.
I'D SUGGEST GETTING COMFY.
OKAY!! WE'LL NEED CUSHIONS, HUH?!
IF IT'LL BE *THAT* LONG, I'D LIKE A DRINK, TOO!
OOH, GOOD CALL! AND SOME SNACKS.
LET'S TURN OFF OUR PHONES SO WE'RE NOT INTERRUPTED.
Hey!
IS THIS A MOVIE THEATER NOW?!
CHATTER
CHATTER

Food, Shelter, Clothing

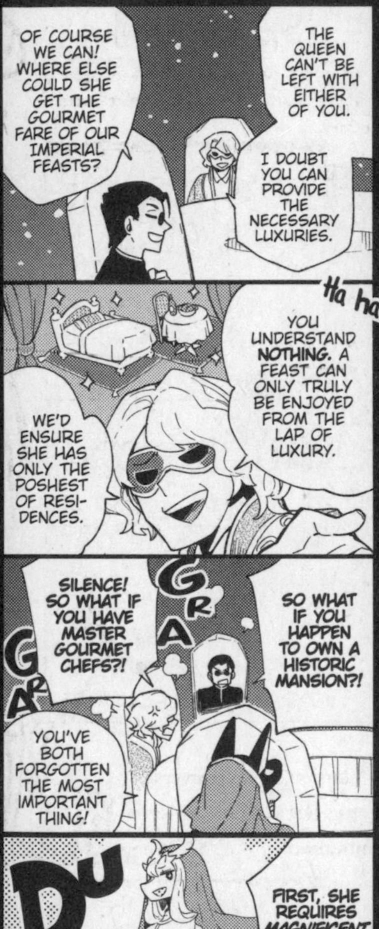
THE QUEEN CAN'T BE LEFT WITH EITHER OF YOU.
I DOUBT YOU CAN PROVIDE THE NECESSARY LUXURIES.
OF COURSE WE CAN! WHERE ELSE COULD SHE GET THE GOURMET FARE OF OUR IMPERIAL FEASTS?
Ha ha!
YOU UNDERSTAND **NOTHING.** A FEAST CAN ONLY TRULY BE ENJOYED FROM THE LAP OF LUXURY.
WE'D ENSURE SHE HAS ONLY THE POSHEST OF RESIDENCES.
SO WHAT IF YOU HAPPEN TO OWN A HISTORIC MANSION?!
GRA
SILENCE! SO WHAT IF YOU HAVE MASTER GOURMET CHEFS?!
GAR
YOU'VE BOTH FORGOTTEN THE MOST IMPORTANT THING!
FIRST, SHE REQUIRES *MAGNIFICENT CLOTHING!*
DUN

The dragon's past, and a prelude to war.

There's been a decisive split amongst the communes of Paris. While Quatre Saisons begins preparing for war, Giselle, the ancient queen of Paris, tells Ao about her history.

What happened in the earliest days of her life, so long ago?

Do her memories hold a clue to preventing her death? Is there anything Ao can do to help, either as an alchemist or as her groom?

Delve deeper into *The Ancient Magus' Bride* universe with *Wizard's Blue's* fresh take on the relationship between the human and the inhuman!

The Ancient Magus' Bride: Wizard's Blue

VOLUME 4 COMING SOON

SEVEN SEAS ENTERTAINMENT PRESENTS

The Ancient Magus' Bride

WIZARD'S BLUE

VOLUME 3

story: MAKOTO SANDA art: ISUO TSUKUMO script supervisor: KORE YAMAZAKI

TRANSLATION
Adrienne Beck

ADAPTATION
Ysabet Reinhardt MacFarlane

LETTERING
Carolina Hernández Mendoza

COVER DESIGN
Nicky Lim

LOGO DESIGN
Kris Aubin

PROOFREADER
Janet Houck

COPY EDITOR
Dawn Davis

EDITOR
Shanti Whitesides

PREPRESS TECHNICIAN
Rhiannon Rasmussen-Silverstein

PRODUCTION ASSOCIATE
Christa Miesner

PRODUCTION MANAGER
Lissa Pattillo

MANAGING EDITOR
Julie Davis

ASSOCIATE PUBLISHER
Adam Arnold

PUBLISHER
Jason DeAngelis

Originally published in Japan in 2020 by MAG Garden Corporation, TOKYO.
English translation rights arranged through TOHAN CORPORATION, Tokyo.

Seven Seas press and purchase enquiries can be sent to Marketing Manager Lianne Sentar at press@gomanga.com. Information regarding the distribution and purchase of digital editions is available from Digital Manager CK Russell at digital@gomanga.com.

ISBN: 978-1-64827-274-5
Printed in Canada
First Printing: August 2021
10 9 8 7 6 5 4 3 2 1

READING DIRECTIONS

This book reads from ***right to left***, Japanese style. If this is your first time reading manga, you start reading from the top right panel on each page and take it from there. If you get lost, just follow the numbered diagram here. It may seem backwards at first, but you'll get the hang of it! Have fun!!

1
2
3
4
5
6
7
8
9

Follow us online: www.SevenSeasEntertainment.com

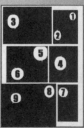